# *Webster's*
# Spanish-English Dictionary

# Webster's
# Spanish-English
# Dictionary

*Features Latin-American Spanish*

*Created in cooperation with the Editors of*

# Merriam-Webster

creative EDGE

This 2008 Edition published by arrangement with Federal Street Press,
a division of Merriam Webster, Incorporated

**creative EDGE**
118 Seaboard Lane, Franklin, TN 37067
CE10886/0208

ISBN 1-40378-430-2

Printed in the United States of America
09 10 11 12 CLI 5 4 3 2

# Contents

# Preface

This Spanish-English dictionary has been edited with an eye to keeping the vocabulary as concise as possible and yet covering the most essential words in everyday use. There are more than 20,000 boldface entries in all, and each one has a translation. In most cases a single word will serve as a translation; in others, where there is no single word that translates, a phrase is used.

All dictionary entries are printed in **bold** type, followed by an *italicized* part of speech label. **Main entries** follow one another in strict alphabetical order, without regard to intervening spaces or hyphens. The Spanish letter combinations *ch* and *ll* are alphabetized within the letters *C* and *L*. However, the Spanish letter *ñ* is a separate letter of the Spanish alphabet, falling after the letter N and before the letter O, so words that contain the *ñ* are alphabetized accordingly. For example, the Spanish word **mañana** falls alphabetically between the entry word **manzana** and the entry word **mapa**.

Words with identical spellings and differing only in part of speech and derived words and phrases are run into a single entry:

> **back** *n* . . . — **back** *adv* . . . — **back** *adj* . . . — **back** *v* **back up** . . . **back down** . . . — **backbone** *n* — **background** *n* . . .

Words spelled the same but unrelated are given a separate entry with a distinguishing superscript numeral:

> **sobre**[1] *nm* envelope
> **sobre**[2] *prep.* on, on top of; over . . .

**Variant spellings** appear at the main entry separated by *or* (as **blond** *or* **blonde** *adj* rubio . . . and **cacahuate** *or* **cacahuete** *nm* peanut). For Spanish nouns and adjectives, the main entry by tradition is the masculine form and the feminine ending is shown, usually cut back to the last element, following a comma: (as **campeón, -peona** *n* . . . champion).

It is not in the scope of this book to give complete grammatical information. Spanish masculine and feminine nouns and adjectives are noted and part of speech functions are indicated, but inflected forms, such as the plurals of nouns and the principal parts of verbs, are not shown except for the most irregular formations. When they are shown, they are in bold type in parentheses following the part of speech label. Plurals are shown for English nouns where there is an internal spelling change, as **calf** . . . (**calves**), or for nouns that end in 'y' and sometimes 'o'. For English verbs the past tense and past participle forms are shown where there is a change in internal spelling, as **break** . . . (**broke; broken**). Comparative and superlative forms are generally not shown for adjectives and adverbs. For Spanish nouns, the plural form is shown only when there is a change in spelling, such as the addition or loss of a diacritic on a letter:

> **abdomen** *nm* (**-dómenes**) abdomen
> **abstención** *nf* (**-ciones**) abstention

# Preface

Where the plural form shown affects only the masculine form, that is indicated by an italic *m* within the parentheses:

**bailarín, -rina** *n* (**-rines** *m*) dancer

The grammatical functions of entry words, including the traditional parts of speech, are indicated by italic abbreviations. These include indications of plural (*pl*) and masculine (*m*) and feminine (*f*) gender of words as well as the following part of speech labels:

| | |
|---|---|
| *art* | article |
| *n* | noun (also *nm* masculine noun; *nf* feminine noun; *npl* plural noun) |
| *v* | verb |
| *vr* | reflexive verb |
| *v impers* | impersonal verb |
| *v aux* | auxiliary verb |
| *v phr* | verb phrase |
| *vr phr* | reflexive verb phrase |
| *adj* | adjective |
| *adv* | adverb |
| *prep* | preposition |
| *prep phr* | prepositional phrase |
| *pron* | pronoun |
| *reflexive pron* | reflexive pronoun |
| *conj* | conjunction |
| *conj phr* | conjunctive phrase |
| *interj* | interjection |

These labels are also sometimes combined: (*nmpl*) or (*n or adj*).

# Spanish-English
# Dictionary

# A

**a**[1] *nf* a, first letter of the Spanish alphabet

**a**[2] *prep* (**al** when contracted with *el*) to; **a las dos** at two o'clock; **al día siguiente** (on) the following day; **a pie** on foot; **de lunes a viernes** from Monday until Friday; **tres veces a la semana** three times per week

**abajo** *adv* down, below, downstairs; **hacia ~** downward

**abandonar** *v* abandon, leave; give up — **abandono** *nm* abandonment, neglect

**abanico** *nm* fan

**abastecer** *v* supply, stock — **abastecimiento** *nm* supply, provisions

**abdomen** *nm* (**-dómenes**) abdomen

**abedul** *nm* birch

**abeja** *nf* bee

**abertura** *nf* opening

**abeto** *nm* fir tree

**abierto, -ta** *adj* open

**abismo** *nm* abyss, chasm

**ablandar** *v* soften up

**abofetear** *v* slap

**abogado, -da** *n* lawyer — **abogacía** *nf* legal profession

**abominable** *adj* abominable

**abonar** *v* pay; fertilize — **abonarse** *vr* subscribe — **abonado, -da** *n* subscriber — **abono** *nm* payment, installment; fertilizer; season ticket

**abordar** *v* approach, deal with; get on board

**aborigen** *nmf* (**-rígenes**) aborigine — **aborigen** *adj* aboriginal, native

**aborrecer** *v* abhor, detest

**abortar** *v* have a miscarriage; abort — **aborto** *nm* abortion, miscarriage

**abotonar** *v* button

**abrazar** *v* hug, embrace — **abrazo** *nm* hug, embrace

**abrelatas** *nms & pl* can opener

**abreviar** *v* shorten, abridge; abbreviate — **abreviatura** *nf* abbreviation

**abrigar** *v* dress warmly — **abrigado, -da** *adj* warm, wrapped up — **abrigo** *nm* coat, overcoat

**abril** *nm* April

**abrir** *v* open, open up; unlock, undo

**abrochar** *v* button, fasten

**absceso** *nm* abscess

**absoluto, -ta** *adj* absolute, unconditional; **en absoluto** not at all — **absolutamente** *adv* absolutely

**absorber** *v* absorb; take up, require — **absorbente** *adj* absorbent; absorbing — **absorto, -ta** *adj* absorbed, engrossed

**abstenerse** *vr* abstain, refrain — **abstención** *nf* (**-ciones**) abstention

**abstracto, -ta** *adj* abstract — **abstraer** *v* abstract — **abstraerse** *vr* lose oneself in thought

**absurdo, -da** *adj* absurd, ridiculous — **absurdo** *nm* absurdity

**abuelo, -la** *n* grandfather, grandmother; **abuelos** *nmpl* grandparents

**abundar** *v* abound, be plentiful — **abundancia** *nf* abundance — **abundante** *adj* abundant

**aburrir** *v* bore — **aburrido, -da** *adj* boring — **aburrimiento** *nm* boredom

**abusar** *v* go too far — **abusivo, -va** *adj* outrageous, excessive — **abuso** *nm* abuse

**acá** *adv* here, over here

**acabar** *v* finish, end; **~ con** put an end to — **acabado, -da** *adj* finished, perfect; old, worn-out

**academia** *nf* academy — **académico, -ca** *adj* academic

**acalorar** *v* stir up, excite — **acalorado, -da** *adj* emotional, heated

**acampar** *v* camp

**acaparar** *v* hoard

**acariciar** *v* caress

**acaso** *adv* perhaps, maybe; **por si ∼** just in case

**acatarrarse** *vr* catch a cold

**acaudalado, -da** *adj* wealthy, rich

**acceder** *v* agree; **∼ a** gain access to

**acceso** *nm* access; entrance

**accesorio** *nm* accessory

**accidentado, -da** *adj* eventful, turbulent; injured — **accidentado, -da** *n* accident victim

**accidente** *nm* accident — **accidentarse** *vr* have an accident

**acción** *nf* (**-ciones**) action; act, deed; share of stock — **accionista** *nmf* stockholder

**aceite** *nm* oil — **aceitar** *v* oil — **aceitoso, -sa** *adj* oily

**aceituna** *nf* olive

**acelerar** *v* accelerate — **acelerarse** *vr* hurry up — **acelerador** *nm* accelerator

**acelga** *nf* Swiss chard

**acento** *nm* accent — **acentuar** *v* accent; emphasize, stress — **acentuarse** *vr* stand out

**acepción** *nf* (**-ciones**) sense, meaning

**aceptar** *v* accept — **aceptable** *adj* acceptable

**acera** *nf* sidewalk

**acerca de** *prep phr* about, concerning

**acercar** *v* bring near or closer

**acero** *nm* steel

**acertar** *v* guess correctly; be accurate — **acertado, -da** *adj* correct, accurate

**achacar** *v* attribute, impute

**achaque** *nm* aches and pains

**achicar** *v* make smaller

**ácido, -da** *adj* acid, sour — **acidez** *nf* (**-deces**) acidity — **ácido** *nm* acid

**acierto** *nm* correct answer; skill; sound judgment

**aclamar** *v* acclaim

**aclarar** *v* clarify, explain; clear up — **aclaración** *nf* (**-ciones**) explanation

**acné** *nm* acne

**acobardar** *v* intimidate

**acoger** *v* shelter; receive, welcome —

**acogedor, -dora** *adj* cozy, welcoming — **acogida** *nf* welcome; refuge

**acogerse a** *vr phr* resort to

**acolchar** *v* pad

**acólito** *nm* altar boy

**acometer** *v* attack

**acomodar** *v* adjust; put; make a place for — **acomodarse** *vr* settle in; **acomodarse a** adapt to — **acomodado, -da** *adj* well-to-do

**acompañar** *v* accompany — **acompañante** *nmf* companion; music accompanist

**acondicionar** *v* fit out, equip

**aconsejar** *v* advise

**acontecimiento** *nm* event

**acoplar** *v* couple, connect — **acoplarse** *vr* fit together

**acordar** *v* agree; **acordarse** *vr* remember

**acordeón** *nm* (**-deones**) accordion

**acortar** *v* shorten, cut short

**acosar** *v* hound, harass

**acostar** *v* put to bed

**acostumbrar** *v* accustom; **∼ a** be in the habit of

**acrecentar** *v* increase

**acreditar** *v* accredit, authorize; prove — **acreditarse** *vr* prove oneself — **acreditado, -da** *adj* reputable; accredited

**acreedor, -dora** *adj* worthy —**acreedor, -dora** *n* creditor

**acribillar** *v* riddle, pepper

**acrílico** *nm* acrylic

**acrobacia** *nf* acrobatics — **acróbata** *nmf* acrobat

**acta** *nf* certificate; meeting minutes *pl*

**actitud** *nf* attitude; posture, position

**activar** *v* activate; stimulate, speed up — **actividad** *nf* activity — **activo, -va** *adj* active

**acto** *nm* act, deed; act (in a play)

**actor** *nm* actor — **actriz** *nf* (**-trices**) actress

**actual** *adj* present, current — **actualidad** *nf* present time — **actualizar** *v* modernize — **actualmente** *adv* at present, nowadays

**actuar** *v* act, perform

**acuarela** *nf* watercolor

**acuario** *nm* aquarium

**acuático, -ca** *adj* aquatic, water

**acudir** *v* go, come; ~ **a** be present at, attend

**acueducto** *nm* aqueduct

**acuerdo** *nm* agreement; de ~ OK, all right

**acumular** *v* accumulate

**acupuntura** *nf* acupuncture

**acurrucarse** *vr* curl up, nestle

**acusar** *v* accuse — **acusado, -da** *n* defendant

**acústica** *nf* acoustics — **acústico, -ca** *adj* acoustic

**adaptar** *v* adapt; adjust, fit — **adaptación** *nf* (-ciones) adaptation — **adaptador** *nm* electrical adapter

**adecuar** *v* adapt, make suitable — **adecuado, -da** *adj* suitable, appropriate

**adelantar** *v* advance, move forward; overtake; pay in advance — **adelantarse** *vr* run fast (of a clock)

**adelante** *adv* ahead, forward; **más** ~ later on, further on — **¡adelante!** *interj* come in!

**adelgazar** *v* lose weight

**además** *adv* besides, furthermore; ~ **de** in addition to, as well as

**adentro** *adv* inside, within

**adherirse** *vr* adhere, stick — **adhesión** *nf* (-siones) adhesion; support — **adhesivo, -va** *adj* adhesive — **adhesivo** *nm* adhesive

**adición** *nf* (-ciones) addition — **adicional** *adj* additional

**adicto, -ta** *adj* addicted — **adicto, -ta** *n* addict

**adiestrar** *v* train

**adinerado, -da** *adj* wealthy

**adiós** *nm* (**adioses**) farewell **¡adiós!** *interj* good-bye!

**adivinar** *v* guess; foretell — **adivinanza** *nf* riddle

**adjetivo** *nm* adjective

**adjudicar** *v* award — **adjudicarse** *vr* appropriate

**administración** *nf* (-ciones) administration; management — **administrador, -dora** *n* administrator, manager — **administrar** *v* manage, run; administer (a drug)

**admirar** *v* admire

**admitir** *v* admit; accept — **admisión** *nf* (-siones) admission; acceptance

**ADN** *nm* DNA

**adolecer de** *v phr* suffer from

**adolescente** *adj & nmf* adolescent — **adolescencia** *nf* adolescence

**adónde** *adv* where

**adoptar** *v* adopt — **adopción** *nf* (-ciones) adoption

**adorar** *v* adore, worship — **adorable** *adj* adorable

**adormecer** *v* make sleepy; numb

**adornar** *v* decorate, adorn — **adorno** *nm* ornament, decoration

**adquirir** *v* acquire; purchase — **adquisición** *nf* (-ciones) acquisition; purchase

**aduana** *nf* customs office

**aduanero, -ra** *adj* customs — **aduanero, -ra** *n* customs officer

**adueñarse de** *vr phr* take possession of

**adular** *v* flatter

**adulterar** *v* adulterate

**adulterio** *nm* adultery

**adulto, -ta** *adj & n* adult

**adverbio** *nm* adverb — **adverbial** *adj* adverbial

**adversario, -ria** *n* adversary, opponent — **adversidad** *nf* adversity

**advertir** *v* warn; notice — **advertencia** *nf* warning

**adyacente** *adj* adjacent

**aéreo, -rea** *adj* aerial, air

**aerolínea** *nf* airline

**aeronave** *nf* aircraft

**aeropuerto** *nm* airport

**afán** *nm* (**afanes**) eagerness; effort, hard work — **afanarse** *vr* toil

**afección** *nf* (**-ciones**) ailment, complaint

**afectivo, -va** *adj* emotional

**afecto** *nm* affection — **afectar** *v* affect

**afeitar** *v* shave

**aferrarse** *vr* cling, hold on

**afianzar** *v* secure, strengthen

**afiche** *nm* poster

**afición** *nf* (**-ciones**) penchant, fondness; hobby — **aficionado, -da** *n* enthusiast, fan; amateur — **aficionarse a** *vr phr* become interested in

**afilar** *v* sharpen

**afiliarse a** *vr phr* join, become a member of — **afiliación** *nf* (**-ciones**) affiliation

**afinar** *v* tune; perfect, refine

**afinidad** *nf* affinity, similarity

**afirmar** *v* state, affirm; strengthen — **afirmación** *nf* (**-ciones**) statement, affirmation

**afligir** *v* afflict; distress

**aflojar** *v* loosen, slacken; ease up

**afortunado, -da** *adj* fortunate, lucky

**africano, -na** *adj* African

**afuera** *adv* out; outside, outdoors — **afueras** *nfpl* outskirts

**agencia** *nf* agency, office — **agente** *nmf* agent, officer

**agenda** *nf* agenda; notebook

**ágil** *adj* agile — **agilidad** *nf* agility

**agitar** *v* agitate; wave, flap; stir up

**aglomerar** *v* amass

**agobiar** *v* oppress; overwhelm

**agonía** *nf* death throes; agony — **agonizar** *v* be dying

**agosto** *nm* August

**agotar** *v* deplete, use up; exhaust

**agradar** *v* be pleasing — **agradable** *adj* pleasant, agreeable

**agradecer** *v* be grateful for, thank

**agrado** *nm* taste, liking; **con ~** with pleasure

**agrandar** *v* enlarge

**agrario, -ria** *adj* agrarian, agricultural

**agravar** *v* make heavier; aggravate, worsen

**agredir** *v* attack

**agregar** *v* add, attach

**agresión** *nf* (**-siones**) aggression, attack — **agresividad** *nf* aggressiveness

**agricultura** *nf* agriculture, farming — **agricultor, -tora** *n* farmer

**agridulce** *adj* bittersweet; sweet-and-sour

**agrietar** *v* crack

**agrio, agria** *adj* sour

**agrupar** *v* group together — **agrupación** *nf* (**-ciones**) group, association

**agua** *nf* water; **~ oxigenada** hydrogen peroxide; **~s negras** *or* **~s residuales** sewage

**aguacate** *nm* avocado

**aguacero** *nm* downpour

**aguantar** *v* bear, withstand; hold; hold out, last — **aguantarse** *vr* restrain oneself

**aguardiente** *nm* clear brandy

**agudo, -da** *adj* acute, sharp; shrill, high-pitched — **agudeza** *nf* sharpness; witticism

**aguijón** *nm* (**-jones**) stinger; goad, stimulus

**águila** *nf* eagle

**aguja** *nf* needle; hand (of a clock); church spire

**aguzar** *v* sharpen; **~ el oído** prick up one's ears

**ahí** *adv* there; **por ~** somewhere, thereabouts

**ahínco** *nm* eagerness, zeal

**ahogar** *v* drown; smother — **ahogo** *nm* breathlessness

**ahondar** *v* deepen; elaborate

**ahora** *adv* now; **~ mismo** right now

**ahorcar** *v* hang, kill by hanging

**ahorrar** *v* save; save up

**ahorro** *nm* saving

**ahumar** *v* smoke, cure

**ahuyentar** *v* scare away, chase away

**airado, -da** *adj* irate, angry

**aire** *nm* air; ~ **acondicionado** air-conditioning; **al** ~ **libre** in the open air, outdoors

**airear** *v* air out

**aislar** *v* isolate; insulate — **aislamiento** *nm* isolation; insulation

**ajedrez** *nm* chess

**ajeno, -na** *adj* someone else's; alien; ~ **a** foreign to

**ají** *nm* (**ajíes**) chili pepper

**ajo** *nm* garlic

**ajustar** *v* adjust, adapt; agree on — **ajustado, -da** *adj* close, tight; tight-fitting

**ajusticiar** *v* execute, put to death

**ala** *nf* wing; brim (of a hat)

**alacrán** *nm* (**-cranes**) scorpion

**alado, -da** *adj* winged

**alargar** *v* extend, lengthen; prolong

**alarmar** *v* alarm — **alarma** *nf* alarm

**alba** *nf* dawn

**albañil** *nm* bricklayer, mason

**albedrío** *nm* will

**albergar** *v* house, lodge — **albergue** *nm* lodging; shelter

**albóndiga** *nf* meatball

**álbum** *nm* album

**alcalde, -desa** *n* mayor

**alcance** *nm* reach; range, scope

**alcancía** *nf* money box

**alcantarilla** *nf* sewer, drain

**alcanzar** *v* reach; catch up with; achieve, attain; suffice, be enough; ~ **a** manage to

**alcaparra** *nf* caper

**alcoba** *nf* bedroom

**alcohol** *nm* alcohol — **alcohólico, -ca** *adj & n* alcoholic

**aleatorio, -ria** *adj* random

**alegoría** *nf* allegory

**alegrar** *v* make happy, cheer up — **alegre** *adj* glad, happy; colorful, bright — **alegría** *nf* joy, cheer

**alejar** *v* remove, move away; estrange

**alemán, -mana** *adj* (**-manes**) German — **alemán** *nm* German language

**alentar** *v* encourage

**alergia** *nf* allergy

**alerta** *adv* on the alert — **alerta** *adj & nf* alert — **alertar** *v* alert

**aleta** *nf* fin, flipper; small wing

**alfabeto** *nm* alphabet — **alfabetismo** *nm* literacy — **alfabetizar** *v* teach literacy; alphabetize

**alfiler** *nm* pin; brooch

**alfombra** *nf* carpet, rug

**alga** *nf* seaweed

**álgebra** *nf* algebra

**algo** *adv* somewhat, rather — **algo** *pron* something; **algo de** some, a little

**algodón** *nm* (**-dones**) cotton

**alguien** *pron* somebody, someone

**alguno** *pron* one, someone, somebody — **alguno, -na** *adj* (**algún** *before masculine singular nouns*) some, any; (*in negative constructions*) not any, not at all; **algunas veces** sometimes

**algunos, -nas** *pron pl* some, a few

**aliado, -da** *n* ally — **aliado, -da** *adj* allied — **alianza** *nf* alliance — **aliarse** *vr* form an alliance

**alicates** *nmpl* pliers

**alienar** *v* alienate — **alienación** *nf* (**-ciones**) alienation

**aliento** *nm* breath; encouragement, strength

**aligerar** *v* lighten; hasten, quicken

**alimentar** *v* feed, nourish — **alimentación** *nf* (**-ciones**) feeding; nourishment

**alineación** *nf* (**-ciones**) alignment; lineup

**alinear** *v* align, line up — **alinearse con** *vr phr* align oneself with

**alisar** *v* smooth

**alistarse** *vr* join up, enlist

**aliviar** *v* relieve, soothe — **alivio** *nm* relief

**allá** *adv* there, over there; **más** ~ farther away; **más** ~ **de** beyond

**allanar** *v* smooth, level out; raid — **allanamiento** *nm* raid

**allí** *adv* there, over there
**alma** *nf* soul
**almacén** *nm* (**-cenes**) warehouse; shop, store; **grandes almacenes** department store — **almacenamiento** *nm* storage — **almacenar** *v* store
**almanaque** *nm* almanac
**almendra** *nf* almond; kernel
**almíbar** *nm* syrup
**almidón** *nm* (**-dones**) starch
**almirante** *nm* admiral
**almohada** *nf* pillow
**almorzar** *v* have lunch; have for lunch — **almuerzo** *nm* lunch
**alojar** *v* house, lodge — **alojamiento** *nm* lodging, accommodations *pl*
**alquilar** *v* rent, lease
**alrededor** *adv* around, about; **~ de** approximately — **alrededor de** *prep phr* around — **alrededores** *nmpl* outskirts
**alta** *nf* discharge; release
**altar** *nm* altar
**altavoz** *nm* (**-voces**) loudspeaker
**alterar** *v* alter, modify; disturb — **alteración** *nf* (**-ciones**) alteration; disturbance
**alternar** *v* alternate; **~ con** socialize with — **alternarse** *vr* take turns — **alternativa** *nf* alternative — **alternativo, -va** *adj* alternating, alternative — **alterno, -na** *adj* alternate
**altiplano** *nm* high plateau
**altitud** *nf* altitude
**altivo, -va** *adj* haughty
**alto** *adv* high; loud, loudly — **alto** *nm* height, elevation; stop, halt — **alto** *interj* halt!, stop!
**alto, -ta** *adj* tall, high; loud
**altruista** *adj* altruistic — **altruismo** *nm* altruism
**altura** *nf* height; altitude; **a la ~ de** near, up by
**alucinar** *v* hallucinate — **alucinación** *nf* (**-ciones**) hallucination
**alud** *nm* avalanche

**aludido, -da** *adj* previously mentioned; **darse por ~** take it personally
**aludir** *v* allude, refer
**alumbrar** *v* light, illuminate; **alumbrado** *nm* lighting
**alumno, -na** *n* pupil, student
**alusión** *nf* (**-siones**) allusion
**aluvión** *nm* (**-viones**) flood, barrage
**alzar** *v* lift, raise — **alza** *nf* rise
**amabilidad** *nf* kindness — **amable** *adj* kind, nice
**amaestrar** *v* train
**amamantar** *v* breast-feed, nurse
**amanecer** *v impers* dawn — **amanecer** *v* wake up — **amanecer** *nm* dawn, daybreak
**amante** *adj* loving; **~ de** fond of
**amante** *nmf* lover
**amapola** *nf* poppy
**amar** *v* love
**amargo, -ga** *adj* bitter — **amargo** *nm* bitterness
**amarillo, -lla** *adj* yellow — **amarillo** *nm* yellow
**amarrar** *v* tie up
**amasar** *v* knead
**amateur** *adj* & *nmf* amateur
**ambición** *nf* (**-ciones**) ambition — **ambicionar** *v* aspire to — **ambicioso, -sa** *adj* ambitious
**ambiente** *nm* atmosphere; environment, surroundings *pl*
**ambigüedad** *nf* ambiguity — **ambiguo, -gua** *adj* ambiguous
**ambos, -bas** *adj* & *pron* both
**ambulancia** *nf* ambulance
**amén** *nm* amen
**amenazar** *v* threaten — **amenaza** *nf* threat, menace
**ameno, -na** *adj* pleasant
**americano, -na** *adj* American
**ametralladora** *nf* machine gun
**amígdala** *nf* tonsil — **amigdalitis** *nf* tonsilitis
**amigo, -ga** *adj* friendly, close — **amigo, -ga** *n* friend

**amistad** *nf* friendship — **amistoso, -sa** *adj* friendly

**amnesia** *nf* amnesia

**amnistía** *nf* amnesty

**amo, ama** *n* master, mistress; **ama de casa** homemaker, housewife

**amoldar** *v* adapt, adjust

**amontonar** *v* pile up

**amor** *nm* love

**amparar** *v* shelter, protect

**ampliar** *v* expand; enlarge — **ampliación** *nf* (**-ciones**) expansion, enlargement

**amplio, -plia** *adj* broad, wide, ample — **amplitud** *nf* breadth, extent; spaciousness

**ampolla** *nf* blister; vial

**amueblar** *v* furnish

**añadir** *v* add

**analfabeto, -ta** *adj* & *n* illiterate — **analfabetismo** *nm* illiteracy

**analgésico** *nm* painkiller, analgesic

**analizar** *v* analyze — **análisis** *nm* analysis

**anaranjado, -da** *adj* orange-colored

**anatomía** *nf* anatomy — **anatómico, -ca** *adj* anatomic, anatomical

**anchoa** *nf* anchovy

**ancho, -cha** *adj* wide, broad, ample — **ancho** *nm* width

**anchura** *nf* width, breadth

**anciano, -na** *adj* aged, elderly — **anciano, -na** *n* elderly person

**andar** *v* walk; go, travel; run, work; ~ **en** rummage around in; ~ **por** be approximately

**andén** *nm* (**-denes**) train platform; sidewalk

**andino, -na** *adj* Andean

**anécdota** *nf* anecdote

**anemia** *nf* anemia — **anémico, -ca** *adj* anemic

**anestesia** *nf* anesthesia — **anestésico, -ca** *adj* anesthetic — **anestésico** *nm* anesthetic

**anexar** *v* annex, attach — **anexo, -xa** *adj* attached — **anexo** *nm* annex

**anfibio, -bia** *adj* amphibious — **anfibio** *nm* amphibian

**ángel** *nm* angel

**angloparlante** *adj* English-speaking

**angosto, -ta** *adj* narrow

**ángulo** *nm* angle; corner

**angustiar** *v* anguish, distress; worry — **angustia** *nf* anguish; worry

**anhelar** *v* yearn for, crave — **anhelo** *nm* longing

**anillo** *nm* ring

**animado, -da** *adj* cheerful, animated — **animador, -dora** *n* television host; cheerleader

**animal** *nm* animal — **animal** *nmf* brute, beast

**animar** *v* encourage; cheer up — **animarse** *vr* take heart; cheer up; **animarse a** get up the nerve to

**ánimo** *nm* mood, spirits *pl*; encouragement

**anís** *nm* anise

**aniversario** *nm* anniversary

**anoche** *adv* last night

**anochecer** *v* get dark — **anochecer** *nm* dusk, nightfall

**anónimo, -ma** *adj* anonymous

**anorexia** *nf* anorexia

**anormal** *adj* abnormal — **anormalidad** *nf* abnormality

**anotar** *v* annotate — **anotación** *nf* (**-ciones**) annotation, note

**ansiedad** *nf* anxiety — **ansioso, -sa** *adj* anxious; eager

**antártico, -ca** *adj* antarctic

**ante** *prep* before, in front of

**anteanoche** *adv* the night before last

**anteayer** *adv* the day before yesterday

**antebrazo** *nm* forearm

**antecedente** *adj* previous, prior — **antecedente** *nm* precedent

**antelación** *nf* (**-ciones**) advance notice; **con** ~ in advance

**antena** *nf* antenna

**anteojos** *nmpl* glasses, eyeglasses

**antepasado, -da** *n* ancestor

**antepenúltimo, -ma** *adj* third from last

**anterioridad** *nf* priority; **con** ∼ beforehand, in advance — **anterior** *adj* previous, earlier; front — **anteriormente** *adv* previously

**antes** *adv* before, earlier; previously; first; rather

**antibiótico** *nm* antibiotic

**anticipación** *nf* (**-ciones**) anticipation; **con** ∼ in advance

**anticipado, -da** *adj* advance, early; **por** ∼ in advance

**anticipar** *v* move up; pay in advance — **anticiparse** *vr* be early; get ahead

**anticonceptivo, -va** *adj* contraceptive — **anticonceptivo** *nm* contraceptive

**anticuado, -da** *adj* antiquated, outdated

**antiguo, -gua** *adj* ancient, old; former; old-fashioned; **antiguamente** *adv* long ago; formerly — **antigüedad** *nf* antiquity

**antihigiénico, -ca** *adj* unsanitary

**antipatía** *nf* aversion, dislike — **antipático, -ca** *adj* unpleasant

**antirreglamentario, -ria** *adj* unlawful

**antirrobo, -ba** *adj* antitheft

**antisemita** *adj* anti-Semitic

**antisocial** *adj* antisocial

**antojo** *nm* whim, craving — **antojarse** *vr* crave

**antropología** *nf* anthropology

**anual** *adj* annual, yearly — **anuario** *nm* yearbook, annual

**anular** *v* annul, cancel

**anunciar** *v* announce; advertise — **anuncio** *nm* announcement; advertisement

**año** *nm* year; **Año Nuevo** New Year

**apachurrar** *v* crush

**apacible** *adj* gentle, mild

**apaciguar** *v* appease, pacify

**apagar** *v* switch off; extinguish, put out — **apagado, -da** *adj* off, out

**aparato** *nm* machine, appliance, apparatus; anatomical system

**aparecer** *v* appear; show up

**aparentar** *v* seem — **aparente** *adj* apparent, seeming

**apariencia** *nf* appearance, look

**apartado** *nm* section, paragraph; ∼ **postal** post office box

**apartamento** *nm* apartment

**apartar** *v* move away; set aside, separate — **aparte** *adv* apart, separately; besides

**apasionar** *v* excite, fascinate — **apasionado, -da** *adj* passionate, excited — **apasionante** *adj* exciting

**apegado, -da** *adj* devoted — **apegarse a** *vr phr* become attached to, grow fond of — **apego** *nm* fondness

**apellido** *nm* last name, surname — **apellidarse** *vr* have for a last name

**apenar** *v* sadden — **apenarse** *vr* grieve; become embarrassed

**apenas** *adv* hardly, scarcely — **apenas** *conj* as soon as

**apéndice** *nm* appendix — **apendicitis** *nf* appendicitis

**aperitivo** *nm* appetizer; aperitif

**apetecer** *v* crave, long for

**apetito** *nm* appetite — **apetitoso, -sa** *adj* appetizing

**apio** *nm* celery

**aplanar** *v* flatten, level

**aplastar** *v* crush — **aplastante** *adj* overwhelming

**aplaudir** *v* applaud — **aplauso** *nm* applause; acclaim

**aplazar** *v* postpone, defer

**aplicar** *v* apply — **aplicable** *adj* applicable — **aplicado, -da** *adj* diligent

**apodo** *nm* nickname

**aportar** *v* contribute — **aportación** *nf* (**-ciones**) contribution

**apostar** *v* bet, wager

**apóstrofo** *nm* apostrophe

**apoyar** *v* support; lean, rest — **apoyo** *nm* support

**apreciar** *v* appreciate — **apreciable** *adj* considerable — **apreciación** *nf* (**-ciones**) appreciation — **aprecio** *nm* esteem

**aprender** *v* learn — **aprenderse** *vr* memorize

**aprendizaje** *nm* apprenticeship

**apresurar** *v* speed up — **apresuradamente** *adv* hurriedly, hastily — **apresurado, -da** *adj* in a rush

**apretar** *v* press, push; tighten; squeeze; press (down); fit too tightly — **apretado, -da** *adj* tight

**aprisa** *adv* quickly

**aprobar** *v* approve of; pass — **aprobación** *nf* (**-ciones**) approval

**apropiación** *nf* (**-ciones**) appropriation — **apropiado, -da** *adj* appropriate

**apropiarse de** *vr phr* take possession of, appropriate

**aprovechar** *v* take advantage of, make good use of; be of use

**aproximar** *v* bring closer — **aproximadamente** *adv* approximately

**apto, -ta** *adj* suitable; capable — **aptitud** *nf* aptitude, capability

**apuesta** *nf* bet, wager

**apuntar** *v* aim, point; jot down; point at; prompt — **apuntarse** *vr* sign up; score, chalk up — **apunte** *nm* note

**apurar** *v* hurry, rush; use up; trouble

**aquél, aquélla** *pron* (**aquéllos**) that (one), those (ones); the former

**aquel, aquella** *adj* (**aquellos**) that, those

**aquello** *pron* that, that matter

**aquí** *adv* here; now; **por ~** hereabouts

**aquietar** *v* calm

**árabe** *adj* Arab, Arabic — **árabe** *nm* Arabic language

**araña** *nf* spider; chandelier

**arañar** *v* scratch, claw

**arbitrario, -ria** *adj* arbitrary — **arbitrio** *nm* (free) will; judgment — **árbitro, -tra** *n* arbitrator; referee, umpire

**árbol** *nm* tree

**arcaico, -ca** *adj* archaic

**archipiélago** *nm* archipelago

**archivar** *v* file — **archivo** *nm* file; archives *pl*

**arco** *nm* arch; bow; arc; **~ iris** rainbow

**ardilla** *nf* squirrel; **~ listada** chipmunk

**ardor** *nm* burning; passion, ardor

**arduo, -dua** *adj* arduous

**área** *nf* area

**arena** *nf* sand; arena

**arete** *nm* earring

**argentino, -na** *adj* Argentinian, Argentine

**argolla** *nf* hoop, ring

**argot** *nm* slang

**argumentar** *v* argue, contend — **argumentación** *nf* (**-ciones**) argument, reason — **argumento** *nm* argument, reasoning; plot, story line

**árido, -da** *adj* dry, arid

**aristocracia** *nf* aristocracy

**aritmética** *nf* arithmetic

**arma** *nf* arm, weapon; **~ de fuego** firearm — **armada** *nf* navy

**armar** *v* arm; assemble

**armario** *nm* closet; cupboard, cabinet

**armonía** *nf* harmony — **armónica** *nf* harmonica

**aroma** *nm* aroma, scent

**arpa** *nf* harp

**arquear** *v* arch, bend

**arqueología** *nf* archaeology — **arqueólogo, -ga** *n* archaeologist

**arquitectura** *nf* architecture — **arquitecto, -ta** *n* architect

**arracimarse** *vr* cluster together

**arraigar** *v* take root, become established

**arrancar** *v* pull out, tear off; start; get going

**arranque** *nm* engine starter; outburst; **punto de ~** starting point

**arrasar** *v* destroy; fill to the brim

**arrastrar** *v* drag; draw, attract; trail — **arrastrarse** *vr* grovel

**arrebatar** *v* snatch, seize; captivate

**arrecife** *nm* reef

**arreglar** *v* fix; tidy up; solve, work out — **arreglarse** *vr* get dressed up

**arreglo** *nm* agreement

**arrendar** *v* rent, lease

**arrepentirse** *vr* regret, be sorry; repent

**arriba** *adv* above, overhead; up, upwards; upstairs; ∼ **de** more than; **de** ∼ **abajo** from top to bottom

**arribar** *v* arrive; dock, put into port — **arribista** *nmf* parvenu, upstart — **arribo** *nm* arrival

**arriesgar** *v* risk, venture

**arrobar** *v* entrance

**arrodillarse** *vr* kneel

**arrogancia** *nf* arrogance

**arrojar** *v* hurl, cast; give off, spew out; yield

**arrollar** *v* sweep away; crush, overwhelm; run over

**arroyo** *nm* stream; gutter

**arroz** *nm* (**arroces**) rice

**arrugar** *v* wrinkle, crease — **arruga** *nf* wrinkle, crease

**arruinar** *v* ruin, wreck — **arruinarse** *vr* go bankrupt

**arrullar** *v* lull to sleep; coo

**arte** *nmf* (*usually m in singular, f in plural*) art; skill; cunning, cleverness

**arteria** *nf* artery

**artesanía** *nm* craftsmanship; handicrafts *pl* — **artesanal** *adj* handmade — **artesano, -na** *n* artisan, craftsman

**ártico, -ca** *adj* arctic

**articular** *v* articulate — **articulación** *nf* (**-ciones**) articulation, pronunciation; joint

**artículo** *nm* article; ∼**s de primera necesidad** essentials; ∼**s de tocador** toiletries

**artificial** *adj* artificial

**artista** *nmf* artist; actor, actress *f* — **artístico, -ca** *adj* artistic

**artritis** *nms* & *pl* arthritis

**arveja** *nf* pea

**asado** *nm* roast

**asalariado, -da** *n* wage earner — **asalariado, -da** *adj* salaried

**asaltar** *v* assault; mug, rob — **asaltante** *nmf* assailant; mugger, robber — **asalto** *nm* assault; mugging, robbery

**asamblea** *nf* assembly, meeting

**asar** *v* roast, grill — **asarse** *vr* feel the heat

**asbesto** *nm* asbestos

**ascender** *v* ascend, rise up; be promoted; promote; ∼ **a** amount to — **ascenso** *nm* ascent, rise; promotion — **ascensor** *nm* elevator

**asco** *nm* disgust; **hacer** ∼**s de** turn up one's nose at; **me da** ∼ it makes me sick

**asear** *v* clean, tidy up

**asegurar** *v* assure; secure; insure

**asemejarse** *vr* be similar; ∼ **a** resemble

**aseo** *nm* cleanliness

**asequible** *adj* accessible, attainable

**asesinar** *v* murder; assassinate — **asesinato** *nm* murder; assassination — **asesino, -na** *n* murderer; assassin

**asesorar** *v* advise, counsel — **asesor, -sora** *n* advisor, consultant

**asfalto** *nm* asphalt

**asfixiar** *v* asphyxiate, suffocate

**así** *adv* like this, like that, thus; ∼ **de** so, that (much); ∼ **que** so, therefore; ∼ **que** as soon as; ∼ **como** as well as — **así** *adj* such, like that — **así** *conj* even though

**asiático, -ca** *adj* Asian, Asiatic

**asignar** *v* assign, allocate; appoint — **asignación** *nf* (**-ciones**) assignment; salary, pay — **asignatura** *nf* subject, course

**asilo** *nm* asylum, home; refuge, shelter — **asilado, -da** *n* inmate

**asimismo** *adv* similarly, likewise

**asistencia** *nf* attendance; assistance

**asistente** *nmf* assistant; **los** ∼**s** those in attendance

**asma** *nf* asthma

**asociar** *v* associate — **asociación** *nf* (**-ciones**) association

**asociarse a** *vr phr* join, become a member of

**asombrar** *v* amaze, astonish — **asombro** *nm* amazement, astonishment

**aspecto** *nm* aspect; appearance, look

**áspero, -ra** *adj* rough, harsh

**aspersión** *nf* (**-siones**) sprinkling — **aspersor** *nm* sprinkler

**aspiración** *nf* (**-ciones**) breathing in; aspiration

**aspiradora** *nf* vacuum cleaner

**aspirar** *v* inhale, breathe in; ~ **a** aspire to — **aspirante** *nmf* applicant, candidate

**aspirina** *nf* aspirin

**asterisco** *nm* asterisk

**asteroide** *nm* asteroid

**astigmatismo** *nm* astigmatism

**astro** *nm* heavenly body; star

**astrología** *nf* astrology

**astronauta** *nmf* astronaut

**astronomía** *nf* astronomy — **astrónomo, -ma** *n* astronomer

**astucia** *nf* astuteness; cunning, guile — **astuto, -ta** *adj* astute; crafty

**asumir** *v* assume — **asunción** *nf* (**-ciones**) assumption

**asunto** *nm* matter, affair; business

**asustar** *v* scare, frighten

**atacar** *v* attack — **atacante** *nmf* attacker

**atañer a** *v phr* concern, have to do with

**ataque** *nm* attack, assault; fit; ~ **de nervios** nervous breakdown

**atar** *v* tie up, tie down

**atardecer** *v impers* get dark — **atardecer** *nm* late afternoon, dusk

**ataúd** *nm* coffin

**ataviar** *v* dress up

**atención** *nf* (**-ciones**) attention; **prestar** ~ pay attention; **llamar la** ~ attract attention — **atención** *interj* attention!, watch out!

**atender** *v* attend to; look after; heed; pay attention

**atentado** *nm* attack — **atentar contra** *v phr* make an attempt on

**atentamente** *adv* attentively; **le saluda** ~ sincerely yours

**atento, -ta** *adj* attentive, mindful; courteous

**ateo, atea** *adj* atheistic — **ateo, atea** *n* atheist

**aterrador, -dora** *adj* terrifying

**aterrizar** *v* land — **aterrizaje** *nm* landing

**atestiguar** *v* testify to

**atlántico, -ca** *adj* Atlantic

**atlas** *nm* atlas

**atleta** *nmf* athlete — **atlético, -ca** *adj* athletic — **atletismo** *nm* athletics

**atmósfera** *nf* atmosphere — **atmosférico, -ca** *adj* atmospheric

**átomo** *nm* atom — **atómico, -ca** *adj* atomic — **atomizador** *nm* atomizer

**atornillar** *v* screw

**atracción** *nf* (**-ciones**) attraction

**atraco** *nm* holdup, robbery

**atractivo, -va** *adj* attractive — **atractivo** *nm* attraction, appeal

**atraer** *v* attract

**atrapar** *v* trap, capture

**atrás** *adv* back, behind; before, earlier; **para** ~ *or* **hacia** ~ backwards

**atrasar** *v* delay; lose time — **atrasado, -da** *adj* late, overdue; backward; slow — **atraso** *nm* delay; backwardness; ~**s** *nmpl* arrears

**atravesar** *v* cross; pierce; go through — **atravesarse** *vr* be in the way

**atreverse** *vr* dare — **atrevido, -da** *adj* bold; insolent — **atrevimiento** *nm* boldness; insolence

**atribuir** *v* attribute; confer — **atribuirse** *vr* take credit for

**atributo** *nm* attribute

**atrocidad** *nf* atrocity

**atropellar** *v* run over; violate, abuse — **atropello** *nm* abuse, outrage

**atropellarse** *vr* rush — **atropellado, -da** *adj* hasty

**atún** *nm* (**atunes**) tuna

**aturdir** *v* stun, shock; bewilder — **aturdido, -da** *adj* dazed, bewildered

**audaz** *adj* (**-daces**) bold, daring — **audacia** *nf* boldness, audacity

**audible** *adj* audible

**audición** *nf* (**-ciones**) hearing; audition

**audiencia** *nf* audience

**audífono** *nm* hearing aid; **∼s** *nmpl* headphones, earphones

**audiovisual** *adj* audiovisual

**auditorio** *nm* auditorium; audience

**auge** *nm* peak; boom, upturn

**augurar** *v* predict, foretell — **augurio** *nm* omen

**aula** *nf* classroom

**aumentar** *v* increase, raise; grow — **aumento** *nm* increase, rise

**aún** *adv* still, yet; **más ∼** furthermore

**aun** *adv* even; **∼ así** even so

**aunque** *conj* though, although, even if; **∼ sea** at least

**aurora** *nf* dawn

**ausentarse** *vr* leave, go away — **ausencia** *nf* absence — **ausente** *adj* absent — **ausente** *nmf* absentee; missing person

**austeridad** *nf* austerity

**australiano, -na** *adj* Australian

**austriaco** *or* **austríaco, -ca** *adj* Austrian

**auténtico, -ca** *adj* authentic, genuine

**autobiografía** *nf* autobiography — **autobiográfico, -ca** *adj* autobiographical

**autobús** *nm* (**-buses**) bus

**autocontrol** *nm* self-control

**autóctono, -na** *adj* indigenous, native

**autodefensa** *nf* self-defense

**autodidacta** *adj* self-taught

**autodisciplina** *nf* self-discipline

**autoestop** hitchhiking — **autostopista** *nmf* hitchhiker

**autografiar** *v* autograph — **autógrafo** *nm* autograph

**automático, -ca** *adj* automatic

**automotor, -triz** *adj* (**-trices** *f*) self-propelled

**automóvil** *nm* automobile — **automovilista** *nmf* motorist

**autonomía** *nf* autonomy — **autónomo, -ma** *adj* autonomous

**autopista** *nf* expressway, highway

**autopsia** *nf* autopsy

**autoridad** *nf* authority — **autoritario, -ria** *adj* authoritarian

**autorizar** *v* authorize, approve — **autorización** *nf* (**-ciones**) authorization

**autor, -tora** *n* author; perpetrator

**autoservicio** *nm* self-service restaurant; supermarket

**autosuficiente** *adj* self-sufficient

**auxiliar** *nmf* assistant, helper; **∼ de vuelo** flight attendant — **auxiliar** *v* aid, assist — **auxiliar** *adj* auxiliary

**auxilio** *nm* aid, assistance; **primeros ∼s** first aid

**avalancha** *nf* avalanche

**avanzar** *v* advance, move forward — **avance** *nm* advance — **avanzado, -da** *adj* advanced

**avaro, -ra** *adj* miserly — **avaro, -ra** *n* miser — **avaricia** *nf* greed, avarice

**ave** *nf* bird

**avellana** *nf* hazelnut

**avena** *nf* oats *pl*; *or* **harina de ∼** oatmeal

**avenida** *nf* avenue

**aventajar** *v* be ahead of, surpass

**aventurar** *v* venture, risk — **aventura** *nf* adventure; risk; love affair

**avergonzar** *v* shame, embarrass

**averiguar** *v* find out; investigate — **averiguación** *nf* (**-ciones**) investigation, inquiry

**aversión** *nf* (**-siones**) aversion, dislike

**avestruz** *nm* (**-truces**) ostrich

**aviación** *nf* (**-ciones**) aviation — **aviador, -dora** *n* aviator

**avión** *nm* (**aviones**) airplane — **avioneta** *nf* light airplane

**aviso** *nm* notice; warning; advertisement, ad; **estar sobre ∼** be on the alert — **avisar** *v* notify; warn

**avispa** *nf* wasp — **avispón** *nm* (**-pones**) hornet

**avispado, -da** *adj* clever, sharp

**axila** *nf* underarm, armpit

**axioma** *nm* axiom

**ay** *interj* oh!; ouch!, ow!

**ayer** *adv* yesterday — **ayer** *nm* yesteryear, days gone by

**ayuda** *nf* help, assistance — **ayudante** *nmf* helper, assistant

**ayudar** *v* help, assist — **ayudarse de** *vr phr* make use of

**azabache** *nm* jet

**azafata** *nf* stewardess *f*

**azafrán** *nm* (**-franes**) saffron

**azalea** *nf* azalea

**azar** *nm* chance; **al ～** at random

**azote** *nm* whip, lash; scourge

**azotea** *nf* flat or terraced roof

**azteca** *adj* Aztec

**azúcar** *nmf* sugar

**azufre** *nm* sulphur

**azul** *adj & nm* blue — **azulado, -da** *adj* bluish

**azulejo** *nm* ceramic tile; bluebird

# B

**b** *nf* b, second letter of the Spanish alphabet

**baba** *nf* saliva, drool

**babero** *nm* bib

**babosa** *nf* slug

**babucha** *nf* slipper

**bacalao** *nm* cod

**bachiller** *nmf* high school graduate — **bachillerato** *nm* high school diploma

**bacteria** *nf* bacterium, germ

**bagre** *nm* catfish

**bahía** *nf* bay

**bailar** *v* dance — **bailarín, -rina** *n* (**-rines** *m*) dancer — **baile** *nm* dance; dance party, ball

**bajar** *v* bring down, lower; go down, come down; descend, drop — **bajarse** *vr* get out of, get off — **bajada** *nf* descent, drop; slope

**bajo** *adv* low — **bajo** *prep* under, below — **bajo, -ja** *adj* low, lower; short

**bala** *nf* bullet

**balada** *nf* ballad

**balancear** *v* balance; swing, rock — **balancearse** *vr* swing, sway — **balance** *nm* balance — **balanceo** *nm* swaying, rocking

**balancín** *nm* (**-cines**) seesaw; rocking chair

**balanza** *nf* scales *pl*, balance

**balcón** *nm* (**-cones**) balcony

**balde** *nm* bucket, pail

**baldosa** *nf* floor tile

**ballena** *nf* whale

**ballet** *nm* ballet

**balneario** *nm* spa

**balompié** *nm* soccer

**balón** *nm* (**-lones**) ball — **baloncesto** *nm* basketball

**balsa** *nf* raft

**bambú** *nm* (**-búes** *or* **-bús**) bamboo

**banal** *adj* banal

**banana** *nf* banana — **banano** *nm* banana

**banca** *nf* banking; bench — **bancario, -ria** *adj* bank, banking — **banco** *nm* bank; stool, bench, pew

**banda** *nf* band, strip; band; gang — **bandada** *nf* flock (of birds), school (of fish)

**bandeja** *nf* tray, platter

**bandera** *nf* flag, banner

**bandido, -da** *n* bandit

**bando** *nm* proclamation, edict; faction, side

**banquero, -ra** *n* banker

**banquete** *nm* banquet

**baño** *nm* bath, swim; ¿dónde está el ∼? where is the bathroom? — **bañar** *v* bathe, wash — **bañera** *nf* bathtub

**bar** *nm* bar, tavern

**baraja** *nf* deck of cards

**baranda** *nf* rail, railing

**barato, -ta** *adj* cheap — **barato** *adv* cheap, cheaply

**barba** *nf* beard, stubble

**barbaridad** *nf* barbarity, cruelty — **bárbaro, -ra** *adj* barbaric

**barbero, -ra** *n* barber — **barbería** *nf* barbershop

**barbilla** *nf* chin

**barbudo, -da** *adj* bearded

**barca** *nf* boat — **barco** *nm* boat, ship

**barman** *nm* bartender

**barra** *nf* bar, rod, stick; counter

**barrer** *v* sweep

**barrera** *nf* barrier

**barriga** *nf* belly

**barril** *nm* barrel, keg

**barrio** *nm* neighborhood

**barro** *nm* mud

**basar** *v* base

**báscula** *nf* scales *pl*

**base** *nf* base; basis, foundation — **básico, -ca** *adj* basic

**basquetbol** *or* **básquetbol** *nm* basketball

**bastante** *adv* fairly, rather; enough — **bastante** *adj* enough, sufficient — **bastante** *pron* enough

**basto, -ta** *adj* coarse, rough

**bastón** *nm* (-tones) cane, walking stick

**basura** *nf* garbage, rubbish — **basurero, -ra** *n* garbage collector

**bata** *nf* bathrobe, housecoat; smock

**batallar** *v* battle, fight — **batalla** *nf* battle, fight, struggle — **batallón** *nm* (-llones) battalion

**batear** *v* bat, hit — **bate** *nm* baseball bat — **bateador, -dora** *n* batter, hitter

**batería** *nf* battery; drums *pl*

**batir** *v* beat, whip — **batido** *nm* milk shake — **batidor** *nm* eggbeater, whisk — **batidora** *nf* electric mixer

**baúl** *nm* trunk, chest

**bautismo** *nm* baptism — **bautizar** *v* baptize — **bautizo** *nm* baptism, christening

**bazar** *nm* bazaar

**bazo** *nm* spleen

**bebé** *nm* baby

**beber** *v* drink — **bebida** *nf* drink, beverage — **bebido, -da** *adj* drunk

**beca** *nf* grant, scholarship

**becerro, -rra** *n* calf

**beige** *adj* & *nm* beige

**beisbol** *or* **béisbol** *nm* baseball — **beisbolista** *nmf* baseball player

**belga** *adj* Belgian

**belleza** *nf* beauty — **bello, -lla** *adj* beautiful; **bellas artes** fine arts

**bellota** *nf* acorn

**bendecir** *v* bless — **bendición** *nf* (-ciones) benediction, blessing — **bendito, -ta** *adj* blessed, holy

**beneficiar** *v* benefit, assist — **beneficio** *nm* gain, profit; benefit — **beneficioso, -sa** *adj* beneficial — **benéfico, -ca** *adj* charitable

**benigno, -na** *adj* benign

**berenjena** *nf* eggplant

**besar** *v* kiss — **besarse** *vr* kiss (each other) — **beso** *nm* kiss

**bestia** *nf* beast, animal — **bestial** *adj* bestial, brutal — **bestialidad** *nf* brutality

**betún** *nm* (-tunes) shoe polish

**bianual** *adj* biannual

**biberón** *nm* (-rones) baby's bottle

**Biblia** *nf* Bible

**bibliografía** *nf* bibliography

**biblioteca** *nf* library — **bibliotecario, -ria** *n* librarian

**bicicleta** *nf* bicycle

**bicolor** *adj* two-tone

**bien** *adv* well, good; correctly, right; very, quite; willingly; **más** ∼ rather — **bien** *adj* all right, well; pleasant, nice;

satisfactory; correct, right — **bien** *nm* good; **bienes** *nmpl* property, goods

**bienestar** *nm* welfare, well-being

**bienhechor, -chora** *n* benefactor

**bienvenido, -da** *adj* welcome — **bienvenida** *nf* welcome

**bigote** *nm* mustache

**bikini** *nm* bikini

**bilingüe** *adj* bilingual

**bilis** *nf* bile

**billar** *nm* pool, billiards

**billete** *nm* bill, banknote; ticket — **billetera** *nf* billfold, wallet

**billón** *nm* (**-llones**) trillion

**bimensual, -suales** *adj* twice a month — **bimestral** *adj* every two months

**bingo** *nm* bingo

**binoculares** *nmpl* binoculars

**biografía** *nf* biography

**biología** *nf* biology — **biológico, -ca** *adj* biological, biologic — **biólogo, -ga** *n* biologist

**biombo** *nm* folding screen

**bis** *adv* twice

**bisabuelo, -la** *n* great-grandfather *m*, great-grandmother *f*

**bisagra** *nf* hinge

**bisexual** *adj* bisexual

**bisiesto** *adj* leap year

**bisnieto, -ta** *n* great-grandson *m*, great-granddaughter *f*

**bisonte** *nm* bison, buffalo

**bistec** *nm* steak

**bit** *nm* bit (unit of information)

**bizco, -ca** *adj* cross-eyed

**bizcocho** *nm* sponge cake

**blanco, -ca** *adj* white — **blanco, -ca** *n* white person — **blanco** *nm* white; target, bull's-eye; blank (space) — **blancura** *nf* whiteness

**blando, -da** *adj* soft, tender; weak-willed; lenient — **blandura** *nf* softness, tenderness; weakness; leniency

**bloc** *nm* (**blocs**) (writing) pad

**bloquear** *v* block, obstruct; blockade

**blusa** *nf* blouse — **blusón** *nm* (**-sones**) smock

**bobo, -ba** *adj* silly, stupid — **bobo, -ba** *n* fool, simpleton

**boca** *nf* mouth; entrance; ~ **arriba** faceup; ~ **abajo** facedown

**bocacalle** *nf* entrance (to a street)

**bocado** *nm* bite, mouthful — **bocadillo** *nm* sandwich

**boceto** *nm* sketch, outline

**bochorno** *nm* muggy weather

**bocina** *nf* horn; mouthpiece

**boda** *nf* wedding

**bodega** *nf* wine cellar; warehouse

**bofetear** *v* slap — **bofetada** *nf or* **bofetón** *nm* slap (in the face)

**boga** *nf* fashion, vogue

**bohemio, -mia** *adj & n* bohemian

**boina** *nf* beret

**bola** *nf* ball

**bolera** *nf* bowling alley

**boleta** *nf* ticket — **boletería** *nf* ticket office

**boletín** *nm* (**-tines**) bulletin

**boleto** *nm* ticket

**bolígrafo** *nm* ballpoint pen

**bolillo** *nm* bobbin

**boliviano, -na** *adj* Bolivian

**bolsa** *nf* bag; — **bolsillo** *nm* pocket — **bolso** *nm* pocketbook, handbag

**bomba** *nf* bomb

**bombardeo** *nm* bombing, bombardment

**bombero, -ra** *n* firefighter

**bombilla** *nf* lightbulb — **bombillo** *nm* lightbulb

**bombo** *nm* bass drum

**bombón** *nm* (**-bones**) candy, chocolate

**bonachón, -chona** *adj* (**-chones** *m*) good-natured

**bonanza** *nf* prosperity

**bondad** *nf* goodness, kindness — **bondadoso, -sa** *adj* kind, good

**bonificación** *nf* (**-ciones**) bonus, extra; discount

**bonito, -ta** *adj* pretty, lovely

**boquiabierto, -ta** *adj* open-mouthed, speechless

**bordar** *v* embroider — **bordado** *nm* embroidery, needlework

**borde** *nm* border, edge; — **bordear** *v* border — **bordillo** *nm* curb

**bordo** *nm* **a** ~ aboard, on board

**borracho, -cha** *adj & n* drunk — **borrachera** *nf* drunkenness

**borrar** *v* erase, blot out — **borrador** *nm* rough draft; eraser

**borroso, -sa** *adj* blurry, smudgy; vague, hazy

**bosque** *nm* woods, forest

**bostezar** *v* yawn — **bostezo** *nm* yawn

**bota** *nf* boot

**botánica** *nf* botany

**botar** *v* throw, hurl; throw away; bounce

**bote** *nm* small boat

**botella** *nf* bottle

**botín** *nm* (**-tines**) ankle boot

**botiquín** *nm* (**-quines**) medicine cabinet; first-aid kit

**botón** *nm* (**-tones**) button

**boutique** *nf* boutique

**bóveda** *nf* vault

**boxear** *v* box — **boxeador, -dora** *n* boxer — **boxeo** *nm* boxing

**bragas** *nf* panties

**bragueta** *nf* fly, pants zipper

**braille** *adj & nm* braille

**brandy** *nm* brandy

**brasa** *nf* ember

**brasier** *nm* brassiere

**brasileño, -ña** *adj* Brazilian

**bravo, -va** *adj* fierce, savage; angry — **bravo, -va** *interj* bravo!, well done!

**brazalete** *nm* bracelet; armband

**brazo** *nm* arm; branch (of a river); ~**s** *nmpl* hands, laborers; ~ **derecho** right-hand man; top aide

**breve** *adj* brief, short; **en** ~ shortly, in short — **brevedad** *nf* brevity, shortness

**brigada** *nf* brigade

**brillar** *v* shine, sparkle — **brillante** *adj* brilliant, shiny — **brillante** *nm* diamond — **brillo** *nm* luster, shine; splendor

**brinco** *nm* jump, skip

**brindar** *v* drink a toast; offer, provide — **brindarse** *vr* offer one's assistance — **brindis** *nm* drink, toast

**brioso, -sa** *adj* spirited, lively

**brisa** *nf* breeze

**británico, -ca** *adj* British

**brocha** *nf* paintbrush

**broche** *nm* fastener, clasp

**brócoli** *nm* broccoli

**bromear** *v* joke, fool around — **broma** *nf* joke, prank — **bromista** *adj* fun-loving, joking — **bromista** *nmf* joker, prankster

**bronce** *nm* bronze — **bronceado, -da** *adj* suntanned — **bronceado** *nm* tan — **broncearse** *vr* get a suntan

**bronquitis** *nf* bronchitis

**brotar** *v* bud, sprout — **brote** *nm* outbreak

**brujería** *nf* witchcraft — **bruja** *nf* witch — **brujo** *nm* warlock, sorcerer — **brujo, -ja** *adj* bewitching

**brújula** *nf* compass

**bruma** *nf* haze, mist

**brusco, -ca** *adj* brusque, rough — **brusquedad** *nf* abruptness, brusqueness

**brutal** *adj* brutal — **brutalidad** *nf* brutality

**bruto, -ta** *adj* brutish, stupid

**bucal** *adj* oral

**bucear** *v* dive, swim underwater — **buceo** *nm* scuba diving

**budismo** *nm* Buddhism — **budista** *adj & nmf* Buddhist

**bueno, -na** *adj* good; kind; appropriate; well, healthy; **buenos días** hello, good day; **buenas noches** good night; **buenas tardes** good afternoon, good evening — **bueno** *interj* OK!, all right!

**buey** *nm* ox, steer

**búfalo** *nm* buffalo

**bufanda** *nf* scarf

**bufete** *nm* writing desk
**búho** *nm* owl
**buitre** *nm* vulture
**búlgaro, -ra** *adj* Bulgarian
**bulto** *nm* package, bundle
**buñuelo** *nm* fried pastry
**buque** *nm* ship
**burbuja** *nf* bubble
**burdel** *nm* brothel
**burdo, -da** *adj* coarse, rough
**burgués, -guesa** *adj & n* (**-gueses** *m*)
  bourgeois — **burguesía** *nf* bour-
  geoisie

**burlar** *v* trick, deceive — **burla** *nf* mock-
  ery, ridicule; joke, trick
**burlón, -lona** *adj* (**-lones** *m*) mocking
**burocracia** *nf* bureaucracy
**burro, -rra** *n* donkey; dunce — **burro,**
  **-rra** *adj* stupid
**bus** *nm* bus
**buscar** *v* look for, seek; search —
  **búsqueda** *nf* search
**butaca** *nf* armchair
**buzo** *nm* diver
**buzón** *nm* (**-zones**) mailbox
**byte** *nm* byte

# C

**c** *nf* c, third letter of the Spanish alphabet
**cabalgar** *v* ride — **cabalgata** *nf* caval-
  cade
**caballería** *nf* cavalry; horse, mount
**caballero** *nm* gentleman
**caballo** *nm* horse; knight (in chess);
  horsepower
**cabaña** *nf* cabin, hut
**cabaret** *nm* (**-rets**) nightclub, cabaret
**cabecilla** *nmf* ringleader
**cabello** *nm* hair
**caber** *v* fit, go (into)
**cabeza** *nf* head
**cabida** *nf* room, capacity
**cabina** *nf* booth; cabin, cockpit
**cable** *nm* cable
**cabra** *nf* goat
**cacahuate** *or* **cacahuete** *nm* peanut
**cacao** *nm* cocoa (drink)
**cacería** *nf* hunt
**cacerola** *nf* pan, saucepan
**cachete** *nm* cheek — **cachetada** *nf* slap
**cacho** *nm* horn
**cachorro, -rra** *n* puppy
**cactus** *or* **cacto** *nm* cactus
**cada** *adj* each, every
**cadáver** *nm* corpse
**cadena** *nf* chain

**cadera** *nf* hip
**cadete** *nmf* cadet
**caducar** *v* expire
**caer** *v* fall, drop; **me cae bien** I like her,
  I like him — **caerse** *vr* drop, fall
  (down)
**café** *nm* coffee; café ∼ *adj* brown —
  **cafetera** *nf* coffeepot — **cafetería** *nf*
  coffee shop, cafeteria
**caída** *nf* fall, drop
**caimán** *nm* (**-manes**) alligator
**caja** *nf* box, case; checkout counter; safe;
  cash register — **cajero, -ra** *n* cashier;
  teller — **cajón** *nm* (**-jones**) drawer
**cajetilla** *nf* pack
**calabaza** *nf* pumpkin, squash, gourd
**calabozo** *nm* cell
**calamar** *nm* squid
**calambre** *nm* cramp
**calavera** *nf* skull
**calcar** *v* trace; copy, imitate
**calcetín** *nm* (**-tines**) sock
**calcio** *nm* calcium
**calcomanía** *nf* decal
**calcular** *v* calculate, estimate — **calcu-**
  **ladora** *nf* calculator — **cálculo** *nm* calculation; calculus
**caldo** *nm* broth, stock

**calefacción** *nf* (**-ciones**) heating, heat

**calendario** *nm* calendar

**calentar** *v* heat (up), warm (up) — **calentarse** *vr* get warm, heat up — **calentador** *nm* heater

**calidad** *nf* quality

**cálido, -da** *adj* hot, warm

**caliente** *adj* hot

**calificar** *v* grade — **calificación** *nf* (**-ciones**) grade

**callar** *v* keep quiet, be silent; hush — **callarse** *vr* remain silent — **callado, -da** *adj* quiet, silent

**calle** *nf* street, road — **callejón** *nm* (**-jones**) alley

**callo** *nm* callus, corn

**calma** *nf* calm, quiet — **calmante** *nm* tranquilizer — **calmar** *v* calm, soothe

**calor** *nm* heat, warmth — **caloría** *nf* calorie

**caluroso, -sa** *adj* warm, enthusiastic

**calvo, -va** *adj* bald — **calvicie** *nf* baldness

**calzada** *nf* roadway

**calzado** *nm* footwear — **calzar** *v* put shoes on (someone)

**calzones** *nmpl* panties — **calzoncillos** *nmpl* underpants, briefs

**cama** *nf* bed

**cámara** *nf* camera

**camarero, -ra** *n* waiter, waitress *f*

**camarón** *nm* (**-rones**) shrimp

**camarote** *nm* cabin, stateroom

**cambiar** *v* change; exchange — **cambio** *nm* change

**camello** *nm* camel

**camilla** *nf* stretcher

**caminar** *v* walk; cover (a distance)

**camino** *nm* road, path; way

**camión** *nm* (**-miones**) truck — **camioneta** *nm* light truck, van

**camisa** *nf* shirt — **camiseta** *nf* T-shirt, undershirt

**campana** *nf* bell

**campeón, -peona** *n* (**-peones** *m*) champion — **campeonato** *nm* championship

**campesino, -na** *n* peasant, farm laborer — **campestre** *adj* rural, rustic

**camping** *nm* campsite

**campo** *nm* field; countryside, country

**cana** *nf* gray hair

**caña** *nf* cane, reed; fishing pole

**canadiense** *adj* Canadian

**canal** *nm* canal; channel

**canario** *nm* canary

**canasta** *nf* basket

**cancelar** *v* cancel; pay off, settle

**cáncer** *nm* cancer

**cancha** *nf* court, field (for sports)

**canciller** *nm* chancellor

**canción** *nf* (**-ciones**) song

**candado** *nm* padlock

**candela** *nf* candle — **candelabro** *nm* candelabra

**candidato, -ta** *n* candidate

**canela** *nf* cinnamon

**cangrejo** *nm* crab

**canguro** *nm* kangaroo

**canino, -na** *adj* canine

**canje** *nm* exchange, trade

**canoa** *nf* canoe

**cañón** *nm* (**-ñones**) cannon

**canoso, -sa** *adj* gray, gray-haired

**cansar** *v* tire (out); be tiring — **cansarse** *vr* get tired — **cansado, -da** *adj* tired; tiresome — **cansancio** *nm* fatigue, weariness

**cantar** *v* sing — **cantar** *nm* song — **cantante** *nmf* singer

**cantidad** *nf* quantity, amount

**cantimplora** *nf* canteen, water bottle

**canto** *nm* singing, song — **cantor, -tora** *adj* singing

**caos** *nm* chaos

**capa** *nf* cape, cloak

**capacidad** *nf* capacity; ability

**capacitar** *v* train, qualify — **capacitación** *nf* (**-ciones**) training

**caparazón** *nm* (**-zones**) shell

**capaz** *adj* (**-paces**) capable, able

**capilla** *nf* chapel

**capital** *adj* capital; ~ *nf* capital (city) — **capitalismo** *nm* capitalism

**capitán, -tana** *n* (**-tanes** *m*) captain

**capítulo** *nm* chapter

**capricho** *nm* whim, caprice — **caprichoso, -sa** *adj* whimsical, capricious

**cápsula** *nf* capsule

**captar** *v* grasp

**capturar** *v* capture, seize — **captura** *nf* capture, seizure

**caqui** *adj & nm* khaki

**cara** *nf* face

**caracol** *nm* snail

**carácter** *nm* (**-racteres**) character — **característica** *nf* characteristic — **característico, -ca** *adj* characteristic — **caracterizar** *v* characterize

**caramba** *interj* oh my!, good grief!

**caramelo** *nm* caramel; candy

**carbohidrato** *nm* carbohydrate

**carbón** *nm* (**-bones**) coal

**carcajada** *nf* loud laugh, guffaw

**cárcel** *nf* jail, prison

**cardenal** *nm* cardinal

**cardíaco** or **cardiaco, -ca** *adj* cardiac, heart

**cardiólogo, -ga** *n* cardiologist

**carecer** *vi* lack — **carencia** *nf* lack, want

**carestía** *nf* high cost

**cargar** *v* charge; carry — **cargamento** *nm* cargo, load — **cargo** *nm* charge; position, office

**caribe** *adj* Caribbean

**caricatura** *nf* caricature

**caricia** *nf* caress

**caridad** *nf* charity

**cariño** *nm* affection, love — **cariñoso, -sa** *adj* affectionate, loving

**caritativo, -va** *adj* charitable

**carnaval** *nm* carnival

**carne** *nf* meat

**carnero** *nm* ram, sheep

**carnet** *nm* ID card; ~ **de conducir** driver's license

**carnicería** *nf* butcher shop

**caro, -ra** *adj* expensive; dear — **caro** *adv* dearly

**carpa** *nf* tent

**carpeta** *nf* folder

**carpintería** *nf* carpentry — **carpintero, -ra** *n* carpenter

**carrera** *nf* running, run; race; course (of studies); career, profession

**carretera** *nf* highway, road

**carril** *nm* lane

**carro** *nm* automobile, car

**carrusel** *nm* merry-go-round, carousel

**carta** *nf* letter; playing card; menu

**cartel** *nm* poster, bill — **cartelera** *nf* billboard

**cartera** *nf* briefcase; wallet; pocketbook — **carterista** *nmf* pickpocket

**cartero, -ra** *nm* mail carrier, mailman *m*

**cartón** *nm* (**-tones**) cardboard

**casa** *nf* house; home

**casar** *v* marry — **casado, -da** *adj* married

**cascabel** *nm* small bell

**cascada** *nf* waterfall

**cáscara** *nf* skin, peel, shell

**casco** *nm* helmet

**caseta** *nf* booth, stall

**casi** *adv* almost, nearly

**casino** *nm* casino

**caso** *nm* case; pay attention

**caspa** *nf* dandruff

**cassette** *nmf* cassette

**castaña** *nf* chestnut

**castaño, -ña** *adj* chestnut (color)

**castañuela** *nf* castanet

**castellano** *nm* Castilian

**castigar** *v* punish — **castigo** *nm* punishment

**castillo** *nm* castle

**casual** *adj* chance, accidental — **casualidad** *nf* coincidence

**catálogo** *nm* catalog

**catarata** *nf* waterfall

**catarro** *nm* cold

**catedral** *nf* cathedral

**categoría** *nf* category; rank; first-rate

**católico, -ca** *adj & n* Catholic — **catolicismo** *nm* Catholicism

**catorce** *adj & nm* fourteen — **catorceavo** *nm* fourteenth

**caucho** *nm* rubber

**causar** *v* cause, provoke — **causa** *nf* cause; reason

**cauteloso, -sa** *adj* cautious

**cavar** *v* dig

**caverna** *nf* cavern, cave

**cavidad** *nf* cavity

**cazar** *v* hunt; go hunting — **caza** *nf* hunt, hunting — **cazador, -dora** *n* hunter

**cazuela** *nf* casserole

**CD** *nm* CD, compact disc

**cebada** *nf* barley

**cebolla** *nf* onion

**cebra** *nf* zebra

**ceder** *v* yield, give way; cede, hand over

**cedro** *nm* cedar

**cédula** *nf* document, certificate

**ceguera** *nf* blindness

**ceja** *nf* eyebrow

**celador, -dora** *n* guard, warden

**celda** *nf* cell

**celebrar** *v* celebrate — **celebración** *nf* (**-ciones**) celebration — **célebre** *adj* famous, celebrated

**celestial** *adj* celestial, heavenly

**celo** *nm* zeal; **~s** *nmpl* jealousy

**célula** *nf* cell — **celular** *adj* cellular

**cementerio** *nm* cemetery

**cemento** *nm* cement

**cena** *nf* supper, dinner

**cenar** *v* have dinner, have supper; have for dinner

**cenicero** *nm* ashtray

**ceniza** *nf* ash

**centavo** *nm* cent; centavo

**centenar** *nm* hundred

**centígrado** *adj* centigrade, Celsius

**centímetro** *nm* centimeter

**central** *adj* central

**centrar** *v* center — **centrarse en** *vr phr* focus on — **centro** *nm* center; downtown

**centroamericano, -na** *adj* Central American

**cepillo** *nm* brush; **~ de dientes** toothbrush — **cepillar** *v* brush

**cera** *nf* wax; beeswax

**cerámica** *nf* ceramics *pl*; pottery

**cerca¹** *nf* fence

**cerca²** *adv* close, near

**cerdo** *nm* pig, hog

**cereal** *adj & nm* cereal

**cerebro** *nm* brain

**ceremonia** *nf* ceremony

**cereza** *nf* cherry

**cerilla** *nf* match

**cero** *nm* zero

**cerrar** *v* close, shut; turn off; lock up — **cerrado, -da** *adj* closed — **cerradura** *nf* lock

**cerro** *nm* hill

**certeza** *nf* certainty — **certidumbre** *nf* certainty

**certificar** *v* certify — **certificado, -da** *adj* certified, registered — **certificado** *nm* certificate

**cerveza** *nf* beer

**cesar** *v* cease, stop; dismiss, lay off — **cesantía** *nf* unemployment

**cesárea** *nf* cesarean

**césped** *nm* lawn, grass

**cesta** *nf* basket — **cesto** *nm* basket; wastebasket

**chal** *nm* shawl

**chaleco** *nm* vest

**champaña** *or* **champán** *nm* champagne

**champiñón** *nm* (**-ñones**) mushroom

**champú** *nm* (**-pús** *or* **-púes**) shampoo

**chance** *nm* chance, opportunity

**chaqueta** *nf* jacket

**charco** *nm* puddle

**charlar** *v* chat — **charla** *nf* chat, talk

**charlatán, -tana** *adj* (**-tanes** *m*) talkative — **charlatán, -tana** *n* chatterbox; charlatan

**charol** *nm* patent leather

**chasis** *nms & pl* chassis
**chatarra** *nf* scrap
**chato, -ta** *adj* pug-nosed
**chaval, -vala** *n* kid, boy *m*, girl *f*
**checo, -ca** *adj* Czech — **checo** *nm* Czech
**chef** *nm* chef
**cheque** *nm* check — **chequera** *nf* checkbook
**chequear** *v* check, inspect, verify; check in — **chequeo** *nm* checkup
**chicharrón** *nm* (-rrones) pork rind
**chichón** *nm* (-chones) bump
**chicle** *nm* chewing gum
**chico, -ca** *adj* little, small — **chico, -ca** *n* child, boy *m*, girl *f*
**chiflar** *v* whistle; whistle at, boo — **chiflado, -da** *adj* crazy, nuts — **chiflido** *nm* whistling
**chile** *nm* chili pepper
**chileno, -na** *adj* Chilean
**chillido** *nm* scream; screech, squeal — **chillón, -llona** *adj* (-llones *m*) shrill, loud
**chimenea** *nf* chimney; fireplace
**chimpancé** *nm* chimpanzee
**chino, -na** *adj* Chinese — **chino** *nm* Chinese
**chiquillo, -lla** *n* kid, child
**chiquito, -ta** *adj* tiny — **chiquito, -ta** *n* little child, tot
**chirriar** *v* squeak, creak; screech — **chirrido** *nm* squeak, creak; screech
**chismoso, -sa** *adj* gossipy — **chismoso, -sa** *n* gossipy person — **chisme** *nm* gossip
**chispa** *nf* spark
**chiste** *nm* joke, funny story — **chistoso, -sa** *adj* funny, witty
**chivo, -va** *n* kid, young goat
**chocar** *v* crash, collide; clash — **chocante** *adj* striking, shocking; unpleasant, rude
**chocolate** *nm* chocolate
**chofer** *or* **chófer** *nm* chauffeur; driver
**choque** *nm* shock; crash, collision

**chorizo** *nm* chorizo, sausage
**chorrear** *v* drip; pour out, gush — **chorro** *nm* stream, jet
**choza** *nf* hut, shack
**chubasco** *nm* downpour, squall
**chueco, -ca** *adj* crooked
**chuleta** *nf* cutlet, chop
**chupar** *v* suck; absorb; suckle — **chupete** *nm* pacifier
**churro** *nm* fried dough
**cicatriz** *nf* (-trices) scar — **cicatrizar** *v* form a scar, heal
**cíclico, -ca** *adj* cyclical
**ciclismo** *nm* cycling — **ciclista** *nmf* cyclist
**ciclón** *nm* (-clones) cyclone
**ciego, -ga** *adj* blind — **ciegamente** *adv* blindly
**cielo** *nm* sky; heaven
**ciempiés** *nms & pl* centipede
**cien** *adj* a hundred, hundred — **cien** *nm* one hundred
**ciénaga** *nf* swamp, bog
**ciencia** *nf* science
**científico, -ca** *adj* scientific — **científico, -ca** *n* scientist
**ciento** *adj* one hundred — **ciento** *nm* hundred, group of a hundred
**cierre** *nm* closing, closure; fastener, clasp
**cierto, -ta** *adj* true; certain
**ciervo, -va** *n* deer, stag *m*, hind *f*
**cifra** *nf* number, figure; sum; code, cipher
**cigarrillo** *nm* cigarette
**cigüeña** *nf* stork
**cilantro** *nm* cilantro, coriander
**cilindro** *nm* cylinder — **cilíndrico, -ca** *adj* cylindrical
**cima** *nf* peak, summit
**cimentar** *v* cement, strengthen; establish — **cimientos** *nmpl* base, foundation(s)
**cinc** *nm* zinc
**cincel** *nm* chisel
**cinco** *adj & nm* five
**cincuenta** *adj & nm* fifty

**cine** *nm* cinema, movies *pl* — **cine-matográfico, -ca** *adj* movie, film
**cínico, -ca** *adj* cynical — **cínico, -ca** *n* cynic — **cinismo** *nm* cynicism
**cinta** *nf* ribbon, band; adhesive tape
**cintura** *nf* waist — **cinturón** *nm* (**-rones**) belt; seat belt
**circo** *nm* circus
**circuito** *nm* circuit
**circular** *v* circulate; drive — **circular** *adj* circular — **circulación** *nf* (**-ciones**) circulation; traffic
**círculo** *nm* circle
**circunferencia** *nf* circumference
**circunstancia** *nf* circumstance
**cirio** *nm* candle
**ciruela** *nf* plum; prune
**cirugía** *nf* surgery — **cirujano, -na** *n* surgeon
**cisne** *nm* swan
**cisterna** *nf* cistern
**cita** *nf* appointment, date; quote, quotation — **citar** *v* quote, cite; make an appointment with
**ciudad** *nf* city, town — **ciudadano, -na** *n* citizen; resident — **ciudadanía** *nf* citizenship
**cívico, -ca** *adj* civic
**civil** *adj* civil — **civil** *nmf* civilian — **civilización** *nf* (**-ciones**) civilization — **civilizar** *v* civilize
**clamar** *v* clamor, cry out — **clamor** *nm* clamor, outcry
**clandestino, -na** *adj* clandestine, secret
**clara** *nf* egg white
**claramente** *adv* clearly
**claridad** *nf* clarity, clearness; light
**clarificar** *v* clarify
**clarinete** *nm* clarinet
**claro** *adv* clearly; of course, surely — **claro** *nm* clearing, glade — **claro, -ra** *adj* clear, bright; light; evident
**clase** *nf* class; sort, kind
**clásico, -ca** *adj* classic, classical — **clásico** *nm* classic
**clasificar** *v* classify, sort out — **clasifi-carse** *vr* qualify — **clasificación** *nf* (**-ciones**) classification; league
**cláusula** *nf* clause
**clausurar** *v* close (down)
**clavar** *v* nail, hammer; drive in, plunge
**clave** *nf* code; key — **clave** *adj* key
**clavel** *nm* carnation
**clavícula** *nf* collarbone
**clavo** *nm* nail; clove (spice)
**clemencia** *nf* clemency, mercy — **clero** *nm* clergy
**cliente, -ta** *n* customer, client — **clientela** *nf* clientele, customers *pl*
**clima** *nm* climate; atmosphere — **climático, -ca** *adj* climatic
**climatizar** *v* air-condition — **climatizado, -da** *adj* air-conditioned
**clímax** *nm* climax
**clínica** *nf* clinic — **clínico, -ca** *adj* clinical
**clip** *nm* (**clips**) clip
**cloro** *nm* chlorine
**clóset** *nm* (**clósets**) closet, cupboard
**club** *nm* club
**cobarde** *nmf* coward — **cobarde** *adj* cowardly — **cobardía** *nf* cowardice
**cobertor** *nm* bedspread
**cobertura** *nf* cover; coverage
**cobijar** *v* shelter — **cobija** *nf* blanket
**cobra** *nf* cobra
**cobrar** *v* charge, collect; earn — **cobrador, -dora** *n* collector
**cobre** *nm* copper
**cobro** *nm* collection, cashing
**cocaína** *nf* cocaine
**cocer** *v* cook; boil
**coche** *nm* car, automobile; coach (of a train) — **cochecito** *nm* baby carriage, stroller
**cochino, -na** *n* pig, hog — **cochino, -na** *adj* dirty, filthy — **cochinillo** *nm* piglet
**cocido, -da** *adj* boiled, cooked
**cocina** *nf* kitchen; stove; cooking, cuisine — **cocinar** *v* cook — **cocinero, -ra** *n* cook, chef
**coco** *nm* coconut

**cocodrilo** *nm* crocodile

**coctel** *or* **cóctel** *nm* cocktail; cocktail party

**código** *nm* code; zip code

**codo** *nm* elbow

**codorniz** *nf* (-nices) quail

**cofre** *nm* chest, coffer

**coger** *v* take; catch; pick up

**coherencia** *nf* coherence — **coherente** *adj* coherent — **cohesión** *nf* (-siones) cohesion

**cohete** *nm* rocket

**coincidir** *v* coincide — **coincidencia** *nf* coincidence

**cojear** *v* limp — **cojera** *nf* limp

**cojín** *nm* (-jines) cushion

**cojo, -ja** *adj* lame — **cojo, -ja** *n* lame person

**col** *nf* cabbage

**cola** *nf* tail; line

**colaborar** *v* collaborate — **colaboración** *nf* (-ciones) collaboration — **colaborador, -dora** *n* collaborator; contributor

**colador** *nm* colander, strainer

**colar** *v* strain, filter — **colarse** *vr* sneak in, gate-crash

**colcha** *nf* bedspread, quilt — **colchón** *nm* (-chones) mattress — **colchoneta** *nf* mat

**colección** *nf* (-ciones) collection — **coleccionar** *v* collect — **coleccionista** *nmf* collector

**colega** *nmf* colleague

**colegio** *nm* school — **colegial, -giala** *n* schoolboy *m*, schoolgirl *f*

**colesterol** *nm* cholesterol

**colgar** *v* hang; hang up

**colibrí** *nm* hummingbird

**cólico** *nm* colic

**coliflor** *nf* cauliflower

**colilla** *nf* (cigarette) butt

**colina** *nf* hill

**coliseo** *nm* coliseum

**collar** *nm* necklace; collar

**colocar** *v* place, put; find a job for —

**colocación** *nf* (-ciones) placement, placing; position, job

**colombiano, -na** *adj* Colombian

**columna** *nf* column; ~ **vertebral** spine, backbone

**columpiar** *v* push

**combinar** *v* combine; put together, match — **combinación** *nf* (-ciones) combination; connection (in travel)

**combustible** *nm* fuel — **combustible** *adj* combustible — **combustión** *nf* (-tiones) combustion

**comedia** *nf* comedy

**comedor** *nm* dining room

**comentar** *v* comment on, discuss; mention — **comentario** *nm* comment; commentary

**comenzar** *v* begin, start

**comer** *v* eat; eat up; eat into; feed

**comercio** *nm* commerce, trade; business — **comerciante** *nmf* merchant, dealer

**cometer** *v* commit; make a mistake

**comicios** *nmpl* elections

**comida** *nf* food; lunch; dinner

**comité** *nm* committee

**como** *conj* as, since; if — **como** *prep* like, as; as well as — **como** *adv* as; around, about

**cómo** *adv* how; by all means; ¿~ **te llamas?** what's your name?

**cómodo, -da** *adj* comfortable; handy, convenient

**compadecer** *v* feel sorry for

**compañero, -ra** *n* companion, partner

**compañía** *nf* company

**comparar** *v* compare — **comparación** *nf* (-ciones) comparison

**compartir** *v* share

**compensar** *v* compensate for

**competir** *v* compete — **competencia** *nf* competition, rivalry — **competente** *adj* competent

**complacer** *v* please

**complejo, -ja** *adj* complex — **complejo** *nm* complex

**complementar** *v* complement

**completar** *v* complete — **completo, -ta** *adj* complete; perfect; full

**complicar** *v* complicate; involve — **complicación** *nf* (**-ciones**) complication

**cómplice** *nmf* accomplice — **cómplice** *adj* conspiratorial, knowing

**componer** *v* make up; compose, write (a song); fix, repair

**comportamiento** *nm* behavior

**composición** *nf* (**-ciones**) composition — **compositor, -tora** *n* composer, songwriter

**comprar** *v* buy, purchase — **compra** *nf* purchase

**comprender** *v* comprehend, understand; cover, include — **comprensión** *nf* (**-siones**) understanding

**comprobar** *v* check; prove — **comprobante** *nm* proof; receipt, voucher

**comprometer** *v* compromise; jeopardize; commit — **comprometerse** *vr* get engaged to

**computadora** *nf or* **computador** *nm* computer; laptop computer

**común** *adj* (**-munes**) common; ordinary; generally

**comunicar** *v* communicate — **comunicarse** *vr* get in touch with

**con** *prep* with; in spite of; (*before an infinitive*) by; so long as

**concebir** *v* conceive

**conceder** *v* grant, bestow; concede

**concentrar** *v* concentrate — **concentración** *nf* (**-ciones**) concentration

**concepto** *nm* concept; opinion

**concertar** *v* arrange, coordinate; (*used before an infinitive*) agree; harmonize

**conciencia** *nf* conscience; consciousness, awareness — **concientizar** *v* make aware

**concierto** *nm* concert; concerto

**conciliar** *v* reconcile — **conciliación** *nf* (**-ciones**) reconciliation

**concluir** *v* conclude — **conclusión** *nf* (**-siones**) conclusion

**concordar** *v* agree; reconcile — **concordancia** *nf* agreement

**concretar** *v* make concrete, specify

**concurrir** *v* come together, meet; ~ **a** take part in

**concursar** *v* compete, participate — **concursante** *nmf* competitor — **concurso** *nm* competition; gathering; help, cooperation

**condenar** *v* condemn, damn; sentence — **condena** *nf* condemnation; sentence

**condición** *nf* (**-ciones**) condition, state; capacity, position — **condicional** *adj* conditional

**condimento** *nm* condiment, seasoning

**condolerse** *vr* sympathize — **condolencia** *nf* condolence

**condominio** *nm* joint ownership; condominium

**conducir** *v* direct, lead; drive; lead to — **conducirse** *vr* behave

**conducta** *nf* behavior, conduct

**conductor, -tora** *n* driver

**conectar** *v* connect; plug in

**conejo, -ja** *n* rabbit

**confabularse** *vr* conspire, plot

**confeccionar** *v* make (up), prepare — **confección** *nf* (**-ciones**) making, preparation; tailoring, dressmaking

**conferencia** *nf* lecture; conference

**conferir** *v* confer, bestow

**confesar** *v* confess — **confesión** *nf* (**-siones**) confession; religion, creed

**confiar** *v* trust; entrust — **confiado, -da** *adj* confident; trusting — **confianza** *nf* trust; confidence

**confidencia** *nf* confidence, secret — **confidencial** *adj* confidential

**configuración** *nf* (**-ciones**) configuration, shape

**confirmar** *v* confirm — **confirmación** *nf* (**-ciones**) confirmation

**confiscar** *v* confiscate

**conflagración** *nf* (**-ciones**) war, conflict; fire

**conflicto** *nm* conflict

**conformar** *v* shape, make up — **conformarse** *vr* content oneself with — **confortable** *adj* comfortable

**confrontar** *v* confront; compare; border — **confrontación** *nf* (**-ciones**) confrontation

**confundir** *v* confuse, mix up — **confusión** *nf* (**-siones**) confusion — **congelar** *v* freeze — **congelador** *nm* freezer

**congestión** *nf* (**-tiones**) congestion

**congregar** *v* bring together

**congreso** *nm* congress — **congresista** *nmf* member of congress

**conjugar** *v* conjugate — **conjugación** *nf* (**-ciones**) conjugation

**conjunción** *nf* (**-ciones**) conjunction

**conjunto, -ta** *adj* joint — **conjunto** *nm* collection; outfit; band

**conmemorar** *v* commemorate — **conmemoración** *nf* (**-ciones**) commemoration

**conmigo** *pron* with me

**conmover** *v* move, touch; shake (up)

**conmutador** *nm* switch; switchboard

**conocer** *v* know; meet; recognize — **conocimiento** *nm* knowledge; consciousness

**conque** *conj* so

**consciente** *adj* conscious, aware

**consecuencia** *nf* consequence; **en ～** accordingly

**consecutivo, -va** *adj* consecutive

**conseguir** *v* get, obtain

**consejo** *nm* advice, counsel; council

**consenso** *nm* consensus

**consentir** *v* allow, permit; pamper, spoil; consent — **consentimiento** *nm* consent, permission

**conservar** *v* preserve; keep, conserve — **conservación** *nf* (**-ciones**) conservation, preservation — **conservador, -dora** *adj & n* conservative — **conservatorio** *nm* conservatory

**considerar** *v* consider; respect

**consigna** *nf* slogan; assignment; checkroom

**consigo** *pron* with her, with him, with you, with oneself

**consiguiente** *adj* consequent; **por ～** consequently

**consistir** *v* consist of; lie in, consist in

**consolar** *v* console, comfort

**consolidar** *v* consolidate — **consolidación** *nf* (**-ciones**) consolidation

**consonante** *adj* consonant, harmonious — **consonante** *nf* consonant

**consorcio** *nm* consortium

**constancia** *nf* record, evidence; perseverance — **constante** *adj* constant

**constar** *v* be evident, be clear; consist of

**constatar** *v* verify; state, affirm

**constituir** *v* constitute, form; establish, set up — **constituirse** *vr* set oneself up as — **constitución** *nf* (**-ciones**) constitution — **constitucional** *adj* constitutional — **constituyente** *adj & nm* constituent

**construir** *v* build, construct — **construcción** *nf* (**-ciones**) construction, building

**consultar** *v* consult — **consulta** *nf* consultation — **consultorio** *nm* office (of a doctor or dentist)

**consumar** *v* consummate, complete; commit

**consumidor, -dora** *n* consumer — **consumo** *nm* consumption

**contabilidad** *nf* accounting, bookkeeping; accountancy

**contacto** *nm* contact

**contagiar** *v* infect; transmit — **contagio** *nm* contagion, infection

**contaminar** *v* contaminate, pollute — **contaminación** *nf* (**-ciones**) contamination, pollution

**contar** *v* count; tell; rely on

**contemplar** *v* look at, behold; contemplate

**contemporáneo, -nea** *adj & n* contemporary

**contener** *v* contain; restrain, hold back — **contenido** *nm* contents *pl*

**contentar** *v* please, make happy — **contentarse con** *vr phr* be satisfied with

**contestar** *v* answer; reply

**contexto** *nm* context

**contigo** *pron* with you

**continuar** *v* continue — **continuación** *nf* (-**ciones**) continuation; next, then — **continuidad** *nf* continuity

**contra** *prep* against — **contra** *nm* opposition, opponent

**contradecir** *v* contradict — **contradicción** *nf* (-**ciones**) contradiction

**contraer** *v* contract; ~ **matrimonio** get married — **contraerse** *vr* tighten up

**contralto** *nmf* contralto

**contrariar** *v* oppose; vex, annoy

**contraseña** *nf* password

**contrastar** *v* check, verify; resist

**contratar** *v* contract for; hire

**contrato** *nm* contract — **contratista** *nmf* contractor

**contribuir** *v* contribute; pay taxes — **contribución** *nf* (-**ciones**) contribution; tax — **contribuyente** *nmf* contributor; taxpayer

**controlar** *v* control; monitor, check — **control** *nm* control; inspection, check

**controversia** *nf* controversy

**contundente** *adj* blunt; forceful, convincing

**convalecencia** *nf* convalescence

**convencer** *v* convince, persuade

**convención** *nf* (-**ciones**) convention — **convencional** *adj* conventional

**convenir** *v* be suitable, be advisable; agree on — **conveniencia** *nf* convenience; suitability (of an action, etc.) — **conveniente** *adj* convenient; suitable, advisable; useful — **convenio** *nm* agreement, pact

**conversar** *v* converse, talk — **conversación** *nf* (-**ciones**) conversation

**convertir** *v* convert

**convexo, -xa** *adj* convex

**convicción** *nf* (-**ciones**) conviction — **convicto, -ta** *adj* convicted

**convincente** *adj* convincing

**convivir** *v* live together

**convocar** *v* convoke, call together

**cónyuge** *nmf* spouse, partner

**cooperar** *v* cooperate — **cooperación** *nf* (-**ciones**) cooperation — **cooperativa** *nf* cooperative, co-op

**coordinar** *v* coordinate — **coordinación** *nf* (-**ciones**) coordination — **coordinador, -dora** *n* coordinator

**copa** *nf* glass, goblet; cup

**copiar** *v* copy

**copioso, -sa** *adj* copious, abundant

**coquetear** *v* flirt

**Corán** *nm* the Koran

**corazón** *nm* (-**zones**) heart; core; **mi** ~ my darling

**corbata** *nf* tie, necktie

**corchete** *nm* hook and eye, clasp; square bracket

**corcho** *nm* cork

**cordero** *nm* lamb

**cordial** *adj* cordial

**cordillera** *nf* mountain range

**cordón** *nm* (-**dones**) cord; (police) cordon; **cordones** *nmpl* shoelaces

**cordura** *nf* sanity

**coro** *nm* chorus; choir

**corporación** *nf* (-**ciones**) corporation

**corporal** *adj* corporal, bodily

**corporativo, -va** *adj* corporate

**corpulento, -ta** *adj* stout

**corrección** *nf* (-**ciones**) correction; correctness, propriety — **correcto, -ta** *adj* correct, right; polite

**corredor, -dora** *n* runner, racer; agent, broker — **corredor** *nm* corridor, hallway

**corregir** *v* correct

**correo** *nm* mail; airmail

**correr** *v* run, race; flow; travel over

**corresponder** *v* correspond; belong; fit; reciprocate, repay — **corresponderse**

*vr* write to each other — **correspondencia** *nf* correspondence; connection
**corriente** *nf* current, draft; tendency,
trend; **al ~** up-to-date; informed —
**corriente** *adj* current; common, ordinary; running
**corroborar** *v* corroborate
**cortar** *v* cut; cut out; cut off — **cortarse**
*vr* curdle; have one's hair cut
**cortauñas** *nms & pl* nail clippers
**corte** *nm* cutting; cut, style; haircut
**cortejo** *nm* entourage; courtship; funeral
procession
**cortés** *adj* courteous, polite — **cortesía**
*nf* courtesy, politeness
**corto, -ta** *adj* short; scarce; timid, shy;
nearsighted — **cortocircuito** *nm* short
circuit
**cosa** *nf* thing; matter, affair; **poca ~**
nothing much
**cosechar** *v* harvest, reap — **cosecha** *nf*
harvest, crop; vintage
**cosmético, -ca** *adj* cosmetic
**cosmopolita** *adj* cosmopolitan
**cosquillas** *nfpl* tickling; tickle
**costa**[1] *nf* cost; **a toda ~** at any cost
**costa**[2] *nf* coast, shore
**costarricense** *or* **costarriqueño, -ña**
*adj* Costa Rican
**costumbre** *nf* custom, habit; usual
**costura** *nf* sewing, dressmaking; seam
**cotidiano, -na** *adj* daily
**cotizar** *v* quote, set a price on — **coti-
zación** *nf* (**-ciones**) quotation, price
**coyuntura** *nf* joint; situation, moment
**cráneo** *nf* cranium, skull
**cráter** *nm* crater
**crear** *v* create — **creación** *nf* (**-ciones**)
creation — **creador, -dora** *n* creator
**crecer** *v* grow; increase — **crecimiento**
*nm* growth; increase
**crédito** *nm* credit
**creer** *v* believe; suppose, think —
**creerse** *vr* regard oneself as — **creencia** *nf* belief
**cremación** *nf* (**-ciones**) cremation

**cremallera** *nf* zipper
**cremoso, -sa** *adj* creamy
**creyente** *nmf* believer
**crimen** *nm* (**crímenes**) crime — **criminal** *adj & nmf* criminal
**criollo, -lla** *adj & n* Creole
**crisis** *nf* crisis; nervous breakdown
**cristal** *nm* crystal; glass, piece of glass
— **cristalería** *nf* glassware — **cristalino, -na** *adj* crystalline — **cristalino**
*nm* lens — **cristalizar** *v* crystallize
**cristiano, -na** *adj & n* Christian — **cristianismo** *nm* Christianity — **Cristo** *nm*
Christ
**criterio** *nm* criterion; judgment, opinion
**crítico, -ca** *adj* critical — **crítico, -ca** *n*
critic, reviewer — **criticar** *v* criticize —
**crítica** *nf* criticism; review, critique
**crónica** *nf* chronicle; (news) report
**crónico, -ca** *adj* chronic
**cronista** *nmf* reporter, newscaster
**cronología** *nf* chronology — **cronológico, -ca** *adj* chronological
**cronometrar** *v* time, clock — **cronó-
metro** *nm* chronometer, stopwatch
**cruce** *nm* crossing; crossroads, intersection; crosswalk
**crucero** *nm* cruise; cruiser (ship)
**crucial** *adj* crucial
**crucificar** *v* crucify — **crucifijo** *nm* crucifix
**crucigrama** *nm* crossword puzzle
**crudo, -da** *adj* harsh, crude; raw —
**crudo** *nm* crude oil
**cruel** *adj* cruel — **crueldad** *nf* cruelty
**cruz** *nf* (**cruces**) cross — **cruzar** *v*
cross; exchange — **cruzarse** *vr* pass
each other
**cuaderno** *nm* notebook
**cuadra** *nf* stable; (city) block
**cuadrado, -da** *adj* square
**cuadrar** *v* conform, agree; tally; square
— **cuadrarse** *vr* stand at attention
**cuadrilátero** *nm* quadrilateral; (boxing)
ring

**cuadro** *nm* square; painting; picture, description; staff, management; check

**cuadrúpedo** *nm* quadruped

**cual** *pron* who, whom, which; which; everyone, everybody — **cual** *prep* like, as

**cuál** *pron* which (one), what (one) ∼ *adj* which, what

**cualidad** *nf* quality, trait

**cualquiera** (**cualquier** *before nouns*) *adj* (**cualesquiera**) any, whatever ∼ *pron* (**cualesquiera**) anyone, whatever

**cuán** *adv* how

**cuando** *conj* when; since, if; ∼ **más** at the most; from time to time — **cuando** *prep* during, at the time of

**cuándo** *adv* when; since when?

**cuanto** *adv* as much as; ∼ **antes** as soon as possible; **en** ∼ as soon as; **en** ∼ **a** as for, as regards

**cuánto** *adv* & *pron* how much, how many — **cuánto, -ta** *adj* how much, how many

**cuanto, -ta** *adj* as many, whatever — **cuanto, -ta** *pron* as much as, all that, everything; **unos cuantos, unas cuantas** a few

**cuarenta** *adj* & *nm* forty

**Cuaresma** *nf* Lent

**cuartel** *nm* barracks *pl*; headquarters; mercy

**cuarteto** *nm* quartet

**cuarto, -ta** *adj* fourth — **cuarto, -ta** fourth one — **cuarto** *nm* quarter, fourth part

**cuatro** *adj* & *nm* four — **cuatrocientos, -tas** *adj* four hundred — **cuatrocientos** *nms* & *pl* four hundred

**cubano, -na** *adj* Cuban

**cúbico, -ca** *adj* cubic, cubed

**cubierta** *nf* cover, covering; tire; deck — **cubierto** *nm* cutlery, place setting; under cover

**cubrecama** *nm* bedspread

**cubrir** *v* cover — **cubrirse** *vr* cloud over

**cuchara** *nf* spoon

**cuchilla** *nf* (kitchen) knife; razor blade — **cuchillo** *nm* knife

**cuello** *nm* neck; collar

**cuenca** *nf* river basin; (eye) socket

**cuenta** *nf* calculation, count; account; check, bill

**cuento** *nm* story, tale; fairy tale

**cuerda** *nf* cord, rope, string; ∼**s vocales** vocal cords

**cuerdo, -da** *adj* sane, sensible

**cuero** *nm* leather, hide

**cuerpo** *nm* body; corps

**cuervo** *nm* crow

**cuesta** *nf* slope; **a** ∼**s** on one's back

**cuestión** *nf* (**-tiones**) matter, affair — **cuestionar** *v* question — **cuestionario** *nm* questionnaire; quiz

**cueva** *nf* cave

**cuidar** *v* take care of, look after; pay attention to — **cuidado** *nm* care; worry, concern — **¡cuidado!** *interj* watch out!, careful!

**culebra** *nf* snake

**culinario, -ria** *adj* culinary

**culminar** *v* culminate — **culminación** *nf* (**-ciones**) culmination

**culpa** *nf* fault, blame; sin; **tener la** ∼ be at fault — **culpar** *v* blame

**culpable** *adj* guilty — **culpable** *nmf* culprit, guilty party

**cultivar** *v* cultivate — **cultivo** *nm* farming, cultivation; crops

**culto, -ta** *adj* cultured, educated — **culto** *nm* worship; cult — **cultura** *nf* culture

**cumpleaños** *nms* & *pl* birthday

**cumplido, -da** *adj* complete, full; courteous — **cumplido** *nm* compliment, courtesy

**cumplir** *v* accomplish, carry out; keep; reach; fall due — **cumplirse** *vr* come true — **cumplimiento** *nm* performance

**cuna** *nf* cradle; birthplace

**cuñado, -da** *n* brother-in-law *m*, sister-in-law *f*

**cuota** *nf* fee, dues; quota; installment, payment

**cupo** *nm* quota, share; capacity
**curar** *v* cure; dress; tan
**curiosidad** *nf* curiosity — **curioso, -sa**
*adj* curious, inquisitive; strange
**currículum** *nm* (**-lums**) *or* **currículo** *nm*
résumé, curriculum vitae
**cursar** *v* take, study; send, pass on
**cursiva** *nf* italics *pl*

**curso** *nm* course; school year
**curva** *nf* curve, bend — **curvo, -va** *adj*
curved, bent
**cutáneo, -nea** *adj* skin
**cutis** *nms & pl* skin, complexion
**cuyo, -ya** *adj* whose, of whom, of
which

# D

**d** *nf* d, fourth letter of the Spanish alphabet
**dados** *nmpl* dice
**dama** *nf* lady; **~s** *nfpl* checkers
**dañar** *v* damage, harm — **daño** *nm* damage, harm
**danés, -nesa** *adj* Danish — **danés** *nm*
Danish
**danzar** *v* dance — **danza** *nf* dance,
dancing
**dar** *v* give; yield, produce
**dardo** *nm* dart
**dátil** *nm* date (fruit)
**dato** *nm* fact
**de** *prep* of
**debajo** *adv* underneath
**debate** *nm* debate
**deber** *v* owe — *v aux* have to, should;
must
**débil** *adj* weak, feeble — **debilidad** *nf*
weakness — **débilmente** *adv* weakly,
faintly
**década** *nf* decade
**decena** *nf* ten, about ten
**decencia** *nf* decency
**decente** *adj* decent
**decidir** *v* decide, determine — **de-**
**cidirse** *vr* make up one's mind — **de-**
**cidido, -da** *adj* determined, resolute
**decimal** *adj* decimal
**décimo, -ma** *adj & n* tenth
**decir** *v* say; tell; **¿comó se dice . . . ?**
how do you say . . . ?

**decisión** *nf* (**-siones**) decision — **deci-**
**sivo, -va** *adj* decisive
**declarar** *v* declare; testify — **de-**
**claración** *nf* (**-ciones**) statement
**decoración** *nf* (**-ciones**) decoration —
**decorado** *nm* stage set — **decorar** *v*
decorate — **decorativo, -va** *adj* decorative
**decretar** *v* decree — **decreto** *nm* decree
**dedicar** *v* dedicate — **dedicación** *nf*
(**-ciones**) dedication
**dedo** *nm* finger
**deducir** *v* deduce; deduct — **deducción**
*nf* (**-ciones**) deduction
**defecto** *nm* defect — **defectuoso, -sa**
*adj* defective, faulty
**defender** *v* defend — **defensa** *nf* defense — **defensor, -sora** *n* defender
**definir** *v* define — **definición** *nf*
(**-ciones**) definition — **definitivo, -va**
*adj* definitive
**deforme** *adj* deformed — **deformidad**
*nf* deformity
**dejar** *v* leave; abandon; allow
**delantal** *nm* apron
**delante** *adv* ahead
**delantero, -ra** *adj* front, forward — **de-**
**lantero, -ra** *n* forward (in sports)
**delegación** *nf* (**-ciones**) delegation —
**delegado, -da** *n* delegate, representative
**deletrear** *v* spell out
**delfín** *nm* (**-fines**) dolphin

**delgado, -da** *adj* thin

**delicadeza** *nf* delicacy, daintiness; gentleness; tact — **delicado, -da** *adj* delicate; sensible; tactful

**delicia** *nf* delight — **delicioso, -sa** *adj* delightful; delicious

**delincuencia** *nf* delinquency, crime — **delincuente** *adj & nmf* delinquent, criminal

**delito** *nm* crime

**demandar** *v* sue; demand

**demás** *pron* **lo (la, los, las)** ~ the rest, others — **demás** *adj* rest of the, other

**demasiado** *adv* too — **demasiado** *adj* too much, too many

**democracia** *nf* democracy — **democrático, -ca** *adj* democratic

**demonio** *nm* devil, demon

**demorar** *v* delay — **demorarse** *vr* take a long time — **demora** *nf* delay

**demostrar** *v* demonstrate; — **demostración** *nf* (**-ciones**) demonstration

**denominador** *nm* denominator

**dentadura** *nf* teeth; ~ **postiza** dentures *pl* — **dentífrico** *nm* toothpaste — **dentista** *nmf* dentist

**dentro** *adv* in, inside

**denunciar** *v* denounce — **denuncia** *nf* accusation

**departamento** *nm* department

**depender** *v* depend — **dependencia** *nf* dependence, dependency; branch office — **dependiente** *adj* dependent — **dependiente, -ta** *n* clerk, salesperson

**deporte** *nm* sport, sports *pl* — **deportista** *nmf* sportsman; sportswoman — **deportivo, -va** *adj* sporty

**depositar** *v* put, place; deposit — **depósito** *nm* deposit; warehouse

**deprimir** *v* depress — **depresión** *nf* (**-siones**) depression

**derecha** *nf* right side — **derecho** *nm* right; law — **derecho** *adv* straight — **derecho, -cha** *adj* right, right-hand; upright; straight

**derramar** *v* spill

**derretir** *v* melt, thaw

**derrotar** *v* defeat — **derrota** *nf* defeat

**derrumbar** *v* demolish, knock down — **derrumbarse** *vr* collapse, break down — **derrumbamiento** *nm* collapse — **derrumbe** *nm* collapse

**desabotonar** *v* unbutton, undo

**desabrochar** *v* unbutton, undo

**desafiar** *v* defy, challenge — **desafiante** *adj* defiant

**desafío** *nm* challenge, defiance

**desafortunadamente** *adv* unfortunately

**desagradar** *v* displease — **desagradable** *adj* disagreeable, unpleasant

**desagradecido, -da** *adj* ungrateful

**desahogar** *v* relieve; give vent to — **desahogarse** *vr* let off steam, unburden oneself — **desahogo** *nm* relief

**desalentar** *v* discourage — **desaliento** *nm* discouragement

**desanimar** *v* discourage — **desanimarse** *vr* get discouraged — **desanimado, -da** *adj* downhearted, despondent

**desaparecer** *v* disappear — **desaparecido, -da** *n* missing person — **desaparición** *nf* (**-ciones**) disappearance

**desapercebido, -da** *adj* unnoticed

**desarrollar** *v* develop — **desarrollarse** *vr* take place — **desarrollo** *nm* development

**desastre** *nm* disaster

**desatar** *v* undo, untie; unleash — **desatarse** *vr* come undone; break out, erupt

**desayunar** *v* have breakfast; have for breakfast — **desayuno** *nm* breakfast

**descafeinado, -da** *adj* decaffeinated

**descalificar** *v* disqualify — **descalificación** *nf* (**-ciones**) disqualification

**descalzo, -za** *adj* barefoot

**descansar** *v* rest — **descanso** *nm* rest; landing; intermission, halftime

**descargar** *v* unload; discharge — **descarga** *nf* unloading; discharge — **des-**

**cargo** *nm* unloading; discharge; defense

**descender** *v* go down; lower; be descended from — **descendiencia** *nf* descendants *pl*; lineage, descent — **descendiente** *nmf* descendant — **descenso** *nm* descent; drop, fall

**desconfiar** *v* distrust — **desconfiado, -da** *adj* distrustful — **desconfianza** *nf* distrust

**desconocer** *v* not know, fail to recognize — **desconocido, -da** *adj* unknown — **desconocido, -da** *n* stranger

**descontar** *v* discount

**descortés** *adj* (**-teses**) rude — **descortesía** *nf* discourtesy, rudeness

**descremado, -da** *adj* nonfat, skim

**describir** *v* describe — **descripción** *nf* (**-ciones**) description — **descriptivo, -va** *adj* descriptive

**descubierto, -ta** *adj* exposed, uncovered — **descubierto** *nm* deficit, overdraft

**descubrir** *v* discover; reveal

**descuento** *nm* discount

**descuidar** *v* neglect — **descuidarse** *vr* be careless; let oneself go

**desde** *prep* from; since; ~ **luego** of course

**desdén** *nm* scorn, disdain — **desdeñar** *v* scorn

**desear** *v* wish, want

**desempeñar** *v* play (a role); redeem, reclaim

**desempeñarse** *vr* get out of debt

**desempleo** *nm* unemployment

**desenlace** *nm* ending, outcome

**deseo** *nm* desire

**desequilibrar** *v* throw off balance — **desequilibrio** *nm* imbalance

**desesperar** *v* exasperate; lose hope — **desesperarse** *vr* become exasperated — **desesperación** *nf* (**-ciones**) desperation, despair

**desfallecer** *v* weaken; faint

**desfavorable** *adj* unfavorable

**desgracia** *nf* misfortune

**deshacer** *v* undo; destroy, ruin; dissolve; break, cancel — **deshacerse** *vr* come undone

**deshonesto, -ta** *adj* dishonest

**desidia** *nf* indolence; sloppiness

**designar** *v* designate — **designación** *nf* (**-ciones**) appointment

**desigual** *adj* unequal; uneven — **desigualdad** *nf* inequality

**desilusionar** *v* disappoint, disillusion — **desilusión** *nf* (**-siones**) disappointment, disillusionment

**desinhibido, -da** *adj* uninhibited

**desistir** *v* stop, desist; ~ **de** give up

**desleal** *adj* disloyal

**desmayar** *v* lose heart — **desmayarse** *vr* faint — **desmayo** *nm* faint

**desmedido, -da** *adj* excessive

**desmesurado, -da** *adj* excessive

**desnudar** *v* undress, strip — **desnudarse** *vr* get undressed — **desnudo, -da** *adj* nude, naked — **desnudo** *nm* nude

**desnutrición** *nf* (**-ciones**) malnutrition

**desocupar** *v* empty, vacate — **desocupado, -da** *adj* vacant, unoccupied; unemployed

**desodorante** *adj* & *nm* deodorant

**desorden** *nm* (**desórdenes**) disorder, mess — **desordenado, -da** *adj* untidy

**desorganizar** *v* disorganize — **desorganización** *nf* (**-ciones**) disorganization

**despacio** *adv* slowly

**despectivo, -va** *adj* pejorative; contemptuous

**despedir** *v* see off; dismiss, fire; emit — **despedirse** *vr* say good-bye — **despedida** *nf* farewell, good-bye

**despeinar** *v* ruffle (hair) — **despeinado, -da** *adj* disheveled, unkempt

**despertar** *v* awaken, wake up; rouse — **despertador** *nm* alarm clock

# despierto

**despierto, -ta** *adj* awake

**desplazar** *v* displace — **desplazarse** *vr* travel

**desprender** *v* detach, remove; give off — **desprenderse** *vr* come off; be inferred, follow

**desprovisto, -ta** *adj* ~ **de** lacking in; devoid of

**después** *adv* afterward; then, next

**destacar** *v* emphasize; stand out — **destacado, -da** *adj* outstanding

**destapar** *v* open, uncover

**destinar** *v* assign, allocate; appoint — **destinado, -da** *adj* destined — **destinatario, -ria** *n* addressee — **destino** *nm* destiny; destination

**destreza** *nf* skill, dexterity

**destrozar** *v* destroy, wreck

**destrucción** *nf* (**-ciones**) destruction — **destructivo, -va** *adj* destructive — **destruir** *v* destroy

**desusado, -da** *adj* obsolete; unusual — **desuso** *nm* disuse

**desvanecer** *v* make disappear — **desvanecerse** *vr* vanish; faint

**desventaja** *nf* disadvantage

**desvestir** *v* undress — **desvestirse** *vr* get undressed

**desviación** *nf* (**-ciones**) deviation; detour — **desviar** *v* divert, deflect — **desviarse** *vr* branch off; stray — **desvío** *nm* diversion, detour

**detener** *v* arrest, detain; stop; delay — **detenerse** *vr* stop; linger

**detergente** *nm* detergent

**deteriorar** *v* damage — **deteriorarse** *vr* wear out, deteriorate — **deterioro** *nm* deterioration, damage

**determinar** *v* determine; bring about; decide — **determinarse** *vr* decide — **determinación** *nf* (**-ciones**) determination — **determinado, -da** *adj* determined; specific

**detrás** *adv* behind

**detrimento** *nm* harm; **en** ~ **de** to the detriment of

**deuda** *nf* debt — **deudor, -dora** *n* debtor

**devaluar** *v* devalue — **devaluarse** *vr* depreciate

**devenir** *v* come about

**devolver** *v* give back; refund, pay back; bring up, vomit — **devolverse** *vr* return, come back

**diagnosticar** *v* diagnose — **diagnóstico, -ca** *adj* diagnostic — **diagnóstico** *nm* diagnosis

**diagonal** *adj* & *nf* diagonal

**diagrama** *nm* diagram

**dialecto** *nm* dialect

**dialogar** *v* have a talk — **diálogo** *nm* dialogue

**diario, -ria** *adj* daily — **diario** *nm* diary; newspaper

**dibujar** *v* draw; portray — **dibujante** *nmf* draftsman, draftswoman — **dibujo** *nm* drawing

**diccionario** *nm* dictionary

**diciembre** *nm* December

**dictar** *v* dictate; pronounce, deliver — **dictado** *nm* dictation

**diecinueve** *adj* & *nm* nineteen

**dieciocho** *adj* & *nm* eighteen

**dieciséis** *adj* & *nm* sixteen

**diecisiete** *adj* & *nm* seventeen

**diente** *nm* tooth; prong, tine

**diestra** *nf* right hand — **diestro, -tra** *adj* right; skillful

**dieta** *nf* diet — **dietético, -ca** *adj* dietetic, dietary

**diez** *adj* & *nm* (**dieces**) ten

**diferencia** *nf* difference — **diferenciar** *v* distinguish between — **diferenciarse** *vr* differ — **diferente** *adj* different

**diferir** *v* postpone; differ

**difícil** *adj* difficult — **dificultad** *nf* difficulty — **dificultar** *v* hinder, obstruct

**difundir** *v* spread (out); broadcast

**difusión** *nf* (**-siones**) spreading

**digerir** *v* digest — **digerible** *adj* digestible — **digestión** *nf* (**-tiones**) digestion

**dígito** *nm* digit — **digital** *adj* digital

**digresión** *nf* (**-siones**) digression

**dilatar** *v* expand, dilate; prolong; postpone

**dilema** *nm* dilemma

**dimensión** *nf* (**-siones**) dimension

**diminuto, -ta** *adj* minute, tiny

**dimitir** *v* resign — **dimisión** *nf* (**-siones**) resignation

**dinámico, -ca** *adj* dynamic

**dinero** *nm* money

**dios, diosa** *n* god, goddess *f* — **Dios** *nm* God

**diploma** *nm* diploma — **diplomado, -da** *adj* qualified, trained

**diplomacia** *nf* diplomacy — **diplomático, -ca** *adj* diplomatic — **diplomático, -ca** *n* diplomat

**diputado, -da** *n* delegate

**dirección** *nf* (**-ciones**) address; direction; management; steering — **direccional** *nf* turn signal, blinker — **directivo, -va** *adj* managerial — **directivo, -va** *n* manager, director — **directo, -ta** *adj* direct; straight — **director, -tora** *n* director, manager; conductor — **directorio** *nm* directory — **directriz** *nf* (**-trices**) guideline

**dirigir** *v* direct, lead; address; aim; conduct — **dirigirse a** *vr phr* go towards

**disciplinar** *v* discipline — **disciplina** *nf* discipline

**discípulo, -la** *n* disciple, follower

**disco** *nm* disc, disk; discus

**discoteca** *nf* disco, discotheque

**discreción** *nf* (**-ciones**) discretion

**discreto, -ta** *adj* discreet

**discriminar** *v* discriminate against; distinguish — **discriminación** *nf* (**-ciones**) discrimination

**disculpar** *v* excuse, pardon — **disculparse** *vr* apologize — **disculpa** *nf* apology; excuse

**discurrir** *v* pass, go by; ponder, reflect

**discurso** *nm* speech, discourse

**discutir** *v* discuss; dispute; argue — **discusión** *nf* (**-siones**) discussion; argument

**diseñar** *v* design — **diseñador, -dora** *n* designer — **diseño** *nm* design

**disertación** *nf* (**-ciones**) lecture; dissertation

**disfrutar** *v* enjoy; have a good time

**disgustar** *v* upset, annoy — **disgustarse** *vr* get annoyed; fall out — **disgusto** *nm* annoyance, displeasure; quarrel

**disimular** *v* conceal, hide; pretend — **disimulo** *nm* pretense

**disipar** *v* dispel; squander

**diskette** *nm* floppy disk, diskette

**dislexia** *nf* dyslexia — **disléxico, -ca** *adj* dyslexic

**disminuir** *v* reduce; decrease, drop — **disminución** *nf* (**-ciones**) decrease

**disociar** *v* dissociate

**disolver** *v* dissolve — **disolverse** *vr* dissolve

**dispensar** *v* dispense, distribute; excuse

**dispersar** *v* disperse, scatter — **dispersarse** *vr* disperse, scatter — **dispersión** *nf* (**-siones**) scattering

**disponer** *v* arrange, lay out; decide, stipulate — **disponerse a** *vr phr* be ready to — **disponibilidad** *nf* availability

**disposición** *nf* (**-ciones**) arrangement; aptitude; order, provision (in law)

**dispositivo** *nm* device, mechanism

**dispuesto, -ta** *adj* prepared, ready

**disputar** *v* argue; compete — **disputa** *nf* dispute, argument

**distanciar** *v* space out — **distanciarse** *vr* grow apart — **distancia** *nf* distance — **distante** *adj* distant

**distinguir** *v* distinguish — **distinguirse** *vr* distinguish oneself, stand out — **distinción** *nf* (**-ciones**) distinction — **distintivo, -va** *adj* distinctive — **distinto, -ta** *adj* different; distinct, clear

**distorsión** *nf* (**-siones**) distortion

**distraer** *v* distract; entertain — **distraerse** *vr* get distracted; amuse oneself

— **distracción** *nf* (**-ciones**) amusement; absentmindedness

**distribuir** *v* distribute — **distribución** *nf* (**-ciones**) distribution — **distribuidor, -dora** *n* distributor

**disturbio** *nm* disturbance

**disuadir** *v* dissuade, discourage — **disuasivo, -va** *adj* deterrent

**diurno, -na** *adj* day, daytime

**divagar** *v* digress

**diversidad** *nf* diversity

**diversificar** *v* diversify

**diversión** *nf* (**-siones**) fun, entertainment

**diverso, -sa** *adj* diverse

**divertir** *v* entertain — **divertirse** *vr* enjoy oneself, have fun

**dividendo** *nm* dividend

**dividir** *v* divide; distribute

**divisar** *v* discern, make out

**división** *nf* (**-siones**) division — **divisor** *nm* denominator

**divorciar** *v* divorce — **divorciarse** *vr* get a divorce — **divorciado, -da** *n* divorcé *m*, divorcée *f* — **divorcio** *nm* divorce

**divulgar** *v* divulge, reveal; spread, circulate

**doblar** *v* double; fold; turn; dub (a film) — **doblarse** *vr* double over — **dobladillo** *nm* hem — **doble** *adj & nm* double — **doble** *nmf* stand-in, double

**doce** *adj & nm* twelve — **docena** *nf* dozen

**docente** *adj* teaching

**dócil** *adj* docile

**doctor, -tora** *n* doctor — **doctorado** *nm* doctorate

**doctrina** *nf* doctrine

**documentar** *v* document — **documentación** *nf* (**-ciones**) documentation — **documental** *adj & nm* documentary — **documento** *nm* document

**dogma** *nm* dogma — **dogmático, -ca** *adj* dogmatic

**dólar** *nm* dollar

**doler** *v* hurt — **dolerse de** *vr phr* complain about — **dolor** *nm* pain; grief

**domicilio** *nm* home, residence

**dominar** *v* dominate, control; master — **dominarse** *vr* control oneself — **dominación** *nf* (**-ciones**) domination

**domingo** *nm* Sunday — **dominical** *adj* Sunday; **periódico** ~ Sunday newspaper

**dominio** *nm* authority; mastery; domain

**donación** *nf* (**-ciones**) donation

**donar** *v* donate — **donante** *nmf* donor — **donativo** *nm* donation

**donde** *conj* where ~ *prep* over by

**dónde** *adv* where

**dondequiera** *adv* anywhere

**doquier** *adv* **por** ~ everywhere

**dormir** *v* sleep; put to sleep — **dormirse** *vr* fall asleep — **dormitorio** *nm* bedroom; dormitory

**dos** *adj & nm* two — **doscientos, -tas** *adj* two hundred — **doscientos** *nms & pl* two hundred

**dosis** *nfs & pl* dose, dosage

**dotar** *v* provide, equip — **dotación** *nf* (**-ciones**) endowment, funding; personnel

**drama** *nm* drama — **dramático, -ca** *adj* dramatic — **dramatizar** *v* dramatize — **dramaturgo, -ga** *n* dramatist, playwright

**drástico, -ca** *adj* drastic

**droguería** *nf* drugstore

**dual** *adj* dual

**ducha** *nf* shower — **ducharse** *vr* take a shower

**dudar** *v* doubt; ~ **en** hesitate to — **duda** *nf* doubt — **dudoso, -sa** *adj* doubtful; questionable

**duelo** *nm* duel; mourning

**dueño, -na** *n* owner; landlord, landlady

**dulce** *adj* sweet; fresh; mild, gentle — **dulce** *nm* candy, sweet — **dulzura** *nf* sweetness

**duplicar** *v* double; duplicate, copy —

**duplicado, -da** *adj* duplicate — **duplicado** *nm* copy
**duración** *nf* (**-ciones**) duration, length
**duradero, -ra** *adj* durable, lasting
**durante** *prep* during

**durar** *v* endure, last
**durazno** *nm* peach
**duro** *adv* hard — **duro, -ra** *adj* hard; harsh — **dureza** *nf* hardness; harshness

# E

**e¹** *nf* e, fifth letter of the Spanish alphabet
**e²** *conj* and
**echar** *v* throw, cast; expel, dismiss
**eclipse** *nm* eclipse
**eco** *nm* echo
**ecología** *nf* ecology — **ecológico, -ca** *adj* ecological — **ecologista** *nmf* ecologist
**economía** *nf* economy; economics — **economico, -ca** *adj* economic, economical; inexpensive — **economista** *nmf* economist — **economizar** *v* save
**ecuatoriano, -na** *adj* Ecuadorian, Ecuadorean, Ecuadoran
**edad** *nf* age; **Edad Media** Middle Ages *pl*
**edición** *nf* (**-ciones**) publishing, publication; edition
**edificar** *v* build — **edificio** *nm* building
**editar** *v* publish — **editor, -tora** *n* publisher — **editorial** *adj* publishing — **editorial** *nm* editorial
**educar** *v* educate; bring up, raise — **educación** *nf* (**-ciones**) education — **educado, -da** *adj* polite
**efectivo, -va** *adj* effective; real — **efectivo** *nm* cash — **efectivamente** *adv* really; yes, indeed — **efecto** *nm* effect — **efectuar** *v* bring about, carry out
**eficaz** *adj* (**-caces**) effective; efficient
**egipcio, -cia** *adj* Egyptian
**egoísmo** *nm* egoism — **egoísta** *adj* egoistic — **egoísta** *nmf* egoist
**ejecutivo, -va** *adj & n* executive
**ejemplo** *nm* example
**ejercicio** *nm* exercise

**ejército** *nm* army
**el, la** *art* (**los, las**) the — **el** *pron* the one
**él** *pron* he, him
**elaborar** *v* manufacture, produce
**elástico, -ca** *adj* elastic — **elástico** *nm* elastic
**elección** *nf* (**-ciones**) election; choice
**electricidad** *nf* electricity — **eléctrico, -ca** *adj* electric, electrical — **electricista** *nmf* electrician
**electrodoméstico** *nm* electric appliance
**electrónico, -ca** *adj* electronic — **electrónica** *nf* electronics
**elefante, -ta** *n* elephant
**elegante** *adj* elegant — **elegancia** *nf* elegance
**elegir** *v* elect; choose, select
**elemento** *nm* element — **elemental** *adj* elementary, basic; fundamental
**elevar** *v* raise, lift — **elevación** *nf* (**-ciones**) elevation
**eliminar** *v* eliminate — **eliminación** *nf* (**-ciones**) elimination
**ella** *pron* she, her — **ello** *pron* it — **ellos, ellas** *pron pl* they, them; **de ellos, de ellas** theirs
**embajada** *nf* embassy — **embajador, -dora** *n* ambassador
**embarazada** *adj* pregnant — **embarazo** *nm* pregnancy — **embarazar** *v* make pregnant
**embarazoso, -sa** *adj* embarrassing
**embarcar** *v* load — **embarcación** *nf* (**-ciones**) boat, craft
**embargo** *nm* embargo; **sin ~** nevertheless

# embarque

**embarque** *nm* loading, boarding

**embellecer** *v* embellish, beautify

**emborracharse** *vr* get drunk

**embrague** *nm* clutch — **embragar** *v* engage the clutch

**embriagado, -da** *adj* intoxicated, drunk — **embriagarse** *vr* get drunk

**embrión** *nm* (**-briones**) embryo

**embutido** *nm* sausage, cold meat

**emergencia** *nf* emergency

**emigrar** *v* emigrate; migrate — **emigración** *nf* (**-ciones**) emigration; migration — **emigrante** *adj* & *nmf* emigrant

**emisora** *nf* radio station

**emoción** *nf* (**-ciones**) emotion — **emocionante** *adj* moving, touching; exciting, thrilling — **emocionar** *v* move, touch; excite, thrill — **emocionarse** *vr* be moved; get excited — **emotivo, -va** *adj* emotional; moving

**empacar** *v* pack

**empanada** *nf* pie, turnover

**empanar** *v* bread

**empapar** *v* soak — **empaparse** *vr* get soaking wet

**empaquetar** *v* pack, package

**emparedado, -da** *adj* walled in, confined — **emparedado** *nm* sandwich

**empaste** *nm* filling

**empatar** *v* result in a draw, be tied — **empate** *nm* draw, tie

**empedernido, -da** *adj* inveterate, hardened

**empeño** *nm* determination, effort

**empeorar** *v* get worse; make worse

**empequeñecer** *v* diminish, make smaller

**empezar** *v* start, begin

**empinar** *v* raise — **empinarse** *vr* stand on tiptoe

**empírico, -ca** *adj* empirical

**emplear** *v* employ, use — **emplearse** *vr* get a job; be used — **empleado, -da** *n* employee — **empleo** *nm* occupation, job

**empobrecer** *v* impoverish — **empobrecerse** *vr* become poor

**empolvarse** *vr* powder one's face

**empresa** *nf* company, firm — **empresario, -ria** *n* businessman, businesswoman

**empujar** *v* push — **empuje** *nm* impetus, drive — **empujón** *nm* (**-jones**) push, shove

**en** *prep* in; into, inside (of); on

**enamorar** *v* win the love of — **enamorarse** *vr* fall in love — **enamorado, -da** *adj* in love — **enamorado, -da** *n* lover, sweetheart

**enano, -na** *adj* & *n* dwarf

**encabezar** *v* head, lead; title

**encaje** *nm* lace

**encarecer** *v* increase, raise — **encarecerse** *vr* become more expensive

**encargar** *v* put in charge of; order — **encargado, -da** *adj* in charge — **encargado, -da** *n* manager, person in charge — **encargo** *nm* errand; assignment; task; order

**encender** *v* light, set fire to; switch on, start; arouse — **encendido, -da** *adj* lit, on

**encerrar** *v* lock up, shut away

**encestar** *v* score

**enchufar** *v* plug in, connect — **enchufe** *nm* plug, socket

**encía** *nf* gum

**enciclopedia** *nf* encyclopedia — **enciclopédico, -ca** *adj* encyclopedic

**encima** *adv* on top; **por ~ de** above, beyond

**encinta** *adj* pregnant

**encoger** *v* shrink — **encogerse** *vr* shrink; cower, cringe

**encontrar** *v* find — **encontrarse** *vr* meet

**encubrir** *v* conceal, cover (up)

**encuentro** *nm* meeting, encounter

**encuestar** *v* poll, survey — **encuesta** *nf* investigation, inquiry; survey — **encuestador, -dora** *n* pollster

**enderezar** *v* straighten (out); put upright, stand on end

**endeudarse** *vr* go into debt — **endeudado, -da** *adj* indebted, in debt

**endosar** *v* endorse — **endoso** *nm* endorsement

**endulzar** *v* sweeten — **endulzante** *nm* sweetener

**endurecer** *v* harden

**enemigo, -ga** *adj* hostile — **enemigo, -ga** *n* enemy — **enemistad** *nf* enmity — **enemistar** *v* make enemies of

**energía** *nf* energy

**enero** *nm* January

**enfadar** *v* annoy, make angry — **enfadarse** *vr* get annoyed — **enfado** *nm* anger, annoyance

**énfasis** *nms & pl* emphasis

**enfermar** *v* make sick; get sick — **enfermedad** *nf* sickness, disease — **enfermería** *nf* infirmary — **enfermero, -ra** *n* nurse — **enfermo, -ma** *adj* sick — **enfermo, -ma** *n* sick person, patient

**enflaquecer** *v* lose weight

**enfocar** *v* focus; consider

**enfrentar** *v* confront, face; bring face to face — **enfrente** *adv* opposite

**enfriar** *v* chill, cool — **enfriarse** *vr* get cold

**enfurecer** *v* infuriate — **enfurecerse** *vr* fly into a rage

**enganchar** *v* hook, snag, catch

**engañar** *v* trick, deceive; cheat on, be unfaithful to — **engaño** *nm* deception, deceit — **engañoso, -sa** *adj* deceptive, deceitful

**engordar** *v* fatten; gain weight

**engrasar** *v* lubricate, grease — **engrase** *nm* lubrication

**engreído, -da** *adj* conceited

**enigma** *nm* enigma — **enigmático, -ca** *adj* enigmatic

**enjabonar** *v* soap (up), lather

**enjaular** *v* cage; jail

**enjuagar** *v* rinse — **enjuague** *nm* rinse

**enlace** *nm* bond, link

**enlatar** *v* can

**enloquecer** *v* drive crazy — **enloquecerse** *vr* go crazy

**enmascarar** *v* mask

**enmudecer** *v* silence; become silent

**enojar** *v* anger; annoy — **enojo** *nm* anger; annoyance

**enorme** *adj* enormous

**enredo** *nm* tangle; confusion, mess

**enriquecer** *v* enrich — **enriquecerse** *vr* get rich

**enrojecer** *v* redden — **enrojecerse** *vr* blush

**enrollar** *v* roll up, coil

**enroscar** *v* roll up; screw in

**ensalada** *nf* salad

**ensanchar** *v* widen; expand — **ensanche** *nm* widening

**ensangrentado, -da** *adj* bloody, bloodstained

**ensayar** *v* rehearse; try out, test — **ensayo** *nm* essay; trial, test; rehearsal

**enseguida** *adv* right away, immediately

**enseñar** *v* teach; show — **enseñanza** *nf* education; teaching

**ensordecer** *v* deafen; go deaf — **ensordecedor, -dora** *adj* deafening

**ensortijar** *v* curl

**ensuciar** *v* soil — **ensuciarse** *vr* get dirty

**entender** *v* understand — **entendido, -da** *adj* understood

**enterar** *v* inform — **enterarse** *vr* find out, learn — **enterado, -da** *adj* well-informed

**enternecer** *v* move, touch

**entero, -ra** *adj* whole; absolute, total; intact — **entero** *nm* integer, whole number

**enterrar** *v* bury

**entidad** *nf* entity; body, organization

**entierro** *nm* burial; funeral

**entonar** *v* sing, intone; be in tune

**entonces** *adv* then

**entorpecer** *v* hinder, obstruct; numb

**entrada** *nf* entrance, entry; ticket; inning (in baseball)

**entrar** *v* enter; begin; introduce, bring in

**entre** *prep* between; among

**entreabrir** *v* leave ajar — **entreabierto, -ta** *adj* half-open, ajar

**entrecortado, -da** *adj* faltering, labored

**entregar** *v* deliver, hand over — **entregarse** *vr* surrender — **entrega** *nf* delivery; dedication, devotion

**entrenar** *v* train, drill — **entrenarse** *vr* train — **entrenador, -dora** *n* trainer, coach — **entranamiento** *nm* training

**entretanto** *adv* meanwhile

**entretener** *v* entertain; distract — **entretenerse** *vr* amuse oneself — **entretenido, -da** *adj* entertaining — **entretenimiento** *nm* entertainment, amusement; pastime

**entrevistar** *v* interview — **entrevista** *nf* interview — **entrevistador, -dora** *n* interviewer

**entristecer** *v* sadden

**entrometerse** *vr* interfere — **entrometido, -da** *adj* meddling, nosy — **entrometido, -da** *n* meddler

**entusiasmar** *v* fill with enthusiasm — **entusiasmarse** *vr* get excited — **entusiasmo** *nm* enthusiasm — **entusiasta** *adj* enthusiastic — **entusiasta** *nmf* enthusiast

**enumerar** *v* enumerate, list — **enumeración** *nf* (**-ciones**) enumeration, count

**envasar** *v* package; bottle, can — **envase** *nm* packaging; container; jar, bottle, can

**envejecer** *v* age — **envejecido, -da** *adj* aged, old — **envejecimiento** *nm* aging

**envenenar** *v* poison — **envenenamiento** *nm* poisoning

**enviar** *v* send — **enviado, -da** *n* envoy, correspondent

**envidiar** *v* envy — **envidia** *nf* envy, jealousy — **envidioso, -sa** *adj* jealous, envious

**envío** *nm* sending, shipment; remittance

**enviudar** *v* be widowed

**envolver** *v* wrap — **envoltorio** *nm* or **envoltura** *nf* wrapping, wrapper

**enyesar** *v* put in a plaster cast

**enzima** *nf* enzyme

**épico, -ca** *adj* epic — **épica** *nf* epic

**epidemia** *nf* epidemic — **epidémico, -ca** *adj* epidemic

**episodio** *nm* episode

**época** *nf* epoch, period; season

**equilibrar** *v* balance — **equilibrado, -da** *adj* well-balanced — **equilibrio** *nm* balance, equilibrium; good sense

**equipaje** *nm* baggage, luggage

**equipar** *v* equip

**equipo** *nm* equipment; team, crew

**equitación** *nf* (**-ciones**) horseback riding

**equivaler** *v* be equivalent — **equivalencia** *nf* equivalence — **equivalente** *adj* & *nm* equivalent

**equivocar** *v* mistake, confuse — **equivocarse** *vr* make a mistake — **equivocación** *nf* (**-ciones**) error, mistake — **equivocado, -da** *adj* mistaken, wrong

**era** *nf* era

**erección** *nf* (**-ciones**) erection

**erizo** *nm* hedgehog

**ermitaño, -ña** *n* hermit

**erosionar** *v* erode — **erosión** *nf* (**-siones**) erosion

**erótico, -ca** *adj* erotic

**erradicar** *v* eradicate

**errar** *v* miss; be wrong, be mistaken; wander — **errado, -da** *adj* wrong, mistaken

**error** *nm* error — **erróneo, -nea** *adj* erroneous, mistaken

**eructar** *v* belch, burp — **eructo** *nm* belch, burp

**erudito, -ta** *adj* erudite, learned

**erupción** *nf* (**-ciones**) eruption; rash

**escalar** *v* climb, scale; escalate — **escala** *nf* scale; ladder; stopover (as of an airplane) — **escalador, -dora** n mountain climber

**escalera** nf stairs pl, staircase; ladder

**escalinata** nf flight of stairs

**escalofrío** nm shiver, chill — **escalofriante** adj chilling, horrifying

**escalón** nm (**-lones**) step, rung

**escama** nf scale (as of fish); flake (of skin)

**escandalizar** v scandalize — **escandalizarse** vr be shocked — **escándalo** nm scandal; scene, commotion — **escandaloso, -sa** adj shocking, scandalous; noisy

**escandinavo, -va** adj Scandinavian

**escáner** nm scanner

**escapar** v escape, run away — **escaparse** vr escape

**escape** nm leak; exhaust

**escarabajo** nm beetle

**escarbar** v dig, scratch, poke

**escarcha** nf frost

**escarpado, -da** adj steep

**escasear** v be scarce — **escasez** nf (**-seces**) shortage, scarcity — **escaso, -sa** adj scarce

**escena** nf scene; stage — **escenario** nm setting, scene; stage

**escepticismo** nm skepticism — **escéptico, -ca** adj skeptical — **escéptico, -ca** n skeptic

**esclavo, -va** n slave — **esclavitud** nf slavery — **esclavizar** v enslave

**escoba** nf broom

**escocés, -cesa** adj (**-ceses** m) Scottish; tartan, plaid — **escocés** nm (**-ceses**) Scotch (whiskey)

**escoger** v choose — **escogido, -da** adj choice, select

**escolar** adj school — **escolar** nmf student, pupil

**escolta** nmf escort — **escoltar** v escort, accompany

**escombros** nmpl ruins, rubble

**esconder** v hide, conceal — **esconderse** vr hide — **escondidas** nfpl

hide-and-seek — **escondite** nm hiding place; hide-and-seek

**escopeta** nf shotgun

**escorpión** nm (**-piones**) scorpion

**escote** nm (low) neckline

**escribir** v write — **escribirse** vr correspond; be spelled — **escrito, -ta** adj written — **escritos** nmpl writings — **escritor, -tora** n writer — **escritorio** nm desk — **escritura** nf handwriting

**escuadra** nf square (instrument)

**escuchar** v listen; listen to; hear

**escudo** nm shield

**escuela** nf school

**escultor, -tora** n sculptor — **escultura** nf sculpture

**escupir** v spit

**escurrir** v drain — **escurrirse** vr drain — **escurridor** nm dish drainer

**ese, esa** adj (**esos** m) that, those

**ése, ésa** pron (**ésos** m) that one, those ones pl

**esencia** nf essence — **esencial** adj essential

**esfera** nf sphere — **esférico, -ca** adj spherical

**esforzar** v strain — **esforzarse** vr make an effort — **esfuerzo** nm effort

**esgrima** nf fencing

**eslabón** nm (**-bones**) link

**eslavo, -va** adj Slavic

**eslogan** nm (**-lóganes**) slogan

**esmalte** nm enamel ~ **de uñas** nail polish

**esmerado, -da** adj careful

**esmeralda** nf emerald

**esmerarse** vr take great care

**esnob** nmf (**esnobs**) snob — **esnob** adj snobbish

**eso** pron (neuter) that

**espaciar** v space out, spread out — **espacial** adj space — **espacio** nm space — **espacioso, -sa** adj spacious

**espada** nf sword

**espagueti** nm or **espaguetis** nmpl spaghetti

**espalda** *nf* back

**espantar** *v* scare, frighten — **espantarse** *vr* become frightened — **espantapájaros** *nms & pl* scarecrow — **espanto** *nm* fright, fear — **espantoso, -sa** *adj* frightening, horrific; awful, terrible

**español, -ñola** *adj* Spanish — **español** *nm* Spanish (language)

**esparcir** *v* scatter, spread

**espárrago** *nm* asparagus

**especia** *nf* spice

**especial** *adj & nm* special — **especialidad** *nf* specialty — **especialista** *nmf* specialist — **especialmente** *adv* especially

**especie** *nf* species; type, kind

**especificar** *v* specify — **especificación** *nf* (-ciones) specification — **específico, -ca** *adj* specific

**espectáculo** *nm* show, performance; spectacle, view — **espectacular** *adj* spectacular — **espectador, -dora** *n* spectator

**espectro** *nm* spectrum; ghost

**especulación** *nf* (-ciones) speculation

**espejo** *nm* mirror — **espejismo** *nm* mirage; illusion

**esperar** *v* wait; wait for; expect — **espera** *nf* wait — **esperanza** *nf* hope, expectation — **esperanzado, -da** *adj* hopeful — **esperanzar** *v* give hope to

**esperma** *nmf* sperm

**espesar** *v* thicken — **espeso, -sa** *adj* thick, heavy — **espesor** *nm* thickness, density — **espesura** *nf* thickness

**espiar** *v* spy; spy on — **espía** *nmf* spy

**espiga** *nf* ear

**espina** *nf* thorn; (fish) bone; ~ **dorsal** spine, backbone

**espinaca** *nf* spinach (plant); ~**s** *nfpl* spinach (food)

**espinilla** *nf* shin; blackhead, pimple

**espinoso, -sa** *adj* prickly; bony

**espionaje** *nm* espionage

**espiral** *adj & nf* spiral

**espirar** *v* breathe out, exhale

**espíritu** *nm* spirit — **espiritual** *adj* spiritual — **espiritualidad** *nf* spirituality

**espléndido, -da** *adj* splendid — **esplendor** *nm* splendor

**esponja** *nf* sponge — **esponjoso, -sa** *adj* spongy

**espontáneo, -nea** *adj* spontaneous

**esposo, -sa** *n* spouse, wife, husband

**espuma** *nf* foam, froth; head — **espumoso, -sa** *adj* foamy, frothy; sparkling

**esqueleto** *nm* skeleton

**esquema** *nf* outline, sketch

**esquí** *nm* ski; skiing — **esquiador, -dora** *n* skier — **esquiar** *v* ski

**esquina** *nf* corner

**esquivar** *v* evade, dodge; avoid — **esquivo, -va** *adj* shy, elusive

**estabilizar** *v* stabilize

**establecer** *v* establish — **establecerse** *vr* establish oneself, settle — **establecimiento** *nm* establishment

**establo** *nm* stable

**estación** *nf* (-ciones) season; ~ **de servicio** gas station — **estacionar** *v* park — **estacionamiento** *nm* parking

**estadía** *nf* stay

**estadio** *nm* stadium; phase, stage

**estadista** *nmf* statesman

**estadística** *nf* statistics

**estado** *nm* state; ~ **civil** marital status

**estadounidense** *adj & nmf* American

**estafar** *v* swindle, defraud — **estafa** *nf* swindle, fraud — **estafador, -dora** *n* cheat, swindler

**estallar** *v* explode

**estampilla** *nf* stamp

**estándar** *adj & nm* standard

**estar** *v aux* be — **estar** *v* be; be at home; stay, remain

**estatua** *nf* statue

**estatura** *nf* height

**estatus** *nm* status, prestige

**estatuto** *nm* statute

**este¹, esta** *adj* (**estos** *m*) this, these

**este**[2] *adj* eastern, east — **este** *nm* east; east wind; **el Este** the Orient

**éste, ésta** *pron* (**éstos** *m*) this one, these ones *pl*; the latter

**estereofónico, -ca** *adj* stereophonic

**estereotipo** *nm* stereotype

**estéril** *adj* sterile; infertile

**estética** *nf* aesthetics

**estigmatizar** *v* stigmatize

**estilo** *nm* style; fashion, manner — **estilista** *nmf* stylist

**estimar** *v* esteem, respect; value, estimate; consider

**estimular** *v* stimulate; encourage — **estimulante** *adj* stimulating — **estimulante** *nm* stimulant — **estímulo** *nm* stimulus

**esto** *pron* (*neuter*) this

**estoico, -ca** *adj* stoic, stoical — **estoico, -ca** *n* stoic

**estómago** *nm* stomach

**estornudar** *v* sneeze

**estrategia** *nf* strategy

**estrato** *nm* stratum

**estrechar** *v* narrow; strengthen (a bond); embrace — **estrecho, -cha** *adj* tight, narrow; close

**estrella** *nf* star; destiny

**estrellar** *v* crash

**estremecer** *v* cause to shudder; tremble, shake — **estremecerse** *vr* shudder, shiver

**estrenar** *v* use for the first time; premiere, open — **estrenarse** *vr* make one's debut

**estrés** *nm* (**estreses**) stress

**estricto, -ta** *adj* strict

**estrofa** *nf* stanza, verse

**estructura** *nf* structure — **estructural** *adj* structural

**estudiar** *v* study — **estudiante** *nmf* student — **estudio** *nm* study; studio, office; ~**s** *nmpl* studies, education

**estupendo, -da** *adj* stupendous, marvelous

**etapa** *nf* stage, phase

**ética** *nf* ethics

**etimología** *nf* etymology

**etíope** *adj* Ethiopian

**etiqueta** *nf* tag, label; etiquette; **de** ~ formal, dressy

**étnico, -ca** *adj* ethnic

**Eucaristía** *nf* Eucharist, communion

**eufemismo** *nm* euphemism

**europeo, -pea** *adj* European

**eutanasia** *nf* euthanasia

**evacuar** *v* evacuate, vacate; have a bowel movement — **evacuación** *nf* (**-ciones**) evacuation

**evadir** *v* evade, avoid

**evaluar** *v* evaluate

**evangelio** *nm* gospel

**evasivo, -va** *adj* evasive

**evento** *nm* event

**eventual** *adj* temporary; possible

**evidencia** *nf* evidence, proof — **evidenciar** *v* demonstrate, show — **evidente** *adj* evident

**evitar** *v* avoid; prevent

**evolución** *nf* (**-ciones**) evolution

**exacto, -ta** *adj* precise, exact

**exagerar** *v* exaggerate — **exageración** *nf* (**-ciones**) exaggeration

**examen** *nm* (**exámenes**) examination, test; investigation — **examinar** *v* examine; study, inspect — **examinarse** *vr* take an exam

**exceder** *v* exceed, surpass — **excederse** *vr* go too far — **excedente** *adj* & *nm* surplus, excess

**excelente** *adj* excellent

**excepción** *nf* (**-ciones**) exception — **excepcional** *adj* exceptional

**excepto** *prep* except (for)

**exceso** *nm* excess — **excesivo, -va** *adj* excessive

**excitar** *v* excite, arouse — **excitación** *nf* (**-ciones**) excitement, agitation, arousal

**exclamar** *v* exclaim — **exclamación** *nf* (**-ciones**) exclamation

# excluir

**44**

**excluir** *v* exclude — **exclusión** *nf* (**-siones**) exclusion — **exclusivo, -va** *adj* exclusive

**excursión** *nf* (**-siones**) excursion — **excursionista** *nmf* tourist, sightseer; hiker

**excusar** *v* excuse; exempt — **excusa** *nf* excuse; apology

**exento, -ta** *adj* exempt

**exequias** *nfpl* funeral rites

**exhaustivo, -va** *adj* exhaustive

**exhibir** *v* exhibit, show — **exhibición** *nf* (**-ciones**) exhibition

**exigir** *v* demand, require — **exigencia** *nf* demand, requirement

**existir** *v* exist — **existencia** *nf* existence; ~s *nfpl* goods, stock

**éxito** *nm* success, hit

**expectativa** *nf* expectation, hope; ~s *nfpl* prospects

**expedición** *nf* (**-ciones**) expedition

**experiencia** *nf* experience

**experimentar** *v* experiment; experiment with, test out; experience, feel — **experimento** *nm* experiment

**experto, -ta** *adj & n* expert

**explicar** *v* explain — **explicarse** *vr* understand

**explícito, -ta** *adj* explicit

**explosión** *nf* (**-siones**) explosion; outburst (as of laughter) — **explosivo, -va** *adj* explosive

**explotar** *v* exploit; operate, run (as a factory), work (a mine); explode — **explotación** *nf* (**-ciones**) exploitation; operating, running

**exponer** *v* expose; explain, set out; exhibit, display — **exponerse a** *vr phr* expose oneself to, submit oneself to

**exportar** *v* export

**exposición** *nf* (**-ciones**) exposure; exhibition; exposition, setting out — **expositor, -tora** *n* exhibitor; exponent

**expresar** *v* express — **expresión** *nf* (**-siones**) expression — **expresivo, -va** *adj* expressive; affectionate

**expulsar** *v* expel, eject — **expulsión** *nf* (**-siones**) expulsion

**extender** *v* spread out; draw up, write out — **extenderse** *vr* extend, spread; last — **extendido, -da** *adj* widespread; outstretched

**extensión** *nf* (**-siones**) extension; expanse; range, extent — **extenso, -sa** *adj* extensive

**exterior** *adj* exterior, external; foreign — **exterior** *nm* outside; **en el** ~ abroad

**externo, -na** *adj* external

**extinguir** *v* extinguish; end, wipe out — **extinción** *nf* (**-ciones**) extinction

**extra** *adv* extra — **extra** *adj* additional; top-quality — **extra** *nmf* extra (in movies); *nm* extra (expense)

**extraer** *v* extract — **extracción** *nf* (**-ciones**) extraction

**extranjero, -ra** *adj* foreign — **extranjero, -ra** *n* foreigner — **extranjero** *nm* foreign countries *pl*

**extrañar** *v* miss — **extrañarse** *vr* be surprised — **extraño, -ña** *adj* foreign; strange, odd — **extraño, -ña** *n* stranger

**extraordinario, -ria** *adj* extraordinary

**extremidad** *nf* tip, end; ~es *nfpl* extremities — **extremista** *adj & nmf* extremist — **extremo, -ma** *adj* extreme; **en caso** ~ as a last resort — **extremo** *nm* end; **en** ~ in the extreme, extremely; **en ultimo** ~ as a last resort

**extrovertido -da** *adj* extroverted — **extrovertido -da** *n* extrovert

**eyacular** *v* ejaculate — **eyaculación** *nf* (**-ciones**) ejaculation

# F

**f** *nf* f, sixth letter of the Spanish alphabet

**fabricar** *v* manufacture; build, construct; fabricate — **fábrica** *nf* factory — **fabricación** *nf* (**-ciones**) manufacture — **fabricante** *nmf* manufacturer

**fábula** *nf* fable; story, lie

**fabuloso, -sa** *adj* fabulous

**facial** *adj* facial

**fácil** *adj* easy; likely — **facilidad** *nf* facility, ease; **∼es** *nfpl* facilities, services — **facilitar** *v* facilitate; provide, supply

**facsímil** *or* **facsímile** *nm* facsimile, copy; fax

**factible** *adj* feasible

**factor** *nm* factor

**factura** *nf* bill, invoice; making, manufacture — **facturar** *v* bill for; check in (as baggage)

**facultad** *nf* faculty, ability; authority; school (of a university)

**falda** *nf* skirt; side, slope (of a mountain)

**fallar** *v* fail, go wrong; pronounce judgment on; miss — **falla** *nf* flaw, defect; (geological) fault

**fallecer** *v* pass away, die — **fallecimiento** *nm* demise, death

**fallo** *nm* error; sentence, verdict

**falso, -sa** *adj* false, untrue; counterfeit, forged

**falta** *nf* lack; defect, fault, error; absence; offense, misdemeanor; foul; **hacer ∼** be lacking, be needed; **sin ∼** without fail — **faltar** *v* be lacking, be needed; be missing; remain, be left; **¡no faltaba más!** don't mention it!

**fama** *nf* fame; reputation

**familia** *nf* family — **familiar** *adj* familial, family; familiar; informal (of language) — **familiar** *nmf* relation, relative — **familiaridad** *nf* familiarity

**famoso, -sa** *adj* famous

**fantástico, -ca** *adj* fantastic

**fascículo** *nm* installment, part (of a publication)

**fascinar** *v* fascinate — **fascinación** *nf* (**-ciones**) fascination — **fascinante** *adj* fascinating

**fascismo** *nm* fascism — **fascista** *adj* & *nmf* fascist

**fase** *nf* phase

**fatiga** *nf* fatigue — **fatigado, -da** *adj* weary, tired — **fatigar** *v* tire

**fauna** *nf* fauna

**favor** *nm* favor; **a ∼ de** in favor of; **por ∼** please — **favorable** *adj* favorable — **favorecer** *v* favor; look well on, suit — **favorito, -ta** *adj* & *n* favorite

**fax** *nm* fax — **faxear** *v* fax

**faz** *nf* (**faces**) face, countenance

**fe** *nf* faith; **dar ∼ de** bear witness to; **de buena ∼** in good faith

**febrero** *nm* February

**fecha** *nf* date

**fecundar** *v* fertilize (an egg); make fertile

**felicidad** *nf* happiness — **felicitación** *nf* (**-ciones**) congratulation — **felicitar** *v* congratulate

**feliz** *adj* (**-lices**) happy; fortunate; **Feliz Navidad** Merry Christmas

**femenino, -na** *adj* feminine; female — **femenino** *nm* feminine (in grammar) — **feminismo** *nm* feminism

**fenómeno** *nm* phenomenon

**feo, fea** *adj* ugly; unpleasant, nasty

**féretro** *nm* coffin

**feria** *nf* fair, market; festival, holiday

**fermentar** *v* ferment — **fermentación** *nf* (**-ciones**) fermentation — **fermento** *nm* ferment

**férreo, -rrea** *adj* iron; **vía férrea** railroad track

**ferretería** *nf* hardware store

**fértil** *adj* fertile, fruitful — **fertilidad** *nf* fertility

**festival** *nm* festival — **festividad** *nf* festivity — **festivo, -va** *adj* festive; **día festivo** holiday

**fiable** *adj* reliable — **fiabilidad** *nf* reliability

**fiado, -da** *adj* on credit — **fiador, -dora** *n* bondsman, guarantor

**fianza** *nf* bail, bond; **dar ~** pay a deposit

**fiar** *v* guarantee; sell on credit; **ser de ~** be trustworthy — **fiarse de** *vr phr* place trust in

**fibra** *nf* fiber

**ficción** *nf* (**-ciones**) fiction

**ficha** *nf* token; index card; counter, chip (in games) — **fichero** *nm* card file; filing cabinet

**ficticio, -cia** *adj* fictitious

**fidelidad** *nf* fidelity, faithfulness

**fiebre** *nf* fever; **~ palúdica** malaria

**fiel** *adj* faithful, loyal; accurate, reliable — **fiel** *nm* pointer (of a scale)

**fiesta** *nf* party; holiday, feast day

**figura** *nf* figure; shape, form — **figurar** *v* figure (in), be included; stand out; represent — **figurarse** *vr* imagine

**fijar** *v* fasten, affix; set, fix — **fijarse** *vr* settle; **fijarse en** notice, pay attention to — **fijo, -ja** *adj* fixed, firm; permanent

**fila** *nf* line, file, row; **ponerse en ~** line up

**filantropía** *nf* philanthropy

**filial** *adj* filial — **filial** *nf* affiliate, subsidiary

**filigrana** *nf* filigree; watermark

**filipino, -na** *adj* Filipino

**filmar** *v* film, shoot — **filme** *or* **film** *nm* film, movie

**filosofía** *nf* philosophy — **filósofo, -fa** *n* philosopher

**filtrar** *v* filter — **filtrarse** *vr* leak out, seep through — **filtro** *nm* filter

**fin** *nm* end; purpose, aim; **en ~** well, in short; **~ de semana** weekend; **por ~** finally, at last

**final** *adj* final — **final** *nm* end, conclusion; *nf* final (in sports) — **finalidad** *nf* purpose, aim — **finalista** *nmf* finalist — **finalizar** *v* finish, end

**financiar** *v* finance, fund — **financiero, -ra** *adj* financial — **financiero, -ra** *n* financier — **finanzas** *nfpl* finance

**finca** *nf* farm, ranch; country house

**fingir** *v* feign, pretend — **fingido, -da** *adj* false, feigned

**finito, -ta** *adj* finite

**finlandés, -desa** *adj* Finnish

**fino, -na** *adj* fine; slender; refined; sharp, keen

**firma** *nf* signature; (act of) signing; firm, company

**firmar** *v* sign

**firme** *adj* firm, resolute; steady, stable — **firmeza** *nf* strength, resolve; firmness, stability

**fiscal** *adj* fiscal — **fiscal** *nmf* district attorney — **fisco** *nm* (national) treasury

**física** *nf* physics — **físico, -ca** *adj* physical — **físico, -ca** *n* physicist — **físico** *nm* physique

**fisiología** *nf* physiology

**fisioterapia** *nf* physical therapy — **fisioterapeuta** *nmf* physical therapist

**fisonomía** *nf* features *pl*, appearance

**flaco, -ca** *adj* thin, skinny; weak

**flamenco, -ca** *adj* flamenco; Flemish

**flauta** *nf* flute; **~ dulce** recorder — **flautista** *nmf* flutist

**flecha** *nf* arrow

**flexible** *adj* flexible — **flexibilidad** *nf* flexibility

**flor** *nf* flower — **florecer** *v* bloom, blossom; flourish — **florero** *nm* vase

**flota** *nf* fleet

**flotar** *v* float — **flotador** *nm* float; life preserver

**fluctuar** *v* fluctuate — **fluctuación** *nf* (**-ciones**) fluctuation

**fluir** *v* flow — **fluidez** *nf* fluidity; fluency — **fluido, -da** *adj* fluid; fluent

**fluvial** *adj* river

**fobia** *nf* phobia

**foca** *nf* seal

**foco** *nm* focus; spotlight, floodlight

**fogata** *nf* bonfire

**folklore** *nm* folklore

**fomentar** *v* promote, encourage — **fomento** *nm* promotion, encouragement

**fondo** *nm* bottom; rear, back, end; depth; ~**s** *nmpl* funds, resources; **a** ~ thoroughly, in depth; **en el** ~ deep down

**fonética** *nf* phonetics

**foráneo, -nea** *adj* foreign, strange

**forense** *adj* forensic

**forjar** *v* forge; build up, create

**forma** *nf* form, shape; manner, way; **en** ~ fit, healthy; ~**s** *nfpl* appearances, conventions — **formación** *nf* (**-ciones**) formation; training

**formal** *adj* formal; serious; dependable, reliable — **formalidad** *nf* formality; seriousness; reliability

**formar** *v* form, shape; constitute; train, educate

**formidable** *adj* tremendous; fantastic, terrific

**fórmula** *nf* formula

**formular** *v* formulate, draw up; make, lodge (as a complaint)

**formulario** *nm* form

**foro** *nm* forum

**fortalecer** *v* strengthen

**fortuna** *nf* fortune, luck; wealth, fortune; **por** ~ fortunately

**forzar** *v* force; strain (one's eyes)

**fosa** *nf* pit, ditch; grave; ~**s nasales** nostrils

**fósforo** *nm* phosphorus; match — **fosforescente** *adj* phosphorescent

**fotocopia** *nf* photocopy

**fotografía** *nf* photography; photograph, picture — **fotografiar** *v* photograph — **fotógrafo, -fa** *n* photographer

**fracasar** *v* fail — **fracaso** *nm* failure

**fracción** *nf* (**-ciones**) fraction; faction (in politics)

**fractura** *nf* fracture — **fracturarse** *vr* fracture, break

**fragancia** *nf* fragrance, scent

**frágil** *adj* fragile; frail, delicate

**fragmento** *nm* fragment

**francés, -cesa** *adj* (**-ceses** *m*) French — **francés** *nm* French (language)

**franco, -ca** *adj* frank, candid; free (in commerce) — **franco** *nm* franc

**frase** *nf* phrase; sentence

**fraternal** *adj* brotherly, fraternal — **fraternidad** *nf* brotherhood, fraternity

**frecuencia** *nf* frequency; **con** ~ often, frequently — **frecuentar** *v* frequent, haunt

**freír** *v* fry

**frenar** *v* brake

**freno** *nm* brake

**frente** *nm* front; facade; **al** ~ **de** at the head of; ~ **a** opposite; **de** ~ (facing) forward; **hacer** ~ **a** face up to, brave — **frente** *nf* forehead

**fresa** *nf* strawberry

**fresco, -ca** *adj* fresh; cool; insolent, nervy — **fresco** *nm* fresh air; coolness; fresco (painting)

**frialdad** *nf* coldness; indifference

**fricción** *nf* (**-ciones**) friction; rubbing, massage — **friccionar** *v* rub

**frigidez** *nf* frigidity

**frijol** *nm* bean

**frío, fría** *adj* cold; cool, indifferent — **frío** *nm* cold; coldness, indifference

**frito, -ta** *adj* fried; fed up

**frívolo, -la** *adj* frivolous — **frivolidad** *nf* frivolity

**frontera** *nf* border, frontier — **fronterizo, -za** *adj* border, on the border

**frotar** *v* rub

**fructífero, -ra** *adj* fruitful

**fruncir** *v* gather (in pleats)

**frustrar** *v* frustrate — **frustrarse** *vr* fail — **frustración** *nf* (**-ciones**) frustration

**fruta** *nf* fruit — **fruto** *nm* fruit; result, consequence

**fuego** *nm* fire; flame, burner; ~**s artificiales** *nmpl* fireworks

**fuente** *nf* fountain; spring; source; platter, serving dish

**fuera** *adv* outside, out; abroad, away; ~ **de** outside of, beyond; aside from, in addition to

**fuerte** strong; bright (of colors), loud (of sounds); intense; hard — **fuerte** *adv* strongly, hard; loudly; abundantly, a lot — **fuerte** *nm* fort; strong point

**fuerza** *nf* strength; force; power, might; ~**s armadas** *nfpl* armed forces; **a ~ de** by dint of; **a la ~** necessarily

**fuga** *nf* flight, escape; fugue (in music); leak — **fugarse** *vr* flee, run away — **fugaz** *adj* (**-gaces**) fleeting — **fugitivo, -va** *adj & n* fugitive

**fumar** *v* smoke — **fumador, -dora** *n* smoker

**función** *nf* (**-ciones**) function; duties; performance, show (in a theater) — **funcional** *adj* functional — **funcionamiento** *nm* functioning — **funcionar** *v* function, run, work; **no funciona** out of order — **funcionario, -ria** *n* civil servant, official

**funda** *nf* cover, sheath

**fundamento** *nm* foundation; ~**s** *nmpl* fundamentals — **fundamental** *adj* fundamental, basic — **fundamentar** *v* lay the foundations for; base

**fundar** *v* found, establish; base — **fundarse en** *vr phr* be based on

**fundir** *v* melt down, smelt; fuse, merge — **fundirse** *vr* blend, merge; melt; burn out — **fundición** *nf* (**-ciones**) smelting; foundry

**fúnebre** *adj* funeral; gloomy

**funeral** *nm* funeral; ~**es** *nmpl* funeral (rites) — **funeral** *adj* funeral, funerary — **funeraria** *nf* funeral home

**funesto, ta** *adj* terrible, disastrous

**furgoneta** *nf* van

**furia** *nf* fury, rage; violence — **furioso, -sa** *adj* furious, irate; intense, violent

**fusión** *nf* (**-siones**) fusion; union, merger — **fusionar** *v* fuse; merge — **fusionarse** *vr* merge

**futbol** *or* **fútbol** *nm* soccer; ~ **americano** football — **futbolista** *nmf* soccer player, football player

**futuro, -ra** *adj* future — **futuro** *nm* future

# G

**g** *nf* g, seventh letter of the Spanish alphabet

**gabardina** *nf* trench coat, raincoat

**gafas** *nfpl* eyeglasses

**galaxia** *nf* galaxy

**galleta** *nf* (sweet) cookie

**gallina** *nf* hen — **gallinero** *nm* henhouse, (chicken) coop — **gallo** *nm* rooster, cock

**galón** *nm* (**-lones**) gallon

**galopar** *v* gallop

**gamuza** *nf* chamois (leather), suede

**gana** *nf* desire, wish; appetite

**ganado** *nm* cattle livestock — **ganadería** *nf* livestock

**ganador, -dora** *adj* winning — **ganador, -dora** *n* winner

**ganancia** *nf* profit

**ganar** *v* earn; win (as in games)

**gancho** *nm* hook; hairpin; (clothes) hanger

**ganga** *nf* bargain

**ganso, -sa** *n* goose, gander *m*

**garaje** *nm* garage

**garantizar** *v* guarantee — **garantía** *nf* guarantee, warranty

**garbanzo** *nm* chickpea

**garganta** *nf* throat

**garza** *nf* heron

**gas** *nm* gas; ~ **lacrimógeno** tear gas

**gasa** *nf* gauze

**gaseosa** *nf* soda, soft drink

**gasolina** *nf* gasoline — **gasolinera** *nf* gas station, service station

**gastar** *v* spend; consume, use up; squander, waste — **gasto** *nm* expense, expenditure

**gastronomía** *nf* gastronomy

**gatear** *v* crawl, creep

**gato, -ta** *n* cat — **gato** *nm* (automobile) jack

**gaveta** *nf* drawer

**gaviota** *nf* gull, seagull

**gay** *adj* gay (homosexual)

**gelatina** *nf* gelatin

**gemelo, -la** *adj & n* twin

**gemir** *v* moan, groan, whine — **gemido** *nm* moan, groan, whine

**generación** *nf* (**-ciones**) generation

**general** *adj* general — **general** *nmf* general — **generalmente** *adv* usually, generally

**género** *nm* kind, sort; gender (in grammar)

**generoso, -sa** *adj* generous, unselfish — **generosidad** *nf* generosity

**genial** *adj* brilliant; great, terrific

**genio** *nm* genius; temper, disposition

**genital** *adj* genital — **genitales** *nmpl* genitals

**gente** *nf* people

**geografía** *nf* geography — **geográfico, -ca** *adj* geographic, geographical

**geología** *nf* geology — **geológico, -ca** *adj* geologic, geological

**geometría** *nf* geometry

**gerencia** *nf* management — **gerente** *nmf* manager

**gesto** *nm* gesture; (facial) expression

**gigante** *adj & nm* giant

**gimnasia** *nf* gymnastics — **gimnasio** *nm* gymnasium, gym

**ginebra** *nf* gin

**ginecología** *nf* gynecology — **ginecólogo, -ga** *n* gynecologist

**gira** *nf* tour

**girar** *v* turn; turn around, revolve; twist, rotate

**girasol** *nm* sunflower

**giro** *nm* turn, rotation

**glándula** *nf* gland

**globo** *nm* globe; balloon — **global** *adj* global; total, overall

**gloria** *nf* glory

**glorieta** *nf* rotary, traffic circle

**glotón, -tona** *adj* (**-tones** *m*) gluttonous — **glotón, -tona** *n* (**-tones** *m*) glutton

**gobernar** *v* govern, rule; direct, manage — **gobernador, -dora** *n* governor — **gobierno** *nm* government

**gol** *nm* goal (in sports)

**golf** *nm* golf — **golfista** *nmf* golfer

**golfo** *nm* gulf

**golondrina** *nf* swallow

**golosina** *nf* sweet, candy — **goloso, -sa** *adj* fond of sweets

**golpe** *nm* blow; punch — **golpear** *v* hit, punch; slam, bang (as a door); knock (at a door)

**goma** *nf* rubber; glue

**gordo, -da** *adj* fat — **gordo, -da** *n* fat person — **gordo** *nm* fat — **gordura** *nf* fatness

**gorila** *nm* gorilla

**gorra** *nf* cap, bonnet

**gorrión** *nm* (**-rriones**) sparrow

**gorro** *nm* cap, bonnet

**gota** *nf* drop

**gozar** *v* enjoy oneself

**grabar** *v* record, tape — **grabación** *nf* (**-ciones**) recording — **grabadora** *nf* tape recorder

**gracia** *nf* grace; humor, wit; ~**s** *nfpl* thanks; ¡(**muchas**) ~**s!** thank you (very much)! — **gracioso, -sa** *adj* funny, amusing

**grado** *nm* degree; grade (in school)

**graduar** *v* regulate, adjust; confer a degree on (in education) — **graduarse** *vr* graduate (from a school) — **graduado, -da** *n* graduate

**gramática** *nf* grammar — **gramatical** *adj* grammatical

**gramo** *nm* gram

**grande** *adj* large, big; tall; great (as in quality, intensity); grown-up

**granizar** *v impers* hail — **granizo** *nm* hail

**granja** *nf* farm — **granjero, -ra** *n* farmer

**grano** *nm* grain; seed

**grapadora** *nf* stapler — **grapar** *v* staple

**grasa** *nf* grease — **graso, -sa** *adj* fatty, greasy, oily — **grasoso, -sa** *adj* greasy, oily

**gratis** *adv & adj* free

**grato, -ta** *adj* pleasant, agreeable

**gratuito, -ta** *adj* gratuitous, unwarranted; free

**grave** *adj* grave, serious — **gravedad** *nf* gravity

**griego, -ga** *adj* Greek — **griego** *nm* Greek (language)

**grieta** *nf* crack, crevice

**grifo** *nm* faucet, tap

**grillo** *nm* cricket

**gringo, -ga** *adj & n* Yankee, gringo

**gripe** *or* **gripa** *nf* flu, influenza

**gris** *adj & nm* gray

**gritar** *v* shout, scream, cry — **grito** *nm* shout, scream, cry

**grosería** *nf* vulgar remark; rudeness — **grosero, -ra** *adj* coarse, vulgar; rude

**grosor** *nm* thickness

**grotesco, -ca** *adj* grotesque, hideous

**grúa** *nf* crane, derrick

**grueso, -sa** *adj* thick — **grueso** *nm* thickness; main body, mass

**gruñir** *v* growl, grunt — **gruñido** *nm* growl, grunt — **gruñón, -ñona** *adj* (-ñones *m*) grumpy, grouchy

**grupo** *nm* group

**guacamole** *nm* guacamole

**guante** *nm* glove

**guapo, -pa** *adj* handsome, good-looking

**guarda** *nmf* keeper, custodian; security guard — **guardabarros** *nms & pl* fender(s) — **guardabosque** *nmf* forest ranger — **guardacostas** *nmfs & pl* coast guard vessel(s) — **guardaespaldas** *nmfs & pl* bodyguard(s) — **guardameta** *nmf* goalkeeper — **guardar** *v* keep; guard, protect; save

**guardería** *nf* nursery, day-care center

**guardia** *nf* guard, vigilance — **guardián, -diana** *n* (-dianes *m*) guardian, keeper; security guard

**guatemalteco, -ca** *adj* Guatemalan

**guayaba** *nf* guava

**gubernamental** *or* **gubernativo, -va** *adj* governmental

**guerra** *nf* war, warfare; conflict, struggle — **guerrilla** *nf* guerrilla warfare — **guerrillero, -ra** *adj & n* guerrilla

**guiar** *v* guide, lead; advise — **guía** *nf* guidebook; guidance; *nmf* guide, leader

**guiño** *nm* wink

**guión** *nm* (guiones) script, screenplay; hyphen, dash (in punctuation)

**guisado** *nm* stew

**guisante** *nm* pea

**guisar** *v* cook — **guiso** *nm* stew, casserole

**guitarra** *nf* guitar — **guitarrista** *nmf* guitarist

**gula** *nf* gluttony

**gusano** *nm* worm; maggot (larva)

**gustar** *v* taste; like; be pleasing

**gusto** *nm* taste; pleasure, liking; **mucho** ~ pleased to meet you

# H

**h** *nf* h, eighth letter of the Spanish alphabet

**haba** *nf* broad bean

**habanero, -ra** *adj* Havanan

**haber** *v aux* have, has — **haber** *v impers, form is* **hay** there is, there are — **haber** *nm* assets

**habichuela** *nf* bean

**hábil** *adj* able, skillful; clever — **habilidad** *nf* ability, skill

**habilitar** *v* equip, furnish; authorize

**habitar** *v* inhabit; reside, dwell — **habitación** *nf* (**-ciones**) room, bedroom — **habitante** *nmf* inhabitant, resident

**hábito** *nm* habit — **habitual** *adj* habitual, usual — **habituar** *v* accustom, habituate

**hablar** *v* talk, speak; speak (a language) — **habla** *nf* speech; language, dialect — **hablador, -dora** *adj* talkative — **hablante** *nmf* speaker

**hacer** *v* do, perform; make; force, oblige; act — **hacer** *v impers* to be; ~ **calor/viento** be hot/be windy; **hace mucho tiempo** a long time ago — **hacerse** *vr* become

**hacha** *nf* hatchet, ax

**hacia** *prep* toward, towards; near, around, about

**hacienda** *nf* estate, ranch; property; **Hacienda** department of revenue

**halagar** *v* flatter — **halagador, -dora** *adj* flattering — **halago** *nm* flattery

**halcón** *nm* (**-cones**) hawk, falcon

**hallar** *v* find; discover, find out — **hallarse** *vr* be, find oneself — **hallazgo** *nm* discovery, find

**hamaca** *nf* hammock

**hambre** *nf* hunger; starvation, famine — **hambriento, -ta** *adj* hungry, starving

**hamburguesa** *nf* hamburger

**harina** *nf* flour

**hasta** *prep* until, up until (in time); as far as, up to (in space); ¡~ **luego!** see you later! — **hasta** *adv* even

**hazaña** *nf* feat, exploit

**hebilla** *nf* buckle

**hebreo, -brea** *adj* Hebrew — **hebreo** *nm* Hebrew (language)

**hechizo** *nm* spell

**hecho, -cha** *adj* made, done; ready-to-wear (of clothing) — **hecho** *nm* fact; event; act, deed

**helar** *v* freeze — **helarse** *vr* freeze up, freeze over — **helado, -da** *adj* freezing cold; frozen — **helada** *nf* frost — **heladería** *nf* ice-cream parlor — **helado** *nm* ice cream

**helecho** *nm* fern

**hélice** *nf* propeller; spiral, helix

**helicóptero** *nm* helicopter

**hembra** *nf* female; woman

**hemisferio** *nm* hemisphere

**hemorragia** *nf* hemorrhage

**hepatitis** *nf* hepatitis

**heredar** *v* inherit — **heredero, -ra** *n* heir, heiress

**herencia** *nf* inheritance; heredity (in biology)

**herir** *v* injure, wound; hurt (as feelings, pride) — **herida** *nf* injury, wound — **herido, -da** *adj* injured, wounded; hurt (as feelings, pride) — **herido, -da** *n* injured person, casualty

**hermano, -na** *n* brother, sister

**hermoso, -sa** *adj* beautiful, lovely — **hermosura** *nf* beauty

**hernia** *nf* hernia

**héroe** *nm* hero — **heroico, -ca** *adj* heroic — **heroína** *nf* heroine; heroin (narcotic) — **heroísmo** *nm* heroism

**herradura** *nf* horseshoe

**herramienta** *nf* tool

# hervir

**52**

**hervir** *v* boil
**heterogéneo, -nea** *adj* heterogeneous
**heterosexual** *adj & nmf* heterosexual
**hiato** *nm* hiatus
**hidratante** *adj* moisturizing
**hielo** *nm* ice; coldness
**hierba** *nf* herb; grass — **hierbabuena** *nf* mint
**hierro** *nm* iron
**hígado** *nm* liver
**higiene** *nf* hygiene — **higiénico, -ca** *adj* hygienic
**higo** *nm* fig
**hijo, -ja** *n* son, daughter; **hijos** *nmpl* children, offspring — **hijastro, -tra** *n* stepson, stepdaughter
**hilo** *nm* thread
**himno** *nm* hymn
**hinchar** *v* inflate, blow up — **hincharse** *vr* swell (up) — **hinchado, -da** *adj* swollen
**hindú** *adj & nmf* Hindu — **hinduismo** *nm* Hinduism
**hiperactivo, -va** *adj* hyperactive
**hipertensión** *nf* (**-siones**) hypertension, high blood pressure
**hipo** *nm* hiccup, hiccups *pl*
**hipocondríaco, -ca** *adj* hypochondriacal — **hipocondríaco, -ca** *n* hypochondriac
**hipocresía** *nf* hypocrisy — **hipócrita** *adj* hypocritical — **hipócrita** *nmf* hypocrite
**hipopótamo** *nm* hippopotamus
**hipoteca** *nf* mortgage — **hipotecar** *v* mortgage
**hipótesis** *nfs & pl* hypothesis
**hispano, -na** *or* **hispánico, -ca** *adj & n* Hispanic — **hispanoamericano, -na** *adj* Latin-American — **hispanoamericano, -na** *n* Latin American — **hispanohablante** *or* **hispanoparlante** *adj* Spanish-speaking
**historia** *nf* history; story — **historiador, -dora** *n* historian — **historial** *nm* record, background — **histórico, -ca**

*adj* historical; historic, important — **historieta** *nf* comic strip
**hocico** *nm* snout, muzzle
**hockey** *nm* hockey
**hogar** *nm* home
**hoguera** *nf* bonfire
**hoja** *nf* leaf; sheet (of paper) — **hojaldre** *nm* puff pastry — **hojear** *v* leaf through — **hojuela** *nf* flake
**hola** *interj* hello!, hi!
**holandés, -desa** *adj* (**-deses** *m*) Dutch
**holocausto** *nm* holocaust
**hombre** *nm* man; **el** ∼ mankind
**hombría** *nf* manliness
**hombro** *nm* shoulder
**homenaje** *nm* homage
**homeopatía** *nf* homeopathy
**homicidio** *nm* homicide, murder — **homicida** *adj* homicidal, murderous — **homicida** *nmf* murderer
**homogéneo, -nea** *adj* homogeneous
**homosexual** *adj & nmf* homosexual — **homosexualidad** *nf* homosexuality
**hondo, -da** *adj* deep — **hondo** *adv* deeply
**hondureño, -ña** *adj* Honduran
**honesto, -ta** *adj* decent, honorable — **honestidad** *nf* honesty, integrity
**hongo** *nm* mushroom; fungus (in botany and medicine)
**honor** *nm* honor — **honorable** *adj* honorable — **honorario, -ria** *adj* honorary — **honorarios** *nmpl* payment, fee — **honradez** *nf* (**-deces**) honesty, integrity — **honrado, -da** *adj* honest, upright — **honrar** *v* honor
**hora** *nf* hour; (specific) time; **¿qué** ∼ **es?** what time is it?; ∼**s extraordinarias** overtime
**horario** *nm* schedule, timetable
**horizonte** *nm* horizon — **horizontal** *adj* horizontal
**hormiga** *nf* ant
**hormigón** *nm* (**-gones**) concrete
**hormiguero** *nm* anthill
**hormona** *nf* hormone

**horno** *nm* oven (for cooking); small furnace, kiln — **hornear** *v* bake

**horóscopo** *nm* horoscope

**horrible** *adj* horrible — **horror** *nm* horror, dread; atrocity — **horrorizar** *v* horrify, terrify

**hortaliza** *nf* (garden) vegetable

**hospedar** *v* put up, lodge — **hospedaje** *nm* lodging

**hospital** *nm* hospital — **hospitalizar** *v* hospitalize

**hostia** *nf* host (in religion)

**hotel** *nm* hotel — **hotelero, -ra** *adj* hotel — **hotelero, -ra** *n* hotel manager, hotelier

**hoy** *adv* today; **~ (en) día** nowadays

**hoyo** *nm* hole

**hueco** *nm* hollow, cavity

**huelga** *nf* strike — **huelguista** *nmf* striker

**huella** *nf* footprint; track, mark; fingerprint

**huérfano, -na** *n* orphan — **huérfano, -na** *adj* orphaned

**huerta** *nf* truck farm — **huerto** *nm* vegetable garden

**hueso** *nm* bone

**huésped, -peda** *n* guest

**huesudo, -da** *adj* bony

**huevo** *nm* egg; **~s revueltos** scrambled eggs

**huida** *nf* flight, escape

**huir** *v* escape, flee

**humano, -na** *adj* human; humane — **humano** *nm* human (being) — **humanidad** *nf* humanity, mankind; **~es** *nfpl* humanities — **humanismo** *nm* humanism — **humanista** *nmf* humanist — **humanitario, -ria** *adj & n* humanitarian

**humedad** *nf* dampness; humidity (in meteorology) — **humedecer** *v* moisten, dampen — **humedecerse** *vr* become moist — **húmedo, -da** *adj* moist, damp; humid (in meteorology)

**humildad** *nf* humility — **humilde** *adj* humble — **humillación** *nf* (-ciones) humiliation — **humillar** *v* humiliate — **humillarse** *vr* humble oneself

**humo** *nm* smoke, steam, fumes

**humor** *nm* humor — **humorismo** *nm* humor, wit — **humorista** *nmf* humorist, comedian

**hundir** *v* sink; destroy, ruin (a building, plans, etc.) — **hundirse** *vr* sink; collapse — **hundido, -da** *adj* sunken — **hundimiento** *nm* sinking; collapse

**húngaro, -ra** *adj* Hungarian

**huracán** *nm* (-canes) hurricane

**hurra** *interj* hurrah!, hooray!

**hurtar** *v* steal — **hurto** *nm* theft; stolen property

**huy** *interj* ow!, ouch!

# I

**i** *nf* i, ninth letter of the Spanish alphabet

**ibérico, -ca** *adj* Iberian — **ibero, -ra** *or* **íbero, -ra** *adj* Iberian

**ida** *nf* outward journey; **~ y vuelta** round-trip

**idea** *nf* idea; opinion

**ideal** *adj & nm* ideal — **idealista** *adj* idealistic — **idealista** *nmf* idealist — **idealizar** *v* idealize

**idear** *v* devise, think up

**identidad** *nf* identity — **idéntico, -ca** *adj* identical — **identificar** *v* identify — **identificarse** *vr* identify oneself — **identificación** *nf* (-ciones) identification

**ideología** *nf* ideology — **ideológico, -ca** *adj* ideological

**idioma** *nm* language — **idiomático, -ca** *adj* idiomatic

**idiota** *adj* idiotic — **idiota** *nmf* idiot — **idiotez** *nf* idiocy

**ídolo** *nm* idol — **idolatrar** *v* idolize

**iglesia** *nf* church

**iglú** *nm* igloo

**ignorar** *v* ignore; be unaware of — **ignorancia** *nf* ignorance — **ignorante** *adj* ignorant — **ignorante** *nmf* ignorant person

**igual** *adv* in the same way — **igual** *adj* equal; the same — **igual** *nmf* equal, peer — **igualar** *v* make equal; be equal to — **igualdad** *nf* equality; uniformity — **igualmente** *adv* likewise

**iguana** *nf* iguana

**ilegal** *adj* illegal

**ilegítimo, -ma** *adj* illegitimate

**ileso, -sa** *adj* unharmed

**ilimitado, -da** *adj* unlimited

**ilógico, -ca** *adj* illogical

**iluminar** *v* illuminate — **iluminación** *nf* (**-ciones**) illumination; lighting

**ilusionar** *v* excite — **ilusión** *nf* (**-siones**) illusion; hope — **ilusionado, -da** *adj* excited

**ilustrar** *v* illustrate; explain — **ilustración** *nf* (**-ciones**) illustration; learning

**ilustre** *adj* illustrious

**imagen** *nf* (**imágenes**) image, picture

**imaginar** *v* imagine — **imaginarse** *vr* imagine — **imaginación** *nf* (**-ciones**) imagination — **imaginario, -ria** *adj* imaginary

**imán** *nm* (**imanes**) magnet

**imbécil** *adj* stupid, idiotic — **imbécil** *nmf* idiot

**imborrable** *adj* indelible

**imitar** *v* imitate, copy; impersonate — **imitación** *nf* (**-ciones**) imitation, copy; impersonation — **imitador, -dora** *n* impersonator

**impaciencia** *nf* impatience — **impacientar** *v* make impatient, exasperate — **impacientarse** *vr* grow impatient — **impaciente** *adj* impatient

**impacto** *nm* impact

**impar** *adj* odd — **impar** *nm* odd number

**imparcial** *adj* impartial — **imparcialidad** *nf* impartiality

**impartir** *v* impart, give

**impecable** *adj* impeccable, spotless

**impedir** *v* prevent; impede, hinder — **impedido, -da** *adj* disabled — **impedimento** *nm* obstacle, impediment

**impenetrable** *adj* impenetrable

**imperativo, -va** *adj* imperative — **imperativo** *nm* imperative

**imperceptible** *adj* imperceptible

**imperdonable** *adj* unforgivable

**imperfección** *nf* (**-ciones**) imperfection — **imperfecto, -ta** *adj* imperfect — **imperfecto** *nm* imperfect (tense)

**imperialismo** *nm* imperialism — **imperialista** *adj & nmf* imperialist

**imperio** *nm* empire

**impermeable** *adj* waterproof — **impermeable** *nm* raincoat

**impersonal** *adj* impersonal

**ímpetu** *nm* impetus; energy, vigor; force — **impetuoso, -sa** *adj* impetuous

**implemento** *nm* implement, tool

**implicar** *v* involve, implicate; imply

**implícito, -ta** *adj* implicit

**imponer** *v* impose; command (as respect); be imposing — **imponerse** *vr* assert oneself, command respect — **imponente** *adj* imposing, impressive

**impopular** *adj* unpopular — **impopularidad** *nf* unpopularity

**importación** *nf* (**-ciones**) importation; **importaciones** *nfpl* imports — **importado, -da** *adj* imported — **importador, -dora** *adj* importing — **importador, -dora** *n* importer

**importancia** *nf* importance — **importante** *adj* important — **importar** *v* matter, be important; **no me importa** I don't care

**importar** *v* import

**imposible** *adj* impossible — **imposibilidad** *nf* impossibility

**impostor, -tora** *n* impostor

**impotente** *adj* powerless, impotent — **impotencia** *nf* impotence

**impracticable** *adj* impracticable

**impreciso, -sa** *adj* vague, imprecise — **imprecisión** *nf* (**-siones**) vagueness; inaccuracy

**impregnar** *v* impregnate

**imprenta** *nf* printing; printing shop, press

**imprescindible** *adj* essential, indispensable

**impresión** *nf* (**-siones**) impression; printing — **impresionante** *adj* impressive — **impresionar** *v* impress; affect, move; make an impression — **impresionarse** *vr* be impressed; be affected

**impreso, -sa** *adj* printed — **impresora** *nf* (computer) printer

**imprimir** *v* print

**improbable** *adj* improbable

**impropio, -pia** *adj* inappropriate; incorrect

**improvisar** *v* improvise — **improvisación** *nf* (**-ciones**) improvisation

**imprudente** *adj* imprudent, rash — **imprudencia** *nf* imprudence, carelessness

**impuesto** *nm* tax

**impulsar** *v* propel, drive — **impulsivo, -va** *adj* impulsive — **impulso** *nm* drive, thrust; impulse

**impuro, -ra** *adj* impure — **impureza** *nf* impurity

**inaceptable** *adj* unacceptable

**inactivo, -va** *adj* inactive — **inactividad** *nf* inactivity

**inadecuado, -da** *adj* inadequate; inappropriate

**inalámbrico, -ca** *adj* wireless, cordless

**inalcanzable** *adj* unreachable, unattainable

**inanimado, -da** *adj* inanimate

**inapropiado, -da** *adj* inappropriate

**inaugurar** *v* inaugurate — **inauguración** *nf* (**-ciones**) inauguration

**incalculable** *adj* incalculable

**incandescente** *adj* incandescent

**incansable** *adj* tireless

**incapacitar** *v* incapacitate, disable — **incapacidad** *nf* incapacity, inability — **incapaz** *adj* (**-paces**) incapable

**incendiar** *v* set fire to, burn (down) — **incendiarse** *vr* catch fire — **incendio** *nm* fire

**incertidumbre** *nf* uncertainty

**incienso** *nm* incense

**incierto, -ta** *adj* uncertain

**incitar** *v* incite, rouse

**incivilizado, -da** *adj* uncivilized

**inclinar** *v* tilt, lean — **inclinarse** *vr* lean (over) — **inclinación** *nf* (**-ciones**) inclination; incline, tilt

**incluir** *v* include; enclose — **inclusive** *adv* up to and including — **incluso** *adv* even, in fact — **incluso, -sa** *adj* enclosed

**incógnito, -ta** *adj* unknown

**incoherente** *adj* incoherent — **incoherencia** *nf* incoherence

**incoloro, -ra** *adj* colorless

**incomodar** *v* inconvenience; bother, annoy — **incomodarse** *vr* take the trouble; get annoyed — **incomodidad** *nf* discomfort — **incómodo, -da** *adj* uncomfortable; inconvenient, awkward

**incomparable** *adj* incomparable

**incompetente** *adj* incompetent — **incompetencia** *nf* incompetence

**incompleto, -ta** *adj* incomplete

**incomprendido, -da** *adj* misunderstood — **incomprensible** *adj* incomprehensible — **incomprensión** *nf* (**-siones**) lack of understanding

**incomunicado, -da** *adj* isolated; in solitary confinement

**inconcebible** *adj* inconceivable

**inconcluso, -sa** *adj* unfinished

**incondicional** *adj* unconditional

**inconfundible** *adj* unmistakable

**inconsciente** *adj* unconscious, unaware; reckless — **inconsciente** *nm* (the) unconscious — **inconsciencia** *nf* unconsciousness; thoughtlessness

**inconsiderado, -da** *adj* inconsiderate

**inconstante** *adj* changeable, unreliable

**inconstitucional** *adj* unconstitutional

**incontable** *adj* countless

**inconveniente** *adj* inconvenient; inappropriate — **inconveniente** *nm* obstacle, problem

**incorrecto, -ta** *adj* incorrect; impolite

**incrédulo, -la** *adj* incredulous

**increíble** *adj* incredible, unbelievable

**incrementar** *v* increase

**inculto, -ta** *adj* uneducated; uncultivated (of land)

**incumplimiento** *nm* noncompliance

**indecisión** *nf* (**-siones**) indecision — **indeciso, -sa** *adj* undecided; indecisive

**indefenso, -sa** *adj* defenseless, helpless

**indefinido, -da** *adj* indefinite

**independiente** *adj* independent — **independencia** *nf* independence

**indicar** *v* indicate; show — **indicación** *nf* (**-ciones**) sign, indication; **indicaciones** *nfpl* directions — **indicador** *nm* sign, signal; gauge, dial, meter — **indicativo, -va** *adj* indicative

**índice** *nm* indication; index (of a book); index finger

**indiferente** *adj* indifferent

**indígena** *adj* indigenous, native — **indígena** *nmf* native

**indigestión** *nf* (**-tiones**) indigestion

**indigno, -na** *adj* unworthy

**indio, -dia** *adj* American Indian; Indian (from India)

**indirecto, -ta** *adj* indirect

**indisciplina** *nf* lack of discipline — **indisciplinado, -da** *adj* undisciplined

**indiscreto, -ta** *adj* indiscreet — **indiscreción** *nf* (**-ciones**) indiscretion; tactless remark

**indiscriminado, -da** *adj* indiscriminate

**indiscutible** *adj* indisputable

**indispensable** *adj* indispensable

**indisponer** *v* upset, make ill; set against, set at odds — **indispuesto, -ta** *adj* unwell, indisposed

**individual** *adj* individual — **individuo** *nm* individual

**indivisible** *adj* indivisible

**índole** *nf* nature, character; type, kind

**indonesio, -sia** *adj* Indonesian

**inducir** *v* induce; infer

**indudable** *adj* beyond doubt

**industria** *nf* industry — **industrial** *adj* industrial — **industrial** *nmf* industrialist, manufacturer

**inédito, -ta** *adj* unpublished

**ineludible** *adj* unavoidable, inescapable

**inesperado, -da** *adj* unexpected

**inestable** *adj* unstable

**inevitable** *adj* inevitable

**inexperto, -ta** *adj* inexperienced, unskilled

**inexplicable** *adj* inexplicable

**infalible** *adj* infallible

**infancia** *nf* infancy — **infantería** *nf* infantry — **infantil** *adj* child's, children's; childish

**infarto** *nm* heart attack

**infectar** *v* infect — **infección** *nf* (**-ciones**) infection — **infeccioso, -sa** *adj* infectious

**inferior** *adj* & *nmf* inferior

**inferir** *v* infer; cause (harm or injury)

**infiel** *adj* unfaithful — **infidelidad** *nf* infidelity

**infinitivo** *nm* infinitive — **infinito, -ta** *adj* infinite — **infinito** *nm* infinity

**inflación** *nf* (**-ciones**) inflation

**inflamar** *v* inflame — **inflamable** *adj* flammable, inflammable — **inflamación** *nf* (**-ciones**) inflammation

**inflexible** *adj* inflexible — **inflexión** *nf* (**-xiones**) inflection

**influir** *v* influence — **influjo** *nm* influence — **influyente** *adj* influential

**información** *nf* (**-ciones**) information; news; (telephone) directory assistance

**informal** *adj* informal; unreliable

**informar** *v* inform — **informática** *nf* information technology — **informativo, -va** *adj* informative

**informe** *adj* shapeless — **informe** *nm* report

**infracción** *nf* (**-ciones**) violation, infraction

**infraestructura** *nf* infrastructure

**infructuoso, -sa** *adj* fruitless

**infundado, -da** *adj* unfounded, baseless

**infundir** *v* instill, infuse

**ingeniería** *nf* engineering — **ingeniero, -ra** *n* engineer

**ingenio** *nm* ingenuity; wit; device, apparatus — **ingenioso, -sa** *adj* ingenious; clever, witty

**ingenuo, -nua** *adj* naive

**ingerir** *v* ingest, consume

**ingle** *nf* groin

**inglés, -glesa** *adj* (**-gleses** *m*) English — **inglés** *nm* English (language)

**ingrato, -ta** *adj* ungrateful; **ingratitud** *nf* ingratitude

**ingrediente** *nm* ingredient

**ingresar** *v* deposit

**ingreso** *nm* entrance, entry; admission (as into a hospital); **~s** *nmpl* income, earnings

**inhabilidad** *nf* unskillfulness

**inherente** *adj* inherent

**inhibir** *v* inhibit — **inhibición** *nf* (**-ciones**) inhibition

**inhóspito, -ta** *adj* inhospitable

**inhumano, -na** *adj* inhuman, inhumane

**iniciar** *v* initiate, begin — **iniciación** *nf* (**-ciones**) initiation; beginning — **inicial** *adj* & *nf* initial — **iniciativa** *nf* initiative — **inicio** *nm* start, beginning

**injusticia** *nf* injustice, unfairness — **injusto, -ta** *adj* unfair, unjust

**inmaduro, -ra** *adj* immature; unripe (of fruit)

**inmediaciones** *nfpl* surrounding area

**inmediato, -ta** *adj* immediate; adjoining

**inmenso, -sa** *adj* immense, vast

**inmigración** *nf* (**-ciones**) immigration — **inmigrante** *adj* & *nmf* immigrant

**inminente** *adj* imminent, impending

**inmoral** *adj* immoral

**inmóvil** *adj* motionless, still — **inmovilizar** *v* immobilize

**inmueble** *nm* building, property

**inmutable** *adj* unchangeable

**innato, -ta** *adj* innate

**innecesario, -ria** *adj* unnecessary, needless

**innegable** *adj* undeniable

**innovar** *v* introduce; innovate — **innovación** *nf* (**-ciones**) innovation — **innovador, -dora** *adj* innovative — **innovador, -dora** *n* innovator

**innumerable** *adj* innumerable

**inocencia** *nf* innocence — **inocente** *adj* & *nmf* innocent

**inodoro, -ra** *adj* odorless — **inodoro** *nm* toilet

**inofensivo, -va** *adj* inoffensive, harmless

**inolvidable** *adj* unforgettable

**inoportuno, -na** *adj* untimely, inopportune

**inquietar** *v* disturb, worry — **inquietante** *adj* disturbing, worrisome — **inquieto, -ta** *adj* anxious, worried — **inquietud** *nf* anxiety, worry

**insatisfecho, -cha** *adj* unsatisfied; dissatisfied

**inscribir** *v* enroll, register; inscribe, engrave — **inscribirse** *vr* register — **inscripción** *nf* (**-ciones**) inscription; registration

**inseguro, -ra** *adj* insecure; unsafe; uncertain — **inseguridad** *nf* insecurity; lack of safety; uncertainty

**insensible** *adj* insensitive, unfeeling; numb (in medicine); imperceptible

**inseparable** *adj* inseparable

**insertar** *v* insert

**insignificante** *adj* insignificant, negligible

**insinuar** *v* insinuate — **insinuante** *adj* insinuating, suggestive

**insistir** *v* insist — **insistente** *adj* insistent

**insólito, -ta** *adj* rare, unusual

**insomnio** *nm* insomnia

**insoportable** *adj* unbearable

**insospechado, -da** *adj* unexpected

**inspirar** *v* inspire; inhale — **inspiración** *nf* (**-ciones**) inspiration; inhalation

**instalar** *v* install — **instalación** *nf* (**-ciones**) installation

**instancia** *nf* request

**instantáneo, -nea** *adj* instantaneous, instant — **instantánea** *nf* snapshot — **instante** *nm* instant

**institución** *nf* (**-ciones**) institution — **institucional** *adj* institutional — **instituto** *nm* institute

**instruir** *v* instruct — **instrucción** *nf* (**-ciones**) instruction; **instrucciones** *nfpl* instructions, directions

**instrumento** *nm* instrument — **instrumental** *adj* instrumental

**insuficiencia** *nf* insufficiency, inadequacy; ~ **cardíaca** heart failure — **insuficiente** *adj* insufficient, inadequate

**insular** *adj* insular, island

**insuperable** *adj* insurmountable

**intacto, -ta** *adj* intact

**intangible** *adj* intangible

**integral** *adj* integral; **pan** ~ whole grain bread — **íntegro, -gra** *adj* honest, upright; whole, complete — **integridad** *nf* integrity; wholeness

**integrar** *v* integrate — **integración** *nf* (**-ciones**) integration

**intelectual** *adj* & *nmf* intellectual

**inteligencia** *nf* intelligence — **inteligente** *adj* intelligent — **inteligible** *adj* intelligible

**intempestivo, -va** *adj* untimely, inopportune

**intención** *nf* (**-ciones**) intention, intent — **intencionado, -da** *adj* intended — **intencional** *adj* intentional

**intensidad** *nf* intensity — **intensificar** *v* intensify — **intensivo, -va** *adj* intensive — **intenso, -sa** *adj* intense

**intentar** *v* attempt, try — **intento** *nm* intention; attempt

**interactuar** *v* interact — **interacción** *nf* (**-ciones**) interaction — **interactivo, -va** *adj* interactive

**intercambiar** *v* exchange, trade

**interceder** *v* intercede

**interés** *nm* (**-reses**) interest — **interesado, -da** *adj* interested; selfish — **interesante** *adj* interesting — **interesar** *v* interest; be of interest

**interfaz** *nf* (**-faces**) interface

**interferir** *v* interfere; interfere with — **interferencia** *nf* interference

**interior** *adj* interior, inner — **interior** *nm* interior, inside

**interjección** *nf* (**-ciones**) interjection

**interlocutor, -tora** *n* speaker

**intermediario, -ria** *adj* & *n* intermediary

**intermedio, -dia** *adj* intermediate — **intermedio** *nm* intermission

**interminable** *adj* interminable, endless

**intermitente** *adj* intermittent — **intermitente** *nm* blinker, turn signal

**internacional** *adj* international

**interponer** *v* interpose — **interponerse** *vr* intervene

**interpretar** *v* interpret; play, perform (in a theater) — **interpretación** *nf* (**-ciones**) interpretation — **intérprete** *nmf* interpreter; performer (of music)

**interrogación** *nf* (**-ciones**) interrogation; **signo de** ~ question mark — **interrogativo, -va** *adj* interrogative — **interrogatorio** *nm* interrogation, questioning — **interrogar** *v* interrogate, question

**interrumpir** *v* interrupt — **interrupción** *nf* (**-ciones**) interruption — **interruptor** *nm* (electrical) switch

**intersección** *nf* (**-ciones**) intersection

**intervalo** *nm* interval

**intervenir** *v* take part; intervene; tap (a

telephone); audit; operate on — **intervención** *nf* (**-ciones**) intervention; audit (in business) — **interventor, -tora** *n* inspector, auditor

**intimidad** *nf* private life; intimacy

**íntimo, -ma** *adj* intimate, close; private

**intolerante** *adj* intolerant

**intoxicar** *v* poison — **intoxicación** *nf* (**-ciones**) poisoning

**intransitable** *adj* impassable

**intransitivo, -va** *adj* intransitive

**intrascendente** *adj* unimportant, insignificant

**intrínseco, -ca** *adj* intrinsic

**introducción** *nf* (**-ciones**) introduction — **introducir** *v* introduce; insert — **introductorio, -ria** *adj* introductory

**intromisión** *nf* (**-siones**) interference

**introvertido, -da** *adj* introverted *n* introvert

**intuir** *v* sense — **intuición** *nf* (**-ciones**) intuition — **intuitivo, -va** *adj* intuitive

**inundar** *v* flood — **inundación** *nf* (**-ciones**) flood

**inútil** *adj* useless; disabled

**invadir** *v* invade

**invalidez** *nf* (**-deces**) invalidity; disability (in medicine) — **inválido, -da** *adj* & *n* invalid

**invariable** *adj* invariable

**invasión** *nf* (**-siones**) invasion — **invasor, -sora** *adj* invading *n* invader

**inventar** *v* invent; fabricate, make up (as a word, an excuse) — **invención** *nf* (**-ciones**) invention; lie, fabrication

**inventario** *nm* inventory

**inventor, -tora** *n* inventor

**inverosímil** *adj* unlikely

**inversión** *nf* (**-siones**) inversion, reversal; investment (of money, time, etc.)

**inverso, -sa** *adj* inverse; opposite

**invertebrado, -da** *adj* invertebrate — **invertebrado** *nm* invertebrate

**invertir** *v* invert, reverse; invest (as money, time); make an investment

**investigar** *v* investigate; research — **in-**

**vestigación** *nf* (**-ciones**) investigation; research — **investigador, -dora** *n* investigator, researcher

**invicto, -ta** *adj* undefeated

**invierno** *nm* winter

**invitar** *v* invite — **invitación** *nf* (**-ciones**) invitation — **invitado, -da** *n* guest

**involuntario, -ria** *adj* involuntary

**inyectar** *v* inject — **inyección** *nf* (**-ciones**) injection, shot

**ir** *v* go; work, function; suit — **irse** *vr* go away, be gone

**ira** *nf* rage, anger

**iraní** *adj* Iranian

**iraquí** *adj* Iraqi

**iris** *nms & pl* iris(es) (of the eye)

**irlandés, -desa** *adj* (**-deses** *m*) Irish

**ironía** *nf* irony — **irónico, -ca** *adj* ironic, ironical

**irracional** *adj* irrational

**irradiar** *v* radiate, irradiate

**irreal** *adj* unreal

**irrefutable** *adj* irrefutable

**irregular** *adj* irregular — **irregularidad** *nf* irregularity

**irrelevante** *adj* irrelevant

**irrespetuoso, -sa** *adj* disrespectful

**irresponsable** *adj* irresponsible — **irresponsabilidad** *nf* irresponsibility

**irreverente** *adj* irreverent

**irreversible** *adj* irreversible

**irrevocable** *adj* irrevocable

**irrigar** *v* irrigate — **irrigación** *nf* (**-ciones**) irrigation

**irrisorio, -ria** *adj* laughable, ridiculous

**irritar** *v* irritate — **irritarse** *vr* get annoyed — **irritación** *nf* (**-ciones**) irritation — **irritante** *adj* irritating

**isla** *nf* island

**islámico, -ca** *adj* Islamic, Muslim

**islandés, -desa** *adj* (**-deses** *m*) Icelandic

**isleño, -ña** *n* islander

**israelí** *adj* Israeli

**istmo** *nm* isthmus

**italiano, -na** *adj* Italian — **italiano** *nm* Italian (language)

**itinerario** *nm* itinerary

**izquierda** *nf* left — **izquierdista** *adj &* *nmf* leftist — **izquierdo, -da** *adj* left

# J

**j** *nf* j, tenth letter of the Spanish alphabet

**jabalina** *nf* javelin

**jabón** *nm* (**-bones**) soap

**jacinto** *nm* hyacinth

**jaguar** *nm* jaguar

**jaiba** *nf* crab

**jalea** *nf* jelly

**jamaicano, -na** *or* **jamaiquino, -na** *adj* Jamaican

**jamás** *adv* never

**jamón** *nm* (**-mones**) ham

**Januká** *nmf* Hanukkah

**japonés, -nesa** *adj* (**-neses** *m*) Japanese — **japonés** *nm* Japanese (language)

**jaque** *nm* check (in chess); ∼ **mate** checkmate

**jaqueca** *nf* headache, migraine

**jarabe** *nm* syrup

**jardín** *nm* (**-dines**) garden; ∼ **infantil** *or* ∼ **de niños** kindergarten — **jardinería** *nf* gardening — **jardinero, -ra** *n* gardener

**jarra** *nf* pitcher, jug

**jaula** *nf* cage

**jazmín** *nm* (**-mines**) jasmine

**jazz** *nm* jazz

**jeans** *nmpl* jeans

**jefe, -fa** *n* chief, leader; boss

**jerarquía** *nf* hierarchy; rank — **jerárquico, -ca** *adj* hierarchical

**jerez** *nm* (**-reces**) sherry

**jerga** *nf* coarse cloth; jargon, slang

**jeringa** *or* **jeringuilla** *nf* syringe

**jeroglífico** *nm* hieroglyphic

**jersey** *nm* (**-seys**) jersey

**jesuita** *adj & nm* Jesuit

**Jesús** *nm* Jesus

**jinete** *nmf* horseman, horsewoman, rider

**jirafa** *nf* giraffe

**jockey** *nmf* (**-keys**) jockey

**jornada** *nf* day's journey; working day

**jota** *nf* iota, jot

**joven** *adj* (**jóvenes**) young — **joven** *nmf* (**jóvenes**) young man, young woman, youth

**joya** *nf* jewel — **joyería** *nf* jewelry store — **joyero, -ra** *n* jeweler — **joyero** *nm* jewelry box

**jubilado, -da** *adj* retired — **jubilado, -da** *nmf* retiree — **jubilar** *v* retire, pension off

**judaísmo** *nm* Judaism

**judía** *nf* bean

**judicial** *adj* judicial

**judío, -día** *adj* Jewish — **judío, -día** *n* Jew

**judo** *nm* judo

**juego** *nm* game; playing (as by children)

**jueves** *nms & pl* Thursday

**juez** *nmf* (**jueces**) judge; umpire, referee

**jugar** *v* play; gamble, bet — **jugarse** *vr* risk, gamble (away) — **jugada** *nf* play, move; (dirty) trick — **jugador, -dora** *n* player; gambler

**jugo** *nm* juice; substance, essence — **jugoso, -sa** *adj* juicy; substantial, important

**juguete** *nm* toy — **juguetería** *nf* toy store

**juicio** *nm* judgment; reason, sense — **juicioso, -sa** *adj* wise, sensible

**julio** *nm* July

**junio** *nm* June

**junta** *nf* board, committee; meeting; (political) junta; joint, gasket — **junto, -ta**

*adj* joined; close, adjacent; (*also used adverbially*) together
**Júpiter** *nm* Jupiter
**jurar** *v* swear — **jurado** *nm* jury; juror, member of a jury — **juramento** *nm* oath
**jurídico, -ca** *adj* legal
**jurisdicción** *nf* (**-ciones**) jurisdiction
**jurisprudencia** *nf* jurisprudence
**justicia** *nf* justice, fairness

**justificar** *v* justify; excuse, vindicate — **justificación** *nf* (**-ciones**) justification
**justo, -ta** *adj* just, fair; exact; tight — **justo** *adv* just, exactly
**juvenil** *adj* youthful — **juventud** *nf* youth; young people
**juzgar** *v* try (a case in court); judge, consider — **juzgado** *nm* court, tribunal

# K

**k** *nf* k, eleventh letter of the Spanish alphabet
**karate** *or* **kárate** *nm* karate

**kilo** *nm* kilo — **kilogramo** *nm* kilogram
**kilómetro** *nm* kilometer — **kilometraje** *nm* distance in kilometers, mileage

# L

**l** *nf* l, twelfth letter of the Spanish alphabet
**la** *pron* her, it
**laberinto** *nm* labyrinth, maze
**labio** *nm* lip
**labor** *nf* work, labor; task — **laborar** *v* work — **laboratorio** *nm* laboratory, lab
**labrar** *v* cultivate, till — **labrado, -da** *adj* cultivated, tilled
**laca** *nf* lacquer; hair spray
**lacio, -cia** *adj* straight (of hair)
**ladera** *nf* slope, hillside
**lado** *nm* side; **al ~** next door, nearby; **al ~ de** beside, next to; **de ~** sideways; **por otro ~** on the other hand; **por todos ~s** everywhere, all around
**ladrar** *v* bark
**ladrillo** *nm* brick
**ladrón, -drona** *n* (**-drones** *m*) thief
**lagarto** *nm* lizard — **lagartija** *nf* (small) lizard
**lago** *nm* lake
**lágrima** *nf* tear
**laguna** *nf* lagoon

**laico, -ca** *adj* lay, secular — **laico, -ca** *n* layman, layperson
**lamentar** *v* regret, be sorry about — **lamentarse** *vr* lament — **lamento** *nm* lament, moan
**lámpara** *nf* lamp
**lampiño, -ña** *adj* beardless, hairless
**lana** *nf* wool
**lancha** *nf* boat, launch
**langosta** *nf* lobster; locust (insect) — **langostino** *nm* prawn, crayfish
**lanudo, -da** *adj* woolly
**lanzar** *v* throw; shoot (a glance), give (as a sigh); launch (a missile, a project) — **lanzamiento** *nm* throwing, launching
**lapicero** *nm* (mechanical) pencil
**lápida** *nf* tombstone
**lápiz** *nm* (**-pices**) pencil; **~ de labios** lipstick
**largo, -ga** *adj* long — **largo** *nm* length — **largometraje** *nm* feature film
**laringe** *nf* larynx — **laringitis** *nfs & pl* laryngitis
**láser** *nm* laser

**lastimar** *v* hurt — **lástima** *nf* pity
**lata** *nf* (tin) can
**lateral** *adj* side, lateral
**latido** *nm* beat, throb
**latín** *nm* Latin (language)
**latino, -na** *adj* Latin; Latin-American — **latino, -na** *n* Latin American — **latinoamericano, -na** *adj* Latin-American — **latinoamericano, -na** *n* Latin American
**latir** *v* beat, throb
**latitud** *nf* latitude
**lavar** *v* wash — **lavabo** *nm* sink — **lavado** *nm* wash, washing — **lavadora** *nf* washing machine — **lavamanos** *nms & pl* washbowl(s) — **lavandería** *nf* laundry (service) — **lavaplatos** *nms & pl* dishwasher(s); kitchen sink(s)
**lazo** *nm* lasso
**le** *pron* (to) her, (to) him, (to) it; (*as direct object*) him, you
**leal** *adj* loyal, faithful — **lealtad** *nf* loyalty, allegiance
**lección** *nf* (**-ciones**) lesson; lecture (in a classroom)
**leche** *nf* milk
**lechuga** *nf* lettuce
**lechuza** *nf* owl
**lector, -tora** *n* reader — **lectura** *nf* reading; reading matter
**leer** *v* read
**legal** *adj* legal — **legalidad** *nf* legality — **legalizar** *v* legalize
**legislar** *v* legislate — **legislación** *nf* (**-ciones**) legislation — **legislador, -dora** *n* legislator
**legítimo, -ma** *adj* legitimate; authentic — **legitimidad** *nf* legitimacy
**legumbre** *nf* vegetable
**lejano, -na** *adj* distant, far away
**lejos** *adv* far (away); **a lo** ∼ in the distance; **de** ∼ *or* **desde** ∼ from afar; ∼ **de** far from
**lengua** *nf* tongue; language
**lenguaje** *nm* language
**lente** *nmf* lens; ∼**s** *nmpl* eyeglasses

**lenteja** *nf* lentil
**lento, -ta** *adj* slow — **lento** *adv* slowly — **lentitud** *nf* slowness
**leña** *nf* firewood
**león, -ona** *n* (**leones** *m*) lion, lioness
**leopardo** *nm* leopard
**les** *pron* (to) them, (to) you; (*as direct object*) them, you
**lesbiano, -na** *adj* lesbian — **lesbiana** *nf* lesbian — **lesbianismo** *nm* lesbianism
**lesión** *nf* (**-siones**) lesion, wound — **lesionado, -da** *adj* injured, wounded — **lesionar** *v* injure, wound; damage
**letra** *nf* letter; handwriting; lyrics (of a song); ∼ **de cambio** bill of exchange; ∼**s** *nfpl* arts — **letrero** *nm* sign, notice
**leucemia** *nf* leukemia
**levadura** *nf* yeast
**levantar** *v* lift, raise; pick up; erect, put up; rouse, stir up — **levantarse** *vr* rise, stand up; get out of bed; rise up
**leve** *adj* light, slight; minor, trivial (as of wounds, sins)
**léxico** *nm* vocabulary, lexicon
**ley** *nf* law
**leyenda** *nf* legend
**libanés, -nesa** *adj* (**-neses** *m*) Lebanese
**libélula** *nf* dragonfly
**liberación** *nf* (**-ciones**) liberation, deliverance
**liberal** *adj & nmf* liberal
**liberar** *v* liberate, free — **libertad** *nf* freedom, liberty; ∼ **condicional** parole — **libertar** *v* set free
**libido** *nf* libido
**libio, -bia** *adj* Libyan
**libra** *nf* pound
**libre** *adj* free; unoccupied (of space), spare (of time); **al aire** ∼ in the open air
**libro** *nm* book — **librería** *nf* bookstore — **librero, -ra** *n* bookseller — **libreta** *nf* notebook
**licencia** *nf* license, permit; permission; (military) leave — **licenciado, -da** *n*

graduate; lawyer — **licenciarse** *vr* graduate — **licenciatura** *nf* degree

**lícito, -ta** *adj* lawful, legal; just, fair

**licor** *nm* liquor; liqueur — **licorera** *nf* decanter

**licuadora** *nf* blender — **licuar** *v* liquefy

**líder** *adj* leading — **líder** *nmf* leader — **liderato** or **liderazgo** *nm* leadership

**liga** *nf* league — **ligamento** *nm* ligament

**ligero, -ra** *adj* light, lightweight; slight; agile; lighthearted, superficial

**lija** *nf* sandpaper

**lila** *nf* lilac

**lima** *n* file — **~ para uñas** nail file — **limar** *v* file

**limitar** *v* limit — **limitación** *nf* (-ciones) limitation, limit — **límite** *nm* limit; boundary, border; **fecha ~** deadline — **limítrofe** *adj* bordering

**limón** *nm* (-mones) lemon — **limonada** *nf* lemonade

**limosna** *nf* alms — **limosnero, -ra** *n* beggar

**limpiabotas** *nmfs & pl* bootblack(s)

**limpiaparabrisas** *nms & pl* windshield wiper(s)

**limpiar** *v* clean, wipe (away) — **limpieza** *nf* cleanliness — **limpio** *adv* cleanly, fairly — **limpio, -pia** *adj* clean, neat

**lindo, -da** *adj* pretty, lovely

**línea** *nf* line; **guardar la ~** watch one's figure — **lineal** *adj* linear

**lingüista** *nmf* linguist — **lingüística** *nf* linguistics — **lingüístico, -ca** *adj* linguistic

**linterna** *nf* lantern; flashlight

**liquidar** *v* liquidate (as merchandise); settle, pay off (as a debt) — **liquidación** *nf* (-ciones) liquidation; clearance sale — **líquido, -da** *adj* liquid

**lírico, -ca** *adj* lyric, lyrical — **lírica** *nf* lyric poetry

**lirio** *nm* iris

**liso, -sa** *adj* smooth; flat; plain; **pelo ~** straight hair

**lista** *nf* stripe; list

**listo, -ta** *adj* clever, smart; ready

**litera** *nf* bunk bed, berth

**literal** *adj* literal

**literatura** *nf* literature — **literario, -ria** *adj* literary

**litografía** *nf* lithograph (picture)

**litoral** *adj nm* shore, seaboard

**litro** *nm* liter

**liturgia** *nf* liturgy — **litúrgico, -ca** *adj* liturgical

**liviano, -na** *adj* light

**llama** *nf* flame; llama (animal)

**llamar** *v* call; call up; phone; knock, ring (at the door) — **llamarse** *vr* be called — **llamada** *nf* call

**llanta** *nf* rim (of a wheel); tire

**llanto** *nm* crying, weeping

**llanura** *nf* plain

**llave** *nf* key; **cerrar con ~** lock; **~ inglesa** monkey wrench — **llavero** *nm* key chain

**llegar** *v* arrive, come; reach; be enough; **~ a ser** become — **llegada** *nf* arrival

**llenar** *v* fill (up), fill in — **lleno, -na** *adj* full

**llevar** *v* take, carry; lead — **llevarse** *vr* take (away)

**llorar** *v* cry, weep — **lloroso, -sa** *adj* tearful

**llover** *v impers* rain — **llovizna** *nf* drizzle — **lloviznar** *v impers* drizzle

**lluvia** *nf* rain — **lluvioso, -sa** *adj* rainy

**lo** *pron* him, it; (*formal, masculine*) you; **~ que** what, that which — **lo** *art* the

**lobo, -ba** *n* wolf

**lóbulo** *nm* lobe

**local** *adj* local — **local** *nm* premises — **localidad** *nf* town, locality — **localizar** *v* localize; locate

**loción** *nf* (-ciones) lotion

**loco, -ca** *adj* crazy, insane — **loco, -ca** *n* crazy person, lunatic

**locución** *nf* (-ciones) expression, phrase

**locura** *nf* insanity, madness
**locutor, -tora** *n* announcer
**lodo** *nm* mud
**lógica** *nf* logic — **lógico, -ca** *adj* logical
**logotipo** *nm* logo
**lograr** *v* achieve, attain; get, obtain — **logro** *nm* achievement, success
**loma** *nf* hill, hillock
**lombriz** *nf* (**-brices**) worm
**lomo** *nm* back (of an animal); spine (of a book)
**longaniza** *nf* sausage
**longitud** *nf* longitude; length
**loro** *nm* parrot
**los, las** *pron* them; you
**losa** *nf* flagstone
**lotería** *nf* lottery
**loto** *nm* lotus
**lubricar** *v* lubricate — **lubricante** *adj* lubricating — **lubricante** *nm* lubricant
**lucero** *nm* bright star
**luchar** *v* fight, struggle; wrestle (in sports) — **lucha** *nf* struggle, fight; wrestling (sport) — **luchador, -dora** *n* fighter, wrestler
**lucidez** *nf* (**-deces**) lucidity — **lúcido, -da** *adj* lucid
**lucido, -da** *adj* magnificent, splendid
**luciérnaga** *nf* firefly, glowworm
**luego** *adv* then; later (on); **desde ~** of course; **¡hasta ~!** see you later! — **luego** *conj* therefore
**lugar** *nm* place; space, room; **en ~ de** instead of
**lujo** *nm* luxury — **lujoso, -sa** *adj* luxurious
**luminoso, -sa** *adj* shining, luminous
**luna** *nf* moon; mirror; **~ de miel** honeymoon — **lunar** *adj* lunar — **lunar** *nm* mole, beauty spot
**lunes** *nms & pl* Monday(s)
**lupa** *nf* magnifying glass
**luto** *nm* mourning
**luz** *nf* (**luces**) light; lighting (in a room); electricity

# M

**m** *nf* m, 13th letter of the Spanish alphabet
**maceta** *nf* flowerpot
**macho** *adj* male; macho — **macho** *nm* male — **machista** *nm* male chauvinist
**macizo, -za** *adj* solid
**madera** *nf* wood; lumber
**madre** *nf* mother — **madrastra** *nf* stepmother
**madrina** *nf* godmother; bridesmaid
**madrugada** *nf* dawn, daybreak
**madurar** *v* mature; ripen (of fruit) — **madurez** *nf* (**-reces**) maturity; ripeness (of fruit) — **maduro, -ra** *adj* mature; ripe
**maestría** *nf* mastery, skill — **maestro, -tra** *adj* masterly, skilled — **maestro, -tra** *n* teacher (in grammar school); expert, master
**magisterio** *nm* teachers, teaching profession
**magistrado, -da** *n* magistrate, judge
**magistral** *adj* masterful; magisterial (as of an attitude)
**magnífico, -ca** *adj* magnificent
**mago, -ga** *n* magician; **los Reyes Magos** the Magi
**mahometano, -na** *adj* Islamic, Muslim — **mahometano, -na** *n* Muslim
**maicena** *nf* cornstarch
**maíz** *nm* corn
**mal** *adv* badly, poorly; incorrectly; with difficulty, hardly — **mal** *nm* evil; harm, damage; illness

**malasio, -sia** *adj* Malaysian
**malayo, -ya** *adj* Malay, Malayan
**maldad** *nf* evil; evil deed
**maleable** *adj* malleable
**maleducado, -da** *adj* rude
**malentendido** *nm* misunderstanding
**malestar** *nm* discomfort; uneasiness
**maleta** *nf* suitcase — **maletero, -ra** *n*
porter — **maletero** *nm* trunk (of an automobile) — **maletín** *nm* (**-tines**)
briefcase; overnight bag
**malo, -la** *adj* bad; poor (in quality); unwell — **malo, -la** *n* villain, bad guy (as in movies)
**maltratar** *v* mistreat
**mamá** *nf* mom, mama
**mamífero, -ra** *adj* mammalian — **mamífero** *nm* mammal
**manantial** *nm* spring; source
**manchar** *v* stain, spot, mark — **mancharse** *vr* get dirty — **mancha** *nf* stain
**manco, -ca** *adj* one-armed, one-handed
**mandar** *v* command, order; send; hurl, throw; be in charge — **mandamiento** *nm* order, warrant; commandment (in religion)
**mandarina** *nf* mandarin orange, tangerine
**mandato** *nm* term of office; mandate — **mandatario, -ria** *n* leader (in politics); agent (in law)
**mandíbula** *nf* jaw, jawbone
**mando** *nm* command, leadership
**manecilla** *nf* hand (of a clock), pointer
**manejar** *v* handle, operate; manage (as a business); drive (a car) — **manejo** *nm* handling, use; management
**manera** *nf* way, manner
**manga** *nf* sleeve
**mango** *nm* hilt, handle; mango (fruit)
**manguera** *nf* hose
**maní** *nm* (**-níes**) peanut
**manía** *nf* mania, obsession; craze, fad
**manicomio** *nm* insane asylum
**manifestar** *v* demonstrate, show; express, declare — **manifestarse** *vr* become evident; demonstrate (in politics)
— **manifestación** *nf* (**-ciones**) manifestation, sign; demonstration (in politics) — **manifestante** *nmf* protester, demonstrator
**manija** *nf* handle
**manipular** *v* manipulate; handle — **manipulación** *nf* (**-ciones**) manipulation
**maniquí** *nmf* (**-quíes**) mannequin, model — **maniquí** *nm* mannequin, dummy
**manjar** *nm* delicacy, special dish
**mano** *nf* hand
**mansión** *nf* (**-siones**) mansion
**manso, -sa** *adj* gentle; tame (of an animal)
**manta** *nf* blanket
**mantel** *nm* tablecloth
**mantener** *v* support; preserve; keep up, maintain (as relations, correspondence); affirm — **mantenimiento** *nm* maintenance; sustenance
**mantequilla** *nf* butter
**manual** *adj* manual — **manual** *nm* manual, handbook
**manubrio** *nm* handle, crank; handlebars
**manzana** *nf* apple; (city) block
**mañana** *adv* tomorrow — **mañana** *nf* morning
**mapa** *nm* map — **mapamundi** *nm* map of the world
**maquillaje** *nm* makeup — **maquillarse** *vr* put on makeup
**máquina** *nf* machine; locomotive — **maquinaria** *nf* machinery; mechanism, works (as of a watch)
**mar** *nmf* sea
**maraca** *nf* maraca
**maratón** *nm* (**-tones**) marathon
**maravilla** *nf* wonder, marvel — **maravillar** *v* astonish — **maravillarse** *vr* be amazed — **maravilloso, -sa** *adj* marvelous
**marca** *nf* mark; brand (on livestock); record (in sports) — **marcador** *nm* scoreboard; marker, felt-tipped pen

**marcar** *v* mark; brand (livestock); indicate, show; dial (as a telephone); score (in sports)

**marchar** *v* go; walk; work, run — **marcharse** *vr* leave, go — **marcha** *nf* march; pace, speed

**marco** *nm* frame; setting, framework

**marea** *nf* tide — **marear** *v* make nauseous or dizzy — **marearse** *vr* become nauseated or dizzy — **mareado, -da** *adj* sick, nauseous; dazed, dizzy

**maremoto** *nm* tidal wave

**mareo** *nm* nausea, seasickness; dizziness

**margarina** *nf* margarine

**margarita** *nf* daisy

**margen** *nm* (**márgenes**) edge, border; margin (as of a page) — **marginado, -da** *adj* alienated — **marginado, -da** *n* outcast — **marginal** *adj* marginal

**marido** *nm* husband

**marimba** *nf* marimba

**marina** *nf* coast

**marinero, -ra** *adj* sea, marine; seaworthy (of a ship) — **marinero** *nm* sailor — **marino, -na** *adj* marine — **marino** *nm* seaman, sailor

**marioneta** *nf* puppet, marionette

**mariposa** *nf* butterfly

**marisco** *nm* shellfish; ~**s** *nmpl* seafood

**marítimo, -ma** *adj* maritime, shipping

**mármol** *nm* marble

**marquesina** *nf* marquee, (glass) canopy

**marrano, -na** *n* pig, hog

**marrón** *adj & nm* (**-rrones**) brown

**marroquí** *adj* Moroccan

**Marte** *nm* Mars

**martes** *nms & pl* Tuesday(s)

**martillo** *nm* hammer — **martillar** *or* **martillear** *v* hammer

**mártir** *nmf* martyr

**marxismo** *nm* Marxism — **marxista** *adj & nmf* Marxist

**marzo** *nm* March

**mas** *conj* but

**más** *adv* more; **el/la/lo** ~ (the) most — **más** *adj* more; most — **más** *prep* plus

**masa** *nf* mass, volume; dough (in cooking); ~**s** *nfpl* people, masses

**masaje** *nm* massage

**mascar** *v* chew

**máscara** *nf* mask (as ceremonial, decorative) — **mascarilla** *nf* mask (as cosmetic, protective)

**mascota** *nf* mascot

**masculino, -na** *adj* masculine, male; manly; masculine (in grammar)

**masivo, -va** *adj* mass, large-scale

**masticar** *v* chew

**matador** *nm* matador, bullfighter

**matar** *v* kill; slaughter (animals) — **matarse** *vr* be killed; commit suicide

**matemáticas** *nfpl* mathematics — **matemático, -ca** *adj* mathematical — **matemático, -ca** *n* mathematician

**materia** *nf* matter; material — **material** *adj* material — **material** *nm* material; equipment, gear

**maternidad** *nf* motherhood; maternity hospital — **materno, -na** *adj* maternal; **lengua materna** native language, mother tongue

**matrícula** *nf* list, roll, register; registration; license plate (of an automobile) — **matricular** *v* register

**matrimonio** *nm* marriage; (married) couple

**matriz** *nf* (**-trices**) uterus, womb

**maullar** *v* meow

**maxilar** *nm* jaw, jawbone

**máxima** *nf* maxim

**máximo, -ma** *adj* maximum, highest

**maya** *adj* Mayan

**mayo** *nm* May

**mayonesa** *nf* mayonnaise

**mayor** *adj* bigger, larger, greater, older; biggest, largest, greatest, oldest ~ **de edad** of (legal) age — **mayor** *nmf* major (in the military); adult; ~**es** *nmfpl* grown-ups

**mayoría** *nf* majority

**mayorista** *adj* wholesale — **mayorista** *nmf* wholesaler

**mayúscula** *nf* capital letter —
  **mayúsculo, -la** *adj* capital, uppercase
**mazapán** *nm* (**-panes**) marzipan
**mazorca** *nf* spike (of a plant) ∼ **de**
  **maíz** corncob
**me** *pron* me; to me, for me, from me; myself, to myself, for myself, from myself
**mecánica** *nf* mechanics — **mecánico,**
  **-ca** *adj* mechanical — **mecánico, -ca**
  *n* mechanic
**mecanismo** *nm* mechanism
**mecedora** *nf* rocking chair
**mecer** *v* rock; push (on a swing) —
  **mecerse** *vr* rock, swing
**media** *nf* stocking
**mediano, -na** *adj* medium, average
**medianoche** *nf* midnight
**mediante** *prep* through, by means of
**medicación** *nf* (**-ciones**) medication —
  **medicamento** *nm* medicine — **medi-**
  **car** *v* medicate — **medicina** *nf* medicine — **medicinal** *adj* medicinal
**medición** *nf* (**-ciones**) measurement
**médico, -ca** *adj* medical — **médico, -ca**
  *n* doctor, physician
**medida** *nf* measurement, measure
**medio, -dia** *adv* half — **medio, -dia** *nm*
  half; means, way; ∼ **ambiente** environment — **medio, -dia** *adj* half; **la**
  **clase media** the middle class
**mediodía** *nm* noon; midday
**medir** *v* measure; weigh, consider —
  **medirse** *vr* be moderate
**meditar** *v* meditate, contemplate; think
  over, consider; plan, work out — **medi-**
  **tación** *nf* (**-ciones**) meditation
**mediterráneo, -nea** *adj* Mediterranean
**megabyte** *nm* megabyte
**mejilla** *nf* cheek
**mejillón** *nm* (**-llones**) mussel
**mejor** *adv* better; best — **mejor** *adj* better; best
**mejorar** *v* improve; get better
**melancolía** *nf* melancholy — **melancó-**
  **lico, -ca** *adj* melancholic, melancholy

**mellizo, -za** *adj* & *n* twin
**melocotón** *nm* (**-tones**) peach
**melodía** *nf* melody
**melón** *nm* (**-lones**) melon
**memoria** *nf* memory; remembrance; report — **memorizar** *v* memorize
**mencionar** *v* mention, refer to —
  **mención** *nf* (**-ciones**) mention
**mendigar** *v* beg
**menopausia** *nf* menopause
**menor** *adj* smaller, lesser, younger;
  smallest, least, youngest — **menor** *nmf*
  minor, juvenile
**menos** *adv* less; least — **menos** *adj*
  less, fewer; least, fewest — **menos**
  *prep* minus; except ∼ *pron* less, fewer
**mensaje** *nm* message — **mensajero,**
  **-ra** *n* messenger
**menstruar** *v* menstruate — **mens-**
  **truación** *nf* menstruation
**mensual** *adj* monthly — **mensualidad**
  *nf* monthly payment; monthly salary
**menta** *nf* mint, peppermint
**mental** *adj* mental — **mentalidad** *nf*
  mentality
**mente** *nf* mind
**mentir** *v* lie — **mentira** *nf* lie — **men-**
  **tiroso, -sa** *adj* lying — **mentiroso,**
  **-sa** *n* liar
**mentón** *nm* (**-tones**) chin
**menú** *nm* (**-nús**) menu
**menudo, -da** *adj* small, insignificant
**meñique** *adj* little — **dedo meñique**
  *nm* little finger, pinkie
**mercado** *nm* market
**mercancía** *nf* merchandise, goods —
  **mercantil** *adj* commercial
**Mercurio** *nm* Mercury (planet)
**merecer** *v* deserve; be worthy
**merienda** *nf* afternoon snack, tea
**mérito** *nm* merit, worth — **mérito** *n* in-
  tern, trainee
**mermelada** *nf* marmalade, jam
**mes** *nm* month
**mesa** *nf* table

**Mesías** *nm* Messiah

**mestizo, -za** *adj* of mixed ancestry; hybrid — **mestizo, -za** *n* person of mixed ancestry

**meta** *nf* goal, objective

**metáfora** *nf* metaphor — **metafórico, -ca** *adj* metaphoric, metaphorical

**metal** *nm* metal — **metálico, -ca** *adj* metallic, metal

**metamorfosis** *nfs & pl* metamorphosis

**meteorología** *nf* meteorology — **meteorólogo, -ga** *adj* meteorological, meteorologic — **meteorólogo, -ga** *n* meteorologist

**meter** *v* put (in); place (as in a job); involve; make, cause — **meterse** *vr* get in, enter

**método** *nm* method — **metódico, -ca** *adj* methodical — **metodología** *nf* methodology

**metro** *nm* meter; subway (train)

**metrópoli** *nf or* **metrópolis** *nfs & pl* metropolis(es) — **metropolitano, -na** *adj* metropolitan

**mexicano, -na** *adj* Mexican

**mezcla** *nf* mixture; mortar — **mezclar** *v* mix, blend; mix up, muddle; involve — **mezclarse** *vr* get mixed up

**mezquita** *nf* mosque

**mi** *adj* my

**mí** *pron* me

**mico** *nm* (long-tailed) monkey

**microbio** *nm* microbe, germ — **microbiología** *nf* microbiology

**micrófono** *nm* microphone

**microonda** *nf* microwave (radiation); **un horno de ~s** *nms & pl* microwave (oven)(s)

**microscopio** *nm* microscope

**miedo** *nm* fear — **miedoso, -sa** *adj* fearful

**miel** *nf* honey

**miembro** *nm* member; limb, extremity

**mientras** *conj* while, as — **mientras** *adv or* **~ tanto** meanwhile, in the meantime

**miércoles** *nms & pl* Wednesday(s)

**migración** *nf* (**-ciones**) migration

**migraña** *nf* migraine

**mil** *adj & nm* thousand

**milagro** *nm* miracle

**milenio** *nm* millennium

**milímetro** *nm* millimeter

**militar** *adj* military — **militar** *nmf* soldier — **militarizar** *v* militarize

**milla** *nf* mile

**millar** *nm* thousand

**millón** *nm* (**-llones**) million — **millonario, -ria** *n* millionaire

**mímica** *nf* mime, sign language; mimicry

**mimo** *nm* pampering, indulgence; ~ *nmf* mime

**mina** *nf* mine; lead (for pencils)

**mineral** *adj* mineral — **mineral** *nm* mineral; ore

**minería** *nf* mining — **minero, -ra** *adj* mining — **minero, -ra** *n* miner

**minifalda** *nf* miniskirt

**minimizar** *v* minimize

**mínimo, -ma** *adj* minimum; minute — **mínimo** *nm* minimum

**ministerio** *nm* ministry — **ministro, -tra** *n* minister, secretary

**minoría** *nf* minority

**minoritario, -ria** *adj* minority

**minusválido, -da** *adj* disabled

**minuto** *nm* minute — **minutero** *nm* minute hand

**mío, mía** *adj* mine

**miope** *adj* nearsighted

**mirar** *v* look; look at; watch; consider — **mirarse** *vr* look at oneself; look at each other — **mirada** *nf* look

**misa** *nf* Mass

**misión** *nf* (**-siones**) mission

**mismo** *adv* right, exactly — **mismo, -ma** *adj* same; very — **mismo** *pron* self **yo ~** myself, etc. (used reflexively)

**misterio** *nm* mystery — **misterioso, -sa** *adj* mysterious

**mística** *nf* mysticism — **místico, -ca** *adj* mystic, mystical — **místico, -ca** *n* mystic

**mitad** *nf* half; middle

**mitin** *nm* (**mítines**) (political) meeting

**mito** *nm* myth — **mitología** *nm* mythology

**mixto, -ta** *adj* mixed, joint; coeducational (of a school)

**mocasín** *nm* (**-sines**) moccasin

**mochila** *nf* backpack, knapsack

**moco** *nm* mucus

**moda** *nf* fashion, style — **modales** *nmpl* manners

**modelo** *adj* model — **modelo** *nm* model, pattern; *nmf* model, mannequin

**módem** *or* **modem** *nm* modem

**moderar** *v* moderate; reduce (as speed)

**moderno, -na** *adj* modern — **modernismo** *nm* modernism

**modesto, -ta** *adj* modest

**modificar** *v* modify, alter — **modificación** *nf* (**-ciones**) alteration

**modismo** *nm* idiom

**modo** *nm* way, manner

**mojar** *v* wet, moisten — **mojado, -da** *adj* wet, damp

**molestar** *v* annoy, bother; be a nuisance — **molestarse** *vr* bother; take offense — **molestia** *nf* annoyance, nuisance; discomfort — **molesto, -ta** *adj* annoyed; annoying; in discomfort

**molinillo** *nm* grinder, mill

**momento** *nm* moment, instant; (period of) time

**moneda** *nf* coin; currency (of a country)

**monetario, -ria** *adj* monetary

**monja** *nf* nun

**mono, -na** *n* monkey — **mono, -na** *adj* lovely, cute

**monografía** *nf* monograph

**monolingüe** *adj* monolingual

**monólogo** *nm* monologue

**monosílabo** *nm* monosyllable

**monoteísta** *adj* monotheistic

**montaje** *nm* assembly; staging (in theater), editing (of films)

**montaña** *nf* mountain — **montañero, -ra** *n* mountain climber — **montañoso, -sa** *adj* mountainous

**montar** *v* mount; establish; assemble, put together

**monte** *nm* mountain; woodland

**montura** *nf* mount (horse); saddle; frame (of eyeglasses)

**monumento** *nm* monument

**monzón** *nm* (**-zones**) monsoon

**moño** *nm* bun (of hair); bow (knot)

**mora** *nf* mulberry; blackberry

**morado, -da** *adj* purple — **morado** *nm* purple

**moral** *adj* moral — **moral** *nf* ethics, morals; morale — **moraleja** *nf* moral (of a story)

**morder** *v* bite

**moreno, -na** *adj* dark-haired, brunette; dark-skinned — **moreno, -na** *n* brunette; dark-skinned person

**morfina** *nf* morphine

**morir** *v* die; die out, go out

**moroso, -sa** *adj* delinquent, in arrears

**morral** *nm* backpack

**mortal** *adj* mortal; deadly (as of a wound, an enemy) — **mortal** *nmf* mortal — **mortalidad** *nf* mortality

**mosca** *nf* fly

**mostaza** *nf* mustard

**mostrador** *nm* counter (in a store)

**mostrar** *v* show

**motín** *nm* (**-tines**) riot, uprising; mutiny (of troops)

**motivo** *nm* motive, cause; motif (as in art, music) — **motivación** *nf* (**-ciones**) motivation — **motivar** *v* cause; motivate

**motocicleta** *nf* motorcycle — **motociclista** *nmf* motorcyclist

**motor, -triz** *or* **-tora** *adj* motor (biology, technology) — **motor** *nm* motor, engine

**mover** *v* move, shift; shake (the head) — **moverse** *vr* move (over)

**móvil** *adj* mobile — **móvil** *nm* motive; mobile — **movilidad** *nf* mobility

**movimiento** *nm* movement, motion

**muchacho, -cha** *n* kid, boy, girl

**mucho** *adv* very much, a lot; long, a long time — **mucho, -cha** *adj* a lot of, many, much — **mucho, -cha** *pron* a lot, many, much

**mudo, -da** *adj* mute; silent

**mueble** *nm* piece of furniture

**muela** *nf* tooth, molar

**muerte** *nf* death — **muerto, -ta** *adj* dead; dull (as of colors) — **muerto, -ta** *nm* dead person, deceased

**muestra** *nf* sample; sign, show

**mujer** *nf* woman; wife

**mulato, -ta** *adj & n* mulatto

**muleta** *nf* crutch; prop, support

**multa** *nf* fine — **multar** *v* fine

**multimedia** *adj* multimedia

**multinacional** *adj* multinational

**multiplicar** *v* multiply — **multiplicarse** *vr* multiply, reproduce — **múltiple** *adj* multiple — **multiplicación** *nf* (-ciones) multiplication — **múltiplo** *nm* multiple

**multitud** *nf* crowd, multitude

**mundo** *nm* world — **mundial** *adj* world, worldwide

**municipal** *adj* municipal — **municipio** *nm* municipality; town council

**muñeca** *nf* wrist; doll — **muñeco** *nm* boy doll; dummy, puppet

**mural** *adj & nm* mural — **muralla** *nf* wall, rampart

**murciélago** *nm* bat (animal)

**muro** *nm* wall

**músculo** *nm* muscle — **muscular** *adj* muscular — **musculoso, -sa** *adj* muscular

**museo** *nm* museum

**música** *nf* music — **musical** *adj* musical — **músico, -ca** *adj* musical — **músico, -ca** *n* musician

**muslo** *nm* thigh

**musulmán, -mana** *adj & n* (-manes *m*) Muslim

**mutuo, -tua** *adj* mutual

**muy** *adv* very, quite; too

# N

**n** *nf* n, 14th letter of the Spanish alphabet

**nacer** *v* be born; arise, spring up

**nacido, -da** *adj* born —**nacido, -da** *n* **recién** ∼ newborn — **nacimiento** *nm* birth

**nación** *nf* (-ciones) nation, country — **nacional** *adj* national — **nacional** *nmf* national, citizen — **nacionalidad** *nf* nationality — **nacionalizar** *v* nationalize; naturalize (as a citizen) — **nacionalizarse** *vr* become naturalized

**nada** *pron* nothing; **de** ∼ you're welcome — **nada** *adv* not at all

**nadar** *v* swim — **nadador, -dora** *n* swimmer

**nadie** *pron* nobody, no one

**naipe** *nm* playing card

**nalgas** *nfpl* buttocks, bottom

**naranja** *adj & nm* orange (color) — **naranja** *nf* orange (fruit)

**narciso** *nm* narcissus, daffodil

**narcótico, -ca** *adj* narcotic — **narcótico** *nm* narcotic — **narcotraficante** *nmf* drug trafficker — **narcotráfico** *nm* drug trafficking

**nariz** *nf* (-rices) nose

**narrar** *v* narrate, tell — **narración** *nf* (-ciones) narration — **narrador, -dora** *n* narrator — **narrativa** *nf* narrative, storytelling

**nasal** *adj* nasal

**natación** *nf* (-ciones) swimming

**natal** *adj* native, birth — **natalidad** *nf* birthrate

**nativo, -va** *adj & n* native

**natural** *adj* natural; normal; ～ **de** native of, from — **natural** *nm* native — **naturaleza** *nf* nature — **naturalidad** *nf* naturalness — **naturalmente** *adv* naturally; of course

**naufragio** *nm* shipwreck — **náufrago, -ga** *adj* shipwrecked

**náusea** *nf* nausea

**navaja** *nf* pocketknife, penknife

**naval** *adj* naval

**nave** *nf* ship; ～ **espacial** spaceship

**navegar** *v* navigate, sail — **navegable** *adj* navigable — **navegación** *nf* (**-ciones**) navigation — **navegante** *adj* sailing, seafaring — **navegante** *nmf* navigator

**Navidad** *nf* Christmas; **feliz** ～ Merry Christmas

**neblina** *nf* mist

**necesario, -ria** *adj* necessary — **necesariamente** *adv* necessarily — **necesidad** *nf* need, necessity; poverty — **necesitado, -da** *adj* needy — **necesitar** *v* need

**necio, -cia** *adj* silly, dumb

**neerlandés, -desa** *adj* (**-deses** *m*) Dutch — **neerlandés** *nm* Dutch (language)

**negar** *v* deny; refuse — **negarse** *vr* refuse — **negación** *nf* (**-ciones**) denial; negative (in grammar) — **negativa** *nf* denial; refusal — **negativo, -va** *adj* negative

**negociar** *v* negotiate; deal, do business — **negociable** *adj* negotiable — **negociación** *nf* (**-ciones**) negotiation — **negociante** *nmf* businessman, businesswoman — **negocio** *nm* business; deal; ～**s** business, commerce

**negro, -gra** *adj* black, dark — **negro, -gra** *n* dark-skinned person — **negro** *nm* black (color)

**nene, -na** *n* baby, small child

**neoyorquino, -na** *adj* of or from New York

**Neptuno** *nm* Neptune

**nervio** *nm* nerve — **nerviosismo** *nf* nervousness — **nervioso, -sa** *adj* nervous, anxious; **sistema nervioso** nervous system

**neumático** *nm* tire

**neumonía** *nf* pneumonia

**neurólogo, -ga** *n* neurologist

**neurosis** *nfs & pl* neurosis (-roses) — **neurótico, -ca** *adj & n* neurotic

**neutral** *adj* neutral — **neutro, -tra** *adj* neutral; neuter (in biology, grammar)

**nevar** *v impers* snow — **nevada** *nf* snowfall — **nevado, -da** *adj* snow-covered, snowy; snow-white

**nevera** *nf* refrigerator

**ni** *conj* neither, nor; ～ **siquiera** not even

**nicaragüense** *adj* Nicaraguan

**nicotina** *nf* nicotine

**nido** *nm* nest

**niebla** *nf* fog, mist

**nieto, -ta** *n* grandson, granddaughter; **nietos** *nmpl* grandchildren

**nieve** *nf* snow

**nigeriano, -na** *adj* Nigerian

**nilón** *or* **nilon** *nm* (**-lones**) nylon

**ninguno, -na** *adj* no, not any — **ninguno, -na** *pron* neither, none; no one, nobody

**niño, -ña** *n* child, boy, girl ～ *adj* young — **niñero, -ra** *n* baby-sitter, nanny — **niñez** *nf* (**-ñeces**) childhood

**nipón, -pona** *adj* Japanese

**nitrógeno** *nm* nitrogen

**nivel** *nm* level, height; ～ **de vida** standard of living — **nivelar** *v* level (out)

**no** *adv* not; no

**noche** *nf* night, evening; **buenas** ～**s** good evening, good night; **de** ～ *or* **por la** ～ at night — **Nochebuena** *nf* Christmas Eve — **Nochevieja** *nf* New Year's Eve

**noción** *nf* (**-ciones**) notion, concept; **nociones** *nfpl* rudiments

**nocturno, -na** *adj* night; nocturnal (as of animals) — **nocturno** *nm* nocturne
**nogal** *nm* walnut tree
**nómada** *nmf* nomad
**nombrar** *v* appoint; mention — **nombrado, -da** *adj* famous, well-known — **nombramiento** *nm* appointment, nomination — **nombre** *nm* name; noun
**nordeste** *or* **noreste** *adj* northeastern — **nordeste** *or* **noreste** *nm* northeast
**nórdico, -ca** *adj* Scandinavian
**norma** *nf* rule, norm, standard — **normal** *adj* normal — **normalidad** *nf* normality — **normalizar** *v* normalize; standardize — **normalmente** *adv* ordinarily, generally
**noroeste** *adj* northwestern — **noroeste** *nm* northwest
**norte** *adj* north, northern — **norte** *nm* north
**norteamericano, -na** *adj* North American
**noruego, -ga** *adj* Norwegian — **noruego** *nm* Norwegian (language)
**nos** *pron* us; to us, for us, from us; ourselves; each other, one another
**nosotros, -tras** *pron* we; us
**nostalgia** *nf* nostalgia
**nota** *nf* note; grade, mark (in school)
**notario, -ria** *n* notary (public)
**noticia** *nf* news item, piece of news — **noticiero** *nm* newscast
**notorio, -ria** *adj* obvious; well-known
**novecientos, -tas** *adj* nine hundred — **novecientos** *nms & pl* nine hundred
**novedad** *nf* newness, innovation — **novedoso, -sa** *adj* original, novel
**novela** *nf* novel; soap opera — **novelista** *nmf* novelist
**noveno, -na** *adj* ninth — **noveno** *nm* ninth

**noventa** *adj & nm* ninety
**noviazgo** *nm* engagement
**noviembre** *nm* November
**novio, -via** *n* boyfriend, girlfriend; bridegroom, bride (at a wedding)
**nube** *nf* cloud — **nubarrón** *nm* (**-rrones**) storm cloud — **nublado, -da** *adj* cloudy — **nublado** *nm* storm cloud — **nublar** *v* cloud — **nublarse** *vr* get cloudy
**nuca** *nf* nape, back of the neck
**nuclear** *adj* nuclear
**nudillo** *nm* knuckle
**nudismo** *nm* nudism — **nudista** *adj & nmf* nudist
**nudo** *nm* knot
**nuera** *nf* daughter-in-law
**nuestro, -tra** *adj* our — **nuestro, -tra** *pron* (*with definite article*) **el/la/lo** ∼ ours, our own
**nuevamente** *adv* again, anew
**nueve** *adj & nm* nine
**nuevo, -va** *adj* new; **de nuevo** again, once more
**nuez** *nf* (**nueces**) nut
**nulo, -la** *adj* null, invalid; useless, inept ∼ **y sin efecto** null and void
**numerar** *v* number — **numeración** *nf* (**-ciones**) numbering; numbers, numerals — **numeral** *adj* numeral — **número** *nm* number, numeral; issue (of a publication) — **numérico, -ca** *adj* numerical — **numeroso, -sa** *adj* numerous
**nunca** *adv* never, ever
**nupcial** *adj* nuptial, wedding — **nupcias** *nfpl* nuptials, wedding
**nutria** *nf* otter
**nutrir** *v* feed, nourish; fuel, foster — **nutrición** *nf* (**-ciones**) nutrition — **nutritivo, -va** *adj* nourishing, nutritious

# Ñ

*nf* 15th letter of the Spanish alphabet

# O

**o**[1] *nf* o, 16th letter of the Spanish alphabet

**o**[2] *conj* or, either; ~ **sea** in other words

**obedecer** *v* obey — **obediencia** *nf* obedience — **obediente** *adj* obedient

**obeso, -sa** *adj* obese — **obesidad** *nf* obesity

**obispo** *nm* bishop

**objeto** *nm* object — **objetivo, -va** *adj* objective — **objetivo** *nm* objective, goal

**oblicuo, -cua** *adj* oblique

**obligar** *v* require, oblige — **obligarse** *vr* commit oneself (to do something) — **obligación** *nf* (**-ciones**) obligation — **obligatorio, -ria** *adj* mandatory

**obra** *nf* deed; work (as of art, literature); construction work — **obrar** *v* work, produce; act, behave — **obrero, -ra** *adj* working; **la clase obrera** the working class — **obrero, -ra** *n* worker, laborer

**obsequiar** *v* give, present — **obsequio** *nm* gift, present

**observar** *v* watch; notice; keep, observe (as a custom, ritual) — **observación** *nf* (**-ciones**) observation — **observador, -dora** *adj* observant — **observador, -dora** *n* observer — **observatorio** *nm* observatory

**obsesionar** *v* obsess — **obsesión** *nf* (**-siones**) obsession — **obsesivo, -va** *adj* obsessive

**obstaculizar** *v* hinder — **obstáculo** *nm* obstacle

**obstar** *v* hinder — **no obstante** *conj phr* nevertheless, however — **no obstante** *prep phr* in spite of, despite

**obstinarse** *vr* be stubborn — **obstinado, -da** *adj* obstinate, stubborn; persistent

**obtener** *v* obtain, get

**obvio, -via** *adj* obvious

**ocasión** *nf* (**-siones**) occasion; opportunity; bargain — **ocasional** *adj* occasional; accidental, chance — **ocasionar** *v* cause

**ocaso** *nm* sunset

**occidente** *nm* west — **occidental** *adj* western, Western

**océano** *nm* ocean

**ochenta** *adj & nm* eighty

**ocho** *adj & nm* eight — **ochocientos, -tas** *adj* eight hundred — **ochocientos** *nms & pl* eight hundred

**ocio** *nm* free time, leisure — **ocioso, -sa** *adj* idle, inactive; useless

**octágono** *nm* octagon

**octavo, -va** *adj & n* eighth

**octubre** *nm* October

**ocular** *adj* ocular, eye — **oculista** *nmf* ophthalmologist

**ocultar** *v* conceal, hide — **ocultarse** *vr* hide — **oculto, -ta** *adj* hidden, occult

**ocupar** *v* occupy; hold (as a position); provide work for — **ocuparse** *vr* concern oneself with; ~ **de** take care of (as children) — **ocupación** *nf* (**-ciones**) occupation; job — **ocupado, -da** *adj* busy; occupied (of a place) — **ocupante** *nmf* occupant

**ocurrir** *v* occur, happen — **ocurrirse** *vr* occur to

**odiar** *v* hate — **odio** *nm* hatred — **odioso, -sa** *adj* hateful

**odontología** *nf* dentistry, dental surgery
— **odontólogo, -ga** *n* dentist, dental surgeon

**oeste** *adj* west, western — **oeste** *nm* west

**ofender** *v* offend — **ofenderse** *vr* take offense — **ofensa** *nf* offense, insult

**oferta** *nf* offer; **de ~** on sale

**oficial** *adj* official; officer (in the military)

**oficina** *nf* office — **oficinista** *nmf* office worker

**oficio** *nm* trade, profession

**ofrecer** *v* offer; provide, present (as an opportunity) — **ofrecerse** *vr* volunteer — **ofrecimiento** *nm* offer

**oftalmología** *nf* ophthalmology — **oftalmólogo, -ga** *n* ophthalmologist

**ogro** *nm* ogre

**oír** *v* hear; listen to — **oído** *nm* ear; (sense of) hearing

**ojal** *nm* buttonhole

**ojalá** *interj* I hope so!, if only!

**ojear** *v* eye, look at — **ojeada** *nf* glimpse, glance

**ojo** *nm* eye — **¡ojo!** *interj* look out!, pay attention!

**ola** *nf* wave — **oleaje** *nm* swell (of the sea)

**olé** *interj* bravo!

**oleada** *nf* wave, swell

**oler** *v* smell

**olfatear** *v* sniff; sense, sniff out — **olfato** *nm* sense of smell

**Olimpiada** *or* **Olimpíada** *nf* Olympics, Olympic Games — **olímpico, -ca** *adj* Olympic

**oliva** *nf* olive — **olivo** *nm* olive tree

**olla** *nf* pot

**olmo** *nm* elm

**olor** *nm* smell — **oloroso, -sa** *adj* fragrant

**olvidar** *v* forget; leave behind; omit — **olvidarse** *vr* forget — **olvidadizo, -za** *adj* forgetful — **olvido** *nm* forgetfulness

**ombligo** *nm* navel

**omitir** *v* omit — **omisión** *nf* (**-siones**) omission

**omnipotente** *adj* omnipotent

**once** *adj* & *nm* eleven

**onda** *nf* wave — **ondear** *v* ripple — **ondulación** *nf* (**-ciones**) undulation — **ondulado, -da** *adj* wavy — **ondular** wave (hair); undulate, ripple

**onza** *nf* ounce

**opaco, -ca** *adj* opaque; dull

**opción** *nf* (**-ciones**) option — **opcional** *adj* optional

**ópera** *nf* opera

**operar** *v* operate; operate on; deal, do business — **operarse** *vr* have an operation — **operación** *nf* (**-ciones**) operation; transaction, deal — **operador, -dora** *n* operator

**opinar** *v* think; express an opinion — **opinión** *nf* (**-niones**) opinion

**opio** *nm* opium

**oponer** *v* raise, put forward (as arguments) — **oponerse** *vr* oppose, be against — **oponente** *nmf* opponent

**oportunidad** *nf* opportunity — **oportunista** *nmf* opportunist — **oportuno, -na** *adj* opportune, timely

**opositor, -tora** *n* opponent — **oposición** *nf* (**-ciones**) opposition

**oprimir** *v* press, squeeze — **opresión** *nf* (**-siones**) oppression

**optar** *v* apply for

**óptica** *nf* optics; optician's (shop) — **óptico, -ca** *adj* optical — **óptico, -ca** *n* optician

**optimismo** *nm* optimism — **optimista** *adj* optimistic — **optimista** *nmf* optimist

**optometría** *nf* optometry

**opuesto** *adj* opposite

**oración** *nf* (**-ciones**) prayer; sentence, clause

**orador, -dora** *n* speaker

**oral** *adj* oral

**orar** *v* pray

**órbita** *nf* orbit (in astronomy)
**orden** *nm* (**órdenes**) order; **orden** *nf* (**órdenes**) order (of food)
**ordenar** *v* order, command; put in order
**ordeñar** *v* milk
**ordinal** *adj & nm* ordinal
**ordinario, -ria** *adj* ordinary; common, vulgar
**oreja** *nf* ear
**orgánico, -ca** *adj* organic
**organismo** *nm* organism; agency, organization
**organizar** *v* organize — **organizarse** *vr* get organized — **organización** *nf* (**-ciones**) organization
**órgano** *nm* organ
**orgasmo** *nm* orgasm
**orgullo** *nm* pride — **orgulloso, -sa** *adj* proud
**orientación** *nf* (**-ciones**) orientation; direction; guidance
**oriental** *adj* eastern; oriental — **oriental** *nmf* Oriental, Asian
**orientar** *v* orient, position; guide, direct
**oriente** *nm* east, East
**origen** *nm* (**orígenes**) origin — **original** *adj & nm* original — **originar** *v* give rise to
**originario, -ria** *adj* original; ～ **de** native to
**orilla** *nf* border, edge
**orinar** *v* urinate — **orina** *nf* urine

**oro** *nm* gold
**orquesta** *nf* orchestra
**orquídea** *nf* orchid
**ortografía** *nf* spelling
**orzuelo** *nm* sty (in the eye)
**os** *pron pl* you, (to) you; yourselves, (to) yourselves; each other, (to) each other
**osado, -da** *adj* bold, daring — **osadía** *nf* boldness, daring
**oscuro, -ra** *adj* dark — **oscurecer** *v* darken — **oscurecer** *v impers* get dark — **oscurecerse** *vr* grow dark — **oscuridad** *nf* darkness
**oso, osa** *n* bear
**osteoporosis** *nf* osteoporosis
**ostra** *nf* oyster
**otoño** *nm* autumn, fall
**otorgar** *v* grant, award
**otro, otra**[1] *adj* another, other; **otra vez** again
**otro, otra**[2] *pron* another (one), other (one)
**óvalo** *nm* oval — **oval** *or* **ovalado, -da** *adj* oval
**ovario** *nm* ovary
**oveja** *nf* sheep, ewe
**overol** *nm* overalls
**ovni** *or* **OVNI** *nm* UFO
**ovular** *v* ovulate — **ovulación** *nf* (**-ciones**) ovulation
**oxígeno** *nm* oxygen
**oyente** *nmf* listener

# P

**p** *nf* p, 17th letter of the Spanish alphabet
**pabellón** *nm* (**-llones**) pavilion; block, building (as in a hospital complex)
**paciencia** *nf* patience — **paciente** *adj & nmf* patient
**pacificar** *v* pacify, calm — **pacífico, -ca** *adj* peaceful, pacific — **pacifista** *adj & nmf* pacifist
**pacto** *nm* pact, agreement

**padecer** *v* suffer, endure
**padre** *nm* father; ～**s** *nmpl* parents — **padrastro** *nm* stepfather — **padrino** *nm* godfather; best man (at a wedding)
**paella** *nf* paella
**pagar** *v* pay, pay for
**página** *nf* page
**pago** *nm* payment

**país** *nm* country, nation; region, land —
**paisaje** *nm* scenery, landscape

**paja** *nf* straw

**pájaro** *nm* bird; ~ **carpintero** wood-
pecker

**pala** *nf* shovel, spade

**palabra** *nf* word; speech

**palacio** *nm* palace, mansion; ~ **de justicia** courthouse

**paladar** *nm* palate

**palanca** *nf* lever, crowbar; leverage, influence; ~ **de cambio** *or* ~ **de ve-
locidades** gearshift

**palco** *nm* box (in a theater)

**palestino, -na** *adj* Palestinian

**pálido, -da** *adj* pale — **palidecer** *v* turn
pale

**palillo** *nm* toothpick

**palma** *nf* palm (of the hand); palm (tree
or leaf) — **palmada** *nf* pat, slap

**palmera** *nf* palm tree

**palo** *nm* stick

**paloma** *nf* pigeon, dove

**palomitas** *nfpl* popcorn

**palpar** *v* feel, touch

**palpitar** *v* palpitate, throb — **palpitación** *nf* (**-ciones**) palpitation

**paludismo** *nm* malaria

**pampa** *nf* pampa

**pan** *nm* bread

**pana** *nf* corduroy

**panadería** *nf* bakery, bread shop —
**panadero, -ra** *n* baker

**panameño, -ña** *adj* Panamanian

**pancarta** *nf* placard, banner

**páncreas** *nms & pl* pancreas

**pandilla** *nf* gang

**pánico** *nm* panic

**panorama** *nm* panorama

**panqueque** *nm* pancake

**pantalla** *nf* screen; lampshade

**pantalón** *nm* (**-lones**) *or* **pantalones**
*nmpl* pants, trousers; **pantalones vaqueros** jeans

**pantera** *nf* panther

**pantorrilla** *nf* calf (of the leg)

**pantufla** *nf* slipper

**pañuelo** *nm* handkerchief

**panza** *nf* belly, paunch

**pañal** *nm* diaper

**paño** *nm* cloth

**papa¹** *nm* pope

**papa²** *nf* potato; ~**s fritas** potato chips,
french fries

**papá** *nm* dad, pop; ~**s** *nmpl* parents,
folks

**papagayo** *nm* parrot

**papaya** *nf* papaya

**papel** *nm* paper, sheet of paper; ~
**higiénico** *or* ~ **de baño** toilet paper
— **papelera** *nf* wastebasket — **pape-
lería** *nf* stationery store

**papilla** *nf* baby food, pap

**paquete** *nm* package, parcel

**paquistaní** *adj* Pakistani

**par** *nm* pair, couple — **par** *adj* even (in
number) — **par** *nf* par

**para** *prep* for; towards; (in order) to;
around, by (a time)

**parabrisas** *nms & pl* windshield(s)

**paracaídas** *nms & pl* parachute(s) —
**paracaidista** *nmf* parachutist; paratrooper

**parada** *nf* stop — **paradero** *nm* bus stop
— **parado, -da** *adj* standing (up)

**parafrasear** *v* paraphrase

**paraguas** *nms & pl* umbrella(s)

**paraguayo, -ya** *adj* Paraguayan

**paraíso** *nm* paradise

**parálisis** *nfs & pl* paralysis (-lyses) —
**paralítico, -ca** *adj* paralytic — **paralizar** *v* paralyze

**páramo** *nm* barren plateau

**parapléjico, -ca** *adj & n* paraplegic

**parar** *v* stop; stand, prop — **pararse** *vr*
stop; stand up

**pararrayos** *nms & pl* lightning rod(s)

**parasol** *nm* parasol

**parcial** *adj* partial

**pardo, -da** *adj* brownish grey

**parecer** *v* seem, look; look like, seem
like — **parecerse a** *vr phr* resemble

**parecido, -da** *adj* similar — **parecido** *nm* resemblance, similarity

**pared** *nf* wall

**pareja** *nf* couple, pair; partner

**parentesco** *nm* relationship, kinship

**paréntesis** *nms & pl* parenthesis (-theses)

**pariente** *nmf* relative, relation

**parlamentario, -ria** *adj* parliamentary — **parlamentario, -ria** *n* member of parliament — **parlamento** *nm* parliament

**paro** *nm* stoppage, shutdown; strike; ∼ **cardíaco** cardiac arrest

**párpado** *nm* eyelid — **parpadear** *v* blink — **parpadeo** *nm* blink

**parque** *nm* park; ∼ **de atracciones** amusement park

**parqué** *nm* parquet

**parquear** *v* park

**parquímetro** *nm* parking meter

**párrafo** *nm* paragraph

**parrilla** *nf* broiler, grill

**párroco** *nm* parish priest — **parroquia** *nf* parish; parish church

**parte**[1] *nm* report; ∼ **meteorológico** weather forecast

**parte**[2] *nf* part; share; side; **de** ∼ **de** on behalf of

**partición** *nf* (-ciones) division, sharing

**participar** *v* participate, take part — **participación** *nf* (-ciones) participation

**participio** *nm* participle

**particular** *adj* particular; private ∼ *nm* matter; individual

**partido** *nm* (political) party; game, match (in sports)

**partir** *v* split, divide; break, crack; depart; ∼ **de** start from; **a** ∼ **de** as of, from — **partida** *nf* departure — **partidario, -ria** *n* follower, supporter

**parto** *nm* childbirth

**pasa** *nf* raisin

**pasado, -da** *adj* past — **pasado** *nm* past

**pasaje** *nm* ticket, fare — **pasajero, -ra** *n* passenger

**pasamanos** *nms & pl* handrail(s), banister(s)

**pasaporte** *nm* passport

**pasar** *v* cross; pass, go (by); come in; happen; **¿qué pasa?** what's the matter?; what's happening?

**pasatiempo** *nm* pastime, hobby

**Pascua** *nf* Easter; Passover; Christmas

**pasear** *v* go for a ride; take a walk; take for a walk — **paseo** *nm* walk, ride

**pasillo** *nm* passage, corridor

**pasión** *nf* (-siones) passion

**pasivo, -va** *adj* passive

**paso** *nm* step; **de** ∼ in passing

**pasta** *nf* paste; pasta

**pastel** *nm* pie — **pastelería** *nf* pastry shop

**pastilla** *nf* pill, tablet

**pasto** *nm* pasture; grass, lawn — **pastor, -tora** *n* shepherd; pastor (in religion)

**pata** *nf* paw, leg (of an animal); foot, leg (of furniture) — **patada** *nf* kick

**patata** *nf* potato

**patear** *v* kick

**paternal** *adj* fatherly, paternal — **paternidad** *nf* fatherhood; paternity — **paterno, -na** *adj* paternal

**patillas** *nfpl* sideburns

**patinar** *v* skate — **patín** *nm* (-tines) skate — **patinador, -dora** *n* skater — **patinaje** *nm* skating

**patio** *nm* courtyard, patio

**pato, -ta** *n* duck

**patria** *nf* native land

**patrimonio** *nm* inheritance; heritage

**patriota** *adj* patriotic — **patriota** *nmf* patriot

**patrocinador, -dora** *n* sponsor — **patrocinar** *v* sponsor

**patrón, -trona** *n* (-trones *m*) patron; boss

**patrulla** *nf* patrol — **patrullar** *v* patrol

**pausa** *nf* pause, break

**pavimento** *nm* pavement — **pavimentar** *v* pave

**pavo, -va** *n* turkey; **pavo real** peacock

**pavor** *nm* dread, terror
**payaso, -sa** *n* clown
**paz** *nf* (**paces**) peace
**peaje** *nm* toll
**peatón** *nm* (**-tones**) pedestrian
**peca** *nf* freckle
**pecado** *nm* sin — **pecador, -dora** *adj* sinful — **pecador, -dora** *n* sinner — **pecar** *v* sin
**pecho** *nm* chest; breast — **pechuga** *nf* breast (of fowl)
**pedagogía** *nf* education, pedagogy — **pedagogo, -ga** *n* educator, teacher
**pedal** *nm* pedal — **pedalear** *v* pedal
**pedazo** *nm* piece, bit
**pediatra** *nmf* pediatrician
**pedir** *v* ask; ask for, request; order (as food, merchandise)
**pegar** *v* stick, glue, paste; hit, strike; hit — **pegarse** *vr* hit oneself, hit each other; stick, adhere — **pegamento** *nm* glue
**peinar** *v* comb — **peinado** *nm* hairstyle, hairdo — **peine** *nm* comb
**pelar** *v* cut the hair of (a person); peel (fruit)
**pelear** *v* fight; quarrel — **pelea** *nf* fight; quarrel
**pelícano** *nm* pelican
**película** *nf* movie, film
**peligro** *nm* danger; risk
**pelirrojo, -ja** *adj* red-haired — **pelirrojo, -ja** *n* redhead
**pellizcar** *v* pinch — **pellizco** *nm* pinch
**pelo** *nm* hair; fur
**pelota** *nf* ball
**peluca** *nf* wig
**peluche** *nm* plush
**peludo, -da** *adj* hairy, furry
**peluquería** *nf* hairdresser's shop, barber shop — **peluquero, -ra** *n* barber, hairdresser
**pelvis** *nfs & pl* pelvis(es)
**pena** *nf* sorrow; suffering, pain; embarrassment
**penal** *adj* penal

**penalty** *nm* penalty (in sports)
**penar** *v* punish; suffer
**pendiente** *adj* pending — **pendiente** *nm* earring
**penetrar** *v* pierce; penetrate; ~ **en** go into — **penetración** *nf* (**-ciones**) penetration; insight — **penetrante** *adj* penetrating; sharp (as of odors), piercing (of sounds)
**penicilina** *nf* penicillin
**península** *nf* peninsula
**penitencia** *nf* penitence; penance
**penoso, -sa** *adj* painful, distressing; difficult; shy
**pensar** *v* think — **pensamiento** *nm* thought; pansy (flower) — **pensativo, -va** *adj* pensive, thoughtful
**pensión** *nf* (**-siones**) boarding house; (retirement) pension
**pentágono** *nm* pentagon
**penúltimo, -ma** *adj* next to last, penultimate
**peón** *nm* (**peones**) laborer, peon; pawn (in chess)
**peor** *adv* worse; worst — **peor** *adj* worse; worst
**pepino** *nm* cucumber — **pepinillo** *nm* pickle, gherkin
**pepita** *nf* seed, pip
**pequeño, -ña** *adj* small, little — **pequeñez** *nf* (**-ñeces**) smallness
**pera** *nf* pear — **peral** *nm* pear tree
**percepción** *nf* (**-ciones**) perception
**percibir** *v* perceive
**percusión** *nf* (**-siones**) percussion
**perder** *v* lose; miss (as an opportunity); waste (time) — **perderse** *vr* get lost; disappear; be wasted — **perdedor, -dora** *n* loser
**perdón** *nm* (**-dones**) forgiveness, pardon — **perdón** *interj* sorry! — **perdonar** *v* forgive; pardon
**perecer** *v* perish, die
**perejil** *nm* parsley
**pereza** *nf* laziness — **perezoso, -sa** *adj* lazy

**perfección** *nf* (**-ciones**) perfection — **perfeccionar** *v* perfect; improve — **perfeccionista** *nmf* perfectionist — **perfecto, -ta** *adj* perfect

**perfil** *nm* profile; outline

**perforar** *v* perforate; drill, bore (a hole) — **perforadora** *nf* (paper) punch

**perfume** *nm* perfume, scent — **perfumar** *v* perfume — **perfumarse** *vr* put perfume on

**periferia** *nf* periphery, outskirts — **periférico, -ca** *adj* peripheral

**periódico, -ca** *adj* periodic — **periódico** *nm* newspaper — **periodismo** *nm* journalism — **periodista** *nmf* journalist

**período** *or* **periodo** *nm* period

**perjudicar** *v* harm, damage — **perjudicial** *adj* harmful

**perla** *nf* pearl

**permanecer** *v* remain — **permanente** *adj* permanent

**permitir** *v* permit, allow — **permiso** *nm* permission; permit, license (document); leave (in the military); **con ~** excuse me

**pero** *conj* but — **pero** *nm* fault; objection

**perpendicular** *adj & nf* perpendicular

**perro, -rra** *n* dog; **perro caliente** hot dog

**perseguir** *v* pursue, chase; persecute — **persecución** *nf* (**-ciones**) pursuit, chase; persecution

**persiana** *nf* (venetian) blind

**persona** *nf* person — **personaje** *nm* character (as in literature); important person, celebrity — **personal** *adj* personal — **personal** *nm* personnel, staff — **personalidad** *nf* personality — **personificar** *v* personify

**perspectiva** *nf* perspective; view; prospect, outlook

**persuadir** *v* persuade

**pertenecer** *v* belong to — **perteneciente** *adj* belonging to

**peruano, -na** *adj* Peruvian

**pesa** *nf* weight; **~s** weights (as for exercise, fitness) — **pesadez** *nf* (**-deces**) heaviness

**pesadilla** *nf* nightmare

**pesado, -da** *adj* heavy; tough, difficult

**pésame** *nm* condolences

**pesar** *v* weigh; be heavy; carry weight (as in importance)

**pescado** *nm* fish — **pesca** *nf* fishing; fish *pl*; catch (of fish) — **pescadería** *nf* fish market — **pescador, -dora** *n* (**-dores** *m*) fisherman — **pescar** *v* fish; fish for; catch, nab

**pesebre** *nm* manger

**pesimista** *adj* pessimistic — **pesimista** *nmf* pessimist

**peso** *nm* weight; burden; peso (currency)

**pestaña** *nf* eyelash

**pétalo** *nm* petal

**petición** *nf* (**-ciones**) petition, request

**petróleo** *nm* oil, petroleum — **petrolero, -ra** *adj* oil — **petrolero** *nm* oil tanker

**peyorativo, -va** *adj* pejorative

**pez** *nm* (**peces**) fish; **~ gordo** big shot

**piano** *nm* piano — **pianista** *nmf* pianist, piano player

**picado, -da** *adj* perforated; minced, chopped (as of meat); decayed (of teeth); choppy (of the sea) — **picada** *nf* bite, sting; sharp descent — **picadura** *nf* sting, bite; (moth) hole

**picante** *adj* hot, spicy

**picar** *v* bite; peck at, nibble on (food); prick, puncture; chop, mince; take the bait; sting, itch; be spicy (of food) — **picarse** *vr* get a cavity

**picnic** *nm* (**-nics**) picnic

**pico** *nm* beak; peak; (sharp) point; pick, pickax (tool)

**pie** *nm* foot (in anatomy); base, bottom, stem; **al ~ de la letra** word for word; **de ~** standing (up)

**piedad** *nf* pity, mercy; piety

**piedra** *nf* stone; flint (of a lighter); hailstone

**piel** *nf* skin; leather; fur, pelt
**pierna** *nf* leg
**pieza** *nf* piece, part; room
**pijama** *nm* pajamas
**pila** *nf* battery; pile; sink; basin (as of a fountain)
**píldora** *nf* pill
**piloto** *nmf* pilot
**pimienta** *nf* pepper (condiment) — **pimentón** *nm* (**-tones**) paprika; cayenne pepper
**pincel** *nm* paintbrush
**pino** *nm* pine (tree)
**pintar** *v* paint — **pintarse** *vr* put on makeup — **pintor, -tora** *n* (**-tores** *m*) painter — **pintura** *nf* paint; painting
**pinza** *nf* clothespin; claw, pincer (as of a crab); **∼s** *nfpl* tweezers
**piña** *nf* pine cone; pineapple
**piñata** *nf* piñata
**piñón** *nm* (**-ñones**) pine nut
**pío, pía** *adj* pious; piebald (of a horse)
**pionero, -ra** *n* pioneer
**pipa** *nf* pipe (for smoking); seed, pip
**piropo** *nm* (flirtatious) compliment
**pisar** *v* step, tread; step on; walk all over, abuse
**piscina** *nf* swimming pool; (fish) pond
**piso** *nm* floor, story; floor (of a room); apartment
**pista** *nf* trail, track; clue; **∼ de aterrizaje** runway, airstrip; **∼ de baile** dance floor
**pistola** *nf* pistol, gun; spray gun
**pistón** *nm* (**-tones**) piston
**pito** *nm* whistle; horn — **pitar** *v* blow a whistle; beep, honk (of a horn); whistle at — **pitillo** *nm* cigarette
**pizza** *nf* pizza — **pizzería** *nf* pizzeria
**placa** *nf* sheet, plate; plaque; (police) badge
**placenta** *nf* placenta
**placer** *v* please — **placer** *nm* pleasure — **placentero, -ra** *adj* pleasant, agreeable
**plagio** *nm* plagiarism
**plan** *nm* plan

**plancha** *nf* iron (for ironing clothes); grill (for cooking); sheet, plate — **planchar** *v* iron (clothes)
**planear** *v* plan; glide
**planeta** *nm* planet
**planificar** *v* plan — **planificación** *nf* (**-ciones**) planning
**planilla** *nf* list, roster
**plano, -na** *adj* flat — **plano** *nm* map, plan; plane (surface); level
**planta** *nf* plant; floor, story; sole (of the foot)
**plantear** *v* expound, set forth; raise (a question); create, pose (a problem) — **plantearse** *vr* think about, consider
**plantel** *nm* staff, team; educational institution
**plantilla** *nf* insole; pattern, template; staff (as of a business)
**plástico, -ca** *adj* plastic
**plata** *nf* silver; money
**plátano** *nm* banana; plantain
**platea** *nf* orchestra seating area (in a theater)
**platillo** *nm* saucer; cymbal; dish, course
**plato** *nm* plate, dish; course (of a meal)
**platónico, -ca** *adj* platonic
**playa** *nf* beach, seashore
**plaza** *nf* square, plaza; seat (in transportation); post, position; market, marketplace
**plazo** *nm* period, term; installment
**pleno, -na** *adj* full, complete — **plenitud** *nf* fullness, abundance
**pliego** *nm* sheet (of paper) — **pliegue** *nm* crease, fold; pleat (in fabric)
**plomero, -ra** *n* plumber
**pluma** *nf* feather; (fountain) pen
**plural** *adj & nm* plural — **pluralidad** *nf* plurality
**Plutón** *nm* Pluto
**población** *nf* (**-ciones**) city, town, village; population
**pobre** *adj* poor — **pobreza** *nf* poverty
**poco, -ca** *adj* little, not much, (a) few — **poco, -ca** *pron* little, few

**poder¹** *v aux* be able to, can; might, may; can, may — **poder** *v* be possible

**poder²** *nm* power; possession — **poderoso, -sa** *adj* powerful

**poema** *nm* poem — **poesía** *nf* poetry; poem — **poeta** *nmf* poet

**polaco, -ca** *adj* Polish

**polarizar** *v* polarize

**polémica** *nf* controversy — **polémico, -ca** *adj* controversial

**policía** *nf* police; *nmf* police officer, policeman, policewoman

**politécnico, -ca** *adj* polytechnic

**política** *nf* politics; policy — **político, -ca** *adj* political; **hermano político** brother-in-law — **político, -ca** *n* politician

**pollo, -lla** *n* chicken, chick; chicken (for cooking)

**polo** *nm* pole; polo (sport); ~ **norte** North Pole

**polución** *nf* (**-ciones**) pollution

**polvo** *nm* powder; dust — **pólvora** *nf* gunpowder

**pómulo** *nm* cheekbone

**poner** *v* put; add; contribute; suppose; arrange, set out; give (a name), call; turn on; set up, establish; lay (eggs) — **ponerse** *vr* move (into a position); put on (as clothing); set (of the sun)

**pontífice** *nm* pontiff

**popular** *adj* popular; colloquial — **popularidad** *nf* popularity

**póquer** *nm* poker (card game)

**por** *prep* for; around; during; about; through, along; because of; per; ~ *or* ~ **medio de** by means of; times (in mathematics); as for, according to; ~ **ciento** percent; ~ **favor** please; ~ **lo tanto** therefore; **¿por qué?** why?

**porcelana** *nf* porcelain, china

**porcentaje** *nm* percentage

**porción** *nf* (**-ciones**) portion, piece

**porque** *conj* because; ~ *or* **por que** in order that — **porqué** *nm* reason

**portada** *nf* facade; title page (of a book), cover (of a magazine)

**portador, -dora** *n* bearer

**portaequipajes** *nms & pl* luggage rack(s)

**portafolio** *or* **portafolios** *nm* (**-lios**) portfolio; briefcase

**portal** *nm* doorway; hall, vestibule

**portar** *v* carry, bear — **portarse** *vr* behave

**portátil** *adj* portable

**portavoz** *nmf* (**-voces**) spokesperson, spokesman; spokeswoman

**porteño, -ña** *adj* of or from Buenos Aires

**portería** *nf* superintendent's office; goal, goalposts (in sports) — **portero, -ra** *n* goalkeeper, goalie; janitor, superintendent

**portugués, -guesa** *adj* (**-gueses** *m*) Portuguese — **portugués** *nm* Portuguese (language)

**porvenir** *nm* future

**posar** *v* pose; place, lay — **posarse** *vr* settle, rest

**poseer** *v* possess, own — **posesionarse de** *vr phr* take possession of, take over — **posesivo, -va** *adj* possessive

**posguerra** *nf* postwar period

**posibilidad** *nf* possibility — **posible** *adj* possible

**posición** *nf* (**-ciones**) position

**positivo, -va** *adj* positive

**posponer** *v* postpone; put behind, subordinate

**postal** *adj* postal — **postal** *nf* postcard

**poste** *nm* post, pole

**postergar** *v* pass over; postpone

**posteridad** *nf* posterity — **posterior** *adj* later, subsequent; back, rear

**postre** *nm* dessert

**postular** *v* advance, propose; nominate

**póstumo, -ma** *adj* posthumous

**postura** *nf* position, stance

**potable** *adj* drinkable, potable

**potencia** *nf* power — **potente** *adj* powerful

**práctica** *nf* practice — **practicar** *v* practice; perform, carry out — **practicar** *v* practice — **práctico, -ca** *adj* practical

**precaución** *nf* (**-ciones**) precaution; caution, care

**precedente** *adj* preceding, previous — **precedente** *nm* precedent

**precio** *nm* price, cost — **precioso, -sa** *adj* beautiful; precious

**precipitar** *v* hasten, speed up; hurl — **precipitarse** *vr* rush; act rashly; throw oneself — **precipitación** *nf* (**-ciones**) precipitation; haste — **precipitado, -da** *adj* hasty

**preciso, -sa** *adj* precise; necessary — **precisar** *v* specify, determine; require — **precisión** *nf* (**-siones**) precision; necessity

**precoz** *adj* (**-coces**) early; precocious (of children)

**predecir** *v* foretell, predict

**predicado** *nm* predicate

**predicar** *v* preach

**predicción** *nf* (**-ciones**) prediction; forecast

**predilección** *nf* (**-ciones**) preference — **predilecto, -ta** *adj* favorite

**predominar** *v* predominate — **predominante** *adj* predominant, prevailing

**prefacio** *nm* preface

**preferir** *v* prefer — **preferido, -da** *adj* favorite

**prefijo** *nm* prefix; area code

**pregunta** *nf* question — **preguntar** *v* ask — **preguntarse** *vr* wonder

**prehistórico, -ca** *adj* prehistoric

**prejuicio** *nm* prejudice

**preliminar** *adj* & *nm* preliminary

**prematrimonial** *adj* premarital

**prematuro, -ra** *adj* premature

**premio** *nm* prize; reward

**premisa** *nf* premise

**prenda** *nf* piece of clothing; pledge; forfeit (in a game)

**prender** *v* pin, fasten; capture; light (as a match); turn on (as a light) catch, burn (of fire); take root — **prenderse** *vr* catch fire

**preocupar** *v* worry — **preocupación** *nf* (**-ciones**) worry

**preparar** *v* prepare — **prepararse** *vr* get ready — **preparación** *nf* (**-ciones**) preparation — **preparado, -da** *adj* prepared, ready

**preposición** *nf* (**-ciones**) preposition

**presentar** *v* present; offer, give; show; introduce (persons) — **presentarse** *vr* show up; arise, come up (as a problem); introduce oneself — **presentación** *nf* (**-ciones**) presentation; introduction (of persons); appearance — **presentador, -dora** *n* presenter, host (as of a television program)

**presente** *adj* present; **tener** ～ keep in mind — **presente** *nm* present

**presentimiento** *nm* premonition

**presidente, -ta** *n* president; chair, chairperson (of a meeting) — **presidencia** *nf* presidency; chairmanship

**presión** *nf* (**-siones**) pressure — **presionar** *v* press; put pressure on

**preso, -sa** *adj* imprisoned — **preso, -sa** *n* prisoner

**prestar** *v* lend, loan; give (aid) — **prestado, -da** *adj* borrowed, on loan — **préstamo** *nm* loan

**prestigio** *nm* prestige

**presupuesto** *nm* budget, estimate; assumption

**pretender** *v* try to; claim; court, woo — **pretensión** *nf* (**-siones**) intention, aspiration; claim (to a throne, etc.)

**pretérito** *nm* past (in grammar)

**pretexto** *nm* pretext, excuse

**prevenir** *v* prevent; warn — **prevención** *nf* (**-ciones**) prevention; precaution; prejudice — **prevenido, -da** *adj* prepared, ready; cautious

**prima** *nf* bonus; (insurance) premium

**primario, -ria** *adj* primary

**primavera** *nf* spring (season); primrose (flower)

**primero, -ra** *adj* first; top, leading; main, basic — **primero, -ra** *n* first one — **primero** *adv* first; rather, sooner

**primitivo, -va** *adj* primitive

**primo, -ma** *n* cousin

**principal** *adj* main, principal

**principio** *nm* principle; beginning, start; origin

**prioridad** *nf* priority

**prisa** *nf* hurry, rush

**prisión** *nf* (**-siones**) prison; imprisonment — **prisionero, -ra** *n* prisoner

**privar** *v* deprive; forbid; knock out — **privación** *nf* (**-ciones**) deprivation — **privado, -da** *adj* private

**privilegio** *nm* privilege

**probabilidad** *nf* probability

**probar** *v* try, test; try on (clothing); prove; taste — **probarse** *vr* try on (clothing)

**problema** *nm* problem

**proceder** *v* proceed, act; be appropriate — **procedimiento** *nm* procedure, method; proceedings (in law)

**procesar** *v* prosecute; process (data) — **procesador** *nm* processor; ~ **de textos** word processor — **proceso** *nm* process; trial, proceedings *pl* (in law)

**procurar** *v* try, endeavor; obtain, procure — **procurador, -dora** *n* attorney

**producir** *v* produce; cause; yield, bear (as interest, fruit) — **producirse** *vr* take place — **producción** *nf* (**-ciones**) production — **producto** *nm* product

**profesar** *v* practice (a profession) — **profesión** *nf* (**-siones**) profession — **profesional** *adj* & *nmf* professional — **profesor, -sora** *n* teacher; professor — **profesorado** *nm* teaching profession; faculty

**profundo, -da** *adj* deep; profound (as of thoughts) — **profundidad** *nf* depth — **profundizar** *v* study in depth

**programa** *nm* program; curriculum —

**programación** *nf* (**-ciones**) programming — **programador, -dora** *n* programmer — **programar** *v* schedule; program (as a computer)

**progreso** *nm* progress — **progresar** *v* (make) progress

**prohibir** *v* prohibit, forbid — **prohibición** *nf* (**-ciones**) ban, prohibition — **prohibido, -da** *adj* forbidden

**proletariado** *nm* proletariat

**prólogo** *nm* prologue, foreword

**prolongar** *v* prolong; lengthen — **prolongarse** *vr* last, continue

**promesa** *nf* promise — **prometer** *v* promise; show promise — **prometerse** *vr* get engaged

**promocionar** *v* promote — **promoción** *nf* (**-ciones**) promotion

**promover** *v* promote; cause — **promotor, -tora** *n* promoter

**pronombre** *nm* pronoun

**pronóstico** *nm* prediction, forecast; (medical) prognosis

**pronto, -ta** *adj* quick, prompt; ready — **pronto** *adv* soon; quickly, promptly; **de** ~ suddenly; **tan** ~ **como** as soon as

**pronunciar** *v* pronounce; give, deliver (a speech) — **pronunciarse** *vr* declare oneself; revolt — **pronunciación** *nf* (**-ciones**) pronunciation

**propiedad** *nf* property; ownership, possession — **propietario, -ria** *n* owner, proprietor

**propio, -pia** *adj* own; proper, appropriate; characteristic, typical; himself, herself, oneself

**proponer** *v* propose; nominate (a person) — **proponerse** *vr* propose, intend

**proporción** *nf* (**-ciones**) proportion — **proporcional** *adj* proportional — **proporcionar** *v* provide; adapt, proportion

**proposición** *nf* (**-ciones**) proposal, proposition

**propósito** *nm* purpose, intention; **a** ~ incidentally, by the way

**propuesta** *nf* proposal; offer (as of employment)

**prosa** *nf* prose

**prosperar** *v* prosper, thrive — **prosperidad** *nf* prosperity — **próspero, -ra** *adj* prosperous, flourishing

**prostituta** *nf* prostitute

**protagonista** *nmf* protagonist

**proteger** *v* protect — **protección** *nf* (**-ciones**) protection — **protector, -tora** *adj* protective — **protector, -tora** *n* protector

**protestar** *v* protest — **protesta** *nf* protest

**provecho** *nm* benefit, advantage

**provisional** *adj* provisional

**provocar** *v* provoke, cause; irritate — **provocación** *nf* (**-ciones**) provocation — **provocativo, -va** *adj* provocative

**próximo, -ma** *adj* near; next — **proximidad** *nf* proximity; ~**es** *nfpl* vicinity

**proyectar** *v* plan; throw, hurl; cast (light); show (a film) — **proyección** *nf* (**-ciones**) projection — **proyecto** *nm* plan, project — **proyector** *nm* projector

**prudente** *adj* prudent, sensible

**prueba** *nf* proof, evidence; test (as in education, medicine); event (in sports)

**psicología** *nf* psychology — **psicológico, -ca** *adj* psychological — **psicólogo, -ga** *n* psychologist

**psiquiatra** *nmf* psychiatrist

**pubertad** *nf* puberty

**publicar** *v* publish; divulge, disclose — **publicación** *nf* (**-ciones**) publication

**publicidad** *nf* publicity; advertising (in marketing) — **publicista** *nmf* publicist

**público, -ca** *adj* public — **público** *nm* public; audience (in a theater), spectators (in sports)

**pudín** *nm* (**-dines**) pudding

**pueblo** *nm* town, village; people, nation

**puente** *nm* bridge

**puerta** *nf* door, gate

**puerto** *nm* port; (mountain) pass; haven

**puertorriqueño, -ña** *adj* Puerto Rican

**pues** *conj* since, because; so, therefore; well, then — **puesto, -ta** *adj* put, set; dressed — **puesto** *nm* place; position, job; stand, stall (in a market)

**pulga** *nf* flea

**pulgada** *nf* inch — **pulgar** *nm* thumb; big toe

**pulir** *v* polish; touch up, perfect

**pulmón** *nm* (**-mones**) lung

**pulsar** *v* press (a button), strike (a key); play (music) — **pulsación** *nf* (**-ciones**) beat, throb; keystroke

**pulsera** *nf* bracelet

**pulso** *nm* pulse; steadiness (of hand)

**punta** *nf* tip, end; point (of a needle, etc.)

**puntilla** *nf* lace edging

**punto** *nm* dot, point; period (in punctuation); item, question; spot, place; moment; point (in a score); stitch; **dos** ~**s** colon; ~ **de partida** starting point; ~ **muerto** deadlock; ~ **y coma** semicolon

**puntuación** *nf* (**-ciones**) punctuation; scoring, score (in sports)

**puntual** *adj* prompt, punctual; accurate, detailed — **puntualidad** *nf* punctuality; accuracy

**puño** *nm* fist; cuff (of a shirt); handle, hilt

**pupila** *nf* pupil (of the eye)

**pupitre** *nm* desk

**puré** *nm* purée

**pureza** *nf* purity

**purificar** *v* purify — **purificación** *nf* (**-ciones**) purification

**puro¹, -ra** *adj* pure; plain, simple; only, just

**puro²** *nm* cigar

# Q

**q** *nf* q, 18th letter of the Spanish alphabet

**que** *conj* that; than; so that, or else — **que** *pron* who, whom; that, which

**qué** *adv* how, what — **qué** *adj* what, which — **qué** *pron* what

**quedar** *v* remain, stay; be; appear; turn out to be; be left — **quedarse** *vr* stay; **quedarse con** remain

**queja** *nf* complaint — **quejarse** *vr* complain

**quemar** *v* burn — **quemarse** *vr* burn oneself; burn (up); get sunburned — **quemado, -da** *adj* burned — **quemadura** *nf* burn

**querer** *v* want; love — **querer** *nm* love

**queso** *nm* cheese

**quiebra** *nf* break

**quien** *pron* (**quienes**) who; whom; whoever, anyone, some people

**quién** *pron* (**quiénes**) who; whom

**quieto, -ta** *adj* calm, quiet; still — **quietud** *nf* stillness

**quijada** *nf* jaw, jawbone (of an animal)

**química** *nf* chemistry

**quince** *adj & nm* fifteen — **quincena** *nf* two-week period, fortnight

**quinientos, -tas** *adj* five hundred — **quinientos** *nms & pl* five hundred

**quinto, -ta** *adj & n* fifth — **quinto** *nm* fifth

**quiosco** *nm* kiosk, newsstand

**quiste** *nm* cyst

**quitar** *v* remove, take away; take off (clothes) — **quitarse** *vr* withdraw, leave — **quitaesmalte** *nm* nail-polish remover — **quitamanchas** *nms & pl* stain remover

**quizá** *or* **quizás** *adv* maybe, perhaps

# R

**r** *nf* r, 19th letter of the Spanish alphabet

**rabia** *nf* rage, anger

**rabo** *nm* tail

**racionamiento** *nm* rationing

**racismo** *nm* racism — **racista** *adj & nmf* racist

**radio** *nmf* radio

**raíz** *nf* (**raíces**) root

**rallar** *v* grate — **rallador** *nm* grater

**rama** *nf* branch

**rana** *nf* frog

**rapar** *v* shave; crop (hair)

**rápido, -da** *adj* rapid, quick — **rápidamente** *adv* rapidly, fast — **rapidez** *nf* speed — **rápido** *adv* quickly, fast

**raqueta** *nf* racket (in sports)

**raro, -ra** *adj* rare; odd, strange — **raramente** *adv* rarely, infrequently — **rareza** *nf* rarity

**rascacielos** *nms & pl* skyscraper(s)

**rascar** *v* scratch; scrape — **rascarse** *vr* scratch oneself

**rasgar** *v* rip, tear

**rasgo** *nm* stroke (of a pen); trait, characteristic; ~**s** *nmpl* features

**rasguñar** *v* scratch — **rasguño** *nm* scratch

**raspar** *v* scrape; file down, smooth; be rough

**rasurar** *v* shave

**rata** *nf* rat

**ratero, -ra** *n* thief

**rato** *nm* while

**ratón** *nm* (**-tones**) mouse

**raya** *nf* line; stripe — **rayar** *v* scratch

**rayo** *nm* ray, beam

**raza** *nf* (human) race

**razón** *nf* (**-zones**) reason; **tener ~** be right

**reacción** *nf* (**-ciones**) reaction — **reaccionar** *v* react

**real** *adj* real, true

**realidad** *nf* reality; **en ~** actually, in fact

**realismo** *nm* realism — **realista** *adj* realistic — **realista** *nmf* realist

**realizar** *v* carry out; achieve (a goal) — **realización** *nf* (**-ciones**) execution, realization

**realmente** *adv* really, actually

**rebajar** *v* lower, reduce — **rebaja** *nf* reduction; discount; **rebajas** *nfpl* sales

**rebanada** *nf* slice

**rebaño** *nm* herd; flock (of sheep)

**rebelarse** *vr* rebel — **rebelde** *adj* rebellious — **rebelde** *nmf* rebel — **rebeldía** *nf* rebelliousness

**rebuznar** *v* bray

**recaída** *nf* relapse

**recargar** *v* overload; recharge (a battery); reload (as a firearm) — **recargo** *nm* surcharge

**recepción** *nf* (**-ciones**) reception — **recepcionista** *nmf* receptionist

**receta** *nf* recipe; prescription (in medicine)

**rechazar** *v* reject, refuse; repel — **rechazo** *nm* rejection

**recibir** *v* receive; welcome; receive visitors — **recibimiento** *nm* reception, welcome — **recibo** *nm* receipt

**reciclar** *v* recycle — **reciclaje** *nm* recycling

**recién** *adv* newly, recently; **~ casados** newlyweds — **reciente** *adj* recent — **recientemente** *adv* recently

**recipiente** *nm* container, receptacle; **~** *nmf* recipient

**recitar** *v* recite — **recital** *nm* recital

**reclamar** *v* demand, ask for; complain

**reclinar** *v* rest, lean

**recoger** *v* collect, gather; pick up; clean up, tidy (up) — **recogerse** *vr* retire, withdraw — **recogedor** *nm* dustpan — **recogido, -da** *adj* quiet, secluded

**recolección** *nf* (**-ciones**) collection; harvest

**recomendar** *v* recommend — **recomendación** *nf* (**-ciones**) recommendation

**recompensar** *v* reward — **recompensa** *nf* reward

**reconocer** *v* recognize; admit

**récord** *nm* (**-cords**) record

**recordar** *v* remember; remind

**recorrer** *v* travel through; cover (a distance) — **recorrido** *nm* journey, trip; route, course

**recortar** *v* reduce; cut (out) — **recorte** *nm* cut, cutting

**recostar** *v* lean, rest

**recreativo, -va** *adj* recreational — **recreo** *nm* recreation, amusement; recess, break (at school)

**rectángulo** *nm* rectangle — **rectangular** *adj* rectangular

**rectificar** *v* rectify, correct; straighten (out) — **rectitud** *nf* straightness; (moral) rectitude — **recto, -ta** *adj* straight; upright, honorable

**rector, -tora** *adj* governing, managing — **rector, -tora** *n* rector — **rectoría** *nf* rectory

**recuerdo** *nm* memory; souvenir, remembrance (of a journey, etc.); **~s** *nmpl* regards

**recuperar** *v* recover, retrieve — **recuperación** *nf* (**-ciones**) recovery

**recurso** *nm* recourse, resort; **~s** *nmpl* resources

**red** *nf* net; network, system; **la Red** the Internet

**redactar** *v* write (up), draft — **redacción** *nf* (**-ciones**) writing, drafting; editing (as of a newspaper) — **redactor, -tora** *n* editor

**redondo, -da** *adj* round

**reducir** *v* reduce — **reducido, -da** *adj* reduced, limited; small

**reembolso** *nm* refund, reimbursement

**reemplazar** *v* replace — **reemplazo** *nm* replacement

**referencia** *nf* reference

**reflejar** *v* reflect — **reflejarse** *vr* be reflected — **reflejo** *nm* reflection; (physical) reflex; **reflejos** *nmpl* highlights (in hair)

**reflexionar** *v* reflect, think — **reflexión** *nf* (**-xiones**) reflection, thought — **reflexivo, -va** *adj* reflective, thoughtful; reflexive (in grammar)

**reforma** *nf* reform; **~s** *nfpl* renovations — **reformar** *v* reform; renovate, repair (as a house) — **reformarse** *vr* mend one's ways

**reforzar** *v* reinforce

**refrán** *nm* (**-franes**) proverb, saying

**refrendar** *v* approve, endorse

**refrescar** *v* cool, turn cooler; refresh; brush up on (knowledge) — **refrescante** *adj* refreshing

**refuerzo** *nm* reinforcement

**refugiar** *v* shelter — **refugio** *nm* refuge, shelter

**regadera** *nf* watering can; shower head, shower

**regalar** *v* give (as a gift)

**regalo** *nm* gift, present; pleasure, delight

**regañar** *v* scold; grumble; quarrel

**régimen** *nm* (**regímenes**) regime; diet

**región** *nf* (**-giones**) region, area — **regional** *adj* regional

**regir** *v* rule; manage, run; govern, determine; apply, be in force

**registrar** *v* register; record, tape; search (as a house), frisk (a person) — **registrarse** *vr* register; be recorded — **registro** *nm* registration; register (book); registry (office); range (as of a voice); search

**regla** *nf* rule, regulation; ruler (for measuring); period — **reglamento** *nm* regulations, rules

**regresar** *v* return, come back, go back; give back — **regreso** *nm* return

**regular** *adj* regular; medium, average — **regular** *v* regulate, control — **regulación** *nf* (**-ciones**) regulation, control

**rehabilitar** *v* rehabilitate; reinstate (in a position); renovate (as a building)

**rehén** *nm* (**-henes**) hostage

**reimpresión** *nf* (**-siones**) reprinting, reprint

**reincidir** *v* backslide, relapse

**reintegrar** *v* reinstate; refund (money), reimburse (as expenses) — **reintegro** *nm* reimbursement

**reír** *v* laugh; laugh at

**reiterar** *v* repeat, reiterate

**reivindicar** *v* claim; restore

**reja** *nf* grille, grating

**rejuvenecer** *v* rejuvenate

**relación** *nf* (**-ciones**) relation, connection; relationship, relations; account; list; **con ~ a** *or* **en ~ a** in relation to — **relacionar** *v* relate, connect

**relámpago** *nm* flash of lightning

**relatar** *v* relate, tell

**relativo, -va** *adj* relative — **relatividad** *nf* relativity

**relato** *nm* account, report; story, tale

**relevante** *adj* outstanding, important

**relevar** *v* relieve, take over from — **relevo** *nm* relief, replacement; **carrera de ~s** relay race

**relieve** *nm* relief (in art); prominence, importance

**religión** *nf* (**-giones**) religion — **religioso, -sa** *adj* religious — **religioso, -sa** *n* monk, nun

**reloj** *nm* clock; **~ de arena** hourglass; **como un ~** like clockwork

**remar** *v* row

**rematar** *v* conclude, finish up; finish off; sell off cheaply; auction; shoot (in sports) — **remate** *nm* shot (in sports); end

**remediar** *v* remedy, repair; solve (a

problem); avoid — **remedio** *nm* remedy, cure; solution; **sin ~** hopeless

**remesa** *nf* remittance; shipment (of merchandise)

**remisión** *nf* (**-siones**) remission

**remitir** *v* send, remit; subside, let up — **remite** *nm* return address — **remitente** *nmf* sender

**remolacha** *nf* beet

**remoto, -ta** *adj* remote

**remover** *v* stir; move around, turn over (as earth); bring up again; fire, dismiss

**remunerar** *v* remunerate

**renacer** *v* be reborn, revive — **renacimiento** *nm* rebirth, revival; **el Renacimiento** the Renaissance

**renacuajo** *nm* tadpole, pollywog

**rencor** *nm* rancor, hostility

**rendido, -da** *adj* submissive; exhausted

**rendir** *v* render, give; yield, produce; exhaust; make progress, go a long way — **rendimiento** *nm* performance; yield, return (as in finance)

**renglón** *nm* (**-glones**) line (of writing); line (of products)

**renovar** *v* renew, restore; renovate (as a building)

**rentar** *v* produce, yield; rent — **renta** *nf* income; rent; **impuesto sobre la renta** income tax — **rentable** *adj* profitable

**renunciar** *v* resign — **renuncia** *nf* renunciation; resignation

**reorganizar** *v* reorganize

**reparar** *v* repair, fix; make amends for

**repartir** *v* allocate; distribute; spread — **reparto** *nm* allocation; delivery; cast (of characters)

**repente** *nm* fit, outburst; **de ~** suddenly — **repentino, -na** *adj* sudden

**repercutir** *v* reverberate — **repercusión** *nf* (**-siones**) repercussion

**repertorio** *nm* repertoire

**repetir** *v* repeat; have a second helping of (food) — **repetirse** *vr* repeat oneself; recur (as an event)

**réplica** *nf* reply; replica, reproduction

**reponer** *v* replace; reply — **reponerse** *vr* recover

**reportar** *v* yield, bring; report — **reportaje** *nm* article, (news) report — **reporte** *nm* report — **reportero, -ra** *n* reporter

**reposar** *v* rest; stand, settle (as liquids, dough) — **reposado, -da** *adj* calm, relaxed — **reposición** *nf* (**-ciones**) replacement; rerun, repeat

**representar** *v* represent; perform (as a play); look, appear as — **representación** *nf* (**-ciones**) representation; performance — **representante** *nmf* representative; performer

**reprimir** *v* repress; suppress

**reproducir** *v* reproduce — **reproducirse** *vr* breed, reproduce; recur (as an event) — **reproducción** *nf* (**-ciones**) reproduction

**reptil** *nm* reptile

**república** *nf* republic

**repuesto** *nm* spare (auto) part

**reputación** *nf* (**-ciones**) reputation

**requerir** *v* require; summon, send for (a person)

**requisito** *nm* requirement

**res** *nf* beast, animal; **~** or **carne de ~** beef

**resaltar** *v* stand out; emphasize

**resbalar** *v* slip, slide; skid (of an automobile) — **resbaloso, -sa** *adj* slippery

**rescatar** *v* rescue, ransom; recover, get back — **rescate** *nm* rescue; ransom (money); recovery

**reseco, -ca** *adj* dry, dried-up

**reseñar** *v* review; describe — **reseña** *nf* review, report; description

**reservar** *v* reserve; keep, save — **reserva** *nf* reservation; reserve; **de reserva** spare, in reserve — **reservación** *nf* (**-ciones**) reservation — **reservado, -da** *adj* reserved; confidential (as of a document)

**resfriar** *v* cool — **resfriado** *nm* cold

**residencia** *nf* residence; ~ *or* ~ **universitaria** dormitory — **residencial** *adj* residential — **residente** *adj & nmf* resident — **residir** *v* reside, live

**residuo** *nm* residue; ~**s** *nmpl* waste

**resignación** *nf* (**-ciones**) resignation

**resistir** *v* stand, bear; withstand; resist — **resistencia** *nf* resistance; endurance, stamina — **resistente** *adj* resistant, strong, tough

**resma** *nf* ream

**resolver** *v* resolve; decide — **resolverse** *vr* make up one's mind — **resolución** *nf* (**-ciones**) resolution; decision; determination, resolve

**respaldar** *v* back, endorse — **respaldarse** *vr* lean back — **respaldo** *nm* back (as of a chair); support, backing

**respetar** *v* respect — **respeto** *nm* respect — **respetuoso, -sa** *adj* respectful

**respirar** *v* breathe — **respiración** *nf* (**-ciones**) respiration, breathing — **respiratorio, -ria** *adj* respiratory

**responder** *v* answer, reply; answer back

**responsable** *adj* responsible

**respuesta** *nf* answer, reply; response

**resta** *nf* subtraction

**restablecer** *v* reestablish, restore — **restablecerse** *vr* recover

**restar** *v* deduct, subtract; minimize; be left

**restaurante** *nm* restaurant

**restaurar** *v* restore

**resto** *nm* rest, remainder; ~**s** *nmpl* leftovers; ~**s** *or* ~**s mortales** mortal remains

**restringir** *v* restrict, limit — **restricción** *nf* (**-ciones**) restrictión, limitation

**resuelto, -ta** *adj* determined, resolved

**resultar** *v* succeed, work out; turn out (to be) — **resultado** *nm* result, outcome

**resumen** *nm* (**-súmenes**) summary; **en** ~ in short — **resumir** *v* summarize, sum up

**resurgir** *v* reappear, revive — **resurgimiento** *nm* resurgence

**retener** *v* retain, keep; withhold (as funds); detain — **retención** *nf* (**-ciones**) retention; deduction, withholding

**retina** *nf* retina

**retirar** *v* remove, take away; withdraw (as funds, statements) — **retirarse** *vr* retreat, withdraw; retire — **retiro** *nm* retreat; retirement; withdrawal

**reto** *nm* challenge, dare

**retórico, -ca** *adj* rhetorical

**retrasar** *v* delay, hold up; postpone; set back (a clock) — **retrasarse** *vr* be late; fall behind — **retrasado, -da** *adj* retarded; in arrears; backward; slow (of a clock) — **retraso** *nm* delay; backwardness; **retraso mental** mental retardation

**retratar** *v* portray; photograph; paint a portrait of — **retrato** *nm* portrayal; portrait; photograph

**retroactivo, -va** *adj* retroactive

**retroceder** *v* go back, turn back; back down — **retroceso** *nm* backward movement; backing down

**retrovisor** *nm* rearview mirror

**reumatismo** *nm* rheumatism

**reunir** *v* unite, join; have, possess; gather, collect — **reunirse** *vr* meet, gather — **reunión** *nf* (**-niones**) meeting; (social) gathering, reunion

**revelar** *v* reveal, disclose; develop (film) — **revelación** *nf* (**-ciones**) revelation — **revelador, -dora** *adj* revealing

**reventar** *v* burst, blow up

**reversa** *nf* reverse (gear)

**reverso** *nm* back, reverse

**revés** *nm* (**-veses**) back, wrong side; setback; slap; backhand (in sports); **al** ~ the other way around, upside down, inside out

**revisar** *v* examine, inspect; check over, overhaul (as machinery); revise —

**revisión** *nf* (**-siones**) revision; inspection, check

**revista** *nf* magazine, journal; revue (in theater); **pasar** ~ review, inspect

**revivir** *v* revive, come alive again; relive

**revocar** *v* revoke

**revolución** *nf* (**-ciones**) revolution — **revolucionario, -ria** *adj & n* revolutionary

**revolver** *v* mix, stir; upset (one's stomach); mess up — **revolverse** *vr* toss and turn; turn around

**revuelto, -ta** *adj* choppy, rough; messed up; **huevos revueltos** scrambled eggs

**rezar** *v* pray; say; recite

**ribera** *nf* bank, shore

**rico, -ca** *adj* rich, wealthy; abundant; rich, tasty — **rico, -ca** *n* rich person

**riesgo** *nm* risk

**rifa** *nf* raffle

**rígido, -da** *adj* rigid, stiff; harsh, strict

**rigor** *nm* rigor, harshness; precision — **riguroso, -sa** *adj* rigorous

**rima** *nf* rhyme; ~s *nfpl* verse, poetry

**rincón** *nm* (**-cones**) corner, nook

**rinoceronte** *nm* rhinoceros

**riña** *nf* fight, brawl; dispute, quarrel

**riñón** *nm* (**-ñones**) kidney

**río** *nm* river; torrent, stream

**riqueza** *nf* wealth; richness; ~s **naturales** natural resources

**risa** *nf* laughter, laugh; **morirse de la** ~ die laughing

**ritmo** *nm* rhythm; pace, speed — **rítmico, -ca** *adj* rhythmical

**rito** *nm* rite, ritual

**rival** *adj & nmf* rival — **rivalidad** *nf* rivalry, competition

**rizado, -da** *adj* curly; choppy (of water) — **rizo** *nm* curl; ripple (in water); loop (in aviation)

**róbalo** *nm* bass (fish)

**robar** *v* steal; burglarize; kidnap — **robo** *nm* robbery, theft

**roble** *nm* oak

**robot** *nm* (**-bots**) robot — **robótica** *nf* robotics

**robusto, -ta** *adj* robust, sturdy

**roca** *nf* rock, boulder

**rocoso, -sa** *adj* rocky

**rodar** *v* roll, roll down, roll along; turn, go around; travel (of a vehicle); shoot, film (as movies); break in (a vehicle) — **rodaje** *nm* filming, shooting; breaking in

**rodear** *v* surround, encircle; round up (cattle)

**rodilla** *nf* knee

**rodillo** *nm* roller; rolling pin

**rogar** *v* beg, request; pray

**rojo, -ja** *adj* red; **ponerse** ~ blush — **rojo** *nm* red

**rollo** *nm* roll, coil; boring speech, lecture

**romance** *nm* romance; Romance (language)

**romano, -na** *adj & n* Roman

**romántico, -ca** *adj* romantic — **romanticismo** *nm* romanticism

**rompecabezas** *nms & pl* puzzle(s)

**romper** *v* break; rip, tear; break off (relations), break (a contract)

**ron** *nm* rum

**roncar** *v* snore — **ronco, -ca** *adj* hoarse

**ronda** *nf* rounds, patrol; round (of drinks)

**ropa** *nf* clothes, clothing; ~ **interior** underwear — **ropero** *nm* wardrobe, closet

**rosa** *nf* rose (flower); ~ *nm* rose (color) — **rosa** *adj* rose-colored — **rosado, -da** *adj* pink — **rosado** *nm* pink (color)

**rosbif** *nm* roast beef

**rosca** *nf* thread (of a screw); ring, coil

**roseta** *nf* rosette

**rostro** *nm* face

**rotación** *nf* (**-ciones**) rotation — **rotativo, -va** *adj* rotary, revolving

**roto, -ta** *adj* broken, torn

**rótulo** *nm* heading, title; label, sign

**rozar** *v* graze, touch lightly; touch on, border on; rub against — **rozarse** *vr* rub, chafe

**rubio, -bia** *adj & n* blond

**rubor** *nm* flush, blush

**rúbrica** *nf* flourish (in writing); title, heading

**rudimentos** *nmpl* rudiments, basics — **rudimentario, -ria** *adj* rudimentary

**rueda** *nf* wheel; circle, ring; (round) slice; **ir sobre ～s** go smoothly

**ruido** *nm* noise

**ruina** *nf* ruin, destruction; collapse; **～s** *nfpl* ruins, remains

**rumano, -na** *adj* Romanian, Rumanian

**rumba** *nf* rumba

**rumbo** *nm* direction, course; lavishness

**rumor** *nm* rumor; murmur

**ruptura** *nf* break, rupture; breach (of a contract); breaking off (of relations)

**rural** *adj* rural

**ruso, -sa** *adj* Russian — **ruso** *nm* Russian (language)

**rústico, -ca** *adj* rural, rustic; **en rústica** in paperback

**ruta** *nf* route

**rutina** *nf* routine — **rutinario, -ria** *adj* routine

# S

**s** *nf* s, 20th letter of the Spanish alphabet

**sábado** *nm* Saturday

**sábana** *nf* sheet

**saber** *v* know; know how to, be able to; learn, find out; taste — **saber** *nm* knowledge — **sabiduría** *nf* wisdom — **sabio, -bia** *adj* learned; wise, sensible

**sabor** *nm* flavor, taste — **saborear** *v* savor

**sabroso, -sa** *adj* delicious, tasty

**sacacorchos** *nms & pl* corkscrew(s)

**sacapuntas** *nms & pl* pencil sharpener(s)

**sacar** *v* take out; get, obtain; extract, withdraw; take (photos), make (copies); remove

**sacerdote, -tisa** *n* priest; priestess

**saco** *nm* bag, sack; jacket

**sacrificar** *v* sacrifice — **sacrificarse** *vr* sacrifice oneself — **sacrificio** *nm* sacrifice

**sacudir** *v* shake; beat — **sacudirse** *vr* shake off

**sagrado, -da** *adj* sacred, holy

**sal** *nf* salt

**sala** *nf* room, hall; living room

**salar** *v* salt — **salado, -da** *adj* salty; witty

**salario** *nm* salary, wage

**salchicha** *nf* sausage — **salchichón** *nf* (**-chones**) salami-like cold cut

**saldo** *nm* balance (of an account); **～s** *nmpl* remainders, sale items — **saldar** *v* settle, pay off; sell off

**salero** *nm* saltshaker

**salir** *v* go out, come out; leave; appear; turn out; rise (of the sun); **～ con** date — **salirse** *vr* leave; leak out, escape; come off — **salida** *nf* exit; (action of) leaving, departure; **salida de emergencia** emergency exit

**saliva** *nf* saliva

**salmón** *nm* (**-mones**) salmon

**salón** *nm* (**-lones**) lounge, sitting room; **～ de belleza** beauty salon; **～ de clase** classroom

**salpicar** *v* splash, spatter

**salsa** *nf* sauce; salsa (music)

**saltamontes** *nms & pl* grasshopper(s)

**saltar** *v* jump, leap; bounce; jump (over)

**salto** *nm* jump, leap

**salud** *nf* health — **¡salud!** *interj* here's to your health!; bless you! (when someone sneezes) — **saludable** *adj* healthy

**saludar** *v* greet, say hello to — **saludo**

*nm* greeting; (military) salute; **saludos** best wishes, regards

**salvación** *nf* (**-ciones**) salvation

**salvadoreño, -ña** *adj* (El) Salvadoran

**salvaje** *adj* wild; savage, primitive — **salvaje** *nmf* savage

**salvar** *v* save, rescue — **salvarse** *vr* save oneself — **salvavidas** *nms & pl* life preserver(s)

**salvo, -va** *adj* safe

**samba** *nf* samba

**sanar** *v* heal, cure; recover

**sanción** *nf* (**-ciones**) sanction — **sancionar** *v* sanction

**sandalia** *nf* sandal

**sandía** *nf* watermelon

**sandwich** *nm* (**-wiches**) sandwich

**sangrar** *v* bleed — **sangre** *nf* blood — **sangriento, -ta** *adj* bloody — **sanguíneo, -nea** *adj* blood

**sano, -na** *adj* healthy — **sanitario** toilet

**santo, -ta** *adj* holy; **Santo, Santa** Saint (as in a name) — **santo, -ta** *n* saint

**sapo** *nm* toad

**sarampión** *nm* measles

**sardina** *nf* sardine

**sargento** *nmf* sergeant

**sartén** *nmf* (**-tenes**) frying pan

**sastre, -tra** *n* tailor — **sastrería** *nf* tailoring; tailor's shop

**satélite** *nm* satellite

**satisfacer** *v* satisfy; fulfill, meet; pay — **satisfacerse** *vr* be satisfied — **satisfacción** *nf* (**-ciones**) satisfaction — **satisfactorio, -ria** *adj* satisfactory — **satisfecho, -cha** *adj* satisfied

**Saturno** *nm* Saturn

**sauce** *nm* willow

**sauna** *nmf* sauna

**sazón** *nf* (**-zones**) seasoning — **sazonar** *v* season

**se** *pron* himself, herself, itself, oneself; yourself, yourselves, themselves; (to) him, (to) her, (to) you, (to) them; each other, one another

**secar** *v* dry — **secarse** *vr* dry (up) —

**secador** *nm* hair dryer — **secadora** *nf* (clothes) dryer

**sección** *nf* (**-ciones**) section

**seco, -ca** *adj* dry; dried (as of fruits)

**secretario, -ria** *n* secretary — **secretaría** *nf* secretariat

**secreto, -ta** *adj* secret — **secreto** *nm* secret; **en secreto** in confidence

**sector** *nm* sector

**secuencia** *nf* sequence

**secuestrar** *v* kidnap — **secuestrador, -dora** *n* kidnapper — **secuestro** *nm* kidnapping

**secundario, -ria** *adj* secondary

**sed** *nf* thirst

**seda** *nf* silk

**sedante** *adj & nm* sedative

**sede** *nf* seat, headquarters

**sedentario, -ria** *adj* sedentary

**sediento, -ta** *adj* thirsty

**sedoso, -sa** *adj* silky, silken

**seducir** *v* seduce; captivate, charm — **seducción** *nf* (**-ciones**) seduction — **seductor, -tora** *adj* seductive; charming — **seductor, -tora** *n* seducer

**seglar** *adj* lay, secular — **seglar** *nm* layperson; layman; laywoman

**segmento** *nm* segment

**seguir** *v* follow; go on, continue — **seguido** *adv* straight (ahead) — **en seguida** *adv phr* right away

**según** *prep* according to — **según** *adv* it depends — **según** *conj* as, just as

**segundo, -da** *adj* second — **segundo, -da** *n* second (one) — **segundo** *nm* second (of time)

**seguro, -ra** *adj* safe; secure; sure, certain; reliable — **seguramente** *adv* for sure, surely — **seguridad** *nf* safety; security; certainty; confidence — **seguro** *adv* certainly — **seguro** *nm* insurance; safety (device)

**seis** *adj & nm* six — **seiscientos, -tas** *adj* six hundred — **seiscientos** *nms & pl* six hundred

**selección** *nf* (**-ciones**) selection — **seleccionar** *v* select, choose

**sellar** *v* seal; stamp — **sello** *nm* seal; stamp

**selva** *nf* jungle; forest

**semáforo** *nm* traffic light

**semana** *nf* week — **semanal** *adj* weekly

**semántica** *nf* semantics

**sembrar** *v* sow

**semejar** *v* resemble — **semejarse** *vr* look alike — **semejante** *adj* similar — **semejanza** *nf* similarity

**semen** *nm* semen

**semestre** *nm* semester

**semifinal** *nf* semifinal

**semilla** *nf* seed

**seminario** *nm* seminary; seminar, course

**senado** *nm* senate — **senador, -dora** *n* senator

**sencillo, -lla** *adj* simple; single — **sencillez** *nf* simplicity

**seno** *nm* breast, bosom

**sensación** *nf* (**-ciones**) feeling, sensation — **sensacional** *adj* sensational

**sensato, -ta** *adj* sensible

**sensible** *adj* sensitive — **sensibilidad** *nf* sensitivity

**sensual** *adj* sensual, sensuous

**sentar** *v* seat, sit — **sentarse** *vr* sit (down)

**sentido** *nm* sense

**sentimiento** *nm* feeling, emotion — **sentimental** *adj* sentimental

**sentir** *v* feel; be sorry for — **sentirse** *vr* feel

**seña** *nf* sign

**señal** *nf* signal; sign — **señalar** *v* indicate, point out; mark; fix, set

**señor, -ñora** *n* gentleman, man; lady, woman; Sir; Madam; Mr.; Mrs.; **señora** wife — **señorita** *nf* young lady, young woman; Miss

**separar** *v* separate; move away — **separarse** *vr* separate — **separación** *nf* (**-ciones**) separation — **separado, -da** *adj* separate

**septiembre** *nm* September

**séptimo, -ma** *adj* seventh — **séptimo, -ma** *n* seventh

**sepultar** *v* bury

**sequedad** *nf* dryness

**ser** *v* be; **a no ~ que** unless; **~ de** belong to; **~ de** come from; **son las diez** it's ten o'clock — **ser** *nm* being; **ser humano** human being

**serbio, -bia** *adj* Serb, Serbian

**serenar** *v* calm — **serenarse** *vr* calm down — **serenata** *nf* serenade — **serenidad** *nf* serenity — **sereno, -na** *adj* serene, calm

**serie** *nf* series

**serio, -ria** *adj* serious; reliable; **en serio** seriously — **seriedad** *nf* seriousness

**sermón** *nm* (**-mones**) sermon

**serpiente** *nf* serpent, snake

**serrucho** *nm* saw, handsaw

**servicio** *nm* service; **los ~s** *nmpl* restroom — **servicial** *adj* obliging, helpful

**servilleta** *nf* napkin

**servir** *v* serve; work, function; be of use

**sesenta** *adj & nm* sixty

**sesión** *nf* (**-siones**) session; showing (of a film), performance (of a play)

**setecientos, -tas** *adj* seven hundred — **setecientos** *nms & pl* seven hundred

**setenta** *adj & nm* seventy

**seudónimo** *nm* pseudonym

**severo, -ra** *adj* harsh, severe; strict

**sexo** *nm* sex — **sexismo** *nm* sexism — **sexista** *adj & nmf* sexist

**sexto, -ta** *adj & n* sixth

**sexual** *adj* sexual — **sexualidad** *nf* sexuality

**si** *conj* if; whether

**sí**[1] *adv* yes — **sí** *nm* consent

**sí**[2] *reflexive pron* **de por ~** *or* **en ~** by itself, in itself, per se; **para ~ (mismo)** to himself, to herself, for himself, for herself

**SIDA** *or* **sida** *nm* AIDS

**sidra** *nf* (hard) cider

**siembra** *nf* sowing

**siempre** *adv* always

**sien** *nf* temple

**sierra** *nf* saw; mountain range

**siervo, -va** *n* slave

**siesta** *nf* nap, siesta

**siete** *adj & nm* seven

**sigla** *nf* acronym, abbreviation

**siglo** *nm* century

**significar** *v* mean, signify; express — **significado, -da** *adj* well-known — **significado** *nm* meaning

**signo** *nm* sign; ~ **de admiración** exclamation point; ~ **de interrogación** question mark

**siguiente** *adj* next, following

**sílaba** *nf* syllable

**silbar** *v* whistle — **silbido** *nm* whistle, whistling

**silencio** *nm* silence — **silencioso, -sa** *adj* silent, quiet

**silla** *nf* chair; ~ *or* ~ **de montar** saddle; ~ **de ruedas** wheelchair — **sillón** *nm* (-llones) armchair, easy chair

**símbolo** *nm* symbol — **simbólico, -ca** *adj* symbolic

**similar** *adj* similar, alike

**simio** *nm* ape

**simpatía** *nf* liking, affection; friendliness — **simpático, -ca** *adj* nice, likeable; pleasant, kind — **simpatizar** *v* get along, hit it off

**simple** *adj* simple — **simplificar** *v* simplify

**simular** *v* simulate

**simultáneo, -nea** *adj* simultaneous

**sin** *prep* without

**sincero, -ra** *adj* sincere — **sinceramente** *adv* sincerely — **sinceridad** *nf* sincerity

**sindicato** *nm* (labor) union

**sinfonía** *nf* symphony

**singular** *adj* exceptional, outstanding; peculiar; singular (in grammar) — **singular** *nm* singular (one)

**sino** *conj* but, rather; except, save

**sinónimo, -ma** *adj* synonymous — **sinónimo** *nm* synonym

**sintaxis** *nfs & pl* syntax(es)

**síntesis** *nfs & pl* synthesis (-theses)

**síntoma** *nm* symptom

**sintonía** *nf* tuning in (of a radio) — **sintonizar** *v* tune (in) to

**sinvergüenza** *nmf* scoundrel

**siquiera** *adv* at least; **ni** ~ not even — **siquiera** *conj* even if

**sirena** *nf* siren

**sirio, -ria** *adj* Syrian

**sistema** *nm* system

**sitio** *nm* place, site; room, space

**situar** *v* situate, place — **situarse** *vr* be located — **situación** *nf* (-ciones) situation, position

**smoking** *nm* tuxedo

**soberbia** *nf* pride, arrogance

**sobornar** *v* bribe — **soborno** *nm* bribe

**sobrar** *v* be more than enough; be left over — **sobrado, -da** *adj* more than enough

**sobre**[1] *nm* envelope

**sobre**[2] *prep* on, on top of; over, above; about; ~ **todo** especially, above all

**sobredosis** *nfs & pl* overdose(s)

**sobregiro** *nm* overdraft

**sobremesa** *nf* **de** ~ after-dinner

**sobrepasar** *v* exceed

**sobresalir** *v* protrude; stand out — **sobresaliente** *adj* outstanding

**sobretodo** *nm* overcoat

**sobrevivir** *v* survive; outlive

**sobriedad** *nf* sobriety; restraint

**sobrino, -na** *n* nephew, niece

**sobrio , -bria** *adj* sober

**social** *adj* social — **socialismo** *nm* socialism — **socialista** *adj & nmf* socialist

**sociedad** *nf* society; company; ~ **anónima** incorporated company

**socio, -cia** *n* partner; member — **socio- logía** *nf* sociology

**soda** *nf* soda (water)

**sodio** *nf* sodium

**sofá** *nm* couch, sofa

**sofocar** *v* suffocate, smother; put out (a fire), stifle (as a rebellion)

**sol** *nm* sun

**solamente** *adv* only, just

**solapa** *nf* lapel (of a jacket); flap (of an envelope)

**soldado** *nm* soldier

**soleado, -da** *adj* sunny

**soledad** *nf* loneliness, solitude

**solicitar** *v* request, solicit; apply for (as a job) — **solicitud** *nf* concern; request; application

**solidaridad** *nf* solidarity

**sólido, -da** *adj* solid; sound (as of an argument)

**solista** *nmf* soloist

**solitario, -ria** *adj* solitary; lonely, deserted — **solitario, -ria** *n* recluse

**solo, -la** *adj* alone; lonely — **solo** *nm* solo

**sólo** *adv* just, only

**soltar** *v* release; let go of, drop; unfasten, undo — **soltarse** *vr* break free; come undone

**soltero, -ra** *adj* single, unmarried — **soltero, -ra** *n* bachelor, single woman

**soltura** *nf* looseness; fluency (in language); agility, ease

**solución** *nf* (-ciones) solution — **solucionar** *v* solve, resolve

**sombra** *nf* shadow; shade; ∼s *nfpl* darkness, shadows

**sombrero** *nm* hat

**sombrilla** *nf* parasol, umbrella

**someter** *v* subjugate; subordinate; subject (as to treatment); submit, present — **someterse** *vr* submit, yield

**somnífero** *nm* sleeping pill

**sonajero** *nm* (baby's) rattle

**sonar** *v* sound; ring (as a bell); look or sound familiar

**sondeo** *nm* sounding, probing; survey, poll

**sonido** *nm* sound

**sonoro, -ra** *adj* resonant, sonorous; loud

**sonreír** *v* smile

**soñar** *v* dream — **soñador, -dora** *adj* dreamy — **soñador, -dora** *n* dreamer

**sopa** *nf* soup

**soplar** *v* blow; blow out, blow off, blow up — **soplo** *nm* puff, gust

**soportar** *v* support; bear

**sorber** *v* sip; absorb; suck up — **sorbete** *nm* sherbet — **sorbo** *nm* sip, swallow

**sordera** *nf* deafness

**sordo, -da** *adj* deaf; muted (of a sound) — **sordomudo, -da** *n* deaf-mute

**sorprender** *v* surprise — **sorprendente** *adj* surprising — **sorpresa** *nf* surprise

**sortear** *v* raffle off, draw lots for; dodge

**sortija** *nf* ring; ringlet (of hair)

**sospechoso, -sa** *adj* suspicious — **sospechoso, -sa** *n* suspect

**sostener** *v* support; hold; sustain, maintain — **sostenerse** *vr* stand (up); remain; support oneself — **sostén** *nm* (-tenes) support; sustenance; brassiere, bra — **sostenido, -da** *adj* sustained; sharp (in music)

**soya** *nf* soy

**Sr.** *nm* Mr. — **Sra.** *nf* Mrs., Ms. — **Srta.** or **Srita.** *nf* Miss, Ms.

**su** *adj* his, her, its, their, one's; your

**suave** *adj* soft; smooth; gentle, mild

**subasta** *nf* auction

**subcampeón, -peona** *n* (-peones *m*) runner-up

**subcomité** *nm* subcommittee

**subconsciente** *adj* & *nm* subconscious

**subdesarrollado, -da** *adj* underdeveloped

**subdirector, -tora** *n* assistant manager

**subir** *v* climb, go up; bring up, take up; raise; come up; ∼ **a** get in (a car), get on (a bus, etc.) — **subida** *nf* ascent, climb; rise; slope — **subido, -da** *adj* bright, strong

**subjetivo, -va** *adj* subjective

**subjuntivo** *nm* subjunctive (case)

**sublevar** *v* stir up, incite to rebellion

**submarino, -na** *adj* underwater — **submarino** *nm* submarine

**subrayar** *v* underline; emphasize, stress

**subsanar** *v* rectify, correct; make up for (a deficiency), overcome (an obstacle)

**subsidio** *nm* subsidy, benefit

**subsistir** *v* live, subsist; survive

**subterráneo, -nea** *adj* underground, subterranean — **subterráneo** *nm* underground passage

**subtítulo** *nm* subtitle

**subversivo, -va** *adj & n* subversive

**subyacente** *adj* underlying

**suceder** *v* happen, occur — **suceso** *nm* event; incident

**sucio, -cia** *adj* dirty, filthy

**sucursal** *nf* branch (of a business)

**sudadera** *nf* sweatshirt

**sudafricano, -na** *adj* South African

**sudamericano, -na** *adj* South American

**sudar** *v* sweat

**sudeste** *adj* southeast, southeastern; southeasterly (as of wind) — **sudeste** *nm* southeast, Southeast

**sudoeste** *adj* southwest, southwestern; southwesterly (as of wind) — **sudoeste** *nm* southwest, Southwest

**sudor** *nm* sweat

**sueco, -ca** *adj* Swedish — **sueco** *nm* Swedish (language)

**suegro, -gra** *n* father-in-law, mother-in-law; **suegros** *nmpl* in-laws

**suela** *nf* sole (of a shoe)

**sueldo** *nm* salary, wage

**suelo** *nm* ground; floor (in a house); soil, land

**suelto, -ta** *adj* loose, free

**sueño** *nm* dream

**suerte** *nf* luck, fortune; chance; fate

**suéter** *nm* sweater

**suficiente** *adj* enough, sufficient; smug

**sufijo** *nm* suffix

**sufragio** *nm* suffrage, vote

**sufrir** *v* suffer; bear, stand — **sufrido, -da** *adj* long-suffering — **sufrimiento** *nm* suffering

**sugerir** *v* suggest — **sugerencia** *nf* suggestion — **sugestivo, -va** *adj* suggestive; interesting, stimulating

**suicidio** *nm* suicide — **suicida** *adj* suicidal — **suicida** *nmf* suicide (victim) — **suicidarse** *vr* commit suicide

**suite** *nf* suite

**suizo, -za** *adj* Swiss

**sujetar** *v* hold (on to); fasten; subdue — **sujeto, -ta** *adj* fastened — **sujeto** *nm* individual; subject (in grammar)

**suma** *nf* sum, total; addition — **sumar** *v* add (up); add up to, total

**sumario** *nm* summary; indictment (in law)

**sumergir** *v* submerge, plunge

**suministrar** *v* supply, provide — **suministro** *n.n* supply, provision

**superar** *v* surpass, outdo; overcome — **superarse** *vr* improve oneself

**superficie** *nf* surface; area — **superficial** *adj* superficial

**superior** *adj* superior; upper (floor) — **superior** *nm* superior (one)

**superlativo, -va** *adj* superlative — **superlativo** *nm* superlative

**supermercado** *nm* supermarket

**supervivencia** *nf* survival — **superviviente** *adj* surviving — **superviviente** *nmf* survivor

**suplente** *adj & nmf* substitute

**suponer** *v* suppose, assume; mean; involve, entail

**supositorio** *nm* suppository

**suprimir** *v* suppress, eliminate; delete

**supuesto, -ta** *adj* supposed, alleged; **por supuesto** of course — **supuesto** *nm* assumption

**sur** *nm* south, South; south wind

**sureño, -ña** *adj* southern, Southern — **sureño, -ña** *n* Southerner

**surf** *or* **surfing** *nm* surfing

**surgir** *v* arise; appear — **surgimiento** *nm* rise, emergence

**surtir** *v* supply, provide — **surtido, -da** *adj* assorted, varied; stocked (with merchandise)

**susceptible** *adj* susceptible, sensitive

**suscribir** *v* sign; endorse — **suscribirse a** *vr phr* subscribe to — **suscripción** *nf* (**-ciones**) subscription

**suspender** *v* suspend; hang; fail (as an exam)

**suspirar** *v* sigh

**sustancia** *nf* substance

**sustantivo** *nm* noun

**sustentar** *v* support; sustain, nourish; maintain — **sustentación** *nf* (**-ciones**) support

**susto** *nm* fright, scare

**sustraer** *v* remove, take away; subtract — **sustracción** *nf* (**-ciones**) subtraction

**susurrar** *v* whisper; murmur (of water); rustle (of leaves)

**sutil** *adj* delicate, fine; subtle (of fragrances, differences, etc.)

**suyo, -ya** *adj* his, her, its, one's, theirs; yours — **suyo, -ya** *pron* his, hers, its (own), one's own, theirs; yours

**switch** *nm* switch

# T

**t** *nf* t, 21st letter of the Spanish alphabet

**tabaco** *nm* tobacco

**tabique** *nm* thin wall, partition

**tabla** *nf* board, plank; table, list — **tablero** *nm* bulletin board; (game) board; blackboard

**tableta** *nf* tablet, pill

**tabú** *adj* taboo — **tabú** *nm* (**-búes** or **-bús**) taboo

**tacaño, -na** *adj* stingy, miserly

**tachar** *v* cross out, delete; ~ **de** accuse of, label as

**tachón** *nm* (**-chones**) stud, hobnail

**tácito, -ta** *adj* tacit

**tacón** *nm* (**-cones**) heel (of a shoe)

**táctica** *nf* tactic, tactics

**tacto** *nm* (sense of) touch, feel; tact

**tailandés, -desa** *adj* Thai

**tajar** *v* cut, slice — **tajada** *nf* slice

**tal** *adj* such, such a; ~ **vez** maybe, perhaps — **tal** *adv* so, in such a way — **tal** *pron* such a one, such a thing

**taladrar** *v* drill — **taladro** *nm* drill

**talco** *nm* talcum powder

**talla** *nf* size (in clothing)

**tallarín** *nf* (**-rines**) noodle

**taller** *nm* workshop; studio (of an artist)

**tallo** *nm* stalk, stem

**talón** *nm* (**-lones**) heel (of the foot)

**tamaño, -ña** *adj* such a, such a big — **tamaño** *nm* size

**también** *adv* too, as well, also

**tambor** *nm* drum

**tampoco** *adv* neither, not either

**tampón** *nm* (**-pones**) tampon

**tan** *adv* so, so very

**tanque** *nm* tank

**tanto** *adv* so much; so long — **tanto** *nm* certain amount — **tanto, -ta** *adj* so much, so many; as much, as many — **tanto, -ta** *pron* so much, so many

**tapa** *nf* cover, top, lid; snack

**tapar** *v* cover, put a lid on

**tapete** *nm* small rug, mat; cover (for a table)

**tapón** *nm* (**-pones**) cork; (bottle) cap

**taquilla** *nf* box office

**tardar** *v* take a long time, be late — **tarde** *adv* late — **tarde** *nf* afternoon, evening; ¡**buenas** ~**s!** good afternoon!, good evening!

**tarea** *nf* task, job; (school) homework

**tarifa** *nf* fare, rate; price list

**tarjeta** *nf* card; ~ **de crédito** credit card; ~ **postal** póstcard

**tarro** *nm* jar, pot

**tasa** *nf* rate; tax

**taxi** *nm* (**taxis**) taxi, taxicab — **taxista** *nmf* taxi driver

**taza** *nf* cup; (toilet) bowl

**te** *pron* you; for you, to you, from you; yourself, for yourself, to yourself, from yourself

**té** *nm* tea

**teatro** *nm* theater

**techo** *nm* roof; ceiling

**tecla** *nf* key (of a musical instrument or a machine)

**técnica** *nf* technique, skill; technology — **técnico, -ca** *adj* technical — **técnico, -ca** *n* technician

**tecnología** *nf* technology

**teja** *nf* tile — **tejado** *nm* roof

**tejer** *v* knit, crochet

**tejido** *nm* fabric, cloth; tissue (of the body)

**tela** *nf* fabric, material — **telar** *nm* loom — **telaraña** *nf* spiderweb, cobweb

**telefonear** *v* telephone, call — **telefónico, -ca** *adj* telephone — **telefonista** *nmf* telephone operator — **teléfono** *nm* telephone; **teléfono celular** *m* cell phone, cellular phone

**telenovela** *nf* soap opera

**telescopio** *nm* telescope

**televidente** *nmf* (television) viewer

**televisión** *nf* (**-siones**) television, TV — **televisar** *v* televise — **televisor** *nm* television set

**tema** *nm* theme

**temblar** *v* tremble, shiver; shake (as of a building, the ground) — **temblor** *nm* shaking, trembling — **tembloroso, -sa** *adj* trembling, shaky

**temer** *v* fear, dread; be afraid — **temeroso, -sa** *adj* fearful — **temor** *nm* fear, dread

**temperamento** *nm* temperament

**temperatura** *nf* temperature

**tempestad** *nf* storm

**templo** *nm* temple, synagogue

**temporada** *nf* season, time; period, spel — **temporal** *adj* temporal; temporary — **temporal** *nm* storm

**temprano, -na** *adj* early — **temprano** *adv* early

**tenaz** *adj* (**-naces**) tenacious — **tenaza** *nf or* **tenazas** *nfpl* pliers

**tendencia** *nf* tendency, trend

**tender** *v* spread out, stretch out; ~ a have a tendency towards

**tendón** *nm* (**-dones**) tendon

**tenebroso, -sa** *adj* gloomy, dark; sinister

**tenedor** *nm* table fork

**tener** *v* have, possess; hold; take; ~ ... años> be ... years old; ~ **frío (hambre,** *etc.*) be cold (hungry, etc.) — **tenerse** *vr* stand up

**teniente** *nmf* lieutenant

**tenis** *nms & pl* tennis; ~ *nmpl* sneakers — **tenista** *nmf* tennis player

**tensión** *nf* (**-siones**) tension; ~ **arterial** blood pressure — **tenso, -sa** *adj* tense

**tentación** *nf* (**-ciones**) temptation

**teoría** *nf* theory — **teórico, -ca** *adj* theoretical

**terapia** *nf* therapy — **terapeuta** *nmf* therapist — **terapéutico, -ca** *adj* therapeutic

**tercermundista** *adj* third-world

**tercero, -ra** *adj* third; **el Tercer Mundo** the Third World — **tercero, -ra** *n* third (in a series)

**terco, -ca** *adj* obstinate, stubborn

**terminar** *v* conclude, finish; come to an end — **terminarse** *vr* run out; come to an end — **terminación** *nf* (**-ciones**) termination, conclusion — **terminal** *adj* terminal, final — **terminal** *nf* terminal, station — **término** *nm* end; period, term — **terminología** *nf* terminology

**termómetro** *nm* thermometer

**ternero, -ra** *n* calf (animal) — **ternera** *nf* veal

**ternura** *nf* tenderness

**terquedad** *nf* obstinacy, stubbornness

**terraza** *nf* terrace; balcony

**terremoto** *nm* earthquake

**terreno** *nm* terrain; earth, ground; plot, tract of land — **terreno, -na** *adj* earthly — **terrestre** *adj* terrestrial

**terrible** *adj* terrible

**territorio** *nm* territory — **territorial** *adj* territorial

**terrón** *nm* (**-rones**) lump

**terror** *nm* terror — **terrorismo** *nm* terrorism — **terrorista** *adj* & *nmf* terrorist

**terso, -sa** *adj* smooth; polished, flowing (of a style) — **tersura** *nf* smoothness

**tertulia** *nf* gathering, group

**tesis** *nfs* & *pl* thesis (theses)

**tesoro** *nm* treasure — **tesorero, -ra** *n* treasurer

**testamento** *nm* testament, will

**testículo** *nm* testicle

**testificar** *v* testify — **testigo** *nmf* witness — **testimoniar** *v* testify — **testimonio** *nm* testimony

**tetera** *nf* teapot

**tetilla** *nf* teat, nipple (of a man)

**textil** *adj* & *nm* textile

**texto** *nm* text — **textual** *adj* textual; literal, exact

**textura** *nf* texture

**tez** *nf* (**teces**) complexion

**ti** *pron* you; ~ **mismo,** ~ **misma** yourself

**tibio, -bia** *adj* lukewarm

**tiburón** *nm* (**-rones**) shark

**tic** *nm* tic

**tiempo** *nm* time; age, period; weather; halftime (in sports); tense (in grammar)

**tienda** *nf* store, shop

**tierno, -na** *adj* tender, fresh, young; affectionate

**tierra** *nf* land; ground, earth; **la Tierra** the Earth; **por** ~ overland

**tieso, -sa** *adj* stiff, rigid

**tigre, -gresa** *n* tiger, tigress

**tijera** *nf or* **tijeras** *nfpl* scissors

**tilde** *nf* tilde; accent mark

**timbre** *nm* bell

**tímido, -da** *adj* timid, shy — **timidez** *nf* timidity, shyness

**timón** *nm* (**-mones**) rudder

**tímpano** *nm* eardrum

**tina** *nf* bathtub

**tinieblas** *nfpl* darkness

**tinta** *nf* ink

**tinto, -ta** *adj* red (of wine)

**tintura** *nf* dye, tint

**tío, tía** *n* uncle, aunt

**tiovivo** *nm* merry-go-round

**típico, -ca** *adj* typical

**tiple** *nm* soprano

**tipo** *nm* type, kind; figure (of a woman), build (of a man) — **tipo, -pa** *n* guy, gal

**tique** *or* **tíquet** *nm* ticket

**tira** *nf* strip, strap

**tirante** *adj* brace, strut; ~**s** *nmpl* suspenders

**tirar** *v* throw; throw away; pull

**tiritar** *v* shiver

**tiro** *nm* shot, gunshot; shot, kick (in sports)

**tiroides** *nmf* thyroid (gland)

**tirón** *nm* (**-rones**) pull, yank

**tirotear** *v* shoot at — **tiroteo** *nm* shooting

**títere** *nm* puppet

**titubear** *v* hesitate

**titular¹** *v* title, call — **titularse** *vr* be called, be titled; receive a degree

**titular²** *adj* titular, official — **titular** *nm* headline; ~ *nmf* holder, incumbent — **título** *nm* title; degree, qualification (in education)

**tiza** *nf* chalk

**toalla** *nf* towel — **toallero** *nm* towel rack

**tobillo** *nm* ankle

**tobogán** *nm* (**-ganes**) toboggan, sled; slide (as on a playground)

**tocador** *nm* dressing table

**tocar** *v* touch, feel; touch on, refer to;

play (a musical instrument); knock, ring

**tocino** *nm* bacon; salt pork — **tocineta** *nf* bacon

**todavía** *adv* still; even; ~ **no** not yet

**todo, -da** *adj* all; every, each; **a toda velocidad** at top speed; **todo el mundo** everyone, everybody — **todo, -da** *pron* everything, all; **todos, -das** *pl* everybody, everyone, all — **todo** *nm* whole

**tolerar** *v* tolerate — **tolerancia** *nf* tolerance — **tolerante** *adj* tolerant

**toma** *nf* inlet; outlet; ~ **de corriente** (electrical) wall outlet

**tomar** *v* take; have (food or drink); drink (alcohol); ~ **el sol** sunbathe

**tomate** *nm* tomato

**tomillo** *nm* thyme

**tomo** *nm* volume

**tonel** *nm* barrel, cask

**tonelada** *nf* ton

**tono** *nm* tone; shade (of colors)

**tontería** *nf* silly thing or remark; foolishness — **tonto, -ta** *adj* stupid, silly — **tonto, -ta** *n* fool, idiot

**tópico** *nm* cliché

**topo** *nm* mole (animal)

**torbellino** *nm* whirlwind

**torcer** *v* turn; twist, bend; turn (a corner); wring (out) — **torcerse** *vr* twist, sprain; go wrong; go astray — **torcedura** *nf* twisting; sprain — **torcido, -da** *adj* twisted, crooked

**torear** *v* fight (bulls); dodge, sidestep — **toreo** *nm* bullfighting — **torero, -ra** *n* bullfighter

**tormenta** *nf* storm — **tormento** *nm* torture; torment, anguish — **tormentoso, -sa** *adj* stormy

**tornado** *nm* tornado

**torneo** *nm* tournament

**tornillo** *nm* screw

**torno** *nm* winch, turning device; **en** ~ **a** around, about

**toro** *nm* bull; ~**s** *nmpl* bullfight

**toronja** *nf* grapefruit

**torpe** *adj* clumsy, awkward; stupid, dull

**torpeza** *nf* clumsiness, awkwardness; slowness, stupidity

**torre** *nf* tower; turret (on a ship); rook, castle (in chess)

**torrente** *nm* torrent; ~ **sanguíneo** bloodstream — **torrencial** *adj* torrential

**torsión** *nf* (**-siones**) twisting

**torta** *nf* torte, cake

**tortícolis** *nfs & pl* stiff neck(s)

**tortilla** *nf* tortilla

**tortuga** *nf* turtle, tortoise; ~ **de agua dulce** terrapin

**tortura** *nf* torture — **torturar** *v* torture

**tosco, -ca** *adj* rough, coarse

**toser** *v* cough — **tos** *nf* cough

**tostar** *v* toast — **tostada** *nf* piece of toast; tostada — **tostador** *nm* toaster

**total** *adj & nm* total — **total** *adv* so, after all — **totalidad** *nf* whole — **totalizar** *v* total, add up to

**tóxico, -ca** *adj* toxic, poisonous — **tóxico** *nm* poison

**trabajar** *v* work; work on, work at; act, perform (as in theater) — **trabajador, -dora** *adj* hard-working — **trabajador, -dora** *n* worker — **trabajo** *nm* work; job; task; effort; **costar trabajo** be difficult; **trabajo en equipo** teamwork; **trabajos** *nmpl* hardships, difficulties — **trabajoso, -sa** *adj* hard, laborious

**trabalenguas** *nms & pl* tongue twister

**trabar** *v* join, connect; impede

**tracción** *nf* traction

**tractor** *nm* tractor

**tradición** *nf* (**-ciones**) tradition — **tradicional** *adj* traditional

**traducir** *v* translate — **traducción** *nf* (**-ciones**) translation — **traductor, -tora** *n* translator

**traer** *v* bring; cause, bring about; carry, have — **traerse** *vr* bring along

**traficar** *v* trade, deal; ~ **en** traffic in — **traficante** *nmf* dealer, trafficker —

**tráfico** *nm* trade (of merchandise); traffic (of vehicles)

**tragar** *v* swallow

**tragedia** *nf* tragedy — **trágico, -ca** *adj* tragic

**trago** *nm* swallow, swig; drink, liquor; ~ *nmf* glutton

**traicionar** *v* betray — **traición** *nf* (**-ciones**) betrayal; treason (in law) — **traidor, -dora** *adj* traitorous, treacherous — **traidor, -dora** *n* traitor

**traje** *nm* dress, costume; (man's) suit; ~ **de baño** bathing suit

**trajinar** *v* rush around — **trajín** *nm* (**-jines**) hustle and bustle

**trama** *nf* plot

**tramitar** *v* negotiate — **trámite** *nm* procedure, step

**tramo** *nm* stretch, section

**trampa** *nf* trap; **hacer** ~**s** cheat

**trampolín** *nm* (**-lines**) diving board; trampoline

**tramposo, -sa** *adj* crooked, cheating — **tramposo, -sa** *n* cheat, swindler

**tranquilo, -la** *adj* calm, tranquil — **tranquilidad** *nf* tranquility, peace — **tranquilizante** *nm* tranquilizer — **tranquilizar** *v* calm, soothe — **tranquilizarse** *vr* calm down

**transacción** *nf* (**-ciones**) transaction

**transatlántico, -ca** *adj* transatlantic — **transatlántico** *nm* ocean liner

**transbordo** *nm* transfer; **hacer** ~ change (as trains)

**transcurrir** *v* elapse, pass — **transcurso** *nm* course, progression

**transferir** *v* transfer — **transferencia** *nf* transfer, transference

**transformar** *v* transform, change; convert — **transformarse** *vr* be transformed — **transformación** *nf* (**-ciones**) transformation — **transformador** *nm* transformer

**transfusión** *nf* (**-siones**) transfusion

**transición** *nf* (**-ciones**) transition

**transitar** *v* go, travel — **transitable** *adj* passable

**transitivo, -va** *adj* transitive

**tránsito** *nm* transit; traffic

**transmitir** *v* transmit; broadcast (as radio, TV); pass on — **transmisión** *nf* (**-siones**) broadcast; transfer

**transparente** *adj* transparent

**transportar** *v* transport, carry — **transportarse** *vr* get carried away — **transporte** *nm* transport, transportation

**tranvía** *nm* streetcar, trolley

**trapear** mop

**trapecio** *nm* trapeze

**trapo** *nm* cloth, rag

**tráquea** *nf* trachea, windpipe

**trascendental** *adj* transcendental; important

**trasero, -ra** *adj* rear, back — **trasero** *nm* buttocks

**trasladar** *v* transfer, move; postpone — **trasladarse** *vr* move, relocate — **traslado** *nm* transfer, move

**trasnochar** *v* stay up all night

**trasplante** *nm* transplant

**trastornar** *v* disturb, disrupt — **trastornado, -da** *adj* disturbed, deranged — **trastorno** *nm* disturbance, disruption; (medical or psychological) disorder

**tratable** *adj* friendly, sociable

**tratar** *v* deal with; treat; handle — **tratarse de** *vr phr* be about, concern — **tratamiento** *nm* treatment — **trato** *nm* treatment; deal, agreement

**trauma** *nm* trauma — **traumático, -ca** *adj* traumatic

**través** *nm* **a** ~ **de** across, through; **de** ~ sideways

**travesía** *nf* voyage, crossing (of the sea)

**travesura** *nf* prank; ~**s** *nfpl* mischief — **travieso, -sa** *adj* mischievous, naughty

**trayecto** *nm* trajectory, path; journey; route — **trayectoria** *nf* path, trajectory

**trazar** *v* trace, outline; draw up (a plan, etc.)

**trébol** *nm* clover, shamrock

**trece** *adj & nm* thirteen

**treinta** *adj & nm* thirty

**tremendo, -da** *adj* tremendous, enormous

**tren** *nm* train; ~ **de aterrizaje** landing gear

**trenza** *nf* braid, pigtail

**trepar** *v* climb; creep, spread (of a plant)

**tres** *adj & nm* three — **trescientos, -tas** *adj* three hundred

**triángulo** *nm* triangle — **triangular** *adj* triangular

**tribu** *nf* tribe

**tribunal** *nm* court, tribunal

**tributar** *v* pay, render; pay taxes — **tributo** *nm* tribute; tax

**triciclo** *nm* tricycle

**trigésimo, -ma** *adj & n* thirtieth

**trigo** *nm* wheat

**trigonometría** *nf* trigonometry

**trillizo, -za** *n* triplet

**trilogía** *nf* trilogy

**trimestral** *adj* quarterly

**trío** *nm* trio

**triple** *adj & nm* triple

**trípode** *nm* tripod

**tripulación** *nf* (**-ciones**) crew — **tripulante** *nmf* crew member

**triste** *adj* sad; dismal, gloomy — **tristeza** *nf* sadness, grief

**triunfo** *nm* triumph, victory

**trivial** *adj* trivial

**trofeo** *nm* trophy

**trombón** *nm* (**-bones**) trombone; trombonist

**trombosis** *nf* thrombosis

**trompa** *nf* trunk (of an elephant), snout; horn (musical instrument); tube (in anatomy)

**trompeta** *nf* trumpet — **trompetista** *nmf* trumpet player

**trompo** *nm* top (toy)

**tronar** *v* thunder, rage; shoot — **tronar** *v impers* thunder

**tropezar** *v* trip, stumble

**tropical** *adj* tropical

**trotar** *v* trot; rush about

**trucha** *nf* trout

**trueno** *nm* thunder

**tu** *adj* your

**tú** *pron* you

**tuberculosis** *nf* tuberculosis

**tubo** *nm* tube, pipe; ~ **de escape** exhaust pipe (of a vehicle); ~ **de desagüe** drainpipe — **tubería** *nf* pipes, tubing

**tuerca** *nf* nut (for a screw)

**tulipán** *nm* (**-panes**) tulip

**tumba** *nf* tomb, grave

**tumor** *nm* tumor

**túnel** *nm* tunnel

**turbio, -bia** *adj* cloudy, murky; blurred (as of vision)

**turco, -ca** *adj* Turkish — **turco** *nm* Turkish (language)

**turista** *nmf* tourist — **turismo** *nm* tourism, tourist industry

**turno** *nm* turn

**tutear** *v* address as *tú*

**tutela** *nf* guardianship (in law)

**tuyo, -ya** *adj* yours, of yours — **tuyo, -ya** *pron* **el tuyo, la tuya, lo tuyo, los tuyos, làs tuyas** yours; **los tuyos** your family, your friends

# U

**u¹** *nf* u, 22d letter of the Spanish alphabet

**u²** *conj* or

**ubicar** *v* place, position; find — **ubicarse** *vr* be located

**ubre** *nf* udder

**último, -ma** *adj* last; latest, most recent (in time); farthest (in space)

**umbilical** *adj* umbilical

**un, una** *art* (**unos** *m*) a, an; **unos** *or* **unas** *pl* some, a few; about, approximately

**unánime** *adj* unanimous — **unanimidad** *nf* unanimity

**undécimo, -ma** *adj & n* eleventh

**único, -ca** *adj* only, sole; unique — **único, -ca** *n* only one

**unidad** *nf* unit; unity — **unido, -da** *adj* united; close (as of friends)

**uniforme** *adj & nm* uniform

**unilateral** *adj* unilateral

**unir** *v* unite, join; combine, mix together — **unirse** *vr* join together — **unión** *nf* (**uniones**) union; joint, coupling

**universal** *adj* universal

**universidad** *nf* university, college — **universitario, -ria** *adj* university, college

**universo** *nm* universe

**uno, una** *adj* one — **uno, una** *pron* one; **unos, unas** *pl* some; **uno(s) a otro(s)** one another, each other; **uno y otro** both — **uno** *nm* one (number)

**untar** *v* smear, grease; bribe

**uña** *nf* nail, fingernail; claw, hoof

**Urano** *nm* Uranus

**urbano, -na** *adj* urban, city — **urbanización** *nf* (**-ciones**) housing development

**urgencia** *nf* urgency; emergency — **urgente** *adj* urgent

**urinario, -ria** *adj* urinary

**urna** *nf* urn; ballot box

**uruguayo, -ya** *adj* Uruguayan

**usar** *v* use; wear — **usarse** be used; be worn, be in fashion — **usado, -da** *adj* used; worn, worn-out — **uso** *nm* use; wear and tear; custom, usage

**usted** *pron* you; ~**es** *pl* you (*pl*)

**usual** *adj* usual

**usuario, -ria** *n* user

**útero** *nm* uterus, womb

**utilizar** *v* use, utilize — **útil** *adj* useful — **útiles** *nmpl* implements, tools — **utilidad** *nf* utility, usefulness

**uva** *nf* grape

# V

**v** *nf* v, 23d letter of the Spanish alphabet

**vaca** *nf* cow

**vacaciones** *nfpl* vacation; **estar de** ~ be on vacation

**vacante** *adj* vacant — **vacante** *nf* vacancy

**vaciar** *v* empty (out); hollow out; cast, mold (a statue, etc.)

**vacío** *nm* void; vacuum (in physics); space, gap

**vacuna** *nf* vaccine

**vacuno, -na** *adj* bovine

**vagina** *nf* vagina

**vagón** *nm* (**-gones**) car (of a train)

**vaho** *nm* breath; vapor, steam

**vainilla** *nf* vanilla

**vajilla** *nf* dishes

**vale** *nm* voucher; IOU

**valentía** *nf* courage, bravery

**valer** *v* be worth; cost; gain, earn; be equal to; be valid, count; be of use

**valeroso, -sa** *adj* courageous

**válido, -da** *adj* valid

**valiente** *adj* brave; fine, great

**valioso, -sa** *adj* valuable

**valla** *nf* fence; hurdle (in sports)

**valle** *nm* valley

**valor** *nm* value, worth; courage, valor; ~**es** *nmpl* values, principles; ~**es** *nmpl* securities, bonds — **valoración** *nf* (**-ciones**) valuation — **valorar** *v* evaluate, assess

**vals** *nm* waltz

**vanagloriarse** *vr* boast, brag

**vanguardia** *nf* vanguard; avant-garde; **a la ~** at/in the forefront

**vanidad** *nf* vanity — **vanidoso, -sa** *adj* vain, conceited

**vapor** *nm* steam, vapor; **al ~** steamed

**variar** *v* vary; change, alter — **variable** *adj & nf* variable — **variante** *nf* variant

**varicela** *nf* chicken pox

**variedad** *nf* variety

**vario, -ria** *adj* varied; **~s** *pl* several

**varón** *nm* (**-rones**) man, male; boy — **varonil** *adj* manly

**vasco, -ca** *adj* Basque — **vasco** *nm* Basque (language)

**vasija** *nf* container, vessel

**vaso** *nm* glass; vessel (in anatomy)

**vecino, -na** *n* neighbor; resident, inhabitant — **vecino, -na** *adj* neighboring — **vecindario** *nm* neighborhood; community, residents

**vegetal** *nm* vegetable, plant — **vegetal** *adj* vegetable — **vegetación** *nf* (**-ciones**) vegetation — **vegetariano, -na** *adj & n* vegetarian

**vehículo** *nm* vehicle

**veinte** *adj & nm* twenty — **veinteavo** *nm* twentieth

**vejez** *nf* old age

**vejiga** *nf* bladder; blister

**vela** *nf* candle; sail (of a ship); vigil

**velar** *v* hold a wake over; watch over; blur (a photograph); veil, mask; stay awake — **velado, -da** *adj* veiled, hidden; blurred

**vello** *nm* body hair; down, fuzz — **velludo, -da** *adj* hairy

**veloz** *adj* (**-loces**) fast, quick — **velocidad** *nf* speed, velocity; gear (of an automobile)

**vena** *nf* vein; grain (of wood); mood

**venado** *nm* deer; venison

**vencer** *v* win; beat, defeat; overcome; expire — **vencedor, -dora** *adj* winning — **vencedor, -dora** *n* winner — **vencimiento** *nm* expiration; maturity (of a loan)

**vender** *v* sell — **venderse** *vr* be sold; **se vende** for sale — **vendedor, -dora** *n* seller; salesman, saleswoman

**veneno** *nm* poison; venom

**venezolano, -na** *adj* Venezuelan

**vengar** *v* avenge — **vengarse** *vr* get even, take revenge — **venganza** *nf* vengeance, revenge

**venir** *v* come; arrive; be, appear; fit

**venta** *nf* sale, selling

**ventaja** *nf* advantage

**ventana** *nf* window — **ventanilla** *nf* window (of a vehicle or airplane); ticket window, box office

**ventilación** *nf* (**-ciones**) ventilation — **ventilador** *nm* fan, ventilator

**ver** *v* see; watch (as television); **a ~** *or* **vamos a ~** let's see — **verse** *vr* see oneself; find oneself; see each other, meet

**verano** *nm* summer

**verbal** *adj* verbal

**verbo** *nm* verb

**verdad** *nf* truth; **de ~** really, truly; **¿verdad?** right?, isn't that so? — **verdadero, -dera** *adj* true, real

**verde** *adj* green; unripe; dirty, risqué — **verde** *nm* green (color)

**verdura** *nf* vegetable(s), green(s)

**vergüenza** *nf* shame; bashfulness, shyness

**verificar** *v* verify, confirm; test, check out — **verificarse** *vr* take place; come true (as of a prophecy)

**vernáculo, -la** *adj* vernacular

**verosímil** *adj* probable, likely; credible

**versátil** *adj* versatile; fickle

**versión** *nf* (**-siones**) version; translation

**verso** *nm* poem, verse; line (of poetry)

**vértebra** *nf* vertebra

**vertical** *adj & nf* vertical

**vértice** *nm* vertex, apex

**vertiente** *nf* slope

**vértigo** *nm* vertigo, dizziness — **vertiginoso, -sa** *adj* dizzy

**vesícula** *nf* blister; **~ biliar** gallbladder

**vestíbulo** *nm* vestibule, hall, foyer

**vestido** *nm* dress; clothing, clothes

**vestir** *v* dress, clothe; wear — **vestuario** *nm* wardrobe, clothes; dressing room (in a theater), locker room

**veterano, -na** *adj & n* veteran

**veterinario, -ria** *adj* veterinary — **veterinario, -ria** *n* veterinarian

**veto** *nm* veto

**vez** *nf* (**veces**) time; turn; **a la ~** at the same time; **a veces** sometimes; **de una ~** all at once; **de una ~ para siempre** once and for all; **de ~ en cuando** from time to time; **en ~ de** instead of **una ~** once

**vía** *nf* way, road, route; means; track, line (of a railroad); (anatomical) tract; **en ~ de** in the process of — **vía** *prep* via

**viable** *adj* viable, feasible

**viaducto** *nm* viaduct

**viajar** *v* travel — **viaje** *nm* trip, journey — **viajero, -ra** *adj* traveling — **viajero, -ra** *n* traveler; passenger

**vial** *adj* road, traffic

**vibrar** *v* vibrate — **vibración** *nf* (**-ciones**) vibration

**vicepresidente, -ta** *n* vice president

**vicio** *nm* vice; bad habit; defect — **viciado, -da** *adj* corrupt; stuffy, stale (as of air)

**víctima** *nf* victim

**victoria** *nf* victory

**vida** *nf* life; lifetime; **de por ~** for life; **estar con ~** be alive

**video** *or* **vídeo** *nm* video; VCR, videocassette recorder

**vidrio** *nm* glass — **vidriera** *nf* stained-glass window; glass door; shopwindow — **vidrioso, -sa** *adj* delicate (of a subject, etc.)

**viejo, -ja** *adj* old; **hacerse ~** get old — **viejo, -ja** *n* old man, old woman

**viento** *nm* wind

**vientre** *nm* abdomen, belly; womb; bowels

**viernes** *nms & pl* Friday(s); **Viernes Santo** Good Friday

**vietnamita** *adj & nm* Vietnamese

**vigencia** *nf* validity — **vigente** *adj* valid, in force

**vigésimo, -ma** *adj & n* twentieth

**vigilar** *v* look after, watch over; keep watch — **vigilancia** *nf* vigilance — **vigilante** *adj* vigilant — **vigilante** *nmf* watchman, guard — **vigilia** *nf* wakefulness; vigil (in religion)

**vigor** *nm* vigor — **vigoroso, -sa** *adj* vigorous

**VIH** *nm* HIV

**villancico** *nm* (Christmas) carol

**vinagre** *nm* vinegar

**vincular** *v* tie, link — **vínculo** *nm* link, tie, bond

**vino** *nm* wine

**violar** *v* violate (as a law); rape — **violación** *nf* (**-ciones**) violation, offense; rape

**violencia** *nf* violence, force — **violento, -ta** *adj* violent; awkward, embarrassing

**violeta** *adj & nm* violet (color) — **violeta** *nf* violet (flower)

**violín** *nm* (**-lines**) violin — **violinista** *nmf* violinist — **violoncelista** *or* **violonchelista** *nmf* cellist — **violoncelo** *or* **violonchelo** *nm* cello

**virar** *v* turn, change direction

**virginidad** *nf* virginity

**viril** *adj* virile

**virtual** *adj* virtual

**virtud** *nf* virtue

**viruela** *nf* smallpox

**virus** *nms & pl* virus(es)

**visa** *nf* visa — **visado** *nm* visa

**visera** *nf* visor

**visible** *adj* visible

**visión** *nf* (**-siones**) eyesight; vision, illusion; view, perspective

**visitar** *v* visit — **visita** *nf* visit

**visón** *nm* (**-sones**) mink

**vista** *nf* vision, eyesight; look, gaze; view, vista; hearing (in court); **a**

**primera ~** *or* **a simple ~** at first sight; **perder de ~** lose sight of

**visto, -ta** *adj* clear, obvious; commonly seen

**visto bueno** *nm* approval

**visual** *adj* visual

**vital** *adj* vital — **vitalicio, -cia** *adj* life, for life — **vitalidad** *nf* vitality

**vitamina** *nf* vitamin

**vitrina** *nf* showcase, display case; shop-window

**viudo, -da** *n* widower, widow — **viudo, -da** *adj* widowed

**víveres** *nmpl* provisions, supplies

**vivero** *nm* nursery (for plants); (fish) hatchery, (oyster) bed

**vivienda** *nf* housing; dwelling

**vivir** *v* experience, live, live (through), be alive; **~ de** live on (as an income) — **vivir** *nm* life, lifestyle — **vivo, -va** *adj* alive; intense, bright; lively; sharp, quick

**vocabulario** *nm* vocabulary

**vocación** *nf* (**-ciones**) vocation

**vocal¹** *adj* vocal — **vocalista** *nmf* singer, vocalist

**vocal²** *nmf* member (as of a committee); **~** *nf* vowel

**volar** *v* fly; blow away (as papers); disappear; blow up — **volante** *adj* flying — **volante** *nm* steering wheel; shuttle-cock; flounce (of fabric); flier, circular

**volcán** *nm* (**-canes**) volcano

**volcar** *v* upset, knock over; empty out; overturn

**voleibol** *nm* volleyball

**voltear** *v* turn over, turn upside down

**volumen** *nm* (**-lúmenes**) volume

**voluntad** *nf* will; wish; intention — **voluntario, -ria** *adj* voluntary — **voluntario, -ria** *n* volunteer

**volver** *v* turn, turn over, turn inside out; turn (into); return, come or go back; **~ a** return to, do again; **~ en sí** come to — **volverse** *vr* turn (around); become

**vomitar** *v* vomit; spew (out) — **vómito** *nm* (action of) vomiting; vomit

**vos** *pron* you

**vosotros, -tras** *pron* you, yourselves

**votar** *v* vote; vote for — **voto** *nm* vote; vow (in religion)

**voz** *nf* (**voces**) voice; shout, yell; word, term; rumor

**vuelo** *nm* flight; (action of) flying; flare (of clothing)

**vuelta** *nf* turn; circle, revolution; bend, curve; return; round, lap (in sports); walk, drive, ride; back, other side; change

**vuestro, -tra** *adj* your, of yours — **vuestro, -tra** *pron* yours

**vulgar** *adj* vulgar; common

**vulnerable** *adj* vulnerable

# W

**w** *nf* w, 24th letter of the Spanish alphabet

**whisky** *nm* (**-skys** *or* **-skies**) whiskey

# X

**x** *nf* x, 25th letter of the Spanish alphabet

**xenofobia** *nf* xenophobia

# Y

**y¹** *nf* y, 26th letter of the Spanish alphabet

**y²** *conj* and

**ya** *adv* already; (right) now; later, soon

**yegua** *nf* mare

**yema** *nf* bud, shoot; yolk (of an egg); ∼ *or* ∼ **del dedo** fingertip

**yerno** *nm* son-in-law

**yeso** *nm* gypsum; plaster (for art, construction)

**yo** *pron* I; me — **yo** *nm* ego, self

**yoga** *nm* yoga

**yogurt** *or* **yogur** *nm* yogurt

**yuca** *nf* yucca

**yugoslavo, -va** *adj* Yugoslavian

**yugular** *adj* jugular

# Z

**z** *nf* z, 27th letter of the Spanish alphabet

**zafar** *v* loosen, untie — **zafarse** *vr* come undone; get free of (an obligation, etc.)

**zafiro** *nm* sapphire

**zanahoria** *nf* carrot

**zancudo** *nm* mosquito

**zapato** *nm* shoe — **zapatilla** *nf* slipper; sneaker

**zarpar** *v* set sail, raise anchor

**zigzag** *nm* (**-zags**) *or* **-zagues** zigzag

**zona** *nf* zone, area

**zoología** *nf* zoology — **zoológico** *nm* zoo — **zoólogo, -ga** *n* zoologist

**zorro, -rra** *n* fox, vixen — **zorro, -rra** *adj* foxy, sly

**zueco** *nm* clog (shoe)

**zurdo, -da** *adj* left-handed — **zurdo, -da** *n* left-handed person

# English-Spanish
# Dictionary

# A

**a¹** *n* (**a's** *or* **as**) a *f*, primera letra del alfabeto inglés

**a²** *art* un *m*, una *f*; por, a la, al

**abandon** *v* abandonar; renunciar a — **abandonment** *n* abandono *m*

**abbreviate** *v* abreviar — **abbreviation** *n* abreviatura *f*, abreviación *f*

**abdomen** *n* abdomen *m*, vientre *m*

**ability** *n* (**-ties**) aptitud *f*, capacidad *f*; habilidad *f*

**able** *adj* **abler; ablest** capaz, hábil; competente

**abnormal** *adj* anormal — **abnormality** *n* (**-ties**) anormalidad *f*

**aboard** *adv* a bordo — **aboard** *prep* a bordo de

**abort** *v* abortar — **abortion** *n* aborto *m*

**abound** *v* ~ **in** abundar en

**about** *adv* aproximadamente, más o menos; alrededor — **about** *prep* alrededor de; acerca de, sobre

**above** *adv* arriba — **above** *prep* encima de

**abroad** *adv* en el extranjero; por todas partes; **go** ~ ir al extranjero

**absence** *n* ausencia *f* — **absent** *adj* ausente — **absentee** *n* ausente *mf*

**absolute** *adj* absoluto — **absolutely** *adv* absolutamente

**absorb** *v* absorber — **absorbent** *adj* absorbente

**abstain** *v* ~ **from** abstenerse de

**abstract** *adj* abstracto — **abstract** *n* resumen *m*

**absurd** *adj* absurdo — **absurdity** *n* absurdo *m*

**abundant** *adj* abundante — **abundance** *n* abundancia *f*

**abuse** *n* abuso *m*

**abyss** *n* abismo *m*

**academy** *n* (**-mies**) academia *f* — **academic** *adj* académico

**accelerate** *v* acelerar

**accent** *v* acentuar — **accent** *n* acento *m*

**accept** *v* aceptar — **acceptable** *adj* aceptable — **acceptance** *n* aprobación *f*

**access** *n* acceso *m*

**accessory** *n* (**-ries**) accesorio *m*

**accident** *n* accidente *m*; casualidad *f* — **accidentally** *adv* por casualidad; sin querer

**acclaim** *v* aclamar

**accommodate** *v* acomodar, adaptar — **accomodations** *npl* alojamiento *m*

**accompany** *v* acompañar

**accomplish** *v* realizar, llevar a cabo — **accomplishment** *n* realización *f*; logro *m*, éxito *m*

**according to** *prep* según

**accordion** *n* acordeón *m*

**account** *n* cuenta *f*; relato *m*, informe *m* — **account for** *v phr* dar cuenta de, explicar — **accountable** *adj* responsable — **accountant** *n* contador *m*, -dora *f* — **accounting** *n* contabilidad *f*

**accumulate** *v* acumular; acumularse

**accuse** *v* acusar

**accustomed** *adj* **become** ~ **to** acostumbrarse a

**ace** *n* as *m*

**ache** *v* doler — **ache** *n* dolor *m*

**achieve** *v* lograr, realizar — **achievement** *n* logro *m*, éxito *m*

**acid** *adj* ácido — **acid** *n* ácido *m*

**acknowledge** *v* admitir; reconocer — **acknowledgment** *n* reconocimiento *m*

**acne** *n* acné *m*

**acorn** *n* bellota *f*

**acquaint** *v* ~ **. . . with** poner a algún al corriente de; **be** ~**ed with** conocer a (una persona), saber (un hecho)

**acquire** *v* adquirir — **acquisition** *n* adquisición *f*

**acrobat** *n* acróbata *mf*

**across** *adv* de un lado a otro; a través —
**across** *prep* a través de

**act** *v* actuar; interpretar (un papel) — **act**
*n* acto *m*, acción *f*

**action** *n* acción *f*

**activate** *v* activar

**active** *adj* activo — **activity** *n* (**-ties**) actividad *f*

**actor** *n* actor *m* — **actress** *n* actriz *f*

**actual** *adj* real, verdadero — **actually**
*adv* realmente, en realidad

**acupuncture** *n* acupuntura *f*

**acute** *adj* agudo

**adapt** *v* adaptar — **adaptation** *n*
adaptación *f* — **adapter** *n* adaptador *m*

**add** *v* añadir; sumar

**addict** *n* adicto *m*, -ta *f*; ~ *or* **drug** ~
drogadicto *m*, -ta *f* — **addiction** *n* dependencia *f*

**addition** *n* suma *f* (en matemáticas); **in**
~ además

**address** *v* dirigirse a (una persona); po-
nerle la dirección a (una carta) — **address** *n* dirección *f*, domicilio *m*

**adhere** *v* adherirse — **adherence** *n* adhesión *f* — **adhesive** *adj* adhesivo

**adjacent** *adj* adyacente, contiguo

**adjective** *n* adjetivo *m*

**adjust** *v* ajustar, arreglar; adaptarse

**administer** *v* administrar — **administration** *n* administración *f* — **administrator** *n* administrador *m*, -dora *f*

**admiral** *n* almirante *m*

**admire** *v* admirar — **admiration** *n* admiración *f*

**admit** *v* admitir, dejar entrar — **admission** *n* entrada *f*, admisión *f*

**adolescent** *n* adolescente *mf* — **adolescence** *n* adolescencia *f*

**adopt** *v* adoptar — **adoption** *n* adopción
*f*

**adore** *v* adorar

**adorn** *v* adornar

**adult** *adj* adulto — **adult** *n* adulto *m*, -ta
*f*

**advance** *v* adelantar — **advance** *n*

avance *m* — **advancement** *n* adelanto
*m*, progreso *m*

**advantage** *n* ventaja *f*; **take** ~ **of**
aprovecharse de

**adventure** *n* aventura *f*

**adverb** *n* adverbio *m*

**adversary** *n* (**-saries**) adversario *m*, -ria
*f*

**adversity** *n* (**-ties**) adversidad *f*

**advertise** *v* anunciar; hacer publicidad
— **advertisement** *n* anuncio *m* — **ad-
vertiser** *n* anunciante *mf* — **advertising** *n* publicidad *f*

**advice** *n* consejo *m*

**advise** *v* aconsejar, asesorar — **adviser**
*n* consejero *m*, -ra *f*; asesor *m*, -sora *f*

**aerial** *adj* aéreo — **aerial** *n* antena *f*

**aerobics** *ns & pl* aeróbic *m*

**affair** *n* asunto *m*, cuestión *f*; ~ *or* **love**
~ amorío *m*, aventura *f*

**affect** *v* afectar — **affection** *n* afecto *m*,
cariño *m*

**affinity** *n* (**-ties**) afinidad *f*

**affirm** *v* afirmar — **affirmative** *adj* afir-
mativo

**afflict** *v* afligir

**afford** *v* tener los recursos para, permi-
tirse (el lujo de); brindar

**afraid** *adj* **be** ~ tener miedo

**African** *adj* africano

**after** *adv* después; detrás, atrás — **after**
*conj* después de (que) — **after** *prep* después de

**afternoon** *n* tarde *f*

**afterward** *or* **afterwards** *adv* después,
más tarde

**again** *adv* otra vez, de nuevo

**against** *prep* contra, en contra de

**age** *n* edad *f*; era *f*, época *f* — **age** *v* envejecer — **aged** *adj* anciano, viejo

**agency** *n* (**-cies**) agencia *f*

**agenda** *n* orden *m* del día

**agent** *n* agente *mf*, representante *mf*

**aggravate** *v* agravar, empeorar

**aggression** *n* agresión *f* — **aggressive**
*adj* agresivo

**agile** *adj* ágil — **agility** *n* agilidad *f*

**agitate** *v* agitar; inquietar — **agitation** *n* agitación *f*, inquietud *f*

**ago** *adv* hace; **long** ~ hace mucho tiempo

**agony** *n* atormentarse

**agree** *v* acordar — **agreement** *n* acuerdo *m*

**agriculture** *n* agricultura *f*

**ahead** *adv* delante, adelante; por adelantado; a la delantera; **get** ~ adelantar

**aid** *v* ayudar — **aid** *n* ayuda *f*, asistencia *f*

**AIDS** *n* SIDA *m*, sida *m*

**aim** *v* apuntar (un arma), dirigir (una observación); apuntar — **aim** *n* propósito *m*, objetivo *m*

**air** *v* ~ *or* ~ **out** airear — **air** *n* aire *m* — **air conditioning** *n* aire *m* acondicionado — **airline** *n* aerolínea *f*, línea *f* aérea — **airmail** *n* correo *m* aéreo — **airplane** *n* avión *m* — **airport** *n* aeropuerto *m*

**ajar** *adj* entreabierto

**alarm** *n* alarma *f* — **alarm** *v* alarmar, asustar — **alarm clock** *n* despertador *m*

**album** *n* álbum *m*

**alcohol** *n* alcohol *m* — **alcoholic** *adj* alcohólico — **alcoholic** *n* alcohólico *m*, -ca *f* — **alcoholism** *n* alcoholismo *m*

**alert** *adj* alerta, atento — **alert** *n* alerta *f* — **alert** *v* alertar, poner sobre aviso

**alga** *n* (**-gae**) alga *f*

**algebra** *n* álgebra *f*

**alien** *adj* extranjero — **alien** *n* extranjero *m*, -ra *f*

**alienation** *n* enajenación *f*

**align** *v* alinear — **alignment** *n* alineación *f*

**alike** *adv* igual, del mismo modo — **alike** *adj* parecido

**alive** *adj* vivo, viviente

**all** *adv* todo, completamente — **all** *adj* todo — **all** *pron* todo, -da; **not at all** de ninguna manera — **all–around** *adj* completo

**allergy** *n* (**-gies**) alergia *f*

**alley** *n* (**-leys**) callejón *m*

**alliance** *n* alianza *f*

**alligator** *n* caimán *m*

**allocation** *n* asignación *f*, reparto *m*

**allow** *v* permitir; dar, conceder

**all right** *adv* sí, de acuerdo; bien — **all right** *adj* bien, bueno

**allusion** *n* alusión *f*

**ally** *v* ~ **oneself with** aliarse con — **ally** *n* aliado *m*, -da *f*

**almanac** *n* almanaque *m*

**almond** *n* almendra *f*

**almost** *adv* casi

**alone** *adv* sólo, solamente, únicamente — **alone** *adj* solo

**along** *adv* adelante; ~ **with** con, junto con — **along** *prep* por, a lo largo de — **alongside** *adv* al costado

**aloud** *adv* en voz alta

**alphabet** *n* alfabeto *m* — **alphabetical** *or* **alphabetic** *adj* alfabético

**already** *adv* ya

**also** *adv* también, además

**altar** *n* altar *m*

**alteration** *n* alteración *f*, modificación *f*

**alternate** *v* alternar — **alternative** *adj* alternativo — **alternative** *n* alternativa *f*

**although** *conj* aunque

**altitude** *n* altitud *f*

**altogether** *adv* completamente, del todo; en suma, en general

**always** *adv* siempre; para siempre

**amateur** *adj* amateur — **amateur** *n* amateur *mf*; aficionado *m*, -da *f*

**amaze** *v* asombrar — **amazement** *n* asombro *m* — **amazing** *adj* asombroso

**ambassador** *n* embajador *m*, -dora *f*

**ambiguous** *adj* ambiguo

**ambition** *n* ambición *f*

**ambulance** *n* ambulancia *f*

**amen** *interj* amén

**American** *adj* americano

**amiss** *adv* **something is** ~ algo anda mal

**amnesia** *n* amnesia *f*

**among** *prep* entre

**amount** *v* ~ **to** equivaler a; sumar, ascender a — **amount** *n* cantidad *f*

**amphibian** *n* anfibio *m* — **amphibious** *adj* anfibio

**amuse** *v* hacer reír, divertir; entretener — **amusement** *n* diversión *f* — **amusing** *adj* divertido

**analyze** *v* analizar

**anatomy** *n* (**-mies**) anatomía *f*

**ancestor** *n* antepasado *m*, -da *f*

**anchor** *n* ancla *f* — **anchor** *v* anclar

**ancient** *adj* antiguo, viejo

**and** *conj* y

**anemia** *n* anemia *f*

**anesthesia** *n* anestesia *f* — **anesthetic** *n* anestésico *m*

**angel** *n* ángel *m*

**anger** *v* enojar, enfadar — **anger** *n* ira *f*, enojo *m*, enfado *m*

**angle** *n* ángulo *m*

**Anglo–Saxon** *adj* anglosajón

**angry** *adj* enojado, enfadado

**anguish** *n* angustia *f*

**animal** *n* animal *m*

**animated** *adj* animado, vivo; ~ **cartoon** dibujos *mpl* animados

**ankle** *n* tobillo *m*

**anniversary** *n* (**-ries**) aniversario *m*

**annotate** *v* anotar — **annotation** *n* anotación *f*

**announce** *v* anunciar — **announcement** *n* anuncio *m* — **announcer** *n* locutor *m*, -tora *f*

**annoy** *v* fastidiar, molestar — **annoyance** *n* fastidio *m*, molestia *f* — **annoying** *adj* molesto, fastidioso

**annual** *adj* anual

**anonymous** *adj* anónimo

**another** *adj* otro — **another** *pron* otro, otra

**answer** *n* respuesta *f*, contestación *f*; solución *f* — **answer** *v* contestar a, responder a

**ant** *n* hormiga *f*

**antarctic** *adj* antártico

**antenna** *n* (**-nae** *or* **-nas**) antena *f*

**anthem** *n* himno *m*

**anthropology** *n* antropología *f*

**antibiotic** *n* antibiótico *m*

**anticipate** *v* anticipar, prever

**antipathy** *n* antipatía *f*

**antiquity** *n* (**-ties**) antigüedad *f*

**antisocial** *adj* antisocial

**antonym** *n* antónimo *m*

**anxiety** *n* (**-eties**) inquietud *f*, ansiedad *f* — **anxious** *adj* ansioso

**any** *adv* algo, un poco — **any** *adj* alguno; ningún; cualquier — **any** *pron* alguno, -na; ninguno, -na

**anyhow** *adv* de todas formas; de cualquier modo

**anymore** *adv* **not** ~ ya no

**anyone** *pron* alguien; quienquiera

**anything** *pron* nada; cualquier cosa, lo que sea

**anytime** *adv* en cualquier momento

**anywhere** *adv* en cualquier parte, dondequiera; en algún sitio

**apart** *adv* aparte; ~ **from** excepto, aparte de

**apartment** *n* apartamento *m*

**ape** *n* simio *m*

**apostrophe** *n* apóstrofo *m*

**apparent** *adj* claro, evidente — **apparently** *adv* al parecer, por lo visto

**apparition** *n* aparición *f*

**appear** *v* aparecer — **appearance** *n* apariencia *f*, aspecto *m*

**appendix** *n* (**-dixes** *or* **-dices**) apéndice *m* — **appendicitis** *n* apendicitis *f*

**appetite** *n* apetito *m* — **appetizer** *n* aperitivo *m* — **appetizing** *adj* apetitoso

**applause** *n* aplauso *m*

**apple** *n* manzana *f*

**appliance** *n* aparato *m*

**apply** *v* aplicar; ~ **for** solicitar, pedir — **applicant** *n* solicitante *mf*; candidato *m*, -ta *f* — **application** *n* solicitud *f* (para un empleo, etc.)

**appoint** *v* fijar, señalar — **appointment** *n* cita *f*

**appreciate** *v* apreciar; darse cuenta de

**apprentice** *n* aprendiz *m*, -diza *f*

**approach** *v* acercarse a; dirigirse a (algún); acercarse — **approach** *n* acercamiento *m*

**appropriate** *v* apropiarse de — **appropriate** *adj* apropiado

**approve** *v* aprobar — **approval** *n* aprobación *f*

**approximate** *adj* aproximado — **approximate** aproximarse a — **approximately** *adv* aproximadamente

**apricot** *n* albaricoque *m*

**April** *n* abril *m*

**apron** *n* delantal *m*

**apt** *adj* apto, apropiado — **aptitude** *n* aptitud *f*

**aquarium** *n* (**-iums** *or* **-ia**) acuario *m*

**aquatic** *adj* acuático

**aqueduct** *n* acueducto *m*

**Arab** *adj* árabe — **Arabic** *adj* árabe — **Arabic** *n* árabe *m* (idioma)

**arch** *n* arco *m*

**archaeology** *or* **archeology** *n* arqueología *f* — **archaeologist** *n* arqueólogo *m*, -ga *f*

**archipelago** *n* (**-goes** *or* **-gos**) archipiélago *m*

**architecture** *n* arquitectura *f* — **architect** *n* arquitecto *m*, -ta *f*

**archives** *npl* archivo *m*

**arctic** *adj* ártico

**area** *n* área *f*, zona *f*; ~ **code** código *m* de la zona, prefijo *m*

**arena** *n* arena *f*, ruedo *m*

**Argentine** *or* **Argentinean** *or* **Argentinian** *adj* argentino

**argue** *v* discutir; argumentar, sostener — **argument** *n* disputa *f*, discusión *f*

**arid** *adj* árido

**arise** *v* (**arose**; **arisen**) levantarse

**arithmetic** *n* aritmética *f*

**arm** *n* brazo *m*; arma *f* — **arm** *v* armar — **armament** *n* armamento *m* — **arm-**

**chair** *n* sillón *m* — **armed** *adj* armed **forces** fuerzas *fpl* armadas

**armpit** *n* axila *f*, sobaco *m*

**army** *n* (**-mies**) ejército *m*

**aroma** *n* aroma *m*

**around** *adv* de circunferencia; por ahí; más o menos, aproximadamente; **all** ~ por todos lados, todo alrededor; **turn** ~ voltearse — **around** *prep* alrededor de; por; cerca de

**arrange** *v* arreglar, poner en orden — **arrangement** *n* arreglo *m*

**arrest** *v* detener — **arrest** *n* arresto *m*, detención *f*

**arrive** *v* llegar — **arrival** *n* llegada *f*

**arrow** *n* flecha *f*

**art** *n* arte *m*; ~**s** *npl* letras *fpl* (en educación)

**artery** *n* (**-teries**) arteria *f*

**arthritis** *n* (**-tides**) artritis *f*

**artichoke** *n* alcachofa *f*

**article** *n* artículo *m*

**articulate** *v* articular

**artificial** *adj* artificial

**artillery** *n* artillería *f*

**artist** *n* artista *mf* — **artistic** *adj* artístico

**as** *adv* tan, tanto; ~ **much** tanto como — **as** *conj* mientras; como; ya que; por más que — **as** *prep* de; como — **as** *pron* que

**as for** *prep* en cuanto a

**ash** *n* ceniza *f*

**ashamed** *adj* avergonzado

**ashore** *adv* en tierra

**ashtray** *n* cenicero *m*

**Asian** *adj* asiático

**aside** *adv* a un lado; aparte — **aside from** *prep* además de; aparte de, menos

**as if** *conj* como si

**ask** *v* preguntar; pedir; invitar

**asleep** *adj* dormido; **fall** ~ dormirse, quedarse dormido

**asparagus** *n* espárrago *m*

**aspect** *n* aspecto *m*

**asphalt** *n* asfalto *m*

**asphyxiate** *v* asfixiar — **asphyxiation** *n* asfixia *f*

**aspire** *v* aspirar — **aspiration** *n* aspiración *f*

**aspirin** *n* (**-in** *or* **-ins**) aspirina *f*

**ass** *n* asno *m*; imbécil *mf*, idiota *mf*

**assault** *n* ataque *m*, asalto *m*

**assign** *v* designar, nombrar; asignar — **assignment** *n* misión *f*; tarea *f*

**assist** *v* ayudar — **assistance** *n* ayuda *f* — **assistant** *n* ayudante *mf*

**associate** *v* asociar; asociarse — **associate** *n* socio *m*, -cia *f* — **association** *n* asociación *f*

**as soon as** *conj* tan pronto como

**assume** *v* suponer; asumir — **assumption** *n* suposición *f*

**assure** *v* asegurar

**asterisk** *n* asterisco *m*

**asthma** *n* asma *m*

**astonish** *v* asombrar — **astonishing** *adj* asombroso — **astonishment** *n* asombro *m*

**astrology** *n* astrología *f*

**astronaut** *n* astronauta *mf*

**astronomy** *n* astronomía *f*

**astute** *adj* astuto, sagaz — **astuteness** *n* astucia *f*

**as well as** *conj* tanto como — **as well as** *prep* además de, aparte de

**asylum** *n* asilo *m*

**at** *prep* a; ~ **night** en la noche, por la noche; ~ **two o'clock** a las dos — **at all** *adv* **not at all** en absoluto, nada

**atheist** *n* ateo *m*, atea *f*

**athlete** *n* atleta *mf* — **athletic** *adj* atlético — **athletics** *ns & pl* atletismo *m*

**atlas** *n* atlas *m*

**atmosphere** *n* atmósfera *f*

**atom** *n* átomo *m* — **atomic** *adj* atómico

**atomizer** *n* atomizador *m*

**atrocity** *n* (**-ties**) atrocidad *f* — **atrocious** *adj* atroz

**atrophy** *v* atrofiarse

**attach** *v* sujetar, atar; adjuntar (un documento, etc.) — **attachment** *n* accesorio *m*

**attack** *v* atacar — **attack** *n* ataque *m*

**attempt** *v* intentar — **attempt** *n* intento *m*

**attend** *v* asistir (a) ~ **to** ocuparse de — **attendance** *n* asistencia *f* — **attendant** *n* encargado *m*, -da *f*; asistente *mf*

**attention** *n* atención *f*; **pay** ~ prestar atención, hacer caso

**attitude** *n* actitud *f*; postura *f*

**attract** *v* atraer — **attraction** *n* atracción *f*; atractivo *m* — **attractive** *adj* atractivo, atrayente

**audacity** *n* audacia *f*, atrevimiento *m*

**audible** *adj* audible

**audience** *n* público *m*

**audiovisual** *adj* audiovisual

**audition** *n* audición *f*

**August** *n* agosto *m*

**aunt** *n* tía *f*

**Australian** *adj* australiano

**authentic** *adj* auténtico

**author** *n* autor *m*, -tora *f*

**authority** *n* autoridad *f* — **authorization** *n* autorización *f* — **authorize** *v* autorizar

**autobiography** *n* (**-phies**) autobiografía *f* — **autobiographical** *adj* autobiográfico

**autograph** *n* autógrafo *m* — **autograph** *v* autografiar

**automatic** *adj* automático

**autonomy** *n* autonomía *f* — **autonomous** *adj* autónomo

**autopsy** *n* (**-sies**) autopsia *f*

**autumn** *n* otoño *m*

**auxiliary** *n* (**-ries**) auxiliar *mf*

**available** *adj* disponible — **availability** *n* disponibilidad *f*

**avenge** *v* vengar

**avenue** *n* avenida *f*; vía *f*

**average** *n* promedio *m* — **average** *adj* medio; regular, ordinario

**aviation** *n* aviación *f* — **aviator** *n* aviador *m*, -dora *f*

**avocado** *n* (**-dos**) aguacate *m*
**avoid** *v* evitar
**awake** *v* (**awoke; awoken**) despertar —
  **awake** *adj* despierto
**aware** *adj* **be** ~ **of** estar consciente de
  — **awareness** *n* conciencia *f*

**away** *adv* de aquí, de distancia; **far** ~
  lejos
**awful** *adj* terrible, espantoso
**awhile** *adv* un rato
**awkward** *adj* torpe
**ax** *or* **axe** *n* hacha *f*
**axis** *n* (**axes**) eje *m*

# B

**b** *n* (**b's** *or* **bs**) b, segunda letra del alfabeto inglés
**baby** *n* (**-bies**) bebé *m;* niño *m,* -ña *f*
**baby–sit** *v* (**-sat**) cuidar a los niños
**bachelor** *n* soltero *m;* licenciado *m,* -da *f*
**back** *n* espalda *f;* reverso *m,* dorso *m,*
  revés *m* — **back** *adv* atrás; **be back**
  estar de vuelta; **go back** volver —
  **back** *adj* de atrás, trasero; atrasado —
  **back** *v* **back up** darle marcha atrás a
  (un vehículo); **back down** volverse
  atrás — **backbone** *n* columna *f* vertebral — **background** *n* fondo *m* (de un
  cuadro, etc.), antecedentes *mpl* (de una
  situación); formación *f* — **backpack** *n*
  mochila *f* — **backup** *n* respaldo *m,*
  apoyo *m;* copia *f* de seguridad (para
  computadoras) — **backward** *or* **backwards** *adv* hacia atrás — **backward**
  *adj* hacia atrás
**bacon** *n* tocino *m,* tocineta *f,* bacon *m*
**bacteria** bacterias *fpl*
**bad** *adj* (**worse; worst**) malo; **too** ~!
  ¡qué lástima!
**badly** *adv* mal; gravemente
**bag** *n* bolsa *f,* saco *m;* bolso *m,* cartera *f;*
  maleta *f* — **bag** *v* poner en una maleta
**baggage** *n* equipaje *m*
**bail** *n* fianza *f* — **bail out** *v phr* poner en
  libertad bajo fianza
**bake** *v* cocer al horno; cocerse (al horno)
  — **baker** *n* panadero *m,* -ra *f* — **bakery**
  *n* (**-ries**) panadería *f*
**balance** *n* balanza *f;* equilibrio *m;* bank

~ saldo *m* — **balance** *v* hacer el balance de (una cuenta); equilibrar
**balcony** *n* (**-nies**) balcón *m*
**bald** *adj* calvo
**ball** *n* pelota *f,* bola *f,* balón *m;* ~ **of
string** ovillo *m* de cuerda
**ballad** *n* balada *f*
**ballerina** *n* bailarina *f*
**ballet** *n* ballet *m*
**balloon** *n* globo *m*
**ballpoint pen** *n* bolígrafo *m*
**bamboo** *n* bambú *m*
**banana** *n* plátano *m,* banana *f,* banano *m*
**band** *n* banda *f;* grupo *m,* conjunto *m*
**bandage** *n* vendaje *m,* venda *f* — **bandage** *v* vendar
**bandit** *n* bandido *m,* -da *f*
**bang** *v* golpear; cerrar de un golpe por-
tazo *m*
**bangle** *n* brazalete *m,* pulsera *f*
**banister** *n* pasamanos *m,* barandal *m*
**bank** *n* banco *m* — **banker** *n* banquero
*m,* -ra *f* — **banking** *n* banca *f*
**banner** *n* bandera *f,* pancarta *f*
**banquet** *n* banquete *m*
**baptize** *v* bautizar — **baptism** *n* bautismo *m*
**bar** *n* barra *f;* mostrador *m;* bar *m*
**barbarian** *n* bárbaro *m,* -ra *f*
**barbecue** *v* asar a la parrilla — **barbecue** *n* barbacoa *f*
**barber** *n* barbero *m,* -ra *f*
**bare** *adj* desnudo — **barefaced** *adj*
descarado — **barefoot** *or* **barefooted**

*adv* & *adj* descalzo — **barely** *adv* apenas, por poco

**bargain** *n* ganga *f* — **bargain** *v* regatear, negociar

**bark** *v* ladrar

**barley** *n* cebada *f*

**barracks** *ns* & *pl* cuartel *m*

**barrel** *n* barril *m*, tonel *m*

**barrier** *n* barrera *f*

**bartender** *n* camarero *m*, -ra *f*

**base** *n* base *f* — **base** *v* basar, fundamentar

**baseball** *n* beisbol *m*, béisbol *m*

**basement** *n* sótano *m*

**basic** *adj* básico, fundamental — **basically** *adv* fundamentalmente

**basil** *n* albahaca *f*

**basis** *n* (**bases**) base *f*

**basket** *n* cesta *f*, cesto *m* — **basketball** *n* baloncesto *m*, basquetbol *m*

**bat¹** *n* murciélago *m* (animal)

**bat²** *n* bate *m* — **bat** *v* batear

**batch** *n* hornada *f* (de pasteles, etc.), lote *m* (de mercancías), montón *m* (de trabajo), grupo *m* (de personas)

**bath** *n* baño *m*; cuarto *m* de baño; **take a ∼** bañarse — **bathe** *v* bañar, lavar; bañarse — **bathrobe** *n* bata *f* (de baño) — **bathroom** *n* baño *m*, cuarto *m* de baño — **bathtub** *n* bañera *f*, tina *f* (de baño)

**baton** *n* batuta *f*

**battalion** *n* batallón *m*

**battery** *n* (**-teries**) batería *f*, pila *f* (de electricidad)

**battle** *n* batalla *f*; lucha *f* — **battle** *v* luchar — **battlefield** *n* campo *m* de batalla

**bay¹** *n* bahía *f*

**bay²** *n or* **∼ leaf** laurel *m*

**bazaar** *n* bazar *m*; venta *f* benéfica

**be** *v* (**was, were; been; being; am, is, are**) ser; (*expressing location*) estar; (*expressing existence*) ser, existir; (*expressing a state of being*) estar, tener — **be** *v impers* (*indicating time*) ser; (*indi-*

*cating a condition*) hacer, estar — **be** *v aux* (*expressing occurrence*) ser; (*expressing possibility*) poderse; (*expressing obligation*) deber; (*expressing progression*) estar

**beach** *n* playa *f*

**beak** *n* pico *m*

**beam** *v* brillar; transmitir, emitir

**bean** *n* habichuela *f*, frijol *m*; **string ∼** judía *f*

**bear¹** *n* (**bears** *or* **bear**) oso *m*, osa *f*

**bear²** *v* (**bore; borne**) portar; soportar

**beard** *n* barba *f*

**bearing** *n* comportamiento *m*; relación *f*, importancia *f*

**beast** *n* bestia *f*

**beat** *v* (**beat; beaten** *or* **beat**) golpear; batir (huevos, etc.); derrotar; latir (dícese del corazón) — **beat** *n* golpe *m*; latido *m* (del corazón); ritmo *m*, tiempo *m* — **beating** *n* paliza *f*; derrota *f*

**beauty** *n* (**-ties**) belleza *f* — **beautiful** *adj* hermoso, lindo — **beautifully** *adv* maravillosamente — **beautify** *v* embellecer

**beaver** *n* castor *m*

**because** *conj* porque — **because of** *prep* por, a causa de, debido a

**become** *v* (**-came; -come**) hacerse, ponerse — **becoming** *adj* apropiado

**bed** *n* cama *f*; **go to ∼** irse a la cama — **bedclothes** *npl* ropa *f* de cama — **bedroom** *n* dormitorio *m* — **bedspread** *n* colcha *f* — **bedtime** *n* hora *f* de acostarse

**bee** *n* abeja *f*

**beech** *n* (**beeches** *or* **beech**) haya *f*

**beef** *n* carne *f* de vaca, carne *f* de res — **beefsteak** *n* bistec *m*

**beeline** *n* **make a ∼ for** irse derecho a

**beep** *n* pitido *m* — **beep** *v* pitar

**beer** *n* cerveza *f*

**beet** *n* remolacha *f*

**beetle** *n* escarabajo *m*

**before** *adv* antes — **before** *prep* (*in space*) delante de, ante; (*in time*) antes de — **before** *conj* antes de que — **beforehand** *adv* antes

**beg** *v* pedir, mendigar; suplicar; pedir limosna

**begin** *v* (**-gan; -gun**) empezar, comenzar — **beginner** *n* principiante *mf* — **beginning** *n* principio *m*, comienzo *m*

**behalf** *n* **on ∼ of** de parte de, en nombre de

**behave** *v* comportarse, portarse — **behavior** *n* comportamiento *m*, conducta *f*

**behind** *adv* detrás; **fall ∼** atrasarse — **behind** *prep* atrás de, detrás de

**behold** *v* (**-held**) contemplar

**beige** *adj & nm* beige

**being** *n* ser *m*; **come into ∼** nacer

**belated** *adj* tardío

**Belgian** *adj* belga

**belie** *v* contradecir, desmentir

**belief** *n* confianza *f*; creencia *f*, convicción *f*; fe *f* — **believable** *adj* creíble — **believe** *v* creer — **believer** *n* creyente *mf*

**Belizean** *adj* beliceño *m*, -ña *f*

**bell** *n* campana *f*; timbre *m* (de teléfono, de la puerta, etc.)

**belly** *n* (**-lies**) vientre *m*

**belong** *v* **∼ to** pertenecer a, ser propiedad de; ser miembro de (un club, etc.) — **belongings** *npl* pertenencias *fpl*, efectos *mpl* personales

**beloved** *adj* querido, amado — **beloved** *n* querido *m*, -da *f*

**below** *adv* abajo — **below** *prep* abajo de, debajo de

**belt** *n* cinturón *m*; cinta *f*, correa *f* — **belt** *v* ceñir con un cinturón

**bench** *n* banco *m*; mesa *f* de trabajo

**bend** *v* (**bent**) doblar, torcer; torcerse; **∼ over** inclinarse — **bend** *n* curva *f*, ángulo *m*

**beneath** *adv* abajo, debajo — **beneath** *prep* bajo, debajo de

**benediction** *n* bendición *f*

**benefit** *n* ventaja *f*, provecho *m* — **benefit** *v* beneficiar

**berry** *n* (**-ries**) baya *f*

**beside** *prep* al lado de, junto a — **besides** *adv* además — **besides** *prep* además de

**best** *adj or adv* mejor

**bestow** *v* otorgar, conceder

**bet** *n* apuesta *f* — **bet** *v* (**bet**) apostar

**betray** *v* traicionar — **betrayal** *n* traición *f*

**better** *adj* mejor; **get ∼** mejorar — **better** *adv* mejor

**between** *prep* entre — **between** *adv* **in ∼** en medio

**beverage** *n* bebida *f*

**beware** *v* **∼ of** tener cuidado con

**bewitch** *v* hechizar, encantar

**beyond** *adv* más allá, más lejos (en el espacio), más adelante (en el tiempo) — **beyond** *prep* más allá de

**bib** *n* babero *m* (para niños)

**Bible** *n* Biblia *f*

**bibliography** *n* (**-phies**) bibliografía *f*

**bicycle** *n* bicicleta *f* — **bicycle** *v* ir en bicicleta

**big** *adj* grande

**bike** *n* bici *f*; moto *f*

**bikini** *n* bikini *m*

**bile** *n* bilis *f*

**bill** *n* cuenta *f*, factura *f*; billete *m* — **bill** *v* pasarle la cuenta a — **billboard** *n* cartelera *f*

**billiards** *n* billar *m*

**billion** *n* (**billions** *or* **billion**) mil millones *mpl*

**bind** *v* (**bound**) atar; unir; vendar — **binder** *n* carpeta *f*

**bingo** *n* (**-gos**) bingo *m*

**binoculars** *npl* binoculares *mpl*, gemelos *mpl*

**biography** *n* (**-phies**) biografía *f*

**biology** *n* biología *f* — **biologist** *n* biólogo *m*, -ga *f*

**birch** *n* abedul *m*

**bird** *n* pájaro *m* (pequeño), ave *f* (grande)

**birth** *n* nacimiento *m*, parto *m*; **give ∼ to** dar a luz a — **birthday** *n* cumpleaños *m* — **birthplace** *n* lugar *m* de nacimiento

**biscuit** *n* bizcocho *m*

**bishop** *n* obispo *m*

**bit** trozo *m,* pedazo *m;* bit *m* (de información); **a ~** un poco

**bite** *v* (**bit; bitten**) morder; picar — **bite** *n* picadura *f* (de un insecto), mordedura *f* (de un animal); bocado *m*

**bitter** *adj* amargo

**black** *adj* negro — **black** *n* negro *m* (color); negro *m,* -gra *f* (persona) — **blackberry** *n* (**-ries**) mora *f* — **blackbird** *n* mirlo *m* — **blackboard** *n* pizarra *f,* pizarrón *m* — **blackout** *n* apagón *m* (de poder eléctrico); desmayo *m*

**bladder** *n* vejiga *f*

**blade** *n* hoja *f* (de un cuchillo), cuchilla *f* (de un patín)

**blame** *v* culpar, echar la culpa a — **blame** *n* culpa *f* — **blameless** *adj* inocente

**blank** *adj* en blanco (de un papel), liso (de una pared); vacío — **blank** *n* espacio *m* en blanco

**blanket** *n* manta *f,* cobija *f* — **blanket** *v* cubrir

**blazer** *n* chaqueta *f* deportiva

**bleach** *n* lejía *f,* blanqueador *m*

**bleed** *v* (**bled**) sangrar

**blend** *v* mezclar, combinar — **blend** *n* mezcla *f,* combinación *f* — **blender** *n* licuadora *f*

**bless** *v* bendecir — **blessed** *or* **blest** *adj* bendito — **blessing** *n* bendición *f*

**blindness** *n* ceguera *f*

**blink** *v* parpadear — **blink** *n* parpadeo *m*

**bliss** *n* dicha *f,* felicidad *f* (absoluta) — **blissful** *adj* feliz

**blister** *n* ampolla *f*

**blizzard** *n* ventisca *f* (de nieve)

**block** *n* bloque *m;* obstrucción *f;* manzana *f,* cuadra *f* (de edificios) — **block** *v* obstruir, bloquear

**blond** *or* **blonde** *adj* rubio — **blond** *or* **blonde** *n* rubio *m,* -bia *f*

**blood** *n* sangre *f* — **blood pressure** *n* tensión *f* (arterial) — **bloodstream** *n* sangre *f,* torrente *m* sanguíneo — **bloody** *adj* ensangrentado, sangriento

**blossom** *n* flor *f* — **blossom** *v* florecer

**blouse** *n* blusa *f*

**blow** *v* (**blew; blown**) soplar; sonar; **~ out** fundirse (dícese de un fusible eléctrico), reventarse (dícese de una llanta) — **blow** *n* golpe *m* — **blow up** *v* estallar, hacer explosión; volar; inflar

**blue** *adj* azul; triste — **blue** *n* azul *m* — **blueberry** *n* (**-ries**) arándano *m* — **bluebird** *n* azulejo *m* — **blues** *npl* tristeza *f*

**bluff** *n* farol *m*

**blur** *n* imágen *f* borrosa — **blur** *v* hacer borroso

**blurb** *n* nota *f* publicitaria

**blush** *n* rubor *m* — **blush** *v* ruborizarse

**boar** *n* cerdo *m* macho

**board** *n* tabla *f,* tablón *m;* junta *f,* consejo *m;* tablero *m* (de juegos); **room and ~** comida y alojamiento — **board** *v* subir a bordo de (una nave, un avión, etc.), subir a (un tren); hospedar — **boarder** *n* huésped *mf*

**boast** *n* jactancia *f* — **boast** *v* alardear, jactarse

**boat** *n* barco *m* (grande), barca *f* (pequeña)

**body** *n* (**bodies**) cuerpo *m;* cadáver *m;* conjunto *m* — **bodily** *adj* corporal — **bodyguard** *n* guardaespaldas *mf*

**boil** *v* hervir

**bold** *adj* audaz; descarado — **boldness** *n* audacia *f*

**Bolivian** *adj* boliviano *m,* -na *f*

**bolt** *n* cerrojo *m;* tornillo *m* — **bolt** *v* atornillar; echar el cerrojo a

**bomb** *n* bomba *f* — **bombardment** *n* bombardeo *m*

**bond** *n* vínculo *m,* lazo *m;* fianza *f;* bono *m* (en finanzas) — **bond** *v* adherirse

**bone** *n* hueso *m*

**bonfire** *n* hoguera *f*

**bonus** *n* prima *f*; beneficio *m* adicional

**bony** *adj* huesudo; lleno de espinas (dícese de pescados)

**book** *n* libro *m*; libreta *f*, cuaderno *m* — **book** *v* reservar — **bookcase** *n* estantería *f* — **bookkeeping** *n* teneduría *f* de libros, contabilidad *f* — **booklet** *n* folleto *m* — **bookmark** *n* marcador *m* de libros — **bookseller** *n* librero *m*, -ra *f* — **bookstore** *n* librería *f*

**boom** *v* tronar, resonar; estar en auge, prosperar

**boost** *v* levantar; aumentar — **boost** *n* aumento *m*; estímulo *m*

**boot** *n* bota *f*, botín *m*

**booth** *n* cabina *f* (de teléfono, de votar), caseta *f* (de información)

**border** *n* borde *m*, orilla *f*

**bore** *v* aburrir — **bore** *n* pesado *m*, -da *f* (persona), lata *f* (cosa, situación) — **boredom** *n* aburrimiento *m* — **boring** *adj* aburrido, pesado

**born** *adj* nacido; **be ~** nacer

**borrow** *v* pedir prestado, tomar prestado

**Bosnian** *adj* bosnio *m*, -nia *f*

**bosom** *n* pecho *m*, seno *m* (de una mujer); **bosom friend** amigo *m* íntimo

**boss** *n* jefe *m*, -fa *f*; patrón *m*, -trona *f* — **boss** *v* dirigir

**botany** *n* botánica *f*

**both** *adj* ambos, los dos, las dos — **both** *pron* ambos *m*, -bas *f*; los dos, las dos

**bother** *v* preocupar; molestar, fastidiar; **~ to** molestarse en — **bother** *n* molestia *f*

**bottle** *n* botella *f*, frasco *m*; **baby ~** biberón *m* — **bottle** *v* embotellar — **bottleneck** *n* embotellamiento *m*

**bottom** *n* fondo *m* (de una caja, del mar, etc.), pie *m* (de una escalera, una montaña, etc.), final *m* (de una lista); nalgas *fpl*, trasero *m* — **bottom** *adj* más bajo, inferior

**bough** *n* rama *f*

**bound**[1] *adj* **be ~ for** ir rumbo a

**bound**[2] *adj* obligado; decidido; **be ~ to** tener que

**boundary** *n* (**-aries**) límite *m*

**bow**[1] *v* inclinarse; **~ one's head** inclinar la cabeza — **bow** *n* reverencia *f*, inclinación *f*

**bow**[2] *n* arco *m*

**bowels** *npl* intestinos *mpl*; entrañas *fpl*

**bowl**[1] *n* tazón *m*, cuenco *m*

**bowl**[2] *v* jugar a los bolos — **bowling** *n* bolos *mpl*

**box**[1] *v* boxear — **boxer** *n* boxeador *m*, -dora *f* — **boxing** *n* boxeo *m*

**box**[2] *n* caja *f*, cajón *m* — **box** *v* empaquetar — **box office** *n* taquilla *f*, boletería *f*

**boy** *n* niño *m*, chico *m*

**boyfriend** *n* novio *m*

**brace** *n* abrazadera *f*; **~s** *npl* aparatos *mpl* (para dientes)

**bracket** *n* corchete *m* (marca de puntuación) — **bracket** *v* poner entre corchetes; catalogar

**braille** *n* braille *m*

**brain** *n* cerebro *m*; **~s** *npl* inteligencia *f* — **brainy** *adj* inteligente, listo

**brake** *n* freno *m* — **brake** *v* frenar

**branch** *n* rama *f* (de una planta)

**brand** *n or* **~ name** marca *f* de fábrica — **brand** *v* tachar, tildar

**brassiere** *n* sostén *m*, brasier *m*

**brave** *adj* valiente, valeroso — **brave** *v* afrontar, hacer frente a — **bravery** *n* valor *m*, valentía *f*

**Brazilian** *adj* brasileño *m*, -ña *f*

**bread** *n* pan *m*; **~ crumbs** migajas *fpl*

**breadth** *n* anchura *f*

**break** *v* (**broke; broken**) romper, quebrar; infringir, violar; interrumpir; **~ down** estropearse (dícese de una máquina), fallar (dícese de un sistema, etc.); **~ into** entrar en; **~ off** interrumpirse; **~ out of** escaparse de; **~ up** separarse — **break** *n* ruptura *f*, fractura *f*; **take a break** tomar(se) un descanso — **breakdown** *n* avería *f* (de máquinas), interrupción *f* (de comunicaciones), fracaso *m* (de negociaciones); **nervous breakdown** crisis *f* nerviosa

**breakfast** *n* desayuno *m*

**breast** *n* seno *m* (de una mujer); pecho *m*

**breath** *n* aliento *m,* respiración *f* — **breathe** *v* respirar

**breed** *v* (**bred**) criar (animales); engendrar, producir — **breed** *n* raza *f*

**breeze** *n* brisa *f*

**brevity** *n* brevedad *f*

**brewery** *n* (**-eries**) cervecería *f*

**bribe** *n* soborno *m* — **bribe** *v* sobornar

**brick** *n* ladrillo *m* — **bricklayer** *n* albañil *mf*

**bride** *n* novia *f* — **bridal** *adj* nupcial, de novia — **bridegroom** *n* novio *m*

**bridge** *n* puente *m* — **bridge** *v* tender un puente sobre

**brief** *adj* breve — **brief** *n* resumen *m,* sumario *m* — **briefcase** *n* portafolio *m,* maletín *m* — **briefly** *adv* brevemente

**bright** *adj* brillante, claro; alegre, animado; listo, inteligente — **brighten** *v* hacerse más brillante; iluminar; alegrar, animar

**brilliant** *adj* brillante — **brilliance** *n* resplandor *m,* brillantez *f*; inteligencia *f*

**bring** *v* (**brought**) traer; ∼ **about** ocasionar; ∼ **back** devolver; ∼ **down** derribar; ∼ **out** sacar; ∼ **to an end** terminar (con); ∼ **up** criar; sacar

**British** *adj* británico

**broad** *adj* ancho; general

**broadcast** *v* (**-cast**) emitir — **broadcast** *n* emisión *f*

**broaden** *v* ampliar, ensanchar; ensancharse — **broadly** *adv* en general — **broad–minded** *adj* de miras amplias, tolerante

**broccoli** *n* brócoli *m,* brécol *m*

**brochure** *n* folleto *m*

**broil** *v* asar a la parrilla

**broken** *adj* roto, quebrado

**bronchitis** *n* bronquitis *f*

**brook** *n* arroyo *m*

**broom** *n* escoba *f*

**broth** *n* caldo *m*

**brother** *n* hermano *m* — **brotherhood** *n* fraternidad *f* — **brother–in–law** *n* (**brothers–** . . . ) cuñado *m*

**brow** *n* frente *f*; cima *f* (de una colina)

**brown** *adj* marrón, castaño (del pelo), moreno (de la piel) — **brown** *n* marrón *m* — **brown** *v* dorar (en cocinar)

**brunet** *or* **brunette** *adj* moreno — **brunet** *or* **brunette** *n* moreno *m,* -na *f*

**brush** *n* cepillo *m,* pincel *m* (de artista), brocha *f* (de pintor); maleza *f* — **brush** *v* cepillar

**bubble** *n* burbuja *f*

**buck** *n* dólar *m*

**bucket** *n* cubo *m*

**buckle** *n* hebilla *f* — **buckle** *v* abrochar

**Buddhism** *n* budismo *m* — **Buddhist** *adj* budista — **Buddhist** *n* budista *mf*

**buddy** *n* (**-dies**) compañero *m,* -ra *f*

**budge** *v* moverse; ceder

**budget** *n* presupuesto *m* — **budget** *v* presupuestar

**buffalo** *n* (**-lo** *or* **-loes**) búfalo *m*

**buffet** *n* bufé *m* (comida)

**bug** *n* bicho *m,* insecto *m* — **bug** *v* fastidiar, molestar; ocultar micrófonos en (una habitación, etc.)

**build** *v* (**built**) construir; desarrollar; ∼ **up** aumentar, intensificar — **builder** *n* constructor *m,* -tora *f* — **building** *n* edificio *m*; construcción *f*

**bulb** *n* bombilla *f*

**bulk** *n* volumen *m,* bulto *m*

**bull** *n* toro *m*; macho *m*

**bullet** *n* bala *f*

**bulletin** *n* boletín *m* — **bulletin board** *n* tablón *m* de anuncios

**bullfight** *n* corrida *f* (de toros) — **bullfighter** *n* torero *m,* -ra *f*; matador *m*

**bully** *n* (**-lies**) matón *m* — **bully** *v* intimidar

**bump** *n* bulto *m,* protuberancia *f*; golpe

*m*; sacudida *f* — **bump** *v* chocar contra
— **bumper** *n* parachoques *mpl*

**bunch** *n* grupo *m* (de personas), racimo
*m* (de frutas, etc.), ramo *m* (de flores),
manojo *m* (de llaves) — **bunch up** *v*
· *phr* amontarse, agruparse

**bunny** *n* (**-nies**) conejo *m*, -ja *f*

**burden** *n* carga *f* — **burden** *v* ~ ...
**with** cargar . . . con

**bureau** *n* departamento *m* (del gobierno); agencia *f*

**burglar** *n* ladrón *m*, -drona *f* — **burglarize** *v* robar — **burglary** *n* (**-glaries**)
robo *m*

**burial** *n* entierro *m*

**burn** *v* (**burned** *or* **burnt**) quemar; ~
**down** incendiar; ~ **up** consumir —
**burn** *n* quemadura *f*

**burst** *v* (**burst** *or* **bursted**) reventarse;
reventar — **burst** *n* estallido *m*, explosión *f*; arranque *m*, arrebato *m*

**bury** *v* enterrar; esconder

**bus** *n* (**buses** *or* **busses**) autobús *m*,
bus *m* — **bus** *v* (**bused** *or* **bussed**)
transportar en autobús

**bush** *n* arbusto *m*, mata *f*

**busily** *adv* afanosamente

**business** *n* negocios *mpl*, comercio *m*;
empresa *f*, negocio *m*; **it's none of
your** ~ no es asunto tuyo — **businessman** *n* (**-men**) empresario *m*,
hombre *m* de negocios — **businesswoman** *n* (**-women**) empresaria *f*,
mujer *f* de negocios

**busy** *adj* ocupado; concurrido

**but** *conj* pero; **not one** ~ **two** no uno
sino dos — **but** *prep* excepto, menos

**butcher** *n* carnicero *m*, -ra *f* — **butcher**
*v* matar

**butter** *n* mantequilla *f* — **butter** *v* untar
con mantequilla

**butterfly** *n* (**-flies**) mariposa *f*

**buttocks** *npl* nalgas *fpl*

**button** *n* botón *m* — **button** *v* abotonar
— **buttonhole** *n* ojal *m*

**buy** *v* (**bought**) comprar — **buy** *n* compra *f* — **buyer** *n* comprador *m*, -dora *f*

**buzz** *v* zumbar — **buzz** *n* zumbido *m* —
**buzzer** *n* timbre *m*

**by** *prep* cerca de; por, por delante de; de,
durante; para; de, a — **by** *adv* **by and
by** poco después; **go by** pasar

**bypass** *v* evitar

**bystander** *n* espectador *m*, -dora *f*

**byte** *n* byte *m*, octeto *m*

**byword** *n* **be a** ~ **for** estar sinónimo de

# C

**c** *n* (**c's** *or* **cs**) c, tercera letra del alfabeto
inglés

**cab** *n* taxi *m*; cabina *f* (de un camión,
etc.)

**cabin** *n* cabaña *f*; cabina *f* (de un avión,
etc.), camarote *m* (de un barco)

**cable** *n* cable *m* — **cable television** *n*
televisión *f* por cable

**cactus** *n* (**cacti** *or* **-tuses**) cactus *m*

**cadet** *n* cadete *mf*

**café** *n* café *m*, cafetería *f* — **cafeteria** *n*
restaurante *m* autoservicio, cantina *f*

**cage** *n* jaula *f* — **cage** *v* enjaular

**cake** *n* pastel *m*, torta *f*

**calcium** *n* calcio *m*

**calculate** *v* calcular — **calculation** *n*
cálculo *m* — **calculator** *n* calculadora *f*

**calendar** *n* calendario *m*

**calf** *n* (**calves**) pantorrilla *f* (de la pierna)

**call** *v* llamar; pasar, hacer (una) visita; ~
**for** requerir; ~ **off** cancelar — **call** *n*
llamada *f*

**calm** *n* calma *f*, tranquilidad *f* — **calm** *v*
calmar; **calm down** calmarse — **calm**
*adj* tranquilo, en calma

**calorie** *n* caloría *f*

**camel** *n* camello *m*

**camera** *n* cámara *f*

**camp** *n* campamento *m* — **camp** *v* acampar, ir de camping

**campaign** *n* campaña *f* — **campaign** *v* hacer (una) campaña

**camping** *n* camping *m*

**campus** *n* ciudad *f* universitaria

**can**[1] *v aux* (**could**) poder; saber

**can**[2] *n* lata *f* — **can** *v* enlatar

**Canadian** *adj* canadiense

**canal** *n* canal *m*

**canary** *n* (**-naries**) canario *m*

**cancel** *v* (**-celed** *or* **-celled**) cancelar — **cancellation** *n* cancelación *f*

**cancer** *n* cáncer *m*

**candid** *adj* franco

**candidate** *n* candidato *m*, -ta *f* — **candidacy** *n* (**-cies**) candidatura *f*

**candle** *n* vela *f* — **candlestick** *n* candelero *m*

**candy** *n* (**-dies**) dulce *m*, caramelo *m*

**cane** *n* bastón *m* (para andar), vara *f* (para castigar); caña *f*, mimbre *m*

**canine** *n* ∼ *or* ∼ **tooth** colmillo *m*, diente *m* canino — **canine** *adj* canino

**cannibal** *n* caníbal *mf*

**cannon** *n* (**-nons** *or* **-non**) cañón *m*

**canoe** *n* canoa *f*, piragua *f* — **canoe** *v* ir en canoa

**canon** *n* canon *m*

**can opener** *n* abrelatas *m*

**canteen** *n* cantimplora *f*; cantina *f*

**canvas** *n* lona *f* (tela); lienzo *m* (de pintar)

**cap** *n* gorro *m*, -ra *f*; tapa *f*, tapón *m* (de botellas) — **cap** *v* tapar, cubrir

**capable** *adj* capaz, competente — **capability** *n* (**-ties**) capacidad *f*

**capacity** *n* (**-ties**) capacidad *f*

**capital** *adj* capital; mayúsculo (de las letras) — **capital** *n* **capital** *or* **capital city** capital *f*; **capital letter** mayúscula *f* — **capitalism** *n* capitalismo *m* — **capitalize** *v* escribir con mayúscula

**capitol** *n* capitolio *m*

**capsule** *n* cápsula *f*

**captain** *n* capitán *m*, -tana *f*

**caption** *n* subtítulo *m*

**captivate** *v* cautivar, encantar

**capture** *n* captura *f*, apresamiento *m* — **capture** *v* capturar, apresar

**car** *n* automóvil *m*, coche *m*, carro *m*; **railroad** ∼ vagón *m*

**caramel** *n* caramelo *m*

**caravan** *n* caravana *f*

**card** *n* tarjeta *f*; ∼ *or* **playing** ∼ carta *f*, naipe *m* — **cardboard** *n* cartón *m*

**cardiac** *adj* cardíaco

**cardinal** *n* cardenal *m* —

**care** *n* cuidado *m*; preocupación; **take** ∼ **of** cuidar (de) — **care** *v* preocuparse, inquietarse; **care for** cuidar (de), atender, querer; **I don't care** no me importa

**career** *n* carrera *f*

**carefree** *adj* despreocupado

**careful** *adj* cuidadoso — **carefully** *adv* con cuidado, cuidadosamente — **careless** *adj* descuidado — **carelessness** *n* descuido *m*

**caress** *n* caricia *f* — **caress** *v* acariciar

**caricature** *n* caricatura *f* — **caricature** *v* caricaturizar

**caring** *adj* solícito, afectuoso

**carnival** *n* carnaval *m*

**carol** *n* villancico *m*

**carpenter** *n* carpintero *m*, -ra *f* — **carpentry** *n* carpintería *f*

**carpet** *n* alfombra *f*

**carriage** *n* transporte *m* (de mercancías); porte *m*; **baby** ∼ cochecito *m*

**carrot** *n* zanahoria *f*

**carry** *v* (**-ried**) llevar; transportar; ∼ **oneself** portarse — **carry on** *v* realizar; portarse inapropiadamente; seguir, continuar — **carry out** *v* llevar a cabo, realizar; cumplir

**carton** *n* caja *f* (de cartón)

**cartoon** *n* caricatura *f*; historieta *f*; **animated** ∼ dibujos *mpl* animados

**case** *n* caso *m*; caja *f*; **in any** ∼ en todo caso

**cash** *n* efectivo *m*, dinero *m* en efectivo — **cash** *v* convertir en efectivo, cobrar

**cashier** *n* cajero *m*, -ra *f*

**cash register** *n* caja *f* registradora

**casino** *n* casino *m*

**cassette** *n* cassette *mf*

**castle** *n* castillo *m*; torre *f* (en ajedrez)

**casual** *adj* casual, fortuito; informal

**cat** *n* gato *m*, -ta *f*

**catalog** *or* **catalogue** *n* catálogo *m* — **catalog** *v* (**-loged** *or* **-logued**) catalogar

**catastrophe** *n* catástrofe *f*

**catch** *v* (**caught**) capturar, atrapar; sorprender; agarrar, captar — **catching** *adj* contagioso

**category** *n* (**-ries**) categoría *f*

**cater** *v* proveer comida

**cathedral** *n* catedral *f*

**catholic** *adj* universal; **Catholic** católico — **catholicism** *n* catolicismo *m*

**cattle** *npl* ganado *m* (vacuno)

**cause** *n* causa *f*; motivo *m* — **cause** *v* causar

**caution** *n* advertencia *f*; precaución *f*, cautela *f* — **caution** *v* advertir

**cave** *n* cueva *f*

**cavern** *n* caverna *f*

**cavity** *n* (**-ties**) cavidad *f*; caries *f* (dental)

**CD** *n* CD *m*, disco *m* compacto

**cease** *v* dejar de; cesar

**ceiling** *n* techo *m*

**celebrate** *v* celebrar — **celebrated** *adj* célebre — **celebration** *n* celebración *f*; fiesta *f* — **celebrity** *n* (**-ties**) celebridad *f*

**celery** *n* apio *m*

**cell** *n* célula *f*; celda *f* (en una cárcel, etc.) — **cell phone** *or* **cellular phone** teléfono celular *m*

**cellar** *n* sótano *m*

**cellular** *adj* celular

**cement** *n* cemento *m*

**cemetery** *n* (**-teries**) cementerio *m*

**cent** *n* centavo *m*

**center** *n* centro *m* — **center** *v* centrar

**centigrade** *adj* centígrado

**centimeter** *n* centímetro *m*

**central** *adj* central

**century** *n* (**-ries**) siglo *m*

**ceramics** *npl* cerámica *f*

**cereal** *n* cereal *m*

**ceremony** *n* (**-nies**) ceremonia *f*

**certain** *adj* cierto; **be ～ of** estar seguro de; **for ～** seguro, con toda seguridad — **certainly** *adv* desde luego, por supuesto — **certainty** *n* certeza *f*, seguridad *f*

**certify** *v* (**-fied**) certificar — **certificate** *n* certificado *m*, partida *f*, acta *f*

**chain** *n* cadena *f*

**chair** *n* silla *f*; cátedra *f* (en una universidad) — **chairman** *n* (**-men**) presidente *m*

**chalk** *n* tiza *f*, gis *m*

**challenge** *v* disputar, poner en duda; desafiar — **challenge** *n* reto *m*, desafío *m*

**champagne** *n* champaña *m*, champán *m*

**champion** *n* campeón *m*, -peona *f* — **championship** *n* campeonato *m*

**chance** *n* azar *m*, suerte *f*; oportunidad *f*; **by ～** por casualidad; **take a ～** arriesgarse — **chance** *v* arriesgar

**change** *v* cambiar; cambiar de — **change** *n* cambio *m*

**channel** *n* canal *m*

**chaos** *n* caos *m*

**chapel** *n* capilla *f*

**chapter** *n* capítulo *m*

**character** *n* carácter *m*; personaje *m* (en una novela, etc.) — **characteristic** *adj* característico — **characteristic** *n* característica *f* — **characterize** *v* caracterizar

**charge** *n* carga *f* (eléctrica); precio *m*; **in ～ of** encargado de; **take ～ of** hacerse cargo de

**charity** *n* (**-ties**) organización *f* benéfica; caridad *f*

**charm** *n* encanto *m* — **charm** *v* encantar, cautivar — **charming** *adj* encantador

**charter** *n* carta *f* — **charter** *v* alquilar, fletar

**chat** *v* charlar — **chat** *n* charla *f*

**cheap** *adj* barato — **cheaply** *adv* barato, a precio bajo

**cheat** *v* hacer trampa(s); ⁓ *or* **cheater** *n* tramposo *m*, -sa *f*

**check** *n* inspección *f*, comprobación *f*; cheque *m*; cuenta *f* — **check** *v* revisar; comprobar; dar jaque (en ajedrez); **check in** enregistrarse (en un hotel)

**checkers** *n* damas *fpl*

**checkup** *n* chequeo *m*, examen *m* médico

**cheek** *n* mejilla *f*

**cheer** *n* alegría *f*; ⁓s! ¡salud! — **cheerful** *adj* alegre

**cheese** *n* queso *m*

**chef** *n* chef *m*

**chemist** *n* químico *m*, -ca *f* — **chemistry** *n* (**-tries**) química *f*

**cherish** *v* querer, apreciar

**cherry** *n* (**-ries**) cereza *f*

**chess** *n* ajedrez *m*

**chest** *n* pecho *m* (del cuerpo)

**chestnut** *n* castaña *f*

**chew** *v* masticar, mascar — **chewing gum** *n* chicle *m*

**chic** *adj* elegante

**chicken** *n* pollo *m*

**chief** *adj* principal — **chief** *n* jefe *m*, -fa *f* — **chiefly** *adv* principalmente

**child** *n* (**children**) niño *m*, -ña *f*; hijo *m*, -ja *f* — **childbirth** *n* parto *m* — **childhood** *n* infancia *f*, niñez *f* — **childish** *adj* infantil — **childlike** *adj* infantil, inocente

**Chilean** *adj* chileno

**chili** *or* **chile** *or* **chilli** *n or* ⁓ **pepper** chile *m*; ⁓ **chile** *m* con carne

**chill** *n* frío *m* — **chill** *v* enfriar — **chilly** *adj* **chillier; -est** fresco, frío

**chimney** *n* (**-neys**) chimenea *f*

**chin** *n* barbilla *f*

**Chinese** *adj* chino — **Chinese** *n* chino *m* (idioma)

**chip** *n or* **computer** ⁓ chip *m*

**chocolate** *n* chocolate *m*

**choice** *n* elección *f*, selección *f*; preferencia *f*

**choir** *n* coro *m*

**choke** *v* asfixiar, estrangular; atascar; asfixiarse, atragantarse (con comida)

**choose** *v* (**chose; chosen**) escoger, elegir; decidir

**chop** *v* cortar, picar (carne, etc.) — **chop** *n* chuleta *f* (de cerdo, etc.) — **choppy** *adj* picado, agitado

**chopsticks** *npl* palillos *mpl*

**chorus** coro *m* (grupo de personas); estribillo *m*

**christening** *n* bautizo *m*

**Christian** *n* cristiano *m*, -na *f* — **Christian** *adj* cristiano — **Christianity** *n* cristianismo *m*

**Christmas** *n* Navidad *f*

**chronic** *adj* crónico

**chronology** *n* (**-gies**) cronología *f* — **chronological** *adj* cronológico

**chubby** *adj* regordete, rechoncho

**chunk** *n* trozo *m*, pedazo *m*

**church** *n* iglesia *f*

**chute** *n* vertedor *m*; tobogán *m*

**cigarette** *n* cigarrillo *m*, cigarro *m*

**cinema** *n* cine *m*

**cinnamon** *n* canela *f*

**cipher** *n* cero *m*; cifra *f*

**circle** *n* círculo *m* — **circle** *v* dar vueltas (alrededor de); trazar un círculo alrededor de (un número, etc.)

**circuit** *n* circuito *m*

**circular** *adj* circular — **circular** *n* circular *f*

**circulate** *v* hacer circular; circular — **circulation** *n* circulación *f*; tirada *f* (de una publicación)

**circumference** *n* circunferencia *f*

**circumstance** *n* circunstancia *f*

**circus** *n* circo *m*

**cite** *v* citar

**citizen** *n* ciudadano *m*, -na *f* — **citizenship** *n* ciudadanía *f*

**city** *n* (**cities**) ciudad *f*
**civic** *adj* cívico
**civil** *adj* civil — **civilization** *n* civilización *f*
**claim** *v* reclamar; afirmar, sostener — **claim** *n*; demanda *f*, reclamación *f*; afirmación *f*
**clap** *v* aplaudir
**clarify** *v* (**-fied**) aclarar — **clarification** *n* clarificación *f*
**clarinet** *n* clarinete *m*
**clarity** *n* claridad *f*
**clash** *v* chocar, enfrentarse — **clash** *n* choque *m*
**class** *n* clase *f*
**classic** *or* **classical** *adj* clásico
**classify** *v* (**-fied**) clasificar — **classification** *n* clasificación *f*
**classmate** *n* compañero *m*, -ra *f* de clase
**classroom** *n* aula *f*, salón *m* de clase
**claw** *n* garra *f*, uña *f* (de un gato), pinza *f* (de un crustáceo) — **claw** *v* arañar
**clean** *adj* limpio — **clean** *v* limpiar — **cleaner** *n* limpiador *m*, -dora *f*; tintorería *f* — **cleanliness** *n* limpieza *f*
**clear** *adj* claro; transparente — **clear** *v* despejar (una superficie), desatascar (un tubo, etc.); **clear the table** levantar la mesa; **clear up** aclarar, resolver — **clearing** *n* claro *m* — **clearly** *adv* claramente; obviamente
**clef** *n* clave *f*
**clerk** *n* oficinista *mf*; empleado *m*, -da *f* de oficina; dependiente *m*, -ta *f*
**clever** *adj* ingenioso, hábil; listo, inteligente — **cleverly** *adv* ingeniosamente — **cleverness** *n* ingenio *m*; inteligencia *f*
**click** *v* chasquear; llevarse bien — **click** *n* chasquido *m*
**client** *n* cliente *m*, -ta *f*
**climate** *n* clima *m*
**climax** *n* clímax *m*, punto *m* culminante
**climb** *v* escalar, subir a, trepar a; ～ *or* ～ **up** subirse, treparse — **climb** *n* subida *f*
**clinic** *n* clínica *f* — **clinical** *adj* clínico

**clip** *v* cortar, recortar; sujetar (con un clip) — **clip** *n* clip *m* — **clipper** *n or* **nail** ～ cortauñas *m*
**clock** *n* reloj *m* (de pared); **around the** ～ las veinticuatro horas
**clockwork** *n* **like** ～ con precisión
**close**[1] *v* cerrar; cerrarse; ～ **in** acercarse
**close**[2] *adj* cercano, próximo; íntimo — **close** *or* **closely** *adv* cerca, de cerca — **closeness** *n* cercanía *f*
**closet** *n* armario *m*, clóset *m*
**cloth** *n* tela *f*
**clothe** *v* vestir — **clothes** *npl* ropa *f*; **put on one's clothes** vestirse — **clothing** *n* ropa *f*
**cloud** *n* nube *f* — **cloud** *v* nublar — **cloudy** *adj* nublado
**clover** *n* trébol *m*
**clown** *n* payaso *m*, -sa *f* — **clown around** *v* payasear
**club** *n* club *m*
**clue** *n* pista *f*, indicio *m*
**clumsy** *adj* torpe
**clutch** *n* embrague *m*, clutch *m* (de un automóvil)
**coach** *n* vagón *m* de pasajeros (de un tren); autobús *m*; entrenador *m*, -dora *f* — **coach** *v* entrenar (un atleta), dar clases particulares a (un alumno)
**coal** *n* carbón *m*
**coast** *n* costa *f*
**coastline** *n* litoral *m*
**coat** *n* abrigo *m* — **coating** *n* capa *f*
**cobweb** *n* telaraña *f*
**cockroach** *n* cucaracha *f*
**cocoa** *n* cacao *m*; chocolate *m* (bebida)
**coconut** *n* coco *m*
**cod** *ns & pl* bacalao *m*
**code** *n* código *m*
**coffee** *n* café *m* — **coffeepot** *n* cafetera *f*
**coffin** *n* ataúd *m*, féretro *m*
**coherent** *adj* coherente
**coil** *v* enrollar; enrollarse
**coin** *n* moneda *f*

# coincide

**coincide** *v* coincidir — **coincidence** *n* coincidencia *f*, casualidad *f*
**cold** *adj* frío; **be** ～ tener frío — **cold** *n* frío *m*; resfriado *m* (en medicina)
**coleslaw** *n* ensalada *f* de col
**collaborate** *v* colaborar — **collaboration** *n* colaboración *f*
**collapse** *v* derrumbarse, hundirse; sufrir un colapso (físico o mental) — **collapse** *n* derrumbamiento *m*; colapso *m*
**collar** *n* cuello *m* (de camisa, etc.) — **collarbone** *n* clavícula *f*
**collect** *v* reunir; coleccionar, juntar (timbres, etc.); acumularse, juntarse — **collect** *adv* **call collect** llamar a cobro revertido, llamar por cobrar — **collection** *n* colección *f*; colecta *f* (de contribuciones) — **collector** *n* coleccionista *mf*
**college** *n* universidad *f*
**cologne** *n* colonia *f*
**Colombian** *adj* colombiano
**colon** *n* (**colons**) dos puntos *mpl* (signo de puntuación)
**color** *n* color *m* — **color** *v* colorear, pintar — **colored** *adj* de color — **colorful** *adj* de vivos colores — **colorless** *adj* incoloro
**column** *n* columna *f* — **columnist** *n* columnista *mf*
**coma** *n* coma *m*
**comb** *n* peine *m* — **comb** *v* peinar
**combat** *n* combate *m*
**combine** *v* combinar — **combination** *n* combinación *f*
**come** *v* (**came; come**) venir; llegar; ～ **about** suceder; ～ **back** regresar, volver; ～ **from** venir de, provenir de; ～ **in** entrar; ～ **out** salir; ～ **to** volver en sí; ～ **on!** ¡ándale!; ～ **up** surgir **how** ～? ¿por qué? — **comeback** *n* retorno *m*
**comedy** *n* (**-dies**) comedia *f* — **comedian** *n* cómico *m*, -ca *f*
**comet** *n* cometa *m*
**comfortable** *adj* cómodo

**comic** *or* **comical** *adj* cómico — **comic** *n* cómico *m*, -ca *f*; **comic book** revista *f* de historietas, cómic *m* — **comic strip** *n* tira *f* cómica, historieta *f*
**command** *v* ordenar, mandar — **command** *n* orden *f*; mando *m*
**commemorate** *v* conmemorar — **commemoration** *n* conmemoración *f*
**comment** *n* comentario *m*, observación *f* — **comment** *v* hacer comentarios — **commentary** *n* (**-taries**) comentario *m*
**commerce** *n* comercio *m* — **commercial** *adj* comercial — **commercial** *n* anuncio *m*, aviso *m* — **commercialize** *v* comercializar
**commission** *n* comisión *f* — **commission** *v* encargar (una obra de arte)
**commit** *v* confiar; cometer (un crimen) — **commitment** *n* compromiso *m*
**committee** *n* comité *m*, comisión *f*
**common** *adj* común; ordinario, común y corriente — **commonly** *adv* comúnmente — **common sense** *n* sentido *m* común
**communicate** *v* comunicar; comunicarse — **communication** *n* comunicación *f* — **communicative** *adj* comunicativo
**communion** *n* comunión *f*
**Communism** *n* comunismo *m* — **Communist** *adj* comunista
**community** *n* (**-ties**) comunidad *f*
**compact** *adj* compacto — **compact** *n* *or* **powder compact** polvera *f* — **compact disc** *n* disco *m* compacto
**company** *n* (**-nies**) compañía *f*; visita *f*
**compare** *v* comparar — **comparable** *adj* comparable — **comparative** *adj* comparativo, relativo — **comparison** *n* comparación *f*
**compass** *n* compás *m*
**compassion** *n* compasión *f*
**compel** *v* obligar — **compelling** *adj* convincente
**compensate** *v* ～ **for** compensar

**compete** *v* competir — **competition** *n* competencia *f*; concurso *m*

**complain** *v* quejarse — **complaint** *n* queja *f*

**complement** *n* complemento *m* — **complement** *v* complementar — **complementary** *adj* complementario

**complete** *adj* completo, entero; terminado; total — **complete** *v* completar — **completion** *n* conclusión *f*

**complex** *adj* complejo

**complexion** *n* cutis *m*, tez *f*

**complicate** *v* complicar — **complicated** *adj* complicado

**compliment** *v* felicitar

**comply** *v* (**-plied**) ~ **with** cumplir, obedecer

**compose** *v* componer; ~ **oneself** serenarse — **composer** *n* compositor *m*, -tora *f* — **composition** *n* composición *f*; ensayo *m*

**compound** *v* componer — **compound** *adj* compuesto

**comprehend** *v* comprender — **comprehension** *n* comprensión *f* — **comprehensive** *adj* inclusivo; amplio

**compromise** *n* acuerdo *m*, arreglo *m* — **compromise** *v* comprometer

**computer** *n* computadora *f*, computador *m*, ordenador *m* — **computerize** *v* informatizar

**conceal** *v* ocultar

**concede** *v* conceder, admitir

**concentrate** *v* concentrar; concentrarse — **concentration** *n* concentración *f*

**concept** *n* concepto *m* — **conception** *n* concepción *f*

**concern** *v* ~ **oneself about** preocuparse por — **concern** *n* asunto *m*; preocupación *f* — **concerning** *prep* con respecto a

**concert** *n* concierto *m*

**conclude** *v* concluir — **conclusion** *n* conclusión *f*

**concrete** *adj* concreto

**condemn** *v* condenar

**condiment** *n* condimento *m*

**condition** *n* condición *f* — **conditional** *adj* condicional

**condolences** *npl* pésame *m*

**conduct** *n* conducta *f* — **conduct** *v* conducir, dirigir; llevar a cabo

**cone** *n* cono *m*; **ice–cream** ~ cucurucho *m*, barquillo *m*

**conference** *n* conferencia *f*

**confess** *v* confesar — **confession** *n* confesión *f*

**confidence** *n* confianza *f*; confidencia *f*

**confirm** *v* confirmar — **confirmation** *n* confirmación *f*

**conflict** *n* conflicto *m* — **conflict** *v* oponerse

**conform** *v* ~ **with** corresponder a — **conformity** *n* (**-ties**) conformidad *f*

**confuse** *v* confundir — **confusing** *adj* confuso, desconcertante — **confusion** *n* confusión *f*, desconcierto *m*

**congested** *adj* congestionado — **congestion** *n* congestión *f*

**congratulate** *v* felicitar — **congratulations** *npl* felicitaciones *fpl*

**congress** *n* congreso *m* — **congressman** *n* (**-men**) congresista *mf*

**conjunction** *n* conjunción *f*

**connect** *v* conectarse — **connection** *n* conexión *f*; enlace *m* (como con un tren)

**conscience** *n* conciencia *f*

**conscious** *adj* consciente — **consciousness** *n* consciencia *f*

**consequence** *n* consecuencia *f*; **of no** ~ sin importancia

**conservative** *adj* conservador — **conservative** *n* conservador *m*, -dora *f*

**consider** *v* considerar — **considerate** *adj* considerado — **consideration** *n* consideración *f* — **considering** *prep* teniendo en cuenta

**consist** *v* ~ **in** consistir en — **consistency** *n* (**-cies**) consistencia *f*

**console** *v* consolar — **consolation** *n* consuelo *m*

**constant** *adj* constante — **constantly** *adv* constantemente

**constitute** *v* constituir — **constitution** *n* constitución *f*

**constraint** *n* restricción *f*, limitación *f*

**construct** *v* construir — **construction** *n* construcción *f*

**consulate** *n* consulado *m*

**consult** *v* consultar — **consultation** *n* consulta *f*

**consume** *v* consumir — **consumer** *n* consumidor *m*, -dora *f* — **consumption** *n* consumo *m*

**contact** *n* contacto *m* — **contact lens** *n* lente *mf* (de contacto)

**contain** *v* contener — **container** *n* recipiente *m*, envase *m*

**contaminate** *v* contaminar — **contamination** *n* contaminación *f*

**contemporary** *adj* contemporáneo

**content¹** *n* contenido *m*; **table of ~s** índice *m* de materias

**content²** *adj* contento — **content oneself with** *v phr* contentarse con

**contest** *v* disputar — **contest** *n* concurso *m*, competencia *f*

**context** *n* contexto *m*

**continent** *n* continente *m*

**continue** *v* continuar

**contract** *n* contrato *m*

**contradiction** *n* contradicción *f* — **contradict** *v* contradecir

**contrary** *n* (**-traries**) contrario — **contrary** *adj* contrario, opuesto

**contribute** *v* contribuir — **contribution** *n* contribución *f* — **contributor** *n* contribuyente *mf*

**control** *v* controlar — **control** *n* control *m*; **controls** *npl* mandos *mpl*

**convene** *v* convocar; reunirse

**conversation** *n* conversación *f*

**convert** *v* convertir

**convex** *adj* convexo

**conviction** *n* condena *f* (de un acusado); convicción *f*

**convince** *v* convencer — **convincing** *adj* convincente

**convoke** *v* convocar

**cook** *n* cocinero *m*, -ra *f* — **cook** *v* cocinar, guisar; preparar (comida)

**cookie** *or* **cooky** *n* (**-ies**) galleta *f* (dulce)

**cooking** *n* cocina *f*

**cool** *adj* fresco; tranquilo — **cool** *v* enfriar — **cooler** *n* nevera *f* portátil

**cooperate** *v* cooperar — **cooperation** *n* cooperación *f* — **cooperative** *adj* cooperativo

**coordinate** *v* coordinar — **coordination** *n* coordinación *f*

**cope** *v* arreglárselas; **~ with** hacer frente a, poder con

**copier** *n* fotocopiadora *f*

**copy** *v* (**copied**) hacer una copia de; copiar — **copyright** *n* derechos *mpl* de autor

**cord** *n* cuerda *f*; *or* **electric ~** cable *m* (eléctrico)

**cordial** *adj* cordial

**core** *n* corazón *m* (de una fruta); núcleo *m*, centro *m*

**corn** *n* grano *m* — **corncob** *n* mazorca *f*

**corner** *n* ángulo *m*, rincón *m* (en una habitación); esquina *f* (de una intersección)

**coronary** *n* (**-naries**) trombosis *f* coronaria

**coronation** *n* coronación *f*

**corps** *n* (**corps**) cuerpo *m*

**corpse** *n* cadáver *m*

**correct** *v* corregir — **correct** *adj* correcto — **correction** *n* corrección *f*

**correspond** *v* **~ to** corresponder a — **correspondence** *n* correspondencia *f*

**corridor** *n* pasillo *m*

**corruption** *n* corrupción *f*

**cosmetic** *n* cosmético *m*

**cosmopolitan** *adj* cosmopolita

**cosmos** *n* cosmos *m*

**cost** *n* costo *m*, coste *m* — **cost** *v* (**cost**) costar

**Costa Rican** *adj* costarricense

**costume** *n* traje *m*; disfraz *m*

**cottage** *n* casita *f* (de campo)

**cotton** *n* algodón *m*

**couch** *n* sofá *m*

**cough** *v* toser — **cough** *n* tos *f*

**councillor** *or* **councilor** *n* concejal *m*, -jala *f*

**counsel** *n* consejo *m* — **counselor** *or* **counsellor** *n* consejero *m*, -ra *f*

**count** *v* contar — **count** *n* cuenta *f*; recuento *m*

**counter** *n* mostrador *m* (de un negocio)

**countless** *adj* incontable, innumerable

**country** *n* (**-tries**) país *m*; campo *m* — **country** *adj* campestre, rural — **countryman** *n* (**-men**) compatriota *mf*

**couple** *n* pareja *f* (de personas); **a ~ of** un par de

**courage** *n* valor *m*

**course** *n* curso *m*; **of ~** desde luego, por supuesto

**court** *n* cancha *f*, pista *f* (en deportes)

**courtesy** *n* (**-sies**) cortesía *f*

**courtyard** *n* patio *m*

**cousin** *n* primo *m*, -ma *f*

**cover** *v* cubrir — **cover** *n* cubierta *f*; abrigo *m*, refugio *m*; tapa *f*; portada *f* (de una revista); **covers** *npl* mantas *fpl*, cobijas *fpl* ; **take cover** ponerse a cubierto

**cow** *n* vaca *f*

**coward** *n* cobarde *mf* — **cowardice** *n* cobardía *f* — **cowardly** *adj* cobarde

**cowboy** *n* vaquero *m*

**crab** *n* cangrejo *m*, jaiba *f*

**crack** *v* rajar, partir

**cracker** *n* galleta *f* (de soda, etc.)

**cradle** *n* cuna *f*

**craft** *n* oficio *m*; (**craft**) embarcación *f* — **craftsman** *n* (**-men**) artesano *m*, -na *f* — **craftsmanship** *n* artesanía *f*, destreza *f*

**cramp** *n* calambre *m*, espasmo *m* (de los músculos)

**crane** *n* grúa *f* (máquina)

**crash** *v* estrellar; estrellarse, chocar — **crash** *n* estrépito *m*; choque *m*

**crawl** *v* arrastrarse, gatear (de un bebé)

**crayon** *n* lápiz *m* de cera

**crazy** *adj* **-zier; -est** loco

**cream** *n* crema *f*, nata *f* — **cream cheese** *n* queso *m* crema — **creamy** *adj* cremoso

**create** *v* crear — **creation** *n* creación *f* — **creator** *n* creador *m*, -dora *f*

**creature** *n* criatura *f*, animal *m*

**credence** *n* **lend ~ to** dar crédito a

**credit** *n* crédito *m* — **credit card** *n* tarjeta *f* de crédito

**creek** *n* arroyo *m*, riachuelo *m*

**creep** *v* (**crept**) **creeping** arrastrarse

**crew** *n* tripulación *f* (de una nave); equipo *m*

**crib** *n* cuna *f* (de un bebé)

**cricket** *n* grillo *m* (insecto); críquet *m* (juego)

**crime** *n* crimen *m*

**crinkle** *v* arrugar

**cripple** *v* lisiar, dejar inválido; inutilizar, paralizar

**crisis** *n* (**crises**) crisis *f*

**crisp** *adj* crujiente; frío y vigorizante (del aire) — **crispy** *adj* **crispier; -est** crujiente

**criterion** *n* (**-ria**) criterio *m*

**critic** *n* crítico *m*, -ca *f* — **critical** *adj* crítico — **criticism** *n* crítica *f* — **criticize** *v* criticar

**crocodile** *n* cocodrilo *m*

**crop** *n* cosecha *f*

**cross** *n* cruz *f*; cruzar, atravesar; cruzar; *or* **~ out** tachar — **cross** *adj* que atraviesa — **cross–eyed** *adj* bizco — **crossing** *n* cruce *m*, paso *m*; travesía *f* (del mar) *f* — **crossroads** *n* cruce *m* — **crosswalk** *n* cruce *m* peatonal, paso *m* de peatones — **crossword puzzle** *n* crucigrama *m*

**crow** *n* cuervo *m*

**crowd** *v* amontonarse; atestar, llenar — **crowd** *n* multitud *f*, muchedumbre *f*

**crucial** *adj* crucial
**crucifix** *n* crucifijo *m*
**crude** *adj* crudo
**cruel** *adj* cruel — **cruelty** *n* crueldad *f*
**cruet** *n* vinagrera *f*
**cruise** *n* crucero *m* — **cruiser** *n* crucero *m*; patrulla *f* (de policía)
**crumb** *n* miga *f*, migaja *f*
**crumble** *v* desmenuzar
**crunch** *v* ronzar (con los dientes), hacer crujir (con los pies, etc.) — **crunchy** *adj* crujiente
**crush** *v* aplastar, apachurrar
**crutch** *n* muleta *f*
**cry** *v* (**cried**) gritar; llorar — **cry** *n* (**cries**) grito *m*
**crystal** *n* cristal *m*
**Cuban** *adj* cubano
**cube** *n* cubo *m* — **cubic** *adj* cúbico
**cucumber** *n* pepino *m*
**cue** *n* señal *f*
**cuff** puño *m* (de una camisa)
**cultivate** *v* cultivar — **cultivation** *n* cultivo *m*
**culture** *n* cultura *f* — **cultural** *adj* cultural — **cultured** *adj* culto
**cunning** *adj* astuto, taimado
**cup** *n* taza *f*; copa *f*
**cupboard** *n* alacena *f*, armario *m*
**curb** *n* freno *m*; borde *m* de la acera

**cure** *n* cura *f*, remedio *m* — **cure** *v* curar
**curious** *adj* curioso — **curiosity** *n* (**-ties**) curiosidad *f*
**curl** *n* rizo *m* — **curler** *n* rulo *m*
**currency** *n* (**-cies**) moneda *f*
**current** *adj* actual — **current** *n* corriente *f*
**curriculum** *n* (**-la**) plan *m* de estudios
**curtain** *n* cortina *f* (de una ventana), telón *m* (en un teatro)
**curve** *v* hacer una curva; encorvar — **curve** *n* curva *f*
**cushion** *n* cojín *m*
**custom** *n* costumbre *f* — **customary** *adj* habitual, acostumbrado — **customer** *n* cliente *m*, -ta *f* — **customs** *npl* aduana *f*
**cut** *v* (**cut**) cortar; reducir, rebajar; ~ **oneself** cortarse; ~ **up** cortar en pedazos; ~ **in** interrumpir — **cut** *n* corte *m*
**cute** *adj* lindo
**cutlery** *n* cubiertos *mpl*
**cutlet** *n* chuleta *f*
**cutting** *adj* cortante, mordaz
**cycle** *n* ciclo *m*; bicicleta *f* — **cycle** *v* ir en bicicleta — **cyclist** *n* ciclista *mf*
**cynic** *n* cínico *m*, -ca *f* — **cynicism** *n* cinismo *m*
**Czech** *adj* checo — **Czech** *n* checo *m* (idioma)

# D

**d** *n* (**d's** *or* **ds**) d *f*, cuarta letra del alfabeto inglés
**dad** *n* papá *m*
**daily** *adj* diario
**daisy** *n* (**-sies**) margarita *f*
**damage** *n* daño *m*, perjuicio *m* — **damage** *v* dañar
**damn** *v* condenar
**damp** *adj* húmedo — **dampen** *v* humedecer — **dampness** *n* humedad *f*

**dance** *v* bailar — **dance** *n* baile *m* — **dancer** *n* bailarín *m*, -rina *f*
**dandruff** *n* caspa *f*
**danger** *n* peligro *m*
**Danish** *adj* danés — **Danish** *n* danés *m* (idioma)
**daring** *adj* atrevido, audaz — **daring** *n* audacia *f*
**dark** *adj* oscuro; moreno (del pelo o de la piel) — **darken** *v* oscurecer; oscurecerse — **darkness** *n* oscuridad *f*

**dart** *n* dardo *m*

**dash** *n* guión *m* largo (signo de puntuación)

**data** *ns & pl* datos *mpl* — **database** *n* base *f* de datos

**date**[1] *n* dátil *m* (fruta)

**date**[2] *n* fecha *f* cita *f*

**daughter** *n* hija *f* — **daughter–in–law** *n* (**daughters–** . . . ) nuera *f*

**dawn** *v* amanecer — **dawn** *n* amanecer *m*

**day** *n* día *m*; *or* **working** ~ jornada *f*; **the** ~ **before** el día anterior; **the** ~ **before yesterday** anteayer; **the** ~ **after** el día siguiente; **the** ~ **after tomorrow** pasada mañana — **daybreak** *n* amanecer *m*

**daze** *v* aturdir — **daze** *n* **in a daze** aturdido

**dead** *adj* muerto — **deadline** *n* fecha *f* límite — **deadlock** *n* punto *m* muerto — **deadly** *adj* mortal, letal

**deaf** *adj* sordo — **deafen** *v* ensordecer — **deafness** *n* sordera *f*

**deal** *v* (**dealt**) ~ **with** tratar con — **dealer** *n* comerciante *mf*

**death** *n* muerte *f*

**debate** *n* debate *m*, discusión *f* — **debate** *v* debatir, discutir

**debt** *n* deuda *f* — **debtor** *n* deudor *m*, -dora *f*

**decade** *n* década *f*

**decal** *n* calcomanía *f*

**decanter** *n* licorera *f*

**deceive** *v* engañar — **deceit** *n* engaño *m* — **deceitful** *adj* engañoso

**December** *n* diciembre *m*

**decent** *adj* decente — **decency** *n* (**-cies**) decencia *f*

**deception** *n* engaño *m* — **deceptive** *adj* engañoso

**decide** *v* decidir; decidirse

**decimal** *adj* decimal — **decimal** *n* número *m* decimal

**decision** *n* decisión *f* — **decisive** *adj* decisivo

**deck** *n* *or* ~ **of cards** baraja *f* (de naipes)

**declare** *v* declarar

**decorate** *v* decorar — **decoration** *n* decoración *f*

**decrease** *v* disminuir — **decrease** *n* disminución *f*

**decree** *n* decreto *m* — **decree** *v* decretar

**dedicate** *v* dedicar — ~ **oneself to** consagrarse a — **dedication** *n* dedicación *f*; dedicatoria *f*

**deduce** *v* deducir; concluir

**deduct** *v* deducir — **deduction** *n* deducción *f*

**deed** *n* acción *f*, hecho *m*

**deep** *adj* hondo, profundo — **deep** *adv* **deep down** en el fondo — **deepen** *v* ahondar

**deer** *ns & pl* ciervo *m*

**defeat** *v* vencer, derrotar — **defeat** *n* derrota *f*

**defect** *n* defecto *m* — **defective** *adj* defectuoso

**defend** *v* defender — **defendant** *n* acusado *m*, -da *f* — **defense** *n* defensa *f* — **defenseless** *adj* indefenso

**defer** *v* diferir, aplazar; ~ **to** deferir a

**defiance** *n* desafío *m* — **defiant** *adj* desafiante

**define** *v* definir — **definite** *adj* definido; seguro, incuestionable — **definition** *n* definición *f* — **definitive** *adj* definitivo

**deflect** *v* desviar; desviarse

**deformity** *n* (**-ties**) deformidad *f*

**defy** *v* (**-fied**) desafiar

**degree** *n* grado *m*; *or* **academic** ~ título *m*

**dehydrate** *v* deshidratar

**delay** *n* retraso *m* — **delay** *v* aplazar; retrasar; demorar

**delegate** *n* delegado *m*, -da *f* — **delegate** *v* delegar — **delegation** *n* delegación *f*

**delicacy** *n* (**-cies**) delicadeza *f*; manjar *m*, exquisitez *f* — **delicate** *adj* delicado

**delicatessen** *n* charcutería *f*

**delicious** *adj* delicioso
**delightful** *adj* delicioso, encantador
**delinquent** *adj* delincuente — **delinquent** *n* delincuente *mf*
**deliver** *v* entregar, repartir; liberar; asistir en el parto de (un niño); pronunciar (un discurso, etc.); asestar (un golpe, etc.) — **delivery** *n* (**-eries**) entrega *f*, reparto *m*; liberación *f*; parto *m*, alumbramiento *m*
**demise** *n* fallecimiento *m*
**democracy** *n* (**-cies**) democracia *f* — **democratic** *adj* democrático
**demon** *n* demonio *m*
**demonstrate** *v* demostrar; manifestarse — **demonstration** *n* demostración *f*; manifestación *f*
**denial** *n* negación *f*, rechazo *m*
**denounce** *v* denunciar
**dentist** *n* dentista *mf* — **dentures** *npl* dentadura *f* postiza
**deny** *v* negar
**deodorant** *n* desodorante *m*
**department** *n* sección *f* (de una tienda, etc.), departamento *m* (de una empresa, etc.), ministerio *m* (del gobierno) — **department store** *n* grandes almacenes *mpl*
**depend** *v* ~ **on** depender de; contar con; **that** ~**s** eso depende — **dependence** *n* dependencia *f* — **dependent** *adj* dependiente
**deplete** *v* agotar, reducir
**deplorable** *adj* lamentable
**deposit** *v* depositar — **deposit** *n* depósito *m*; entrega *f* inicial
**depress** *v* deprimir — **depression** *n* depresión *f*
**deprive** *v* privar
**depth** *n* profundidad *f*
**deranged** *adj* trastornado
**descendant** *n* descendiente *mf* — **descent** *n* descenso *m*; descendencia *f*
**describe** *v* describir — **description** *n* descripción *f* — **descriptive** *adj* descriptivo

**deserve** *v* merecer
**design** *v* diseñar; proyectar — **design** *n* diseño *m*; plan *m*, proyecto *m*
**designate** *v* nombrar, designar
**designer** *n* diseñador *m*, -dora *f*
**desire** *v* desear — **desire** *n* deseo *m*
**desk** *n* escritorio *m*, pupitre *m* (en la escuela)
**despair** *v* desesperar — **despair** *n* desesperación *f*
**desperation** *n* desesperación *f*
**despondent** *adj* desanimado
**dessert** *n* postre *m*
**destination** *n* destino *m* — **destined** *adj* destinado; **destined for** con destino a — **destiny** *n* destino *m*
**destroy** *v* destruir — **destruction** *n* destrucción *f* — **destructive** *adj* destructivo
**detergent** *n* detergente *m*
**deteriorate** *v* deteriorarse — **deterioration** *n* deterioro *m*
**determine** *v* determinar — **determined** *adj* decidido — **determination** *n* determinación *f*
**deterrent** *n* medida *f* disuasiva
**detest** *v* detestar
**devalue** *v* devaluar
**devastation** *n* devastación *f*
**develop** *v* aparecer; desarrollar; desarrollarse; ~ **an illness** contraer una enfermedad — **development** *n* desarrollo *m*
**deviation** *n* desviación *f*
**device** *n* dispositivo *m*, mecanismo *m*
**devil** *n* diablo *m*, demonio *m*
**devise** *v* idear, concebir
**devoid** *adj* desprovisto
**dexterity** *n* (**-ties**) destreza *f*
**diagnosis** *n* (**-noses**) diagnóstico *m* — **diagnose** *v* diagnosticar — **diagnostic** *adj* diagnóstico
**diagonal** *adj* diagonal — **diagonal** *n* diagonal *f*
**diagram** *n* diagrama *m*
**dial** *v* marcar

**ialect** *n* dialecto *m*

**ialogue** *n* diálogo *m*

**iamond** *n* diamante *m*; **baseball** ~ cuadro *m*, diamante *m*

**iaper** *n* pañal *m*

**iaphragm** *n* diafragma *m*

**iary** *n* (**-ries**) diario *m*

**ice** *ns & pl* dados *mpl* (juego)

**ictate** *v* dictar — **dictation** *n* dictado *m*

**ictionary** *n* (**-naries**) diccionario *m*

**ie** *v* morir; ~ **down** amainar, disminuir; ~ **out** extinguirse; **be dying for** morirse por

**iffer** *v* diferir, ser distinto; no estar de acuerdo — **difference** *n* diferencia *f* — **different** *adj* distinto, diferente

**ifficult** *adj* difícil — **difficulty** *n* (**-ties**) dificultad *f*

**ig** *v* (**dug**) cavar

**igest** digerir — **digestible** *adj* digerible — **digestion** *n* digestión *f*

**igit** *n* dígito *m*, número *m*; dedo *m* — **digital** *adj* digital

**igress** *v* desviarse del tema, divagar — **digression** *n* digresión *f*

**ilate** *v* dilatar; dilatarse

**ilemma** *n* dilema *m*

**imension** *n* dimensión *f*

**inner** *n* cena *f*, comida *f*

**int** *n* **by** ~ **of** a fuerza de

**iploma** *n* (**-mas**) diploma *m*

**iplomacy** *n* diplomacia *f* — **diplomat** *n* diplomático *m*, -ca *f* — **diplomatic** *adj* diplomático

**irect** *v* dirigir; mandar — **direct** *adj* directo; franco — **direct** *adv* directamente — **direction** *n* dirección *f*; **ask directions** pedir indicaciones — **director** *n* director *m*, -tora *f*

**irty** *adj* sucio; obsceno, cochino

**isability** *n* (**-ties**) minusvalía *f*, invalidez *f* — **disable** *v* incapacitar — **disabled** *adj* minusválido

**isadvantage** *n* desventaja *f*

**isagreeable** *adj* desagradable

**disappear** *v* desaparecer — **disappearance** *n* desaparición *f*

**disaster** *n* desastre *m*

**discharge** *v* descargar; liberar, poner en libertad; despedir; cumplir con (una obligación) — **discharge** *n* descarga *f* (de electricidad), emisión *f* (de humo, etc.); despido *m*; alta *f* (de un paciente), puesta *f* en libertad (de un preso); supuración *f* (en medicina)

**disciple** *n* discípulo *m*, -la *f*

**discipline** *n* disciplina *f*; castigo *m* — **discipline** *v* disciplinar; castigar

**disclose** *v* revelar

**discomfort** *n* incomodidad *f*; malestar *m*; inquietud *f*

**disconnect** *v* desconectar

**discount** *n* descuento *m*, rebaja *f* — **discount** *v* descontar (precios); descartar

**discourage** *v* desalentar, desanimar

**discover** *v* descubrir

**discreet** *adj* discreto

**discretion** *n* discreción *f*

**discriminate** *v* ~ **against** discriminar; ~ **between** distinguir entre — **discrimination** *n* discriminación *f*; discernimiento *m*

**discuss** *v* hablar de, discutir — **discussion** *n* discusión *f*

**disdain** *n* desdén *m* — **disdain** *v* desdeñar

**disease** *n* enfermedad *f*

**disgust** *n* asco *m*, repugnancia *f*

**dish** *n* plato *m*; *or* **serving** ~ fuente *f*; **wash the** ~**es** lavar los platos — **dish** *vt or* **dish up** servir

**disheveled** *or* **dishevelled** *adj* desaliñado, despeinado (del pelo)

**dishonest** *adj* deshonesto

**dishwasher** *n* lavaplatos *m*, lavavajillas *m*

**disillusion** *v* desilusionar — **disillusionment** *n* desilusión *f*

**disk** *or* **disc** *n* disco *m*

**dislike** *n* aversión *f*, antipatía *f* — **dislike** *v* tener aversión a

# disloyal

**disloyal** *adj* desleal
**dismiss** *v* despedir, destituir
**disorder** *n* desorden *m*
**disorganize** *v* desorganizar
**dispel** *v* disipar
**dispense** *v* repartir, distribuir; ~ **with** prescindir de
**disperse** *v* dispersar; dispersarse
**displace** *v* desplazar; reemplazar
**display** *v* exponer, exhibir — **display** *n* muestra *f*, exposición *f*
**displease** *v* desagradar
**disposal** *n* **have at one's** ~ tener a su disposición — **disposition** *n* temperamento *m*, carácter *m*
**dispute** *v* cuestionar; discutir — **dispute** *n* disputa *f*, conflicto *m*
**disqualification** *n* descalificación *f* — **disqualify** *v* (**-fied**) descalificar
**disrespectful** *adj* irrespetuoso
**disruption** *n* trastorno *m*
**dissolve** *v* disolver; disolverse
**dissuade** *v* disuadir
**distance** *n* distancia *f*; **in the** ~ a lo lejos — **distant** *adj* distante
**distinct** *adj* distinto; claro — **distinction** *n* distinción *f*
**distinguish** *v* distinguir
**distract** *v* distraer
**distress** *n* angustia *f*, aflicción *f*; **in** ~ en peligro — **distress** *v* afligir — **distressing** *adj* penoso
**distribute** *v* distribuir, repartir — **distribution** *n* distribución *f* — **distributor** *n* distribuidor *m*, -dora *f*
**district** *n* distrito *m* (zona política)
**distrust** *n* desconfianza *f* — **distrust** *v* desconfiar de
**disturbance** *n* alboroto *m*, disturbio *m*; interrupción *f*
**disuse** *n* **fall into** ~ caer en desuso
**ditto** *n* ~ **marks** comillas *fpl*
**diverse** *adj* diverso — **diversify** *v* (**-fied**) diversificar; diversificarse
**diversity** *n* diversidad *f*
**divert** *v* desviar

**divide** *v* dividir; dividirse
**dividend** *n* dividendo *m*
**division** *n* división *f*
**divorce** *n* divorcio *m* — **divorce** *v* divorciar; divorciarse — **divorcée** *n* divorciada *f*
**divulge** *v* revelar, divulgar
**dizzy** *adj* mareado — **dizziness** *n* mareo *m*, vértigo *m*
**DNA** *n* ADN *m*
**do** *v* (**did**; **done**) hacer; preparar; estar; ir, andar; ser suficiente; ~ **away with** abolir, eliminar; **how are you doing?** ¿cómo estás? — **do** *v aux* **do you know her?** ¿la conoces? **I don't know** yo no se; **do you speak English?** ¿habla inglés?
**doctor** *n* médico *m*, -ca; doctor *m*, -tora
**doctrine** *n* doctrina *f*
**document** *n* documento *m* — **document** *v* documentar — **documentary** *n* (**-ries**) documental *m*
**dodge** *v* esquivar, eludir
**dog** *n* perro *m*, -rra *f*
**dogma** *n* dogma *m* — **dogmatic** *adj* dogmático
**doll** *n* muñeco *m*, -ca *f*
**dollar** *n* dólar *m*
**dolphin** *n* delfín *m*
**domain** *n* dominio *m*; campo *m*, esfera *f*
**domination** *n* dominación *f* — **dominate** *v* dominar
**donate** *v* donar, hacer un donativo de — **donation** *n* donativo *m*
**done** *adj* terminado, hecho; cocido
**donkey** *n* (**-keys**) burro *m*
**donor** *n* donante *mf*
**door** *n* puerta *f* — **doorway** *n* entrada *f*, portal *m*
**dormitory** *n* (**-ries**) dormitorio *m*
**dose** *n* dosis *f* — **dosage** *n* dosis *f*
**dot** *n* punto *m*; **on the** ~ en punto
**double** *adj* doble — **double** *v* doblar; doblarse — **double** *adv* (el) doble — **double** *n* doble *mf* — **double bass** *n* contrabajo *m*

**doubt** *v* dudar; desconfiar de, dudar de — **doubt** *n* duda *f* — **doubtful** *adj* dudoso

**dough** *n* masa *f*

**dove** *n* paloma *f*

**down** *adv* hacia abajo; **come/go** ~ bajar; ~ **here** aquí abajo; **fall** ~ caer; **lie** ~ acostarse; **sit** ~ sentarse — **down** *prep* a lo largo de; a través de; **down the hill** cuesta abajo — **down** *adj* de bajada — **downhearted** *adj* desanimado — **downstairs** *adv* abajo — **downstairs** *adj* de abajo — **downtown** *n* centro *m* (de la ciudad) — **downtown** *adv* al centro, en el centro — **downtown** *adj* del centro

**dozen** *n* docena *f*

**draft** *n or* **rough** ~ borrador *m*; conscripción *f* (militar) — **draft** *v*; hacer el borrador de; reclutar

**drag** *v* arrastrar; arrastrarse

**drain** escurrir(se) (de los platos); alcantarilla *f*; agotamiento *m* — **drainpipe** *n* tubo *m* de desagüe

**drama** *n* drama *m* — **dramatic** *adj* dramático — **dramatist** *n* dramaturgo *m*, -ga *f* — **dramatize** *v* dramatizar

**drastic** *adj* drástico

**draw** *v* (**drew; drawn**) tirar de; dibujar, trazar; ~ **a conclusion** llegar a una conclusión; ~ **up** redactar — **draw** *n* empate *m*; atracción *f* — **drawer** *n* gaveta *f*, cajón *m* (en un mueble)

**dread** *v* temer — **dread** *n* pavor *m*, temor *m*

**dream** *n* sueño *m* — **dream** *v* (**dreamed** *or* **dreamt**) soñar; **dream up** idear — **dreamy** *adj* soñador

**dress** *v* vestir; vestirse — **dress** *n* ropa *f*; vestido *m* (de mujer)

**drill** *n* taladro *m* — **drill** *v* perforar, taladrar

**drink** *v* (**drank; drunk** *or* **drank**) beber — **drink** *n* bebida *f*

**drive** *v* (**drove; driven**) conducir; manejar; impulsar; ~ **one to (do . . . )** llevar a algún a (hacer . . . ) — **drive** *n* paseo *m* (en coche); energía *f*; instinto *m*

**driver** *n* conductor *m*, -tora *f*; chofer *m*

**drizzle** *n* llovizna *f* — **drizzle** *v* lloviznar

**drool** *v* babear — **drool** *n* baba *f*

**drop** *n* gota *f* (de líquido); caída *f* — **drop** *v* caer(se); bajar, descender; abandonar, dejar; **drop off** dejar

**drown** *v* ahogar; ahogarse

**drugstore** *n* farmacia *f*

**drum** *n* tambor *m*

**drunk** *adj* borracho

**dry** *adj* seco — **dry** *v* (**dried**) secar; secarse — **dryer** *n* secadora *f* — **dryness** *n* sequedad *f*, aridez *f*

**duck** *n* (**duck** *or* **ducks**) pato *m*, -ta *f*

**due** *adj* esperado; debido — **dues** *npl* cuota *f*

**duel** *n* duelo *m*

**dull** *adj* torpe — **dull** *v* entorpecer (los sentidos), aliviar (el dolor)

**duplicate** *adj* duplicado — **duplicate** *v* duplicar, hacer copias de — **duplicate** *n* duplicado *m*, copia *f*

**durable** *adj* duradero

**duration** *n* duración *f*

**during** *prep* durante

**dusk** *n* anochecer *m*, crepúsculo *m*

**dust** *n* polvo *m* — **dustpan** *n* recogedor *m*

**Dutch** *adj* holandés — **Dutch** *n* holandés *m* (idioma)

**dwarf** *n* (**dwarfs**) enano *m*, -na *f*

**dynamic** *adj* dinámico

# E

**e** *n* (**e's** *or* **es**) e *f*, quinta letra del alfabeto inglés

**each** *adj* cada — **each** *pron* cada uno *m*, cada una *f*; **each other** el uno al otro — **each** *adv* cada uno, por persona

**eager** *adj* entusiasta; impaciente — **eagerness** *n* entusiasmo *m*, impaciencia *f*

**eagle** *n* águila *f*

**ear** *n* oreja *f*

**early** *adv* temprano — **early** *adj* primero; **be early** llegar temprano

**earn** *v* ganar

**earnings** *npl* ingresos *mpl*; ganancias *fpl*

**earphone** *n* audífono *m*

**earring** *n* pendiente *m*, arete *m*

**earth** *n* tierra *f* — **earthquake** *n* terremoto *m* — **earthworm** *n* lombriz *f* (de tierra)

**ease** *n* facilidad *f*; comodidad *f*

**easily** *adv* fácilmente, con facilidad

**east** *adv* al este — **east** *n* este *m*; **the East** el Oriente

**easy** *adj* fácil — **easygoing** *adj* tolerante, relajado

**eat** *v* (**ate; eaten**) comer

**eccentricity** *n* excentricidad *f*

**echo** *n* (**echoes**) eco *m*

**eclipse** *n* eclipse *m*

**ecology** *n* ecología *f* — **ecological** *adj* ecológico

**economy** *n* economía *f* — **economic** *or* **economical** *adj* económico — **economics** *n* economía *f* — **economist** *n* economista *mf* — **economize** *v* economizar

**Ecuadoran** *or* **Ecuadorean** *or* **Ecuadorian** *adj* ecuatoriano

**edge** *n* borde *m*; filo *m* (de un cuchillo)

**edit** *v* editar, redactar, corregir — **edition** *n* edición *f* — **editor** *n* director *m*, -tora *f* (de un periódico); redactor *m*, -tora *f* (de un libro) — **editorial** *n* editorial *m*

**educate** *v* educar, instruir; informar — **education** *n* educación *f* — **educator** *n* educador *m*, -dora *f*

**effect** *n* efecto *m*; **go into** ∼ entrar en vigor — **effective** *adj* eficaz; efectivo, vigente — **effectiveness** *n* eficacia *f*

**efficient** *adj* eficiente — **efficiency** *n* eficiencia *f*

**effort** *n* esfuerzo *m*

**egg** *n* huevo *m* — **eggplant** *n* berenjena *f*

**eight** *n* ocho *m* — **eight** *adj* ocho — **eight hundred** *n* ochocientos *m*

**eighteen** *n* dieciocho *m* — **eighteen** *adj* dieciocho

**eighth** *n* octavo *m*, -va *f* (en una serie)

**eighty** *n* (**eighties**) ochenta *m* — **eighty** *adj* ochenta

**either** *adj* cualquiera (de los dos); ninguno; cada — **either** *pron* cualquiera *mf* (de los dos); ninguno *m*, -na *f* (de los dos); **either** *or* **either one** algún *m*, alguna *f* — **either** *conj* o; ni

**eject** *v* expulsar, expeler

**elaborate** *adj* detallado — **elaborate** *v* elaborar

**elastic** *adj* elástico — **elastic** *n* elástico *m*; goma *f* (elástica) — **elasticity** *n* elasticidad *f*

**elbow** *n* codo *m*

**elder** *adj* mayor — **elder** *n* mayor *mf*; anciano *m*, -na *f* (de un tribu, etc.) — **elderly** *adj* mayor, anciano

**elect** *v* elegir — **election** *n* elección *f* — **electoral** *adj* electoral — **electorate** *n* electorado *m*

**electricity** *n* electricidad *f* — **electrician** *n* electricista *mf* — **electrify** *v* (**-fied**) electrificar

**electronic** *adj* electrónico — **electronic mail** *or* **E-mail** *n* correo *m* electrónico

**elegant** *adj* elegante — **elegance** *n* elegancia *f*

**element** *n* elemento *m* — **elementary school** *n* escuela *f* primaria

**elephant** *n* elefante *m*, -ta *f*

**elevate** *v* elevar — **elevator** *n* ascensor *m*

**eleven** *n* once *m* — **eleven** *adj* once — **eleventh** *adj* undécimo — **eleventh** *n* undécimo *m*, -ma *f* (en una serie); onceavo *m*, onceava parte *f*

**eliminate** *v* eliminar — **elimination** *n* eliminación *f*

**elliptical** *or* **elliptic** *adj* elíptico

**elm** *n* olmo *m*

**else**[1] *adv* **how** ~ **?** ¿de qué otro modo?; **where** ~ **?** ¿en qué otro sitio?; **or** ~ si no, de lo contrario — **elsewhere** *adv* en otra parte

**else**[2] *adj* **everyone** ~ todos los demás; **nobody** ~ ningún otro, nadie más; **nothing** ~ nada más

**embark** *v* embarcar

**embarrass** *v* avergonzar — **embarrassing** *adj* embarazoso — **embarrassment** *n* vergüenza *f*

**embellish** *v* adornar, embellecer — **embellishment** *n* adorno *m*

**embrace** *v* abrazar — **embrace** *n* abrazo *m*

**embryo** *n* (**embryos**) embrión *m*

**emerald** *n* esmeralda *f*

**emerge** *v* salir, aparecer

**emergency** *n* (**-cies**) emergencia *f*; ~ **exit** salida *f* de emergencia; ~ **room** sala *f* de urgencias, sala *f* de guardia

**emigrant** *n* emigrante *mf* — **emigrate** *v* emigrar — **emigration** *n* emigración *f*

**emotion** *n* emoción *f* — **emotional** *adj* emocional; emotivo

**emphasis** *n* (**-phases**) énfasis *m* — **emphasize** *v* subrayar — **emphatic** *adj* enérgico, categórico

**employ** *v* emplear — **employee** *n* empleado *m*, -da *f* — **employer** *n* patrón *m*, -trona *f*; empleador *m*, -dora *f* — **employment** *n* trabajo *m*, empleo *m*

**empty** *adj* vacío — **empty** *v* (**-tied**) vaciar — **emptiness** *n* vacío *m*

**enable** *v* hacer posible, permitir

**enclose** *v* encerrar, cercar — **enclosure** *n* anexo *m* (con una carta)

**encourage** *v* animar, alentar — **encouragement** *n* aliento *m*; fomento *m*

**encyclopedia** *n* enciclopedia *f*

**end** *n* fin; extremo *m*, punta *f* — **end** *v* terminar

**endeavor** *v* ~ **to** esforzarse por — **endeavor** *n* esfuerzo *m*

**ending** *n* final *m*, desenlace *m*

**endless** *adj* interminable; innumerable

**endure** *v* soportar, aguantar; durar

**enemy** *n* (**-mies**) enemigo *m*, -ga *f*

**energy** *n* energía *f* — **energetic** *adj* enérgico

**engage** *v* captar, atraer (la atención, etc.) — **engagement** *n* cita *f*, hora *f*; compromiso *m* — **engaging** *adj* atractivo

**engine** *n* motor *m* — **engineer** *n* ingeniero *m*, -ra *f*; maquinista *mf* (de locomotoras) — **engineering** *n* ingeniería *f*

**English** *adj* inglés — **English** *n* inglés *m* (idioma) — **Englishman** *n* (**-men**) inglés *m* — **Englishwoman** *n* (**-women**) inglesa *f*

**enhance** *v* aumentar, mejorar

**enjoy** *v* disfrutar, gozar de — **enjoyable** *adj* agradable — **enjoyment** *n* placer *m*

**enlarge** *v* agrandar, agrandarse; ampliar — **enlargement** *n* ampliación *f*

**enlist** *v* alistar

**enormous** *adj* enorme

**enough** *adj* bastante, suficiente — **enough** *adv* bastante — **enough** *pron* (lo) suficiente, (lo) bastante; **not enough** no basta

**enrage** *v* enfurecer

**enrich** *v* enriquecer

**enroll** *v* matricular, inscribir

**ensure** *v* asegurar

**entail** *v* suponer, conllevar

**entangle** *v* enredar — **entanglement** *n* enredo *m*

**enter** *v* entrar (en); ~ **into** firmar (un acuerdo), entablar (negociaciones, etc.)

**enterprise** *n* empresa *f* — **enterprising** *adj* emprendedor

**entertain** *v* entretener, divertir; considerar — **entertainment** *n* entretenimiento *m,* diversión *f*

**enthrall** *or* **enthral** *v* cautivar, embelesar

**enthusiasm** *n* entusiasmo *m* — **enthusiast** *n* entusiasta *mf* — **enthusiastic** *adj* entusiasta

**entire** *adj* entero, completo — **entirely** *adv* completamente

**entitle** *v* titular

**entity** *n* (**-ties**) entidad *f*

**entrance**[1] *v* encantar, fascinar

**entrance**[2] *n* entrada *f*

**entrust** *v* confiar

**entry** *n* (**-tries**) entrada *f*; entrada *f,* anotación *f*

**envelop** *v* envolver — **envelope** *n* sobre *m*

**envious** *adj* envidioso

**environment** *n* medio *m* ambiente

**envy** *n* envidia *f* — **envy** *v* (**-vied**) envidiar

**enzyme** *n* enzima *f*

**epidemic** *n* epidemia *f*

**episode** *n* episodio *m*

**epoch** *n* época *f*

**equal** *adj* igual; **be** ~ **to** estar a la altura de (una tarea, etc.) — **equal** *n* igual *mf* — **equal** *v* igualar — **equality** *n* igualdad *f*

**equation** *n* ecuación *f*

**equator** *n* ecuador *m*

**equilibrium** *n* (**-riums** *or* **-ria**) equilibrio *m*

**equipment** *n* equipo *m*

**equivalent** *adj* equivalente — **equivalent** *n* equivalente *m*

**era** *n* era *f,* época *f*

**erase** *v* borrar — **eraser** *n* goma *f* de borrar, borrador *m*

**errand** *n* mandado *m,* recado *m*

**error** *n* error *m* — **erroneous** *adj* erróneo

**eruption** *n* erupción *f*

**escalator** *n* escalera *f* mecánica

**escape** *v* escapar a, evitar; escaparse, fugarse — **escape** *n* fuga *f*; **escape from reality** evasión *f* de la realidad

**Eskimo** *adj* esquimal

**especially** *adv* especialmente

**espresso** *n* (**-sos**) café *m* exprés

**essay** *n* ensayo *m* (literario), composición *f* (académica)

**essence** *n* esencia *f* — **essential** *adj* esencial

**establish** *v* establecer — **establishment** *n* establecimiento *m*

**estimate** *v* calcular, estimar — **estimate** *n* cálculo *m* (aproximado); **estimate of costs** presupuesto *m* — **estimation** *n* juicio *m*; estima *f*

**eternal** *adj* eterno — **eternity** *n* (**-ties**) eternidad *f*

**ethics** *ns & pl* ética *f,* moralidad *f*

**ethnic** *adj* étnico

**euphemism** *n* eufemismo *m*

**European** *adj* europeo

**evaluate** *v* evaluar

**eve** *n* víspera *f*

**even** *adj* regular, constante; igual; ~ **number** número *m* par — **even** *adv* hasta, incluso

**evening** *n* tarde *f,* noche *f*

**event** *n* acontecimiento *m,* suceso *m*; prueba *f* (en deportes); **in the** ~ **of** en caso de

**ever** *adv* siempre

**every** *adj* cada; ~ **month** todos los meses; ~ **other day** cada dos días — **everybody** *pron* todos *mpl,* -das *fpl;* todo el mundo — **everyday** *adj* cotidiano, de todos los días — **everything** *pron* todo — **everywhere** *adv* en todas partes, por todas partes

**evidence** *n* pruebas *fpl*; testimonio *m*, declaración *f*

**evil** *adj* malvado, malo — **evil** *n* mal *m*, maldad *f*

**evolution** *n* evolución *f*, desarrollo *m*

**exact** *adj* exacto, preciso — **exact** *v* exigir — **exactly** *adv* exactamente

**exaggerate** *v* exagerar — **exaggeration** *n* exageración *f*

**examine** *v* examinar — **exam** *n* examen *m* — **examination** *n* examen *m*

**example** *n* ejemplo *m*

**excellent** *adj* excelente

**except** *prep or* ∼ **for** excepto, menos, salvo — **except** *v* exceptuar — **exception** *n* excepción *f* — **exceptional** *adj* excepcional

**excess** *n* exceso *m* — **excess** *adj* excesivo, de sobra

**exchange** *n* intercambio *m* — **exchange** *v* cambiar, intercambiar

**excite** *v* excitar, emocionar — **excited** *adj* excitado, entusiasmado — **excitement** *n* entusiasmo *m*, emoción *f*

**exclaim** *v* exclamar — **exclamation** *n* exclamación *f* — **exclamation point** *n* signo *m* de admiración

**excluding** *prep* excepto, con excepción de — **exclusion** *n* exclusión *f* — **exclusive** *adj* exclusivo

**excuse** *v* perdonar; ∼ **me** perdóne, perdón — **excuse** *n* excusa *f*

**execute** *v* **-cuted; -cuting** ejecutar

**executive** *adj* ejecutivo — **executive** *n* ejecutivo *m*, -va *f*

**exemplify** *v* (**-fied**) ejemplificar

**exercise** *n* ejercicio *m* — **exercise** *v* hacer ejercicio

**exhaust** *v* agotar — **exhaustive** *adj* exhaustivo

**exhibit** *v* exponer; mostrar — **exhibition** *n* exposición *f*

**exist** *v* existir — **existence** *n* existencia *f*

**exit** *n* salida *f* — **exit** *v* salir

**expect** *v* esperar; contar con

**expedition** *n* expedición *f*

**expend** *v* gastar — **expense** *n* gasto *m*; **expenses** *npl* gastos *mpl*, expensas *fpl* — **expensive** *adj* caro

**experience** *n* experiencia *f* — **experience** *v* experimentar — **experiment** *n* experimento *m*

**expert** *adj* experto — **expert** *n* experto *m*, -ta *f* — **expertise** *n* pericia *f*, competencia *f*

**expire** *v* caducar, vencer — **expiration** *n* vencimiento *m*, caducidad *f*

**explain** *v* explicar — **explanation** *n* explicación *f*

**explicit** *adj* explícito

**export** *v* exportar — **export** *n* exportación *f*

**expose** *v* exponer; descubrir, revelar

**express** *adj* expreso, rápido — **express** *adv* por correo urgente — **express** *v* expresar — **expression** *n* expresión *f*

**extend** *v* extender; prolongar; ampliar — **extension** *n* extensión *f*; **extension cord** alargador, extensión *m*

**exterior** *adj* exterior — **exterior** *n* exterior *m*

**external** *adj* externo

**extra** *adj* suplementario, de más — **extra** *n* extra *m* — **extra** *adv* extra, más

**extraordinary** *adj* extraordinario

**extreme** *adj* extremo — **extremity** *n* (**-ties**) extremidad *f*

**extrovert** *n* extrovertido *m*, -da *f* — **extroverted** *adj* extrovertido

**eye** *n* ojo *m*; visión *f*, vista *f*; mirada *f* — **eye** *v* mirar — **eyebrow** *n* ceja *f* — **eyeglasses** *npl* anteojos *mpl*, lentes *mpl* — **eyelash** *n* pestaña *f* — **eyelid** *n* párpado *m* — **eyesight** *n* vista *f*, visión *f*

# F

**f** *n* (**f's** *or* **fs**) f, sexta letra del alfabeto inglés

**fable** *n* fábula *f*

**fabric** *n* tela *f*, tejido *m*

**fabulous** *adj* fabuloso

**facade** *n* fachada *f*

**face** *n* cara *f*, rostro *m* (de una persona); fisonomía *f*, aspecto *m*; cara *f* (de una moneda), fachada *f* (de un edificio); ~ **value** valor *m* nominal; **in the ~ of** en medio de, ante — **face** *v* estar frente a; enfrentarse a; dar a — **facedown** *adv* boca abajo — **faceless** *adj* anónimo

**facial** *adj* de la cara, facial

**facetious** *adj* gracioso, burlón

**facility** *n* (**-ties**) facilidad *f*

**facsimile** *n* facsímile *m*, facsímil *m*

**fact** *n* hecho *m*; **in ~** en realidad

**faction** *n* facción *m*, bando *m*

**factor** *n* factor *m*

**factory** *n* (**-ries**) fábrica *f*

**faculty** *n* (**-ties**) facultad *f*

**fad** *n* moda *f* pasajera, manía *f*

**fail** *v* fracasar (de una empresa, un matrimonio, etc.); fallar; ~ **in** faltar a, no cumplir con; suspender, ser reprobado ~ **to do** no hacer; reprobar — **fail** *n* **without fail** sin falta — **failure** *n* fracaso *m*; falla *f*

**faint** *v* desmayarse — **faint** *n* desmayo *m* — **faintly** *adv* débilmente

**fair**[1] *n* feria *f*

**fair**[2] *adj* justo — **fair** *adv* **play fair** jugar limpio — **fairly** *adv* bastante — **fairness** *n* justicia *f*

**fairy** *n* (**fairies**) hada; ~ **tale** cuento *m* de hadas

**faith** *n* fe *f* — **faithful** *adj* fiel — **faithfulness** *n* fidelidad *f*

**fall** *v* (**fell; fallen**) caer, bajar (de los precios), descender (de la temperatura); ~ **asleep** dormirse; ~ **in love** ena-

morarse; ~ **through** fracasar — **fall** *n* caída *f*, bajada *f* (de precios), descenso *m* (de temperatura); otoño *m*

**false** *adj* falso; ~ **teeth** dentadura *f* postiza

**fame** *n* fama *f*

**familiar** *adj* familiar — **familiarity** *n* familiaridad *f*

**family** *n* (**-lies**) familia *f*

**famous** *adj* famoso

**fan** *n* ventilador *m*, abanico *m*; aficionado *m*, -da *f* (a un pasatiempo); admirador *m*, -dora *f* (de una persona) — **fan** *v* avivar (un fuego)

**fantasy** *n* (**-sies**) fantasía *f* — **fantastic** *adj* fantástico

**far** *adv* (**farther** *or* **further; farthest** *or* **furthest**) lejos; **as ~ as** hasta (un lugar), con respecto a (un tema); ~ **away** a lo lejos; ~ **from it!** ¡todo lo contrario!; **so ~** hasta ahora, todavía — **far** *adj* (**farther** *or* **further; farthest** *or* **furthest**) lejano — **faraway** *adj* remoto, lejano

**farewell** *n* despedida *f*

**farm** *n* granja *f*, hacienda *f* — **farm** *v* cultivar (la tierra), criar (animales); ser agricultor — **farmer** *n* agricultor *m*, -tora *f*; granjero *m*, -jera *f* — **farmhand** *n* peón *m* — **farming** *n* agricultura *f*, cultivo *m* (de plantas), crianza *f* (de animales)

**fascinate** *v* fascinar — **fascination** *n* fascinación *f*

**fashion** *n* manera *f*; moda *f*; **out of ~** pasada de moda

**fast** *adj* rápido; ~ **friends** amigos *mpl* leales — **fast** *adv* firmemente; rápidamente; **fast asleep** profundamente dormido

**fasten** *v* sujetar (papeles, etc.), abrochar (una blusa, etc.), abrocharse; cerrar (una maleta, etc.) — **fastener** *n* cierre *m*

**fat** *adj* gordo — **fat** *n* grasa *f*

**fatal** *adj* mortal — **fatality** *n* (**-ties**) víctima *f* mortal

**fate** *n* suerte *f*

**father** *n* padre *m* — **fatherhood** *n* paternidad *f* — **father–in–law** *n* (**fathers– . . .**) suegro *m* — **fatherly** *adj* paternal

**fatigue** *n* fatiga *f*

**fatten** *v* engordar

**faucet** *n* grifo *m*

**fault** *n* defecto *m*; culpa *f*; falla *f* (geológica) — **faulty** *adj* defectuoso

**fauna** *n* fauna *f*

**favor** *n* favor *m*; **in ∼ of** a favor de — **favor** *v* favorecer; estar a favor de — **favorable** *adj* favorable — **favorite** *n* favorito *m*, -ta *f* — **favorite** *adj* favorito

**fear** *n* miedo *m*, temor *m* — **fear** *v* temer — **fearful** *adj* temeroso

**feasible** *adj* viable, factible

**feast** *n* fiesta *f* — **feast** *v* **feast upon** darse un festín de

**feat** *n* hazaña *f*

**feather** *n* pluma *f*

**feature** *n* rasgo *m* (de la cara); **∼ film** largometraje *m*

**February** *n* febrero *m*

**fed up** *adj* harto

**fee** *n* honorarios *mpl*

**feeble** *adj* débil

**feed** *v* (**fed**) dar de comer a, alimentar(se); comer

**feel** *v* (**felt**) sentir (una sensación, etc.); tocar, palpar — **feel** *n* tacto *m*, sensación *f* — **feeling** *n* sensación *f*; sentimiento *m*

**feign** *v* fingir

**female** *adj* femenino — **female** *n* mujer *f* (persona); hembra *f* (animal)

**feminine** *adj* femenino — **feminism** *n* feminismo *m*

**fence** *n* cerco *m*, -ca *f*; valla *f* — **fence** *v*

hacer esgrima — **fencing** *n* esgrima *m* (deporte)

**fender** *n* guardabarros *mpl*

**ferment** *v* fermentar — **fermentation** *n* fermentación *f*

**fertility** *n* fertilidad *f* — **fertilize** *v* fecundar (un huevo), abonar (el suelo)

**festive** *adj* festivo — **festivity** *n* (**-ties**) festividad *f*

**fever** *n* fiebre *f*

**few** *adj* pocos; **a ∼ times** varias veces — **few** *pron* pocos; **a few** algunos, unos cuantos — **fewer** *adj or pron* menos

**fiber** *or* **fibre** *n* fibra *f*

**fiction** *n* ficción *f* — **fictional** *or* **fictitious** *adj* ficticio

**fidelity** *n* fidelidad *f*

**field** *n* campo *m*

**fifteen** *n* quince *m* — **fifteen** *adj* quince

**fifth** *n* quinto *m*, -ta *f* (en una serie); quinto *m* (en matemáticas) — **fifth** *adj* quinto

**fifty** *n* (**-ties**) cincuenta *m* — **fifty** *adj* cincuenta

**fight** *v* (**fought**) luchar (contra); pelear — **fight** *n* lucha *f*; pelea *f* — **fighter** *n* luchador *m*, -dora *f*

**figure** *n* número *m*, cifra *f*; figura *f*; **watch one's ∼** cuidar la línea — **figure** *v* figurar

**file**[1] *n* lima *f* (instrumento) — **file** *v* limar

**file**[2] *v* archivar (documentos) — **file** *n* archivo *m*

**file**[3] *n* fila *f*

**fill** *v* llenar, rellenar

**film** *n* película *f* — **film** *v* filmar

**filter** *n* filtro *m* — **filter** *v* filtrar

**fin** *n* aleta *f*

**final** *adj* final — **final** *n* final *f* (en deportes) — **finalist** *n* finalista *mf* — **finalize** *v* finalizar

**finance** *n* finanzas *fpl*; **∼s** *npl* recursos *mpl* financieros — **finance** *v* financiar — **financial** *adj* financiero

**find** *v* (**found**) encontrar; darse cuenta

de; ~ **out** enterarse — **find** *n* hallazgo
*m* — **finding** *n* hallazgo *m*

**fine¹** *n* multa *f* — **fine** *v* multar

**fine²** *adj* fino; sutil — **fine** *adv* bien —
**fine arts** *npl* bellas artes *fpl* — **finely**
*adv* fino, menudo

**finger** *n* dedo *m* — **fingernail** *n* uña *f* —
**fingerprint** *n* huella *f* digital

**finish** *v* acabar, terminar

**finite** *adj* finito

**fire** *n* fuego *m*; incendio *m*; **catch** ~ incendiarse (de bosques, etc.), prenderse
(de fósforos, etc.) — **firearm** *n* arma *f*
de fuego — **firefighter** *n* bombero *m*,
-ra *f* — **firefly** *n* (**-flies**) luciérnaga *f* —
**fireplace** *n* hogar *m*, chimenea *f* —
**firewood** *n* leña *f* — **fireworks** *npl*
fuegos *mpl* artificiales

**firm¹** *n* empresa *f*

**firm²** *adj* firme — **firmness** *n* firmeza *f*

**first** *adj* primero; **at** ~ **sight** a primera
vista; **for the** ~ **time** por primera vez
— **first** *adv* primero; **first of all** en
primer lugar — **first** *n* primero *m*, -ra *f*
— **first aid** *n* primeros auxilios *mpl*

**fiscal** *adj* fiscal

**fish** *n* (**fish**) pez *m* (vivo), pescado *m*
(para comer) — **fish** *v* pescar — **fisherman** *n* (**-men**) pescador *m*, -dora *f* —
**fishing** *n* pesca *f* — **fish market** *n*
pescadería *f*

**fit¹** *n* ataque *m*

**fit²** *adj* en forma — **fit** *v* quedar bien a (de
la ropa); caber (en una caja, etc.), enca-
jar (en un hueco, etc.) — **fitness** *n*
salud *f*

**five** *n* cinco *m* — **five** *adj* cinco — **five
hundred** *n* quinientos *m* — **five hundred** *adj* quinientos

**fix** *v* fijar, sujetar; arreglar — **fixed** *adj*
fijo

**flag** *n* bandera *f* — **flagpole** *n* asta *f*

**flame** *n* llama *f*

**flammable** *adj* inflamable

**flap** *n* solapa *f* (de un sobre, un libro,
etc.), tapa *f* (de un recipiente) — **flap** *v*
batir, agitar

**flash** *n* ~ **of lightning** relámpago *m*; **in
a** ~ de repente — **flashlight** *n* linterna
*f*

**flatter** *v* halagar — **flattering** *adj* halagador — **flattery** *n* halagos *mpl*

**flavor** *n* gusto *m*, sabor *m*

**flaw** *n* defecto *m*

**flea** *n* pulga *f*

**flee** *v* (**fled**) huir (de)

**fleet** *n* flota *f*

**fleeting** *adj* fugaz

**Flemish** *adj* flamenco

**flexibility** *n* flexibilidad *f* — **flexible** *adj*
flexible

**flier** *n* folleto *m*

**flight** *n* vuelo *m*

**flipper** *n* aleta *f*

**float** *n* flotador *m* — **float** *v* flotar; hacer
flotar

**flock** *n* rebaño *m* (de ovejas), bandada *f*
(de pájaros)

**flood** *n* inundación *f* — **flood** *v* inundar
— **floodlight** *n* foco *m*

**floor** *n* suelo *m*, piso *m*; **dance** ~ pista *f*
de baile

**floppy disk** *n* diskette *m*, disquete *m*

**flour** *n* harina *f*

**flourish** *v* florecer

**flow** *v* fluir, correr

**flower** *n* flor *f* — **flower** *v* florecer —
**flowerpot** *n* maceta *f*

**flu** *n* gripe *f*

**fluctuate** *v* fluctuar — **fluctuation** *n*
fluctuación *f*

**fluency** *n* fluidez *f* — **fluent** *adj* fluido

**fluid** *adj* fluido

**flush** *n* rubor *m*, sonrojo *m*

**flute** *n* flauta *f*

**fly¹** *v* (**flew; flown**) volar; ir en avión;
correr — **flyer** *n* volante *m*

**fly²** *n* (**flies**) mosca *f* (insecto)

**foamy** *adj* espumoso

**focus** *n* (**-ci**) foco *m*; **be in** ~ estar enfo-
cado; ~ **of attention** centro *m* de

atención — **focus** v v enfocar; centrar (la atención, etc.); **focus on** enfocar (con los ojos), concentrarse en (con la mente)

**fog** n niebla f

**fold** v doblar, plegar; or ～ **up** doblarse, plegarse — **fold** n pliegue m — **folder** n carpeta f

**folklore** n folklore m

**follow** v seguir; ～ **up on** seguir con — **following** adj siguiente — **following** n seguidores mpl

**fondness** n afición f

**food** n comida f, alimento m

**fool** v bromear — **foolishness** n tontería f

**foot** n (**feet**) pie m — **football** n fútbol m americano — **footprint** n huella f — **footwear** n calzado m

**for** prep para; por; durante; con respecto a — **for** conj puesto que, porque

**forage** v ～ **for** buscar

**forbid** v (**-bade**; **-bidden**) prohibir

**force** n fuerza f; **by** ～ por la fuerza; **in** ～ en vigor, en vigencia; **armed** ～**s** fuerzas fpl armadas — **force** v forzar

**forearm** n antebrazo m

**forecast** v (**-cast**) predecir, pronosticar — **forecast** n predicción f, pronóstico m

**forefinger** n índice m, dedo m índice

**forefront** n **at/in the** ～ a la vanguardia

**forehead** n frente f

**foreign** adj extranjero — **foreigner** n extranjero m, -ra f

**forest** n bosque m

**foretell** v (**-told**) predecir

**forever** adv para siempre

**forfeit** n prenda f (en un juego)

**forge** n herrería — **forge** v forjar (metal, etc.); falsificar

**forget** v (**-got**; **-gotten** or **-got**) olvidar(se), olvidarse de — **forgetful** adj olvidadizo

**forgive** v (**-gave**; **-given**) perdonar — **forgiveness** n perdón m

**form** n forma f; formulario m — **form** v formar(se)

**formal** adj formal — **formality** n formalidad f

**formation** n forma f

**former** adj antiguo, anterior

**formula** n (**-las** or **-lae**) fórmula f

**fortunate** adj afortunado — **fortunately** adv afortunadamente — **fortune** n fortuna f

**forty** n (**forties**) cuarenta m — **forty** adj cuarenta

**forward** adj hacia adelante (en dirección), delantero (en posición) — **forward** adv (hacia) adelante — **forward** n delantero m, -ra f (en deportes)

**foul** n falta f (en deportes) — **foul** v cometer faltas (en deportes)

**found** v fundar, establecer — **foundation** n fundamento m; cimientos mpl (de un edificio)

**fountain** n fuente f

**four** n cuatro m — **four** adj cuatro — **four hundred** adj cuatrocientos — **four hundred** n cuatrocientos m

**fourteen** n catorce m — **fourteen** adj catorce

**fourth** n cuarto m, -ta f (en una serie); cuarto m, cuarta parte f — **fourth** adj cuarto

**fox** n zorro m, -ra f

**foyer** n vestíbulo m

**fraction** n fracción f

**fracture** n fractura f — **fracture** v fracturar

**fragile** adj frágil

**fragment** n fragmento m

**fragrance** n fragancia f, aroma m

**frail** adj débil, delicado

**frame** n marco m (de un cuadro, una puerta, etc.); or ～**s** npl montura f (para anteojos) — **frame** v enmarcar; formular

**frank** adj franco

**fraternal** adj fraterno, fraternal — **fraternity** n (**-ties**) fraternidad f

**freckle** *n* peca *f*

**free** *adj* libre; *or* ∿ **of charge** gratuito, gratis; suelto — **free** *v* liberar, poner en libertad; soltar, desatar — **free** *adv or* **for free** gratis — **freedom** *n* libertad *f* — **free will** *n* libre albedrío *m*

**freeze** *v* (**froze**; **frozen**) congelar(se); helar(se) — **freezer** *n* congelador *m* — **freezing** *adj* helado

**French** *adj* francés — **French** *n* francés *m* (idioma) — **Frenchman** *n* francés *m* — **french fries** *npl* papas *fpl* fritas

**frequent** *v* frecuentar — **frequency** *n* frecuencia *f* — **frequently** *adv* a menudo, frecuentemente

**fresh** *adj* fresco; ∿ **water** agua *m* dulce

**friction** *n* fricción *f*

**Friday** *n* viernes *m*

**friend** *n* amigo *m*, -ga *f* — **friendliness** *n* simpatía *f* — **friendship** *n* amistad *f*

**fright** *n* miedo *m*, susto *m* — **frighten** *v* asustar, espantar — **frightening** *adj* espantoso

**frill** *n* volante *m*

**frisk** *v* cachear, registrar

**frivolous** *adj* frívolo — **frivolity** *n* frivolidad *f*

**frog** *n* rana *f*

**from** *prep* de; desde; de, por; ∿ **now on** a partir de ahora

**front** *n* parte *f* delantera — **front** *vi or* **front on** dar a, estar orientado a — **front** *adj* delantero, de adelante

**frontier** *n* frontera *f*

**frost** *n* helada *f*; escarcha *f* (en una superficie)

**froth** *n* espuma *f* — **frothy** *adj* espumoso

**fruit** *n* fruta *f*; fruto *m* — **fruitful** *adj* fructífero — **fruitless** *adj* infructuoso

**frustrate** *v* frustrar — **frustration** *n* frustración *f*

**fry** *v* (**fried**) freír — **frying pan** *n* sartén *mf*

**fuel** *n* combustible *m*

**fugitive** *n* fugitivo *m*, -va *f*

**full** *adj* lleno; completo, detallado; de lleno

**fun** *n* diversión *f*; **have** ∿ divertirse — **fun** *adj* divertido

**function** *n* función *f* — **function** *v* funcionar — **functional** *adj* funcional

**fund** *n* fondo *m*; ∿**s** *npl* fondos *mpl* — **fund** *v* financiar

**fundamental** *adj* fundamental — **fundamentals** *npl* fundamentos *mpl*

**funeral** *adj* funeral, fúnebre — **funeral** *n* funeral *m*, funerales *mpl* — **funeral home** *or* **funeral parlor** *n* funeraria *f*

**fungus** *n* (**fungi**) hongo *m*

**funny** *adj* divertido, gracioso

**furious** *adj* furioso

**furnace** *n* horno *m*

**furnish** *v* amueblar (una casa, etc.) — **furniture** *n* muebles *mpl*, mobiliario *m*

**furry** *adj* peludo (de un animal), de peluche (de un juguete, etc.)

**furthermore** *adv* además

**fuse**[1] *n* mecha *f* (de una bomba, etc.)

**fuse**[2] *v* fundir(se); fusionar(se) — **fusion** *n* fusión *f*

**fuss** *n* jaleo *m*, alboroto *m*

**future** *adj* futuro — **future** *n* futuro *m*

# G

**g** *n* (**g's** *or* **gs**) g *f*, séptima letra del alfabeto inglés

**gaiety** *n* alegría *f* — **gaily** *adv* alegremente

**gain** *n* ganancia *f*; aumento *m* — **gain** *v* ganar, adquirir

**galaxy** *n* (**-axies**) galaxia *f*

**gallery** *n* (**-leries**) galería *f*

**gallon** *n* galón *m*

**gallop** *v* galopar — **gallop** *n* galope *m*

**gamble** *v* jugar; jugarse — **gamble** *n* apuesta *f* — **gambler** *n* jugador *m*, -dora *f*

**game** *n* juego *m*; partido *m*

**gang** *n* banda *f*, pandilla *f*

**gap** *n* espacio *m*; intervalo *m*; brecha *f*, distancia *f*

**garage** *n* garaje *m*

**garbage** *n* basura *f* — **garbage can** *n* cubo *m* de la basura

**garden** *n* jardín *m* — **gardener** *n* jardinero *m*, -ra *f*

**garlic** *n* ajo *m*

**gas** *n* (**gases**) gas *m*; gasolina *f*

**gasoline** *n* gasolina *f*

**gasp** *v* dar un grito ahogado

**gas station** *n* gasolinera *f*

**gastronomy** *n* gastronomía *f*

**gate** *n* puerta *f*; barrera *f* — **gateway** *n* puerta *f*

**gather** *v* reunir; recoger; deducir; reunirse (de personas), acumularse (de cosas) — **gathering** *n* reunión *f*

**gauze** *n* gasa *f*

**gay** *adj* alegre; gay, homosexual

**gaze** *v* mirar (fijamente) — **gaze** *n* mirada *f*

**gear** *n* equipo *m*; efectos *mpl* personales; marcha *f* (de un vehículo)

**gelatin** *n* gelatina *f*

**gender** *n* sexo *m*; género *m* (en la gramática)

**gene** *n* gen *m*, gene *m*

**genealogy** *n* genealogía *f*

**general** *adj* general — **general** *n* general *mf* (militar); **in general** en general, por lo general — **generalize** *v* generalizar — **generally** *adv* generalmente, en general

**generate** *v* generar — **generation** *n* generación *f*

**generous** *adj* generoso; abundante — **generosity** *n* generosidad *f*

**genial** *adj* afable, simpático

**genius** *n* genio *m*

**gentle** *adj* suave, dulce; ligero — **gentleman** *n* (**-men**) caballero *m*, señor *m* — **gentleness** *n* delicadeza *f*, ternura *f*

**genuine** *adj* verdadero, auténtico

**geography** *n* geografía *f*

**geology** *n* geología *f*

**geometry** *n* geometría *f*

**geriatric** *adj* geriátrico — **geriatrics** *n* geriatría *f*

**German** *adj* alemán — **German** *n* alemán *m* (idioma)

**gesture** *n* gesto *m*

**get** *v* (**got; got** *or* **gotten**) conseguir, obtener; recibir; ganar; traer; coger, agarrar; entender; preparar; ponerse, hacerse; ir; avanzar; **have got** tener; **have got to** tener que; **get up** levantarse

**ghost** *n* fantasma *f*, espectro *m* — **ghostly** *adv* fantasmal

**giant** *n* gigante *m*, -ta *f* — **giant** *adj* gigantesco

**gift** *n* regalo *m*; don *m*

**gigantic** *adj* gigantesco

**gild** *v* (**gilded** *or* **gilt**) dorar

**ginger** *n* jengibre *m*

**giraffe** *n* jirafa *f*

**girl** *n* niña *f*, muchacha *f*, chica *f* — **girlfriend** *n* novia *f*, amiga *f*

**gist** *n* essencia *f* **get the ～ of** comprender lo esencial de

**give** *v* (**gave; given**) dar; señalar; presentar; ceder; **～ out** repartir; agotarse; **～ up** rendirse — **given** *adj* determinado; dado, inclinado — **given name** *n* nombre *m* de pila

**glad** *adj* alegre, contento; **be ～** alegrarse; **～ to meet you!** ¡mucho gusto! — **gladden** *v* alegrar — **gladly** *adv* con mucho gusto — **gladness** *n* alegría *f*, gozo *m*

**glance** *v* **～ at** mirar, dar un vistazo a — **glance** *n* mirada *f*, vistazo *m*

**glare** *v* brillar, relumbrar

**glass** *n* vidrio *m*, cristal *m*; **a ～ of milk**

un vaso de leche; **~es** *npl* anteojos *mpl*, lentes *fpl* — **glassware** *n* cristalería *f*

**gleam** *n* destello *m*

**glide** *v* deslizarse (en una superficie), planear (en el aire)

**glimmer** *n* luz *f* trémula, luz *f* tenue

**globe** *n* globo *m* — **global** *adj* global, mundial

**gloom** *n* oscuridad *f*; tristeza *f* — **gloomy** *adj* sombrío, tenebroso; deprimente, lúgubre; pesimista

**glory** *n* (**-ries**) gloria *f*

**glossary** *n* (**-ries**) glosario *m*

**glove** *n* guante *m*

**glow** *v* brillar, resplandecer — **glow** *n* resplandor *m*, brillo *m*

**glue** *n* pegamento *m*, cola *f* — **glue** *v* pegar

**glum** *adj* sombrío, triste

**go** *v* (**went; gone**) ir; irse, salir; ir, extenderse; venderse; funcionar, marchar; desaparecer — **go** *v aux* **be going to** ir a — **go** *n* (**goes**) **be on the ~** no parar

**goal** *n* meta *m*, objetivo *m*; gol *m* (en deportes) — **goalkeeper** *or* **goalie** *n* portero *m*, -ra *f*; arquero *m*, -ra *f*

**goat** *n* cabra *f*

**god** *n* dios *m*; **God** Dios *m* — **godchild** *n* (**-children**) ahijado *m*, -da *f* — **godfather** *n* padrino *m* — **godmother** *n* madrina *f* — **godparents** *npl* padrinos *mpl*

**gold** *n* oro *m* — **golden** *adj* (hecho) de oro; dorado — **goldsmith** *n* orfebre *mf*

**golf** *n* golf *m* — **golf** *v* jugar (al) golf — **golfer** *n* golfista *mf*

**gone** *adj* ido, pasado; muerto; desaparecido

**good** *adj* (**better; best**) bueno; amable; **~ afternoon (evening)** buenas tardes; **be ~ at** tener facilidad para; **feel ~** sentirse bien; **have a ~ time** divertirse; **~ morning** buenos días; **~ night** buenas noches — **good** *n* bien *m*;

bondad *f*; **goods** *npl* bienes *mpl*; mercancías *fpl*, mercaderías *fpl* — **good** *adv* bien — **good–bye** *or* **good–by** *n* adiós *m* — **good–looking** *adj* bello, guapo — **goodness** *n* bondad *f* — **goodwill** *n* buena voluntad *f* — **goody** *n* (**goodies**) golosina *f*

**goose** *n* (**geese**) ganso *m*, -sa *f*; oca *f*

**gorilla** *n* gorila *m*

**gossip** *n* chismoso *m*, -sa *f* (persona); chisme *m* — **gossip** *v* chismear, contar chismes — **gossipy** *adj* chismoso

**gourmet** *n* gastrónomo *m*, -ma *f*

**govern** *v* gobernar — **government** *n* gobierno *m* — **governor** *n* gobernador *m*, -dora *f*

**gown** *n* vestido *m*

**grace** *n* gracia *f* — **graceful** *adj* grácil — **gracious** *adj* cortés, gentil

**grade** *n* grado *m*, año *m* (a la escuela); nota *f*

**gradual** *adj* gradual — **gradually** *adv* gradualmente, poco a poco

**graduate** *n* licenciado *m*, -da *f* (de la universidad), bachiller *mf* (de la escuela secundaria) — **graduate** *v* graduar; graduarse, licenciarse — **graduation** *n* graduación *f*

**graffiti** *npl* graffiti *mpl*

**grain** *n* grano *m*; cereales *mpl*; veta *f*, vena *f* (de madera)

**gram** *n* gramo *m*

**grammar** *n* gramática *f*

**grand** *adj* magnífico, espléndido; fabuloso, estupendo — **grandchild** *n* (**-children**) nieto *m*, -ta *f* — **granddaughter** *n* nieta *f* — **grandfather** *n* abuelo *m* — **grandmother** *n* abuela *f* — **grandparents** *npl* abuelos *mpl* — **grandson** *n* nieto *m*

**grant** *v* conceder; reconocer, admitir; **take for granted** dar (algo) por sentado — **grant** *n* subvención *f*; beca *f*

**grape** *n* uva *f*

**grapefruit** *n* toronja *f*, pomelo *m*

**graph** *n* gráfico *m*, -ca *f* — **graphic** *adj* gráfico

**grasp** *v* agarrar; comprender, captar — **grasp** *n* agarre *m*; comprensión *f*; alcance *m*

**grass** *n* hierba *f* (planta); césped *m*, pasto *m* — **grasshopper** *n* saltamontes *m* — **grassy** *adj* cubierto de hierba

**grateful** *adj* agradecido — **gratefully** *adv* con agradecimiento — **gratefulness** *n* gratitud *f*, agradecimiento *m*

**gratify** *v* (**-fied**) complacer; satisfacer

**gratitude** *n* gratitud *f*

**grave¹** *n* tumba *f*, sepultura *f*

**grave²** *adj* grave

**graveyard** *n* cementerio *m*

**gravity** *n* gravedad *f*

**gray** *adj* gris; ∼ **hair** pelo *m* canoso — **gray** *n* gris *m* — **gray** *vi or* **turn gray** encanecer, ponerse gris

**grease** *n* grasa *f* — **grease** *v* engrasar — **greasy** *adj* grasiento; graso, grasoso

**great** *adj* grande; estupendo, fabuloso — **great–grandchild** *n* (**-children**) bisnieto *m*, -ta *f* — **great–grandfather** *n* bisabuelo *m* — **great–grandmother** *n* bisabuela *f* — **greatly** *adv* mucho; muy — **greatness** *n* grandeza *f*

**Greek** *adj* griego — **Greek** *n* griego *m* (idioma)

**green** *adj* verde — **green** verde *m* (color); **greens** *npl* verduras *fpl*

**greet** *v* saludar; recibir — **greeting** *n* saludo *m*; ∼**s** *npl* saludos *mpl*, recuerdos *mpl*

**grid** *n* red *f*

**grief** *n* dolor *m*, pesar *m* — **grieve** *v* entristecer

**grill** *v* asar a la parrilla — **grill** *n* parrilla *f* (para cocinar) — **grille** *or* **grill** *n* reja *f*, rejilla *f*

**grim** *adj* severo; sombrío

**grime** *n* mugre *f*, suciedad *f* — **grimy** *adj* **grimier; -est** mugriento, sucio

**grinder** *n* molinillo *m*

**grip** *v* agarrar, asir — **grip** *n*; agarre *m*; control *m*, dominio *m*

**groan** *v* gemir — **groan** *n* gemido *m*

**groceries** *npl* comestibles *mpl* — **grocer** *n* tendero *m*, -ra *f*

**groggy** *adj* atontado

**groin** *n* ingle *f*

**groom** *n* novio *m* — **groom** *v* almohazar (un animal); preparar

**ground** *n* suelo *m*, tierra *f* — **ground** *v* fundar, basar

**group** *n* grupo *m* — **group** *v* agrupar; **group together** agruparse

**grove** *n* arboleda *f*

**grow** *v* (**grew; grown**) cultivar; dejarse crecer (el pelo, etc.); crecer; aumentar; volverse, ponerse; ∼ **dark** oscurecerse; ∼ **up** hacerse mayor — **grower** *n* cultivador *m*, -dora *f*

**growl** *v* gruñir — **growl** *n* gruñido *m*

**grown–up** *adj* mayor — **grown–up** *n* persona *f* mayor

**growth** *n* crecimiento *m*; aumento *m*; desarrollo *m*

**grumble** *v* refunfuñar, rezongar

**grunt** *v* gruñir — **grunt** *n* gruñido *m*

**guarantee** *n* garantía *f* — **guarantee** *v* garantizar

**guard** *n* guardia *f*; protección *f* — **guard** *v* proteger, vigilar — **guardian** *n* guardián *m*, -diana *f*

**guess** *v* adivinar; suponer, creer; ∼ **at** adivinar — **guess** *n* conjetura *f*, suposición *f*

**guest** *n* invitado *m*, -da *f*; huésped *mf* (a un hotel)

**guide** *n* guía *mf* (persona), guía *f* (libro, etc.) — **guide** *v* guiar — **guidance** *n* orientación *f* — **guidebook** *n* guía *f* — **guideline** *n* pauta *f*, directriz *f*

**guilt** *n* culpa *f*, culpabilidad *f* — **guilty** *adj* **guiltier; -est** culpable

**guitar** *n* guitarra *f*

**gulf** *n* golfo *m*; abismo *m*

**gull** *n* gaviota *f*

**gulp** *vt or* ∼ **down** tragarse, engullir

**gum¹** *n* encía *f* (de la boca)
**gum²** *n* goma *f* de mascar, chicle *m*
**gun** *n* arma *f* de fuego — **gun** ∼ *v or* ∼
    **down** matar a tiros, asesinar — **gun-**
    **man** *n* (**-men**) pistolero *m*
**gut** *n* intestino *m*

**guy** *n* tipo *m*
**gym** *or* **gymnasium** *n* (**-siums**) *or* **-sia**
    gimnasio *m* — **gymnast** *n* gimnasta *mf*
    — **gymnastics** *ns & pl* gimnasia *f*
**gynecology** *n* ginecología *f* — **gyne-**
    **cologist** *n* ginecólogo *m*, -ga *f*

# H

**h** *n* (**h's** *or* **hs**) h *f*, octava letra del alfa-
    beto inglés
**habit** *n* hábito *m*, costumbre *f*
**habitual** *adj* habitual
**hack** *v or* ∼ **into** piratear (un sistema in-
    formático)
**hail¹** *v* llamar (un taxi)
**hail²** *n* granizo *m* (en meteorología) —
    **hail** *v* granizar — **hailstone** *n* piedra *f*
    de granizo
**hair** *n* pelo *m*, cabello *m*; vello *m* (en las
    piernas, etc.) — **hairbrush** *n* cepillo *m*
    (para el pelo) — **haircut** *n* corte *m* de
    pelo; **get a haircut** cortarse el pelo —
    **hairdo** *n* (**-dos**) peinado *m* — **hair-**
    **dresser** *n* peluquero *m*, -ra *f* — **hair-**
    **less** *adj* calvo — **hair spray** *n* laca *f*
    (para el pelo) — **hairy** *adj* peludo, vel-
    ludo
**hale** *adj* saludable, robusto
**half** *n* (**halves**) mitad *f*; *or* **halftime**
    tiempo *m* (en deportes); **in** ∼ por la
    mitad — **half** *adj* medio; **half an hour**
    una media hora — **half** *adv* medio —
    **half brother** *n* medio hermano *m*, her-
    manastro *m* — **halfhearted** *adj* sin
    ánimo, poco entusiasta — **half sister** *n*
    media hermana *f*, hermanastra *f* —
    **halfway** *adv* a medio camino —
    **halfway** *adj* medio
**hall** *n* corredor *m*, pasillo *m*; sala *f*;
    vestíbulo *m*; residencia *f* universitaria
**hallmark** *n* sello *m* (distintivo)
**Halloween** *n* víspera *f* de Todos los San-
    tos

**hallucination** *n* alucinación *f*
**hallway** *n* entrada *f*; corredor *m*, pasillo
    *m*
**halt** *n* **call a** ∼ **to** poner fin a; **come to**
    **a** ∼ pararse — **halt** *v* parar; pararse
**halve** *v* partir por la mitad; reducir a la
    mitad
**ham** *n* jamón *m*
**hamburger** *or* **hamburg** *n* hamburguesa
    *f*
**hammer** *n* martillo *m* — **hammer** *v* mar-
    tillar, martillear
**hammock** *n* hamaca *f*
**hamper¹** *v* obstaculizar, dificultar
**hamper²** *n* cesto *m*, canasta *f* (para ropa
    sucia)
**hamster** *n* hámster *m*
**hand** *n* mano *f*; manecilla *f*, aguja *f* (de un
    reloj, etc.); letra *f*, escritura *f*; obrero *m*,
    -ra *f*; **by** ∼ a mano; **lend a** ∼ echar
    una mano **on** ∼ a mano, disponible;
    **on the other** ∼ por otro lado — **hand**
    *v* pasar, dar; **hand out** distribuir; **hand**
    **over** entregar — **handbag** *n* cartera *f*,
    bolso *m* — **handbook** *n* manual *m*
**handicap** *n* minusvalía *f* (física) —
    **handicapped** *adj* minusválido
**handicrafts** *npl* artesanía(s) *f(pl)*
**handkerchief** *n* (**-chiefs**) pañuelo *m*
**handle** *n* asa *m* (de una taza, etc.), mango
    *m* (de un utensilio), pomo *m* (de una
    puerta), tirador *m* (de un cajón) — **han-**
    **dle** *v* tratar, manejar — **handlebars**
    *npl* manillar *m*, manubrio *m*
**handout** *n* dádiva *f*, limosna *f*

**handrail** *n* pasamanos *m*

**handshake** *n* apretón *m* de manos

**handsome** *adj* apuesto, guapo

**handwriting** *n* letra *f*, escritura *f*

**hang** *v* (**hung**) colgar; ahorcar; pender; caer (de la ropa, etc.); ~ **one's head** bajar la cabeza; ~ **up on . . .** colgar a . . . — **hang** *n* caída *f*

**haphazard** *adj* casual, fortuito

**happen** *v* pasar, suceder, ocurrir; **it so happens that . . .** da la casualidad de que . . . — **happening** *n* suceso *m*, acontecimiento *m*

**happy** *adj* feliz; **be ~** alegrarse; **be ~ with** estar contento con — **happiness** *n* felicidad *f*

**harass** *v* acosar

**harbor** *n* puerto *m*

**hard** *adj* duro; difícil; **be a ~ worker** ser muy trabajador; ~ **liquor** bebidas *fpl* fuertes; ~ **water** agua *f* dura — **hard** *adv* fuerte; **work hard** trabajar duro; **take . . . hard** tomarse . . . muy mal — **harden** *v* endurecer — **hardly** *adv* apenas; **hardly ever** casi nunca — **hardness** *n* dureza *f*; dificultad *f* — **hardware** *n* hardware *m* (en informática) — **hardworking** *adj* trabajador

**hardy** *adj* fuerte (de personas), resistente (de las plantas)

**harm** *n* daño *m* — **harm** *v* hacer daño a (una persona), dañar (una cosa), perjudicar (la reputación de algún, etc.) — **harmful** *adj* perjudicial — **harmless** *adj* inofensivo

**harmony** *n* armonía *f*

**harness** *n* arnés *m* — **harness** *v* enjaezar; utilizar

**harsh** *adj* áspero; fuerte (dícese de una luz), discordante (dícese de sonidos)

**harvest** *n* cosecha *f* — **harvest** *v* cosechar

**haste** *n* prisa *f*, apuro *m*; **make ~** darse prisa, apurarse — **hasten** *v* acelerar; apresurarse, apurarse — **hasty** *adj* precipitado

**hat** *n* sombrero *m*

**hatchet** *n* hacha *f*

**hate** *n* odio *m* — **hate** *v* odiar, aborrecer — **hateful** *adj* odioso — **hatred** *n* odio *m*

**haughty** *adj* altanero, altivo

**haul** *v* tirar; arrastrar — **haul** *n* **a long haul** un trayecto largo

**haunt** *v* frecuentar, rondar; inquietar — **haunt** *n* sitio *m* predilecto

**have** *v* (**had**) tener; comer, tomar; permitir; dar (una fiesta, etc.), convocar (una reunión); ~ **one's hair cut** cortarse el pelo; ~ **something done** mandar hacer algo — **have** *v aux* haber

**haven** *n* refugio *m*

**hawk** *n* halcón *m*

**hazard** *n* peligro *m*, riesgo *m* — **hazard** *v* arriesgar, aventurar

**haze** *n* bruma *f*, neblina *f*

**he** *pron* él

**head** *n* cabeza *f*; cabeza *f* (de un clavo, etc.), cabecera *f* (de una mesa); jefe *m*, -fa *f*; **be out of one's ~** estar loco; **come to a ~** llegar a un punto crítico **~s or tails** cara o cruz; **per ~** por cabeza — **head** *adj* principal — **head** *v* encabeza; dirigirse — **headache** *n* dolor *m* de cabeza — **headline** *n* titular *m* — **headphones** *npl* auriculares *mpl*, audífonos *mpl*

**heal** *v* curar; cicatrizar

**health** *n* salud *f* — **healthy** *adj* sano, saludable

**hear** *v* (**heard**) oír; oír; ~ **about** enterarse de ~ **from** tener noticias de — **hearing** *n* oído *m* — **hearing aid** *n* audífono *m*

**heart** *n* corazón *m*; **at ~** en el fondo; **by ~** de memoria; **lose ~** descorazonarse; **take ~** animarse — **heart attack** *n* infarto *m*, ataque *m* al corazón

**heat** *v* calentar — **heat** *n* calor *m*;

calefacción *f* — **heated** *adj* acalorado — **heater** *n* calentador *m*

**heaven** *n* cielo *m*

**heavy** *adj* pesado

**Hebrew** *adj* hebreo — **Hebrew** *n* hebreo *m* (idioma)

**heel** *n* talón *m* (del pie), tacón *m* (de un zapato)

**height** *n* estatura *f* (de una persona), altura *f* (de un objeto); cumbre *f*; **what is your ~ ?** ¿cuánto mides?

**heir** *n* heredero *m*, -ra *f* — **heiress** *n* heredera *f*

**helicopter** *n* helicóptero *m*

**hello** *interj* ¡hola!

**helmet** *n* casco *m*

**help** *v* ayudar; **~ oneself** servirse; **I can't ~ it** no lo puedo remediar — **help** *n* ayuda *f*; personal *m*; **help!** ¡socorro!, ¡auxilio! — **helper** *n* ayudante *mf* — **helpful** *adj* servicial, amable; útil — **helpless** *adj* incapaz; indefenso

**hem** *n* dobladillo *m*

**hemisphere** *n* hemisferio *m*

**hemorrhage** *n* hemorragia *f*

**hen** *n* gallina *f*

**her** *adj* su, sus — **her** *pron* la; le; se; ella — **herself** *pron* se; ella misma

**herb** *n* hierba *f*

**here** *adv* aquí, acá; **~ you are!** ¡toma!

**hero** *n* (**-roes**) héroe *m* — **heroic** *adj* heroico — **heroine** *n* heroína *f* — **heroism** *n* heroísmo *m*

**hers** *pron* (el) suyo, (la) suya, (los) suyos, (las) suyas; **some friends of ~** unos amigos suyos, unos amigos de ella

**heterosexual** *adj* heterosexual —.*n* heterosexual *mf*

**hi** *interj* ¡hola!

**hiccup** *n* hipo

**hide**[1] *n* piel *f*, cuero *m*

**hide**[2] *v* (**hid; hidden** *or* **hid**) esconderse; esconder; ocultar (motivos, etc.) — **hide–and–seek** *n* escondite *m*, escondidas *fpl*

**hierarchy** *n* (**-chies**) jerarquía *f* — **hierarchical** *adj* jerárquico

**high** *adj* alto; borracho, drogado — **high** *adv* alto — **high** *n* récord *m*, máximo *m* — **higher** *adj* superior; **higher education** enseñanza *f* superior — **high school** *n* escuela *f* superior, escuela *f* secundaria — **highway** *n* carretera *f*

**hiker** *n* excursionista *mf*

**hill** *n* colina *f*, cerro *m*; cuesta *f* — **hillside** *n* ladera *f*, cuesta *f*

**hilt** *n* puño *m*

**him** *pron* lo; le; se; él — **himself** *pron* se; él mismo

**Hindu** *adj* hindú

**hinge** *n* bisagra *f*, gozne *m*

**hip** *n* cadera *f*

**his** *adj* su, sus, de él — **his** *pron* (el) suyo, (la) suya, (los) suyos, (las) suyas; **some friends of ~** unos amigos suyos, unos amigos de él

**Hispanic** *adj* hispano, hispánico

**history** *n* (**-ries**) historia *f*; historial *m* — **historian** *n* historiador *m*, -dora *f* — **historic** *or* **historical** *adj* histórico

**hit** *v* (**hit**) golpear, pegar; dar (con un proyectil); afectar; alcanzar; chocar — **hit** *n* golpe *m*; éxito *m*

**HIV** *n* VIH *m*, virus *m* del sida

**hoarse** *adj* ronco

**hobby** *n* (**-bies**) pasatiempo *m*

**hockey** *n* hockey *m*

**hog** *n* cerdo *m*

**hold** *v* (**held**) tener; sostener; contener; considerar; *or* **~ back** detener; **~ up** retrasar — **holdup** *n* atraco *m*; retraso *m*, demora *f*

**hole** *n* agujero *m*, hoyo *m*

**holiday** *n* día *m* feriado, fiesta *f*

**hollow** *n* hueco *m*; hondonada *f*

**holocaust** *n* holocausto *m*

**holy** *adj* santo, sagrado

**homage** *n* homenaje *m*

**home** *n* casa *f*; hogar *m*; residencia *f*, asilo *m* — **home** *adv* **go home** ir a

casa — **homemaker** *n* ama *f* de casa —
**homework** *n* tarea *f*, deberes *mpl*

**homicide** *n* homicidio *m*

**homogeneous** *adj* homogéneo

**honest** *adj* honrado; sincero — **honestly** *adv* sinceramente — **honesty** *n* honradez *f*

**honey** *n* miel *f* — **honeymoon** *n* luna *f* de miel

**honor** *n* honor *m* — **honor** *v* honrar — **honorable** *adj* honorable, honroso — **honorary** *adj* honorario

**hook** *n* gancho *m*; *or* ~ **and eye** corchete *m*; **off the** ~ descolgado — **hook** *v* enganchar; engancharse

**hope** *v* esperar que — **hope** *n* esperanza *f* — **hopeful** *adj* esperanzado

**horizon** *n* horizonte *m* — **horizontal** *adj* horizontal

**hormone** *n* hormona *f*

**horn** *n* cuerno *m* (de un animal); trompa *f* (instrumento musical); bocina *f*, claxon *m* (de un vehículo)

**horoscope** *n* horóscopo *m*

**horror** *n* horror *m* — **horrible** *adj* horrible — **horrify** *v* (**-fied**) horrorizar

**horse** *n* caballo *m* — **horseman** *n* (**-men**) jinete *m* — **horsepower** *n* caballo *m* de fuerza — **horseshoe** *n* herradura *f* — **horsewoman** *n* (**-women**) jinete *f*

**hose** *n* manguera *f*, manga *f*

**hospital** *n* hospital *m* — **hospitalize** *v* hospitalizar

**host**[1] *n* anfitrión *m*, -triona *f*; presentador *m*, -dora *f* (de televisión, etc.) — **host** *v* ofrecer; presentar (un programa de televisión, etc.)

**host**[2] *n* hostia *f*, Eucaristía *f*

**hostage** *n* rehén *m*

**hostel** *n or* **youth** ~ albergue *m* juvenil

**hot** *adj* caliente, caluroso (del tiempo), cálido (del clima)

**hot dog** *n* perro *m* caliente

**hotel** *n* hotel *m*

**hound** *n* perro de caza — *v* acosar, perseguir

**hour** *n* hora *f* — **hourglass** *n* reloj *m* de arena

**house** *n* casa *f*; cámara *f* (del gobierno) — **house** *v* albergar — **housewife** *n* (**-wives**) ama *f* de casa — **housing** *n* viviendas *fpl*; caja *f* protectora

**how** *adv* cómo; qué; ~ **are you?** ¿cómo está Ud.?; ~ **come** por qué; ~ **much** cuánto; ~ **do you do?** mucho gusto; ~ **old are you?** ¿cuántos años tienes? — **how** *conj* como

**however**[1] *conj* de cualquier manera que ~ **you like** como quieras

**however**[2] *adv* sin embargo, no obstante ~ **difficult it is** por díficil que sea ~ **hard I try** por más que me esfuerce

**hug** *v* abrazar — **hug** *n* abrazo *m*

**human** *adj* humano — **human** *n* (ser *m*) humano *m* — **humane** *adj* humano, humanitario — **humanitarian** *adj* humanitario — **humanity** *n* humanidad *f*

**humble** *v* humillar; ~ **oneself** humillarse — **humble** *adj* humilde

**humid** *adj* húmedo — **humidity** *n* humedad *f*

**humiliate** *v* humillar — **humiliation** *n* humillación *f* — **humility** *n* humildad *f*

**humor** *n* humor *m* — **humor** *v* seguir la corriente a, complacer

**hundred** *adj* cien, ciento — **hundred** *n* ciento *m*

**Hungarian** *adj* húngaro — **Hungarian** *n* húngaro *m* (idioma)

**hunger** *n* hambre *m* — **hungry** *adj* hambriento

**hunt** *v* cazar; ~ **for** buscar — **hunt** *n* caza *f*, cacería *f*; búsqueda *f*, busca *f* — **hunter** *n* cazador *m*, -dora *f* — **hunting** *n* caza *f*

**hurdle** *n* valla *f* (en deportes); obstáculo *m*

**hurl** *v* lanzar, arrojar

**hurrah** *interj* ¡hurra!

**hurricane** *n* huracán *m*

**hurry** *n* prisa *f*, apuro *f* — **hurry** *v* (**-ried**) darse prisa, apurarse; apurar, dar prisa a — **hurried** *adj* apresurado — **hurriedly** *adv* apresuradamente, de prisa

**hurt** *v* (**hurt**) hacer daño a, lastimar; ofender, herir; doler; **my foot hurts** me duele el pie

**husband** *n* esposo *m*, marido *m*

**hut** *n* cabaña *f*

**hygiene** *n* higiene *f* — **hygienic** *adj* higiénico

**hymn** *n* himno *m*

**hyperactive** *adj* hiperactivo

**hyphen** *n* guión *m*

**hypocrisy** *n* hipocresía *f* — **hypocrite** *n* hipócrita *mf* — **hypocritical** *adj* hipócrita

**hypothesis** *n* (**-eses**) hipótesis *f*

**hysteria** *n* histeria *f*, histerismo *m* — **hysterical** *adj* histérico

# I

**i** *n* (**i's** *or* **is**) i *f*, novena letra del alfabeto inglés

**I** *pron* yo

**ice** *n* hielo *m* — **ice cream** *n* helado *m*

**idea** *n* idea *f*

**ideal** *adj* ideal — **ideal** *n* ideal *m* — **idealist** *n* idealista *mf* — **idealistic** *adj* idealista — **idealize** *v* idealizar

**identity** *n* identidad *f* — **identical** *adj* idéntico — **identify** *v* (**-fied**) identificar; **identify with** identificarse con — **identification** *n* identificación *f*; **identification card** carnet *m*, carné *m*

**ideology** *n* ideología *f* — **ideological** *adj* ideológico

**idiocy** *n* idiotez *f*

**idiom** *n* modismo *m* — **idiomatic** *adj* idiomático

**idiot** *n* idiota *mf* — **idiotic** *adj* idiota

**idol** *n* ídolo *m* — **idolize** *v* idolatrar

**if** *conj* si; aunque, si bien; ~ **so** si es así

**ignore** *v* ignorar, no hacer caso de — **ignorance** *n* ignorancia *f* — **ignorant** *adj* ignorante

**ill** *adj* (**worse; worst**) enfermo; malo — **ill** *adv* (**worse; worst**) mal

**illegal** *adj* ilegal

**illegitimate** *adj* ilegítimo

**illiterate** *adj* analfabeto — **illiteracy** *n* analfabetismo *m*

**illogical** *adj* ilógico

**illuminate** *v* iluminar — **illumination** *n* iluminación *f*

**illusion** *n* ilusión *f*

**illustrate** *v* ilustrar — **illustration** *n* ilustración *f*

**illustrious** *adj* ilustre, glorioso

**ill will** *n* animadversión *f*, mala voluntad *f*

**image** *n* imagen *f* — **imaginary** *adj* imaginario — **imagination** *n* imaginación *f* — **imagine** *v* imaginar(se)

**imbalance** *n* desequilibrio *m*

**imitation** *n* imitación *f* — **imitation** *adj* de imitación, artificial — **imitate** *v* imitar, remedar

**immature** *adj* inmaduro

**immediate** *adj* inmediato

**immense** *adj* inmenso

**immigrant** *n* inmigrante *mf* — **immigration** *n* inmigración *f*

**imminent** *adj* inminente

**immobile** *adj* inmóvil — **immobilize** *v* inmovilizar

**immoral** *adj* inmoral

**impact** *n* impacto *m*

**impartial** *adj* imparcial — **impartiality** *n* imparcialidad *f*

**impatience** *n* impaciencia *f* — **impatient** *adj* impaciente — **impatiently** *adv* con impaciencia

**impeccable** *adj* impecable

**impede** *v* dificultar — **impediment** *n* impedimento *m*, obstáculo *m*

**impending** *adj* inminente

**impenetrable** *adj* impenetrable

**imperative** *adj* imperativo

**imperceptible** *adj* imperceptible

**imperfection** *n* imperfección *f* — **imperfect** *adj* imperfecto

**imperialism** *n* imperialismo *m*

**impersonal** *adj* impersonal

**impersonation** *n* imitación *f* — **impersonator** *n* imitador *m*, -dora *f*

**impetuous** *adj* impetuoso, impulsivo

**impetus** *n* ímpetu *m*, impulso *m*

**implement** *n* instrumento *m*, implemento *m* — **implement** *v* poner en práctica

**implicate** *v* implicar

**imply** *v* (**-plied**) implicar

**impolite** *adj* descortés, maleducado

**import** *v* importar (mercancías) — **important** *adj* importante — **importance** *n* importancia *f* — **importation** *n* importación *f* — **importer** *n* importador *m*, -dora *f*

**impose** *v* imponer — **imposing** *adj* imponente

**impossible** *adj* imposible — **impossibility** *n* imposibilidad *f*

**impostor** *or* **imposter** *n* impostor *m*, -tora *f*

**impotent** *adj* impotente — **impotence** *n* impotencia *f*

**impracticable** *adj* impracticable

**imprecise** *adj* impreciso — **imprecision** *n* imprecisión *f*

**impregnable** *adj* impenetrable

**impregnate** *v* impregnar; fecundar

**impress** *v* impresionar — **impression** *n* impresión *f* — **impressive** *adj* impresionante

**improbable** *adj* improbable

**improve** *v* mejorar

**improvise** *v* improvisar — **improvisation** *n* improvisación *f*

**impulse** *n* impulso *m* — **impulsive** *adj* impulsivo

**impure** *adj* impuro — **impurity** *n* impureza *f*

**in** *prep* en; por; dentro de — **in** *adv* dentro, adentro — **in** *adj* de moda

**inability** *n* incapacidad *f*

**inactive** *n* inactivo — **inactivity** *n* inactividad *f*

**inadequate** *adj* insuficiente

**inanimate** *adj* inanimado

**inappropriate** *adj* impropio, inoportuno

**inaugurate** *v* investir (a un presidente, etc.); inaugurar — **inauguration** *n* investidura *f* (de una persona), inauguración *f* (de un edificio, etc.)

**incalculable** *adj* incalculable

**incapable** *adj* incapaz — **incapacitate** *v* incapacitar — **incapacity** *n* incapacidad *f*

**incense** *n* incienso *m*

**inch** *n* pulgada *f*

**incidentally** *adv* a propósito

**incite** *v* incitar, instigar

**incline** *v* inclinar; **be ~ed to** inclinarse a, tender a — **incline** *n* pendiente *f* — **inclination** *n* inclinación *f*; deseo *m*, ganas *fpl*

**include** *v* incluir — **inclusion** *n* inclusión *f*

**incoherent** *adj* incoherente — **incoherence** *n* incoherencia *f*

**income** *n* ingresos *mpl* — **income tax** *n* impuesto *m* sobre la renta

**incomparable** *adj* incomparable

**incompetent** *adj* incompetente — **incompetence** *n* incompetencia *f*

**incomplete** *adj* incompleto

**incomprehensible** *adj* incomprensible

**inconceivable** *adj* inconcebible

**inconsiderate** *adj* desconsiderado

**inconvenient** *adj* incómodo, inconveniente — **inconvenience** *n* incomodidad *f*, molestia *f*; inconveniente *m*

**incorrect** *adj* incorrecto

**increase** n aumento m — **increase** v aumentar

**incredible** adj increíble

**incredulous** adj incrédulo

**indebted** adj endeudado

**indecisive** adj indeciso

**indefinite** adj indefinido

**indelible** adj indeleble

**independent** adj independiente — **independence** n independencia f

**index** n (-**dexes** or -**dices**) índice m — **index finger** n dedo m índice

**Indian** adj indio m, -dia f

**indication** n indicio m, señal f — **indicate** v indicar — **indicative** adj indicativo

**indifferent** adj indiferente

**indigenous** adj indígena

**indigestion** n indigestión f

**indirect** adj indirecto

**indiscreet** adj indiscreto — **indiscretion** n indiscreción f

**indiscriminate** adj indiscriminado

**indispensable** adj indispensable, imprescindible

**indisputable** adj indiscutible

**individual** adj individual; particular — **individual** n individuo m — **individually** adv individualmente

**induce** v inducir; provocar

**industry** n industria f; diligencia f — **industrial** adj industrial

**inequality** n desigualdad f

**inescapable** adj ineludible

**inevitable** adj inevitable

**inexplicable** adj inexplicable

**infallible** adj infalible

**infancy** n infancia f

**infect** v infectar — **infection** n infección f — **infectious** adj contagioso

**infer** v deducir, inferir

**inferior** adj inferior — **inferior** n inferior mf

**infidelity** n infidelidad f

**infinite** adj infinito

**infinitive** n infinitivo m

**infinity** n infinito m

**infirmary** n enfermería f

**inflame** v inflamar — **inflammable** adj inflamable — **inflammation** n inflamación f

**inflation** n inflación f

**inflexible** adj inflexible

**influential** adj influyente

**influx** n afluencia f

**inform** v informar

**informal** adj informal; familiar (del lenguaje) — **informality** n falta f de ceremonia — **informally** adv de manera informal

**information** n información f — **informative** adj informativo

**infrastructure** n infraestructura f

**infrequently** adv raramente

**infuse** v infundir

**ingenious** adj ingenioso — **ingenuity** n ingenio

**ingest** v ingerir

**ingratitude** n ingratitud f

**ingredient** n ingrediente m

**inhabit** v habitar — **inhabitant** n habitante mf

**inhale** v aspirar

**inherent** adj inherente

**inherit** v heredar — **inheritance** n herencia f

**inhibit** v inhibir — **inhibition** n inhibición f

**inhuman** adj inhumano — **inhumane** adj inhumano

**initial** adj inicial — **initial** n inicial f — **initial** v poner las iniciales a

**initiate** v iniciar — **initiation** n iniciación f — **initiative** n iniciativa f

**inject** v inyectar — **injection** n inyección f

**injure** v herir; ~ **oneself** hacerse daño — **injury** n herida f

**injustice** n injusticia f

**ink** n tinta f

**in–laws** npl suegros mpl

**inn** n posada f, hostería f

**innate** *adj* innato

**inner** *adj* interior, interno

**inning** *n* entrada *f*

**innocent** *adj* inocente — **innocent** *n* inocente *mf* — **innocence** *n* inocencia *f*

**innovate** *v* innovar — **innovation** *n* innovación *f* — **innovative** *adj* innovador — **innovator** *n* innovador *m*, -dora *f*

**innumerable** *adj* innumerable

**inoffensive** *adj* inofensivo

**input** *n* contribución *f*; entrada *f* (de datos) — **input** *v* (**-putted** *or* **-put**) entrar (datos, etc.)

**inquire** *v* preguntar; ∼ **about** informarse sobre; ∼ **into** investigar — **inquisitive** *adj* curioso

**insane** *adj* loco — **insanity** *n* locura *f*

**inscription** *n* inscripción *f*

**insecure** *adj* inseguro, poco seguro — **insecurity** *n* inseguridad *f*

**insensitive** *adj* insensible

**inseparable** *adj* inseparable

**insert** *v* insertar (texto), introducir (una moneda, etc.)

**inside** *n* interior *m*; ∼ **out** al revés — **inside** *adv* dentro, adentro — **inside** *adj* interior — **inside** *prep or* **inside of** dentro de

**insignificant** *adj* insignificante

**insinuate** *v* insinuar

**insist** *v* insistir — **insistent** *adj* insistente

**insomnia** *n* insomnio *m*

**inspection** *n* inspección *f*

**inspire** *v* inspirar — **inspiration** *n* inspiración *f* — **inspirational** *adj* inspirador

**install** *v* instalar — **installation** *n* instalación *f* — **installment** *n* plazo *m*, cuota *f*; entrega *f* (de una publicación o telenovela)

**instance** *n* ejemplo *m*

**instant** *n* instante *m* — **instantaneous** *adj* instantáneo

**instead of** *prep* en vez de, en lugar de

**institute** *n* instituto *m* — **institution** *n* institución *f*

**instruct** *v* instruir — **instruction** *n* instrucción *f*

**instrument** *n* instrumento *m* — **instrumental** *adj* instrumental; **be instrumental in** jugar un papel fundamental en

**insufficient** *adj* insuficiente

**insular** *adj* insular; estrecho de miras

**insulate** *v* aislar — **insulation** *n* aislamiento *m*

**insure** *v* asegurar — **insurance** *n* seguro *m*

**insurmountable** *adj* insuperable

**intact** *adj* intacto

**intake** *n* consumo *m* (de alimentos), entrada *f* (de aire, etc.)

**intangible** *adj* intangible

**integral** *adj* integral

**integrate** *v* integrar(se)

**integrity** *n* integridad *f*

**intellectual** *adj* intelectual — **intellectual** *n* intelectual *mf* — **intelligence** *n* inteligencia *f* — **intelligent** *adj* inteligente — **intelligible** *adj* inteligible

**intend** *v* **be** ∼**ed for** ser para; ∼ **to do** pensar hacer — **intended** *adj* intencionado, deliberado

**intense** *adj* intenso — **intensify** *v* (**-fied**) intensificar(se) — **intensity** *n* intensidad *f* — **intensive** *adj* intensivo

**intent** *n* intención *f* — **intent** *adj* atento, concentrado; **intent on doing** resuelto a hacer — **intention** *n* intención *f* — **intentional** *adj* intencional, deliberado

**interact** *v* interactuar; ∼ **with** relacionarse con — **interaction** *n* interacción *f* — **interactive** *adj* interactivo

**intercede** *v* interceder

**interest** *n* interés *m* — **interest** *v* interesar — **interested** *adj* interesado — **interesting** *adj* interesante

**interface** *n* interfaz *mf* (de una computadora)

**interior** *adj* interior — **interior** *n* interior *m*

**interjection** *n* interjección *f*

**interlude** *n* intervalo *m*; interludio *m* (en música, etc.)

**intermediate** *adj* intermedio — **intermediary** *n* intermediario *m*, -ria *f*

**intermission** *n* intervalo *m*, intermedio *m*

**intermittent** *adj* intermitente

**international** *adj* internacional

**interpret** *v* interpretar — **interpretation** *n* interpretación *f* — **interpreter** *n* intérprete *mf*

**interrogate** *v* interrogar — **interrogation** *n* interrogatorio *m* — **interrogative** *adj* interrogativo

**interrupt** *v* interrumpir — **interruption** *n* interrupción *f*

**intersect** *v* cruzar (de calles), cruzarse; cortar (de líneas) — **intersection** *n* cruce *m*, intersección *f*

**interval** *n* intervalo *m*

**intervene** *v* intervenir; transcurrir, pasar — **intervention** *n* intervención *f*

**interview** *n* entrevista *f* — **interview** *v* entrevistar — **interviewer** *n* entrevistador *m*, -dora *f*

**intimate** *adj* íntimo — **intimacy** *n* intimidad *f*

**into** *prep* en, a; **bump ∼** darse contra; **3 ∼ 12** 12 dividido por 3

**intolerant** *adj* intolerante

**intoxicated** *adj* embriagado; **∼ with** ebrio de

**intransitive** *adj* intransitivo

**intrinsic** *adj* intrínseco

**introduce** *v* introducir; presentar (a una persona) — **introduction** *n* introducción *f*; presentación *f* (de una persona) — **introductory** *adj* introductorio

**introvert** *n* introvertido *m*, -da *f* — **introverted** *adj* introvertido

**intuition** *n* intuición *f* — **intuitive** *adj* intuitivo

**invade** *v* invadir

**invalid**[1] *adj* inválido

**invalid**[2] *n* inválido *m*, -da *f*

**invariable** *adj* invariable

**invasion** *n* invasión *f*

**invention** *n* invención *f* — **inventor** *n* inventor *m*, -tora *f*

**inventory** *n* inventario *m*

**invert** *v* invertir

**invertebrate** *adj* invertebrado — **invertebrate** *n* invertebrado *m*

**investigator** *n* investigador *m*, -dora *f*

**investment** *n* inversión *f*

**invitation** *n* invitación *f* — **invite** *v* invitar; buscar (problemas, etc.)

**invoice** *n* factura *f*

**involuntary** *adj* involuntario

**involve** *v* concernir, afectar; suponer

**IOU** *n* pagaré *m*, vale *m*

**Iranian** *adj* iraní

**Iraqi** *adj* iraquí

**irate** *adj* furioso

**iris** *n* (**irises**) lirio *m* (planta); (**irises** *or* **irides**) iris *m* (del ojo)

**Irish** *adj* irlandés

**iron** *n* hierro *m*, fierro *m* (metal); plancha *f* (para la ropa) — **iron** *v* planchar

**ironic** *adj* irónico

**irony** *n* ironía *f*

**irrational** *adj* irracional

**irrefutable** *adj* irrefutable

**irregular** *adj* irregular — **irregularity** *n* irregularidad *f*

**irrelevant** *adj* irrelevante

**irresponsible** *adj* irresponsable — **irresponsibility** *n* irresponsabilidad *f*

**irreverent** *adj* irreverente

**irreversible** *adj* irreversible, irrevocable

**irrigate** *v* irrigar, regar — **irrigation** *n* irrigación *f*, riego *m*

**irritate** *v* irritar — **irritating** *adj* irritante — **irritation** *n* irritación *f*

**Islamic** *adj* islámico

**island** *n* isla *f*

**isolate** *v* aislar — **isolation** *n* aislamiento *m*

**Israeli** *adj* israelí
**issue** *n* número *m* (de una revista, etc.)
**isthmus** *n* istmo *m*
**it** *pron* él, ella; le, se; lo, la; él, ella
**Italian** *adj* italiano — **Italian** *n* italiano *m* (idioma)
**italics** *n* cursiva *f*

**item** *n* punto *m* (en una agenda); **news** ～ noticia *f*
**itinerant** *adj* ambulante
**itinerary** *n* itinerario *m*
**its** *adj* su, sus
**itself** *pron* se; (él) mismo, (ella) misma, sí (mismo); **by** ～ solo

# J

**j** *n* (**j's** *or* **js**) j *f*, décima letra del alfabeto inglés
**jab** *n* golpe *m* abrupto
**jack** *n* gato *m* (mecanismo) — **jack** *vt or* ～ **up** levantar (con un gato); subir
**jacket** *n* chaqueta *f*
**jail** *n* cárcel *f* — *v* encarcelar
**jam**[1] *v* apiñar, embutir; atascar, atorar; atascarse, atrancarse — **jam** *n or* **traffic jam** embotellamiento *m* (de tráfico)
**jam**[2] *n* mermelada *f*
**jangle** *v* hacer un ruido metálico; hacer sonar
**January** *n* enero *m*
**Japanese** *adj* japonés — **Japanese** *n* japonés *m* (idioma)
**jar** *n* tarro *m*
**jargon** *n* jerga *f*
**jaw** *n* mandíbula *f* (de una persona), quijada *f* (de un animal)
**jazz** *n* jazz *m*
**jealous** *adj* celoso — **jealousy** *n* celos *mpl*, envidia *f*
**jeans** *npl* jeans *mpl*, vaqueros *mpl*
**jersey** *n* (**-seys**) jersey *m*
**jet** *n* chorro *m*; *or* ～ **airplane** avión *m* a reacción, reactor *m*
**jewel** *n* joya *f* — **jeweler** *or* **jeweller** *n* joyero *m*, -ra *f* — **jewelry** *n* joyas *fpl*, alhajas *fpl*
**Jewish** *adj* judío
**jiggle** *v* sacudir, zarandear — **jiggle** *n* sacudida *f*

**jingle** *v* tintinear; hacer sonar — **jingle** *n* tintineo *m*
**job** *n* empleo *m*, trabajo *m*; trabajo *m*
**jockey** *n* (**-eys**) jockey *mf*
**jog** *v* hacer footing; ～ **one's memory** refrescarle la memoria a algún — **jogging** *n* footing *m*
**join** *v* unir, juntar; reunirse con; *or* ～ **together** unirse; hacerse socio (de una organización, etc.)
**joint** *n* articulación *f* (en anatomía); juntura *f*, unión *f* — **jointly** *adv* conjuntamente
**joke** *n* chiste *m*, broma *f* — **joke** *v* bromear — **joker** *n* bromista *mf*; comodín *m* (en los naipes)
**jolly** *adj* alegre, jovial
**jot** *v or* ～ **down** anotar, apuntar
**journal** *n* diario *m*; revista *f* — **journalism** *n* periodismo *m* — **journalist** *n* periodista *mf*
**journey** *n* (**-neys**) viaje *m* — **journey** *v* (**-neyed**) viajar
**jovial** *adj* jovial
**joy** *n* alegría *f* — **joyful** *adj* alegre, feliz
**Judaism** *n* judaísmo *m*
**judge** *v* juzgar — *n* juez *mf* — **judgment** *or* **judgement** *n* fallo *m*, sentencia *f*; juicio *m*
**judicial** *adj* judicial — **judicious** *adj* juicioso
**juice** *n* jugo *m* — **juicy** *adj* jugoso
**July** *n* julio *m*
**jumble** *v* mezclar

**jumbo** *adj* gigante

**jump** *v* saltar; ~ **at** no dejar escapar (una oportunidad, etc.) — **jump** *n* salto *m*

**June** *n* junio *m*

**jungle** *n* selva *f*

**junior** *adj* más joven; subalterno — **junior** *n* persona *f* de menor edad; subalterno *m*, -na *f*; estudiante *mf* de penúltimo año

**junk** *n* trastos *mpl* (viejos) — **junk** *v* echar a la basura

**jury** *n* (**-ries**) jurado *m*

**just** *adj* justo — **just** *adv* apenas; exactamente; sólo, solamente; **just now** ahora mismo

**justice** *n* justicia *f*; juez *mf*

**justify** *v* (**-fied**) justificar — **justification** *n* justificación *f*

# K

**k** *n* (**k's** *or* **ks**) k *f*, undécima letra del alfabeto inglés

**kangaroo** *n* (**-roos**) canguro *m*

**karate** *n* karate *m*

**keen** *adj* afilado; cortante, penetrante; entusiasta

**keep** *v* (**kept**) guardar; cumplir (una promesa), acudir a (una cita); hacer quedar, detener; impedir; ~ **up** mantener(se); conservarse; *or* ~ **on** no dejar — **keep** *n* **earn one's keep** ganarse el pan; **for keeps** para siempre — **keeper** *n* guarda *mf*

**kernel** *n* almendra *f*; meollo *m*

**ketchup** *n* salsa *f* de tomate

**key** *n* llave *f*; tecla *f* (de un piano o una máquina) — **key** *adj* clave — **key ring** *n* llavero *m*

**kick** *v* dar una patada a; ~ **out** echar a patadas; dar patadas (de una persona), cocear (de un animal) — **kick** *n* patada *f*, coz *f* (de un animal); placer *m*

**kid** *n* niño *m*, -ña *f*; chivo *m*, -va *f*; cabrito *m*; — **kid** *v or* ~ **around** bromear — **kidnap** *v* secuestrar, raptar

**kidney** *n* (**-neys**) riñón *m*

**kill** *v* matar; acabar con; ~ **time** matar el tiempo — **kill** *n* presa *f* — **killer** *n* asesino *m*, -na *f*

**kilo** *n* (**-los**) kilo *m* — **kilogram** *n* kilogramo *m* — **kilometer** *n* kilómetro *m*

**kin** *n* parientes *mpl*

**kind** *n* tipo *m*, clase *f* — **kind** *adj* amable — **kindness** *n* bondad *f*

**kindergarten** *n* jardín *m* infantil, jardín *m* de niños

**kindle** *v* encender (un fuego); despertar

**kindly** *adv* amablemente; **take** ~ **to** aceptar de buena gana

**kinship** *n* parentesco *m*

**kiss** *v* besar(se) — **kiss** *n* beso *m*

**kit** *n* **first–aid** ~ botiquín *m*

**kitchen** *n* cocina *f*

**knapsack** *n* mochila *f*

**knead** *v* amasar, sobar; masajear

**knee** *n* rodilla *f*

**kneel** *v* (**knelt** *or* **kneeled**) arrodillarse

**knife** *n* (**knives**) cuchillo *m*

**knight** *n* caballo *m* (en ajedrez)

**knit** *v* (**knit** *or* **knitted**) tejer — **knit** *n* prenda *f* tejida

**knock** *v* golpear; criticar; dar un golpe, llamar (a la puerta); darse, chocar — **knock** *n* golpe *m*, llamada *f* (a la puerta)

**knot** *n* nudo *m*

**know** *v* (**knew; known**) saber; conocer (a una persona, un lugar); ~ **how to** saber — **knowing** *adj* cómplice — **knowingly** *adv* de manera cómplice; a sabiendas — **knowledge** *n* conocimiento *m*; conocimientos *mpl*, saber *m* — **knowledgeable** *adj* informado, entendido

**knuckle** *n* nudillo *m*
**Koran (the)** *n* el Corán *m*

**Korean** *adj* coreano *m*, -na *f* — **Korean**
*n* coreano *m* (idioma)

# L

*n* (**l's** *or* **ls**) l *f*, duodécima letra del alfabeto inglés

**label** *n* etiqueta *f*; marca *f*

**labor** *n* trabajo *m* — **labor** *v* trabajar

**laboratory** *n* (**-ries**) laboratorio *m*

**lace** *n* encaje *m*; cordón *m* (de zapatos)
— **lace** *v* atar

**lack** *v* carecer de, no tener; **be lacking**
faltar — **lack** *n* falta *f*, carencia *f*

**ladder** *n* escalera *f*

**lady** *n* (**-dies**) señora *f*, dama *f*

**lake** *n* lago *m*

**lamb** *n* cordero *m*

**lame** *adj* cojo, renco

**lament** *v* lamentar — **lament** *n* lamento
*m*

**lamp** *n* lámpara *f* — **lampshade** *n* pantalla *f*

**land** *n* tierra *f*; país *m* — **land** *v* desembarcar (pasajeros de un barco), hacer
aterrizar (un avión); aterrizar (de un
avión) — **landing** *n* aterrizaje *m* (de
aviones) — **landscape** *n* paisaje *m*

**lane** *n* carril *m* (de una carretera); camino
*m*

**language** *n* idioma *m*, lengua *f*; lenguaje
*m*

**laptop** *adj* portátil

**large** *adj* grande — **largely** *adv* en gran
parte

**lasagna** *n* lasaña *f*

**laser** *n* láser *m*

**lash** *n* pestaña *f*

**last** *v* durar — **last** *n* último *m*, -ma *f*; **at
last** por fin, finalmente — **last** *adv* por
última vez, en último lugar — **last** *adj*;
último — **lastly** *adv* por último, finalmente

**late** *adj* tarde; avanzado (de la hora) —

**late** *adv* tarde — **lately** *adv* recientemente, últimamente

**Latin–American** *adj* latinoamericano

**laugh** *v* reír(se) — **laugh** *n* risa *f* —
**laughter** *n* risa *f*, risas *fpl*

**launch** *v* lanzar — **launch** *n* lanzamiento *m*

**launder** *v* lavar y planchar (ropa) —
**laundry** *n*, *pl* -**dries** ropa *f* sucia; lavandería *f* (servicio); **do the laundry** lavar
la ropa

**lavatory** *n* (**-ries**) baño *m*, cuarto *m* de
baño

**law** *n* ley *f*; derecho *m* (profesión, etc.) —
**lawyer** *n* abogado *m*, -da *f*

**lawn** *n* césped *m*

**lay** *v* (**laid**) poner, colocar; ~ **out** presentar, exponer

**layer** *n* capa *f*

**lazy** *adj* perezoso — **laziness** *n* pereza *f*

**lead** *v* (**led**) dirigir; encabezar, ir al frente
de ; llevar, conducir (a algo) — **lead** *n*
delantera *f* — **leader** *n* jefe *m*, -fa *f* —
**leadership** *n* mando *m*, dirección *f*

**leaf** *n* (**leaves**) hoja *f* — **leaf** *v* **leaf
through** hojear (un libro, etc.)

**league** *n* liga *f*

**lean** *v* inclinarse

**leap** *v* (**leapt** *or* **leaped**) saltar, brincar
— **leap** *n* salto *m*, brinco *m* — **leap
year** *n* año *m* bisiesto

**learn** *v* aprender — **learned** *adj* sabio,
erudito — **learner** *n* principiante *mf*,
estudiante *mf* — **learning** *n* erudición *f*,
saber *m*

**lease** *n* contrato *m* de arrendamiento —
**lease** *v* arrendar

**least** *adj* menor; más mínimo — **least** *n*

**at least** por lo menos — **least** *adv* menos

**leather** *n* cuero *m*

**leave** *v* (**left**) dejar; salir(se) de (un lugar); irse — **leave** *n or* **leave of absence** permiso *m*, licencia *f*

**lecture** *n* conferencia *f* — **lecture** *v* dar clase, dar una conferencia

**left** *adj* izquierdo — **left** *adv* a la izquierda — **left** *n* izquierda *f* — **left-handed** *adj* zurdo

**leg** *n* pierna *f* (de una persona, de ropa), pata *f* (de un animal, de muebles); etapa *f* (de un viaje)

**legal** *adj* legítimo, legal; legal, jurídico — **legality** *n* (**-ties**) legalidad *f* — **legalize** *v* legalizar

**legible** *adj* legible

**legislate** *v* legislar — **legislation** *n* legislación *f*

**legitimate** *adj* legítimo — **legitimacy** *n* legitimidad *f*

**leisure** *n* ocio *m*, tiempo *m* libre

**lemon** *n* limón *m* — **lemonade** *n* limonada *f*

**lend** *v* (**lent**) prestar

**length** *n* largo *m*; duración *f* — **lengthen** *v* alargar

**lens** *n* lente *mf* (de un instrumento)

**less** *adv or adj or pron or prep* menos

**lesson** *n* clase *f*, curso *m*

**let** *v* (**let**) dejar, permitir; alquilar; ~**'s go!** ¡vamos!, ¡vámonos!

**letter** *n* carta *f*; letra *f* (del alfabeto)

**lettuce** *n* lechuga *f*

**level** *n* nivel *m* — **level** *v* nivelar

**lever** *n* palanca *f*

**liable** *adj* responsable; probable — **liability** *n* (**-ties**) responsabilidad *f*; desventaja *f*

**liberal** *adj* liberal — **liberal** *n* liberal *mf*

**liberate** *v* liberar — **liberation** *n* liberación *f*

**liberty** *n* (**-ties**) libertad *f*

**library** *n* (**-braries**) biblioteca *f* — **librarian** *n* bibliotecario *m*, -ria *f*

**license** *or* **licence** *n* licencia *f*; permiso *m* — **license** *v* autorizar

**lie¹** *v* (**lay; lain**) acostarse; estar situado, encontrarse

**lie²** *v* (**lied**) mentir — **lie** *n* mentira *f*

**life** *n* (**lives**) vida *f* — **lifeboat** *n* bote *m* salvavidas — **lifeguard** *n* socorrista *m* — **lifestyle** *n* estilo *m* de vida

**lift** *v* levantar — **lift** *n*; levantamiento *m*

**light¹** *n* luz *f*; lámpara *f* — **light** *v* (**lit** *or* **lighted**) encender (un fuego); iluminar — **lightbulb** *n* bombilla *f*, bombillo *m* — **lighten** *v* iluminar — **lighter** *n* encendedor *m* — **lightning** *n* relámpago *m*, rayo *m*

**light²** *adj* ligero — **lighten** *v* aligerar — **lightly** *adv* suavemente

**like¹** *v* gustarle (a uno); querer; **if you** ~ si quieres

**like²** *adj* parecido — **like** *conj* como; como si — **likely** *adj* probable — **likewise** *adv* lo mismo; también

**limb** *n* miembro *m* (en anatomía); rama *f* (de un árbol)

**limit** *n* límite *m* — **limit** *v* limitar, restringir — **limitation** *n* limitación *f*, restricción *f* — **limited** *adj* limitado

**limp** *v* cojear — **limp** *n* cojera *f*

**line** *n* línea *f*; cuerda *f*; fila *f*; cola *f*

**lingerie** *n* ropa *f* íntima femenina, lencería *f*

**linguistics** *n* lingüística *f* — **linguist** *n* lingüista *mf* — **linguistic** *adj* lingüístico

**link** *n* eslabón *m* (de una cadena); lazo *m*; conexión *f* — **link** *v* enlazar, conectar

**lion** *n* león *m* — **lioness** *n* leona *f*

**lip** *n* labio *m*; borde *m* — **lipstick** *n* lápiz *m* de labios

**liquid** *adj* líquido — **liquid** *n* líquido *m* — **liquidate** *v* liquidar — **liquidation** *n* liquidación *f*

**list** *n* lista *f* — **list** *v* enumerar; incluir (en una lista)

**listen** *v* escuchar — **listener** *n* oyente *mf*

**liter** *n* litro *m*

**literacy** *n* alfabetismo *m*

**literal** *adj* literal — **literally** *adv* literalmente, al pie de la letra

**literature** *n* literatura *f* — **literary** *adj* literario

**little** *adj* (**littler** *or* **less** *or* **lesser; littlest** *or* **least**) pequeño; **a** ∼ un poco de — **little** *adv* (**less; least**) poco — **little** *pron* poco *m*, -ca *f*

**live** *v* vivir; residir; llevar (una vida) — **live** *adj* vivo — **livelihood** *n* sustento *m*, medio *m* de vida — **lively** *adj* animado, alegre — **liven** *v* *or* **liven up** animar(se)

**liver** *n* hígado *m*

**living** *adj* vivo — **living room** *n* living *m*, sala *f* (de estar)

**lizard** *n* lagarto *m*

**load** *n* carga *f*; carga *f*, peso *m* — **load** *v* cargar

**loaf** *n* (**loaves**) pan *m*, barra *f* (de pan)

**loan** *n* préstamo *m* — **loan** *v* prestar

**lobby** *n* (**-bies**) vestíbulo *m*

**lobster** *n* langosta *f*

**local** *adj* local — **locality** *n* (**-ties**) localidad *f*

**locate** *v* situar, ubicar; localizar — **location** *n* situación *f*, lugar *m*

**lock** *n* cerradura *f* (de una puerta, etc.) — **lock** *v* cerrar (con llave); *or* **lock up** encerrar — **locker** *n* armario *m*

**lodge** *v* hospedar(se), alojar(se); presentar — **lodging** *n* alojamiento *m*

**loft** *n* desván *m* (en una casa) — **lofty** *adj* noble, elevado

**log** *n* ∼ **on** entrar (en el sistema); ∼ **off** salir (del sistema) — **logger** *n* leñador *m*, -dora *f*

**logic** *n* lógica *f*

**loin** *n* lomo *m*

**lollipop** *or* **lollypop** *n* pirulí *m*, chupete *m*

**lone** *adj* solitario — **loneliness** *n* soledad *f* — **lonely** *adj* solitario, solo — **loner** *n* solitario *m*, -ria *f*

**long** *adv* mucho tiempo; **as** ∼ **as** mientras; **no** ∼**er** ya no; **so** ∼! ¡hasta luego!, ¡adiós! — **long** *adj* largo

**longitude** *n* longitud *f*

**look** *v* mirar; parecer; ∼ **after** cuidar (de); ∼ **for** esperar; ∼ **for** buscar; ∼ **into** investigar; ∼ **out** tener cuidado; ∼ **over** revisar — **look** *n* mirada *f*; aspecto *m*, aire *m* — **lookout** *n* puesto *m* de observación; vigía *mf*

**loom** *v* aparecer, surgir; ser inminente

**loose** *adj* flojo, suelto — **loosely** *adv* sin apretar; aproximadamente — **loosen** *v* aflojar

**lord** *n* señor *m*, noble *m*; **the Lord** el Señor

**lose** *v* (**lost**) perder; ∼ **one's way** perderse; ∼ **time** atrasarse (de un reloj) — **loser** *n* perdedor *m*, -dora *f* — **loss** *n* pérdida *f*; derrota *f* — **lost** *adj* perdido; **get lost** perderse

**lot** *n* suerte *f*; **a** ∼ **of** *or* ∼**s of** mucho, un montón de

**lotion** *n* loción *f*

**lottery** *n* (**-teries**) lotería *f*

**loud** *adj* alto, fuerte; ruidoso; llamativo — **loud** *adv* fuerte; **out loud** en voz alta — **loudly** *adv* en voz alta — **loudspeaker** *n* altavoz *m*

**love** *n* amor *m*; **fall in** ∼ enamorarse — **love** *v* querer, amar — **lovable** *adj* adorable — **lovely** *adj* lindo, precioso — **lover** *n* amante *mf* — **loving** *adj* cariñoso

**low** *adj* bajo; escaso — **low** *adv* bajo — **lower** *adj* inferior, más bajo — **lower** *v* bajar

**loyal** *adj* leal, fiel — **loyalty** *n* (**-ties**) lealtad *f*

**lubricate** *v* lubricar — **lubricant** *n* lubricante *m* — **lubrication** *n* lubricación *f*

**lucid** *adj* lúcido — **lucidity** *n* lucidez *f*

**luck** *n* suerte *f*; **good** ∼! ¡buena suerte! — **luckily** *adv* afortunadamente — **lucky** *adj* afortunado

**luggage** *n* equipaje *m*

**lumber** *n* madera *f*

**luminous** *adj* luminoso

**lunar** *adj* lunar
**lunch** *n* almuerzo *m*, comida *f* — **lunch**
*v* almorzar, comer — **luncheon** *n* comida *f*, almuerzo *m*

**lung** *n* pulmón *m*
**luxurious** *adj* lujoso — **luxury** *n* (**-ries**)
lujo *m*

# M

**m** *n* (**m's** *or* **ms**) m *f*, decimotercera letra
del alfabeto inglés
**machine** *n* máquina *f* — **machinery** *n*
(**-eries**) maquinaria *f*; mecanismo *m*
**mad** *adj* loco; insensato; furioso
**madam** *n* (**mesdames**) señora *f*
**madness** *n* locura *f*
**magazine** *n* revista *f*
**magic** *n* magia *f* — **magician** *n* mago *m*,
-ga *f*
**magistrate** *n* magistrado *m*, -da *f*
**magnificent** *adj* magnífico
**magnifying glass** *n* lupa *f*
**mail** *n* correo *m*; correspondencia *f* —
**mail** *v* enviar por correo — **mailbox** *n*
buzón *m* — **mailman** *n* (**-men**) cartero
*m*
**main** *adj* principal
**maintain** *v* mantener — **maintenance** *n*
mantenimiento *m*
**majority** *n* (**-ties**) mayoría *f*
**make** *v* (**made**) hacer; fabricar; constituir; preparar; poner; obligar; ~ **a decision** tomar una decisión; ~ **a living**
ganar la vida; ~ **do** arreglárselas; ~
**for** dirigirse a; ~ **good** tener éxito —
**make** *n* marca *f* — **make–believe** *n*
fantasía *f* — **make–believe** *adj* imaginario — **make out** *v* hacer (un cheque,
etc.); distinguir; comprender; **how did
you make out?** ¿qué tal te fue? —
**makeup** *n* maquillaje *m* — **make up** *v*
preparar; inventar; formar; hacer las
paces
**male** *n* macho *m* (de animales o plantas),
varón *m* (de personas) — **male** *adj*
macho; masculino

**malnutrition** *n* desnutrición *f*
**mama** *or* **mamma** *n* mamá *f*
**mammal** *n* mamífero *m*
**man** *n* (**men**) hombre *m*
**manage** *v v* manejar; administrar, dirigir
— **management** *n* dirección *f* — **manager** *n* director *m*, -tora *f*; gerente *mf*
**mandate** *n* mandato *m* — **mandatory**
*adj* obligatorio
**maneuver** *n* maniobra *f* — **maneuver** *v*
maniobrar
**mania** *n* manía *f*
**manipulate** *v* manipular — **manipulation** *n* manipulación *f*
**mankind** *n* género *m* humano, humanidad *f*
**manly** *adj* viril
**manner** *n* manera *f*; clase *f*; ~**s** *npl*
modales *mpl*, educación *f*
**mansion** *n* mansión *f*
**manual** *adj* manual — **manual** *n* manual
*m*
**manufacture** *v* fabricar — **manufacturer** *n* fabricante *mf*
**many** *adj* **more; most** muchos; **as** ~
tantos; **how** ~ cuántos; **too** ~ de-
masiados — **many** *pron* muchos *pl*,
-chas *pl*
**map** *n* mapa *m* — **map** *v* trazar el mapa
de; *or* **map out** planear, proyectar
**march** *n* marcha *f* — **march** *v* marchar,
desfilar
**March** *n* marzo *m*
**margarine** *n* margarina *f*
**margin** *n* margen *m* — **marginal** *adj*
marginal
**mark** *n* marca *f*; mancha *f*; huella *f*;

blanco *m*; nota *f* — **mark** *v* marcar; manchar; señalar; calificar (un examen, etc.); conmemorar; caracterizar; **mark off** delimitar — **marked** *adj* marcado, notable — **markedly** *adv* notablemente — **marker** *n* marcador *m*

**market** *n* mercado *m* — **market** *v* vender, comercializar — **marketplace** *n* mercado *m*

**marriage** *n* matrimonio *m*; casamiento *m*, boda *f* — **married** *adj* casado; **get married** casarse

**marry** *v* (**-ried**) casar(se) (con)

**Mars** *n* Marte *m*

**martyr** *n* mártir *mf*

**marvel** *n* maravilla *f* — **marvel** *v* maravillarse — **marvelous** *or* **marvellous** *adj* maravilloso

**masculine** *adj* masculino

**mask** *n* máscara *f* — **mask** *v* enmascarar

**mass** *n* masa *f*; cantidad *f*; **the ~es** las masas

**Mass** *n* misa *f*

**massage** *n* masaje *m* — **massage** *v* masajear

**massive** *adj* enorme, masivo

**master** *n* maestro *m*, -tra *f*; **~'s degree** maestría *f* — **master** *v* dominar — **masterful** *adj* magistral — **mastery** *n* maestría *f*

**match** *n* fósforo *m*, cerilla *f* (para encender); partido *m*, combate *m* (en boxeo); **be a good ~** hacer buena pareja — **match** *v* concordar, coincidir; igualar; combinar con, hacer juego con (ropa, colores, etc.); *or* **match up** emparejar

**material** *adj* material; importante — **material** *n* material *m*; tela *f*, tejido *m*

**maternal** *adj* maternal — **maternity** *n* maternidad *f* — **maternity** *adj* de maternidad; **maternity clothes** ropa *f* de futura mamá

**mathematics** *ns* & *pl* matemáticas *fpl* — **mathematical** *adj* matemático — **mathematician** *n* matemático *m*, -ca *f*

**matter** *n* materia *f*; asunto *m*, cuestión *f*;

as a ~ of fact en efecto, en realidad; for that ~ de hecho; to make ~s worse para colmo de males; what's the ~? ¿qué pasa? — **matter** *v* importar

**mattress** *n* colchón *m*

**mature** *adj* maduro — **mature** *v* madurar — **maturity** *n* madurez *f*

**maximum** *n* (**-ma** *or* **-mums**) máximo *m* — **maximum** *adj* máximo

**may** *v aux* (**might**) poder; **come what ~** pase lo que pase; **it ~ happen** puede pasar; **~ the best man win** que gane el mejor

**May** *n* mayo *m*

**maybe** *adv* quizás, tal vez

**mayonnaise** *n* mayonesa *f*

**mayor** *n* alcalde *m*, -desa *f*

**me** *pron* me; **for ~** para mí; **give it to ~!** ¡dámelo!; **it's ~** soy yo; **with ~** conmigo

**mean¹** *v* (**meant**) querer decir; querer, tener la intención de; **be meant for** estar destinado a; **he didn't ~ it** no lo dijo en serio

**mean²** *adj* malo; mezquino, tacaño; humilde

**mean³** *n* promedio *m*

**meander** *v* serpentear; vagar

**meaning** *n* significado *m*, sentido *m*

**means** *n* medio *m*; **by all ~** por supuesto; **by ~ of** por medio de; **by no ~** de ninguna manera

**meanwhile** *adv* mientras tanto

**measure** *n* medida *f* — **measure** *v* medir — **measurement** *n* medida *f* — **measure up** *v* measure up to estar a la altura de

**meat** *n* carne *f* — **meatball** *n* albóndiga *f*

**mechanic** *n* mecánico *m*, -ca *f* — **mechanical** *adj* mecánico — **mechanics** *ns* & *pl* mecánica *f*; **mechanism** *n* mecanismo *m*

**media** *or* **mass ~** *npl* medios *mpl* de comunicación

**medical** *adj* médico — **medicinal** *adj*

medicinal — **medicine** n medicina f; medicina f, medicamento m

**meditate** v meditar — **meditation** n meditación f

**meet** v (**met**) reunirse; conocerse; encontrarse (con); satisfacer; **pleased to ∼ you** encantado de conocerlo — **meet** n encuentro m — **meeting** n reunión f

**megabyte** n megabyte m

**melancholy** n melancolía f — **melancholy** adj melancólico, triste

**melody** n (-dies) melodía f

**melon** n melón m

**melt** v derretir(se), fundirse

**member** n miembro m

**memory** n (-ries) memoria f; recuerdo m

**menace** n amenaza f — **menace** v amenazar

**mental** adj mental — **mentality** n mentalidad f

**mention** n mención f — **mention** v mencionar; **don't mention it!** ¡de nada!, ¡no hay de qué!

**menu** n menú m

**merchant** n comerciante mf — **merchandise** n mercancía f, mercadería f

**merciful** adj misericordioso, compasivo — **merciless** adj despiadado

**Mercury** n Mercurio m

**merge** v combinar; unir(se), fusionar(se) (de las compañías), confluir (de los ríos, las calles, etc.) — **merger** n unión f, fusión f

**merit** n mérito m

**mess** n desorden m — **mess** v **mess around** entretenerse; **mess up** desordenar; echar a perder; **mess with** meterse con

**message** n mensaje m — **messenger** n mensajero m, -ra f

**metal** n metal m — **metallic** adj metálico

**metamorphosis** n metamorfosis f

**metaphor** n metáfora f

**meteorological** adj meteorológico —

**meteorologist** n meteorólogo m, -ga f — **meteorology** n meteorología f

**meter** n metro m

**method** n método m — **methodical** adj metódico

**metropolis** n metrópoli f — **metropolitan** adj metropolitano

**Mexican** adj mexicano

**microbe** n microbio m

**microphone** n micrófono m

**microscope** n microscopio m

**microwave** n microonda f; or **∼ oven** microondas; un horno de microondas m

**mid** adj **∼ morning** a media mañana; **in ∼-August** a mediados de agosto; **she is in her mid thirties** tiene alrededor de 35 años — **midair** n **in midair** en el aire — **midday** n mediodía m

**middle** adj de en medio, del medio — **middle** n medio m; centro m; **in the middle of** en medio de (un espacio), a mitad de (una actividad); **in the middle of the month** a mediados del mes — **middle–aged** adj de mediana edad — **Middle Ages** npl Edad f Media — **middle class** n clase f media

**midnight** n medianoche f

**might** n fuerza f, poder m

**mile** n milla f — **mileage** n distancia f recorrida (en millas), kilometraje m

**military** adj militar

**milk** n leche f — **milk** v ordeñar (una vaca, etc.)

**millennium** n (-nia) or -niums milenio m

**millimeter** n milímetro m

**million** n millón m; **a ∼ people** un millón de personas — **millionaire** n millonario m, -ria f

**mimic** v (-icked) remedar — **mimicry** n imitación f

**mind** n mente f; capacidad f intelectual; opinión f; razón f; **have a ∼ to** tener intención de — **mind** v cuidar; obedecer; tener cuidado con; **I don't mind** no me importa, me es igual; **I don't mind**

**the heat** no me molesta el calor —
**mindful** *adj* atento — **mindless** *adj*
sin sentido

**mine**[1] *pron* (el) mío, (la) mía, (los) míos,
(las) mías

**mine**[2] *n* mina *f* — **miner** *n* minero *m*, -ra
*f* — **mining** *n* minería *f*

**mineral** *n* mineral *m*

**minimize** *v* minimizar — **minimum** *adj*
mínimo — **minimum** *n* (**-ma** *or*
**-mums**) mínimo *m*

**minister** *n* ministro *m*, -tra *f* (en política)
— **minister** *v* **minister to** cuidar (de),
atender a — **ministry** *n* (**-tries**) ministerio *m*

**minor** *adj* menor; sin importancia —
**minor** *n* menor *mf* (de edad) — **minority** *n* (**-ties**) minoría *f*

**mint** *n* menta *f* (planta)

**minus** *prep* menos

**minute**[1] *n* minuto *m*; ~**s** *npl* actas *fpl*
(de una reunión)

**minute**[2] *adj* diminuto, minúsculo

**miracle** *n* milagro *m*

**mirror** *n* espejo *m*

**mischief** *n* travesuras *fpl* — **mischievous** *adj* travieso

**miss** *v* errar, faltar; perder (una oportunidad, un vuelo, etc.); **I ~ you** te echo
de menos

**Miss** *n* señorita *f*

**missing** *adj* perdido, desaparecido

**mission** *n* misión *f*

**mist** *n* neblina *f*, bruma *f*

**mistake** *v* (**mistook; mistaken**) entender mal; confundir — **mistake** *n* error
*m*; **make a mistake** equivocarse —
**mistaken** *adj* equivocado

**mistreat** *v* maltratar

**misunderstanding** *n* malentendido *m*

**mix** *v* mezclar(se); ~ **up** confundir —
**mix** *n* mezcla *f* — **mixture** *n* mezcla *f*

**moan** *n* gemido *m* — **moan** *v* gemir

**mobile** *adj* móvil — **mobile** *n* móvil *m*
— **mobility** *n* movilidad *f*

**moccasin** *n* mocasín *m*

**model** *n* modelo *m*; modelo *mf* (persona)
— **model** *adj* modelo

**modem** *n* módem *m*

**moderate** *adj* moderado — **moderate** *n*
moderado *m*, -da *f* — **moderate** *v* moderar

**modern** *adj* moderno

**modest** *adj* modesto

**modify** *v* (**-fied**) modificar

**moist** *adj* húmedo — **moisten** *v*
humedecer

**molar** *n* muela *f*

**mom** *n* mamá *f*

**moment** *n* momento *m*

**Monday** *n* lunes *m*

**money** *n* dinero *m* — **monetary** *adj*
monetario

**monitor** *v* controlar

**monkey** *n* (**-keys**) mono *m*, -na *f* —
**monkey wrench** *n* llave *f* inglesa

**monologue** *n* monólogo *m*

**month** *n* mes *m* — **monthly** *adv* mensu-
almente — **monthly** *adj* mensual

**monument** *n* monumento *m*

**moon** *n* luna *f*

**mop** *v* trapear, pasar la fregona a

**moral** *adj* moral — **moral** *n* moraleja *f*
(de un cuento, etc.); **morals** *npl* moral
*f*, moralidad *f*

**more** *adj* más — **more** *adv* más; **more
and more** cada vez más; **more or less**
más o menos; **once more** una vez más
— **more** *n* más *m* — **more** *pron* más —
**moreover** *adv* además

**morning** *n* mañana *f*; **good ~!** ¡buenos
días!; **in the ~** por la mañana

**mortal** *adj* mortal — **mortal** *n* mortal *mf*
— **mortality** *n* mortalidad *f*

**mortgage** *n* hipoteca *f* — **mortgage** *v*
hipotecar

**mosque** *n* mezquita *f*

**most** *adj* la mayoría de, la mayor parte
de; **(the) ~** más — **most** *adv* más —
**most** *n* más *m*, máximo *m* — **most**
*pron* la mayoría, la mayor parte

**mother** *n* madre *f* — **motherhood** *n*

maternidad *f* — **mother–in–law** *n* (**mothers– . . .** ) suegra *f*

**motion** *n* movimiento *m*; moción *f*; **set in** ~ poner en marcha — **motion** *v* **motion to** hacer una señal a — **motionless** *adj* inmóvil — **motion picture** *n* película *f*

**motive** *n* motivo *m* — **motivate** *v* motivar — **motivation** *n* motivación *f*

**motor** *n* motor *m* — **motorcycle** *n* motocicleta *f* — **motorist** *n* automovilista *mf*, motorista *mf*

**mount**[1] *n* montura *f* — **mount** *v* subir (una escalera)

**mount**[2] *n* monte *m* — **mountain** *n* montaña *f* — **mountainous** *adj* montañoso

**mourning** *n* luto *m*

**mouse** *n* (**mice**) ratón *m* (animal); (**mice** *or* **mouses**) ratón *m* (de computador) — **mousetrap** *n* ratonera *f*

**mouth** *n* boca *f* (de una persona o un animal), desembocadura *f* (de un río) — **mouthful** *n* bocado *m*

**move** *v* ir; conmover; transportar, trasladar; proponer; mudarse; mover(se); tomar medidas — **move** *n* movimiento *m*; mudanza *f*; medida *f* — **movable** *or* **moveable** *adj* movible, móvil — **movement** *n* movimiento *m*

**movie** *n* película *f*; ~**s** *npl* cine *m*

**Mr.** *n* (**Messrs.**) señor *m*

**Mrs.** *n* (**Mesdames**) señora *f*

**Ms.** *n* señora *f*, señorita *f*

**much** *adj* (**more; most**) mucho —

**much** *adv* (**more; most**) mucho; **as much as** tanto como; **how much?** ¿cuánto?; **too much** demasiado — **much** *pron* mucho, -cha

**mud** *n* barro *m*, lodo *m*

**muddy** *adj* fangoso, lleno de barro

**mug** *v* asaltar, atracar

**multimedia** *adj* multimedia

**multinational** *adj* multinacional

**multiple** *adj* múltiple — **multiple** *n* múltiplo *m* — **multiplication** *n* multiplicación *f* — **multiply** *v* (**-plied**) multiplicar(se)

**multitude** *n* multitud *f*

**municipal** *adj* municipal — **municipality** *n* (**-ties**) municipio *m*

**muscle** *n* músculo *m* — **muscular** *adj* muscular; musculoso

**museum** *n* museo *m*

**mushroom** *n* hongo *m*, seta *f*; champiñón *m* (en la cocina)

**music** *n* música *f* — **musical** *adj* musical — **musician** *n* músico *m*, -ca *f*

**Muslim** *adj* musulmán — **Muslim** *n* musulmán *m*, -mana *f*

**must** *v aux* deber, tener que; **you** ~ **come** tienes que venir; **you** ~ **be tired** debes (de) estar cansado

**mustache** *n* bigote *m*, bigotes *mpl*

**mute** *adj* mudo — **mute** *n* mudo *m*, -da *f*

**mutiny** *n* (**-nies**) motín *m*

**my** *adj* mi

**myself** *pron* me; yo mismo; **by** ~ solo

**mystery** *n* (**-teries**) misterio *m* — **mysterious** *adj* misterioso

**myth** *n* mito *m*

# N

**n** *n* (**n's** *or* **ns**) *nf*, decimocuarta letra del alfabeto inglés

**nail** *n* clavo *m*; uña *f* (de un dedo) — **nail** *vt or* **nail down** clavar — **nail file** *n* lima *f* de uñas

**naive** *or* **naïve** *adj* ingenuo

**naked** *adj* desnudo

**name** *n* nombre *m*; fama *f*; **first name** nombre *m*; **surname** apellido *m* — **name** *v* poner nombre a; nombrar —

**nameless** *adj* anónimo — **namely** *adv* a saber

**nap** *v* echarse una siesta — **nap** *n* siesta *f*

**nape** *n or* ∼ **of the neck** nuca *f*

**napkin** *n* servilleta *f*

**narrate** *v* narrar — **narration** *n* narración *f* — **narrative** *n* narración *f* — **narrator** *n* narrador *m*, -dora *f*

**narrow** *adj* estrecho, angosto; limitado — **narrow** *v* estrecharse

**nasal** *adj* nasal

**nasty** *adj* malo, cruel; desagradable; asqueroso

**nation** *n* nación *f* — **national** *adj* nacional — **nationality** *n* (**-ties**) nacionalidad *f* — **nationalize** *v* nacionalizar

**native** *adj* natal (de un país, etc.); ∼ **language** lengua *f* materna — **native** *n* nativo *m*, -va *f*; **be a native of** ser natural de — **nativity** *n* (**-ties**) **the Nativity** la Navidad

**nature** *n* naturaleza *f*; índole, *f*, clase *f* — **natural** *adj* natural — **naturally** *adv* naturalmente

**naughty** *adj* travieso, pícaro

**naval** *adj* naval

**navel** *n* ombligo *m*

**navigate** *v* navegar; gobernar (un barco), pilotar (un avión); navegar por (un río, etc.) — **navigation** *n* navegación *f* — **navigator** *n* navegante *mf*

**near** *adv* cerca — **near** *prep* cerca de — **near** *adj* cercano, próximo — **near** *v* acercarse a —**nearby** *adv* cerca — **nearby** *adj* cercano —**nearly** *adv* casi — **nearsighted** *adj* miope

**neat** *adj* ordenado, limpio; pulcro — **neatly** *adv* muy arreglado; hábil, ingenioso hábilmente

**necessary** *adj* necesario — **necessarily** *adv* necesariamente — **necessity** *n* (**-ties**) necesidad *f*

**neck** *n* cuello *m* (de una persona o una botella), pescuezo *m* (de un animal); cuello *m* — **necklace** *n* collar *m*

**need** *n* necesidad *f* — **need** *v* necesitar, exigir; **need to** tener que — **need** *v aux* tener que

**needle** *n* aguja *f*

**negative** *adj* negativo — **negative** *n* negación *f* (en gramática); negativo *m* (en fotografía)

**neglect** *v* descuidar *m*

**negotiate** *v* negociar — **negotiable** *adj* negociable — **negotiation** *n* negociación *f*

**Negro** *n* (**-groes**) negro *m*, -gra *f*

**neighbor** *n* vecino *m*, -na *f* — **neighborhood** *n* barrio *m*, vecindario *m*; **in the neighborhood of** alrededor de

**neither** *conj* ∼ **...** **nor** ni **...** ni; ∼ **am/do I** yo tampoco — **neither** *pron* ninguno, -na — **neither** *adj* ninguno (de los dos)

**nephew** *n* sobrino *m*

**nerve** *n* nervio *m*; ∼**s** *npl* nervios *mpl* — **nervous** *adj* nervioso — **nervousness** *n* nerviosismo *m*

**nest** *n* nido *m* — **nest** *v* anidar

**net** *n* red *f* — **net** *v* pescar, atrapar (con una red)

**network** *n* red *f*

**neutral** *adj* neutral — **neutrality** *n* neutralidad *f*

**never** *adv* nunca, jamás; no; ∼ **mind** no importa — **nevermore** *adv* nunca jamás — **nevertheless** *adv* sin embargo, no obstante

**new** *adj* nuevo — **newborn** *adj* recién nacido — **newly** *adv* recién, recientemente — **news** *n* noticias *fpl* — **newscast** *n* noticiario *m*, noticiero *m* — **newscaster** *n* presentador *m*, -dora *f* (de un noticiario) — **newspaper** *n* periódico *m*, diario *m*

**New Year's Day** *n* día *m* del Año Nuevo

**next** *adj* próximo; siguiente — **next** *adv* la próxima vez; después, luego; ahora — **next to** *adv* casi — **next to** *prep* al lado de

**Nicaraguan** *adj* nicaragüense

# nice

**nice** *adj* agradable, bueno; amable — **nicely** *adv* bien; amablemente

**nickname** *n* apodo *m*, sobrenombre *m*

**niece** *n* sobrina *f*

**night** *n* noche *f*; **at** ～ de noche; **last** ～ anoche — **nightclub** *n* club *m* nocturno — **nightfall** *n* anochecer *m* — **nightgown** *n* camisón *m* (de noche) — **nightmare** *n* pesadilla *f*

**nine** *adj* nueve — **nine** *n* nueve *m* — **nine hundred** *adj* novecientos — **nine hundred** *n* novecientos *m* — **nineteen** *adj* diecinueve — **nineteen** *n* diecinueve *m* — **nineteenth** *adj* decimonoveno, decimonono — **nineteenth** *n* decimonoveno *m*, -na *f*; decimonono *m*, -na *f* (en una serie) — **ninetieth** *adj* nonagésimo — **ninetieth** *n* nonagésimo *m*, -ma *f* (en una serie); noventavo *m* (en matemáticas) — **ninety** *adj* noventa — **ninety** *n* (**-ties**) noventa *m* — **ninth** *adj* noveno — **ninth** *n* noveno *m*, -na *f* (en una serie); noveno *m* (en matemáticas)

**nipple** *n* pezón *m* (de una mujer)

**no** *adv* no — **no** *adj* ninguno — **no** *n* (**noes** *or* **nos**) no *m*

**nobody** *pron* nadie

**nod** *v* saludar con la cabeza; ～ **off** dormirse; *or* ～ **yes** asentir con la cabeza

**noise** *n* ruido *m*

**nominate** *v* proponer, postular; nombrar

**none** *pron* ninguno, ninguna

**nonetheless** *adv* sin embargo, no obstante

**nonsense** *n* tonterías *fpl*, disparates *mpl*

**nonstop** *adj* directo — **nonstop** *adv* sin parar

**noodle** *n* fideo *m*

**noon** *n* mediodía *m*

**no one** *pron* nadie

**nor** *conj* **neither . . .** ～ ni . . . ni

**norm** *n* norma *f* — **normal** *adj* normal

**north** *adv* al norte — **north** *adj* norte, del norte — **north** *n* norte *m* — **North**

**American** *adj* norteamericano — **northern** *adj* del norte, norteño

**Norwegian** *adj* noruego

**nose** *n* nariz *f* (de una persona), hocico *m* (de un animal)

**nostalgia** *n* nostalgia *f* — **nostalgic** *adj* nostálgico

**not** *adv* no

**note** *v* observar, notar; anotar — **note** *n* nota *f*; **take notes** apuntar — **notebook** *n* libreta *f*, cuaderno *m*

**nothing** *pron* nada

**notice** *n* letrero *m*, aviso *m* — **notice** *v* notar

**notion** *n* noción *f*, idea *f*

**notwithstanding** *prep* a pesar de, no obstante — **notwithstanding** *adv* sin embargo — **notwithstanding** *conj* a pesar de que

**noun** *n* nombre *m*, sustantivo *m*

**nourish** *v* nutrir — **nourishment** *n* alimento *m*

**novel** *adj* original — **novel** *n* novela *f* — **novelist** *n* novelista *mf* — **novelty** *n* (**-ties**) novedad *f*

**November** *n* noviembre *m*

**now** *adv* ahora; entonces; **from** ～ **on** de ahora en adelante; **right** ～ ahora mismo — **now** *conj* *or* **now that** ahora que, ya que — **nowadays** *adv* hoy en día

**nowhere** *adv* por ninguna parte, por ningún lado; a ninguna parte, a ningún lado — **nowhere** *n* ninguna parte *f*

**nuclear** *adj* nuclear

**nude** *adj* desnudo — **nude** *n* desnudo *m*

**number** *n* número *m* — **number** *v*; numerar; contar, incluir

**nun** *n* monja *f*

**nurse** *n* enfermero *m*, -ra *f* — **nurse** *v* cuidar (de), atender; amamantar — **nursery** *n* (**-eries**) *or* **day nursery** guardería *f* — **nursing home** *n* asilo *m* de ancianos

**nurture** *v* nutrir

**nut** *n* nuez *f*; ～**s and bolts** tuercas y

tornillos — **nutcracker** *n* cascanueces *m*

**nutrition** *n* nutrición *f*
**nylon** *n* nilón *m*

# O

**o** *n* (**o's** *or* **os**) o *f*, decimoquinta letra del alfabeto inglés; cero *m*

**oak** *n* (**oaks** *or* **oak**) roble *m*

**oath** *n* juramento *m*

**oats** *npl* avena *f* — **oatmeal** *n* harina *f* de avena

**obedient** *adj* obediente

**obey** *v* obedecer

**object** *n* objeto *m*; objetivo *m*; complemento *m* (en gramática) — **objective** *adj* objetivo — **objective** *n* objetivo *m*

**obligation** *n* obligación *f* — **obligatory** *adj* obligatorio

**obscurity** *n* oscuridad *f* — **obscure** *adj* oscuro — **obscure** *v* oscurecer; ocultar

**observe** *v* observar; mirar — **observation** *n* observación *f*

**obsession** *n* obsesión *f* — **obsessive** *adj* obsesivo

**obstacle** *n* obstáculo *m*

**obtain** *v* obtener, conseguir

**obvious** *adj* obvio, evidente

**occasion** *n* ocasión *f* — **occasional** *adj* poco frecuente, ocasional — **occasionally** *adv* de vez en cuando

**occult** *adj* oculto

**occupy** *v* (**-pied**) ocupar — **occupant** *n* ocupante *mf* — **occupation** *n* ocupación *f*

**occur** *v* ocurrir

**ocean** *n* océano *m*

**o'clock** *adv* **at 6 ~** a las seis; **it's one ~** es la una

**October** *n* octubre *m*

**odd** *adj* extraño, raro; **~ number** número *m* impar

**of** *prep* de; **five minutes ~ ten** las diez menos cinco

**off** *adv* **be ~** irse **cut ~** cortar **day ~** día *m* de descanso; **fall ~** caerse; **shut ~** apagar — **off** *prep* de — **off** *adj* cancelado; apagado

**offend** *v* ofender — **offense** *or* **offence** *n* ataque *m*; ofensiva *f* (en deportes); delito *m* — **offensive** *adj* ofensivo

**offer** *v* ofrecer — **offer** *n* oferta *f*

**office** *n* oficina *f*; cargo *m* — **officer** *n* oficial *mf*; *or* **police officer** agente *mf* (de policía)

**often** *adv* muchas veces, a menudo, con frecuencia; **every so ~** de vez en cuando

**oh** *interj* ¡oh!, ¡ah!

**oil** *n* aceite *m*; petróleo *m* — **oily** *adj* aceitoso, grasiento

**OK** *or* **okay** *adv* muy bien; **~!** ¡de acuerdo!, ¡bueno! — *adj* bien

**old** *adj* viejo; antiguo; **be ten years ~** tener diez años (de edad); **~ man** anciano *m*; **~ woman** anciana *f* — **old** *n* **the old** los viejos, los ancianos — **old–fashioned** *adj* anticuado

**olive** *n* aceituna *f* (fruta)

**Olympic** *adj* olímpico — **Olympics** *npl* **the Olympics** las Olimpiadas, las Olimpíadas

**omit** *v* omitir — **omission** *n* omisión *f*

**on** *prep* en; sobre; **~ foot** a pie; **~ Monday** el lunes — **on** *adv* **and so on** etcétera; **keep on** seguir; **later on** más tarde; **put on** ponerse (ropa), poner (música, etc.); **turn on** encender (una luz, etc.), abrir (una llave) — **on** *adj* encendido (de luces, etc.), abierto (de llaves)

**once** *adv* una vez; antes — **once** *n* **at once** al mismo tiempo; **at once** inmediatamente — *conj* una vez que

**oncoming** *adj* que viene

**one** *adj* un, uno; único — **one** *n*; uno *m* (número); **one by one** uno a uno — **one** *pron* uno, una; **that one** aquél, aquella; **which one?** ¿cuál? — **oneself** *pron* se; sí mismo, sí misma; uno mismo, una misma; **by oneself** solo — **one–way** *adj* de sentido único (de una calle)

**ongoing** *adj* en curso, corriente

**onion** *n* cebolla *f*

**only** *adj* único — **only** *adv* sólo, solamente; **if only** ojalá, por lo menos — **only** *conj* pero

**onto** *prep* sobre

**open** *adj* abierto; vacante, libre — **open** *v* abrir; comenzar — **open** *n* **in the open** al aire libre; sacado a la luz — **open–air** *adj* al aire libre — **opener** *n* **or can ~** abrelatas *m* — **opening** *n* abertura *f*; comienzo *m*, apertura *f*

**operate** *v* funcionar; hacer funcionar (una máquina); dirigir, manejar — **operation** *n* operación *f* funcionamiento *m*

**opinion** *n* opinión *f*

**opponent** *n* adversario *m*, -ria *f*; contrincante *mf* (en deportes)

**opportunity** *n* (**-ties**) oportunidad *f* — **opportune** *adj* oportuno

**oppose** *v* oponerse a — **opposed** *adj* **opposed to** en contra de

**opposite** *adj* de enfrente; opuesto — **opposite** *n* **the opposite** lo contrario, lo opuesto — **opposite** *adv* enfrente — **opposite** *prep* enfrente de, frente a — **opposition** *n* oposición *f*; **in opposition to** en contra de

**oppress** *v* oprimir

**optimism** *n* optimismo *m* — **optimist** *n* optimista *mf* — **optimistic** *adj* optimista

**option** *n* opción *f*

**or** *conj* o; ni; **~ else** si no

**oral** *adj* oral

**orange** *n* naranja *f* (fruta); naranja *m* (color)

**orchestra** *n* orquesta *f*

**orchid** *n* orquídea *f*

**order** *v* ordenar; pedir (mercancías, etc.); hacer un pedido — **order** *n* orden *m*; orden *f*; pedido *m*; **in order that** para que; **in order to** para

**ordinary** *adj* normal, corriente; ordinario — **ordinarily** *adv* generalmente

**organ** *n* órgano *m* — **organic** *adj* orgánico — **organism** *n* organismo *m* — **organize** *v* organizar — **organization** *n* organización *f*

**orgasm** *n* orgasmo *m*

**oriental** *adj* del Oriente, oriental — **orientation** *n* orientación *f*.

**origin** *n* origen *m* — **original** *n* original *m* — **original** *adj* original — **originality** *n* originalidad *f* — **originally** *adv* originariamente — **originate** *v* originar

**ornament** *n* adorno *m*

**orphan** *n* huérfano *m*, -na *f*

**ostrich** *n* avestruz *m*

**other** *adj* otro; **every ~ day** cada dos días; **on the ~ hand** por otra parte, por otro lado — **other** *pron* otro, otra; **the others** los otros, las otras, los demás, las demás — **otherwise** *adv* eso aparte, por lo demás; de otro modo; si no

**ought** *v aux* deber

**ounce** *n* onza *f*

**our** *adj* nuestro — **ours** *pron* (el) nuestro, (la) nuestra, (los) nuestros, (las) nuestras — **ourselves** *pron* nos; nosotros, nosotras; nosotros mismos, nosotras mismas

**out** *adv* fuera, afuera; **cry ~** gritar; **go ~** salir; **look ~** mirar para afuera; **run ~ of** agotar; **turn ~** apagar (una luz); **take ~** sacar — **out** *adj* ausente; fuera de moda; apagado

**outcome** *n* resultado *m*

**outdo** *v* (**-did; -done**) superar

**outdoor** *adj* al aire libre — **outdoors** *adv* al aire libre

**outer** *adj* exterior

**outgoing** *adj* extrovertido

**outlay** *n* desembolso *m*

**outlet** *n* salida *f*; *or* **electrical** ∼ toma *f* de corriente

**outline** *n* contorno *m*; bosquejo *m*, boceto *m*; esquema *m* — **outline** *v* bosquejar; delinear, esbozar

**outlook** *n* perspectivas *fpl*; punto *m* de vista

**out of** *prep* de; por; sin

**output** *n* producción *f*, rendimiento *m*; salida *f* (informática) — **output** *v* (**-putted** *or* **-put**) producir

**outrage** *n* atrocidad *f*, escándalo *m*; ira *f*, indignación *f* — **outrageous** *adj* escandaloso

**outright** *adv* por completo; en el acto — **outright** *adj* completo, absoluto

**outset** *n* comienzo *m*, principio *m*

**outside** *n* exterior *m*; **from the** ∼ desde fuera, desde afuera — **outside** *adj* exterior, externo — **outside** *adv* fuera, afuera — **outsider** *n* forastero *m*, -ra *f*

**outskirts** *npl* afueras *fpl*, alrededores *mpl*

**outspoken** *adj* franco, directo

**outstanding** *adj* pendiente; excepcional

**outward** *adj* hacia afuera; externo, external — **outward** *or* **outwards** *adv* hacia afuera

**oval** *n* óvalo *m* — **oval** *adj* ovalado

**ovary** *n* (**-ries**) ovario *m*

**oven** *n* horno *m*

**over** *adv* por encima; otra vez, de nuevo; más; **all** ∼ por todas partes; **cross** ∼ cruzar; **fall** ∼ caerse; ∼ **and** ∼ una y otra vez; ∼ **here** aquí ∼ **there** allí — **over** *prep* encima de, sobre; por encima de, sobre; en, durante; **over $5** más de $5 — **over** *adj* terminado, acabado

**overall** *adv* en general — **overall** *adj* total, en conjunto — **overalls** *npl* overol *m*

**overcoat** *n* abrigo *m*

**overcome** *v* (**-came; -come**) vencer; agobiar

**overdo** *v* (**-did; -done**) hacer demasiado; exagerar

**overdose** *n* sobredosis *f*

**overdraft** *n* sobregiro *m*, descubierto *m*

**overhand** *adv* por encima de la cabeza

**overhead** *adv* por encima — **overhead** *adj* de arriba

**overland** *adv or adj* por tierra

**overlook** *v* dar a (un jardín, el mar, etc.); pasar por alto

**overly** *adv* demasiado

**overnight** *adv* por la noche; de la noche a la mañana — **overnight** *adj* de noche

**overpass** *n* paso *m* elevado

**overseas** *adv* en el extranjero — **overseas** *adj* extranjero, exterior

**oversleep** *v* (**-slept**) quedarse dormido

**overt** *adj* manifiesto

**overtake** *v* (**-took; -taken**) adelantar; superar

**overtime** *n* horas *fpl* extras (de trabajo)

**overwhelm** *v* agobiar; aplastar (a un enemigo)

**owe** *v* deber — **owing to** *prep* debido a

**owl** *n* búho *m*

**own** *adj* propio — **own** *v* poseer, tener — **own** *pron* (**my, your, his/her/their, our**) el mío, la mía; el tuyo, la tuya; el suyo, la suya; el nuestro, la nuestra; **be on one's own** estar solo; **to each his own** cada uno a lo suyo — **owner** *n* propietario *m*, -ria *f* — **ownership** *n* propiedad *f*

**oxygen** *n* oxígeno *m*

# P

**p** *n* (**p's** *or* **ps**) p *f*, decimosexta letra del alfabeto inglés

**pace** *n* ritmo *m*; **keep ~ with** andar al mismo paso que

**pacify** *v* (**-fied**) apaciguar — **pacifier** *n* chupete *m* — **pacifist** *n* pacifista *mf*

**pack** *n* mochila *f*; paquete *m* — **pack** *v* empaquetar; llenar; hacer (una maleta) — **package** *v* empaquetar — **package** *n* paquete *m*

**pact** *n* pacto *m*, acuerdo *m*

**pad** *n* bloc *m* (de papel)

**padlock** *n* candado *m*

**page** *n* página *f* (de un libro, etc.)

**pain** *n* dolor *m*; pena *f* (mental); **~s** *npl* esfuerzos *mpl* — **pain** *v* doler — **painkiller** *n* analgésico *m*

**paint** *v* pintar — **paint** *n* pintura *f* — **paintbrush** *n* pincel *m* (de un artista), brocha *f* (para casas) — **painter** *n* pintor *m*, -tora *f* — **painting** *n* pintura *f*

**pair** *n* par *m*; pareja *f*

**pajamas** *npl* pijama *m*, piyama *mf*

**Pakistani** *adj* paquistaní

**palace** *n* palacio *m*

**palate** *n* paladar *m*

**pale** *adj* pálido — **pale** *v* palidecer

**Palestinian** *adj* palestino

**palm**[1] *n* palma *f* (de la mano)

**palm**[2] *or* **~ tree** palmera *f*

**palpitate** *v* palpitar — **palpitation** *n* palpitación *f*

**pan** *n* cacerola *f*; sartén *mf*

**pancake** *n* crepe *mf*, panqueque *m*

**panic** *n* pánico *m*

**panorama** *n* panorama *m*

**panther** *n* pantera *f*

**panties** *npl* bragas *fpl*, calzones *mpl*

**pants** *npl* pantalón *m*, pantalones *mpl*

**papaya** *n* papaya *f*

**paper** *n* papel *m* — **paperback** *n* libro *m* en rústica

**paprika** *n* pimentón *m*

**parachute** *n* paracaídas *m*

**paradise** *n* paraíso *m*

**paragraph** *n* párrafo *m*

**Paraguayan** *adj* paraguayo

**paralysis** *n* parálisis *f* — **paralyze** *v* paralizar

**paraphrase** *n* paráfrasis *f* — **paraphrase** *v* parafrasear

**paraplegic** *n* parapléjico *m*, -ca *f*

**paratrooper** *n* paracaidista *mf* (militar)

**parcel** *n* paquete *m*

**pardon** *n* perdón *m*

**parent** *n* madre *f*, padre *m*; **~s** *npl* padres *mpl*

**parenthesis** *n* (**-theses**) paréntesis *m*

**parish** *n* parroquia *f*

**park** *n* parque *m* — **park** *v* estacionar, parquear

**parking** *n* estacionamiento *m*

**parliament** *n* parlamento *m* — **parliamentary** *adj* parlamentario

**parole** *n* libertad *f* condicional

**parrot** *n* loro *m*, papagayo *m*

**parsley** *n* perejil *m*

**part** *n* parte *f*; pieza *f*

**partial** *adj* parcial

**participate** *v* participar

**participle** *n* participio *m*

**particular** *adj* particular; **in ~** en particular, en especial

**partition** *n* tabique *m*

**partner** *n* pareja *f* (en un juego, etc.)

**party** *n* (**-ties**) partido *m* (político); fiesta *f*

**pass** *v* pasar; aprobar (en un examen, una ley, etc.); **~ down** transmitir — **passable** *adj* transitable (de un camino, etc.) — **passage** *n* pasillo *m* (dentro de un edificio), pasaje *m* (entre edificios)

**passenger** *n* pasajero *m*, -ra *f*

**passion** *n* pasión *f* — **passionate** *adj* apasionado
**passive** *adj* pasivo
**Passover** *n* Pascua *f* (en el judaísmo)
**passport** *n* pasaporte *m*
**password** *n* contraseña *f*
**past** *adj* pasado; anterior — **past** *prep* por delante de; más allá de; **half past two** las dos y media — **past** *n* pasado *m* — **past** *adv* por delante
**paste** *n* pasta *f* — **paste** *v* pegar
**pastime** *n* pasatiempo *m*
**pastor** *n* pastor *m*, -tora *f*
**pasture** *n* pasto *m*
**paternal** *adj* paternal — **paternity** *n* paternidad *f*
**path** *n* camino *m*, sendero *m*; trayectoria *f*
**patience** *n* paciencia *f* — **patient** *adj* paciente — **patient** *n* paciente *mf*
**patio** *n* (**-tios**) patio *m*
**patriot** *n* patriota *mf* — **patriotic** *adj* patriótico
**patrol** *n* patrulla *f* — **patrol** *v* patrullar
**pattern** *n* modelo *m*
**paunch** *n* panza *f*
**pause** *n* pausa *f*
**pave** *v* pavimentar — **pavement** *n* pavimento *m*
**pavilion** *n* pabellón *m*
**paw** *n* pata *f*
**pawn** *n* peón *m* (en ajedrez)
**pay** *v* (**paid**) pagar; ∼ **attention** prestar atención; ∼ **back** devolver — **payment** *n* pago *m*
**pea** *n* guisante *m*, arveja *f*
**peace** *n* paz *f* — **peaceful** *adj* pacífico
**peach** *n* melocotón *m*, durazno *m*
**peak** *n* cumbre *f*, cima *f*, pico *m* (de una montaña)
**peanut** *n* cacajuete *m*, maní *m*
**pear** *n* pera *f*
**pearl** *n* perla *f*
**peasant** *n* campesino *m*, -na *f*
**pedal** *n* pedal *m* — **pedal** *v or* **pedalling** pedalear

**pedestrian** *n* peatón *m*, -tona *f*
**pediatrician** *n* pediatra *mf*
**peel** *v* pelar (fruta, etc.) pelarse (de la piel), desconcharse (de la pintura) — **peel** *n* piel *f*, cáscara *f*
**pelt** *n* piel *f* (de un animal)
**pelvis** *n* (**-vises** *or* **-ves**) pelvis *f*
**pen** *n or* **ballpoint** ∼ bolígrafo *m*; *or* **fountain** ∼ pluma *f*
**penal** *adj* penal
**penance** *n* penitencia *f*
**pencil** *n* lápiz *m* — **pencil sharpener** *n* sacapuntas *m*
**pending** *adj* pendiente
**penetrate** *v* penetrar — **penetrating** *adj* penetrante — **penetration** *n* penetración *f*
**penicillin** *n* penicilina *f*
**peninsula** *n* península *f*
**pension** *n* pensión *m*, jubilación *f*
**pensive** *adj* pensativo
**pentagon** *n* pentágono *m*
**people** *ns & pl* **people** *npl* gente *f*, personas *fpl*; *pl* ∼**s** pueblo *m*
**pepper** *n* pimienta *f* (condimento); pimiento *m* (fruta)
**peppermint** *n* menta *f*
**perceive** *v* percibir
**percent** *adv* por ciento — **percentage** *n* porcentaje *m*
**perception** *n* percepción *f*
**percussion** *n* percusión *f*
**perfect** *adj* perfecto — **perfect** *v* perfeccionar — **perfection** *n* perfección *f* — **perfectionist** *n* perfeccionista *mf*
**perforate** *v* perforar
**perform** *v* representar (una obra teatral), interpretar (una obra musical); actuar — **performance** *n* representación *f* — **performer** *n* actor *m*, -triz *f*; intérprete *mf* (de música)
**perfume** *n* perfume *m*
**perhaps** *adv* tal vez, quizá, quizás
**peril** *n* peligro *m*
**period** *n* período *m* (de tiempo); punto *m*

(en puntuación); época *f* — **periodic** *adj* periódico

**peripheral** *adj* periférico

**perish** *v* perecer

**permanent** *adj* permanente — **permanent** *n* permanente *f*

**permission** *n* permiso *m* — **permit** *v* permitir — **permit** *n* permiso *m*

**perpendicular** *adj* perpendicular

**persecute** *v* perseguir — **persecution** *n* persecución *f*

**person** *n* persona *f* — **personality** *n* (**-ties**) personalidad *f* — **personnel** *n* personal *m*

**perspective** *n* perspectiva *f*

**persuade** *v* persuadir

**Peruvian** *adj* peruano

**perverse** *adj* obstinado

**pessimist** *n* pesimista *mf* — **pessimistic** *adj* pesimista

**petal** *n* pétalo *m*

**petition** *n* petición *f* — **petition** *v* dirigir una petición a

**petroleum** *n* petróleo *m*

**phenomenon** *n* (**-na** *or* **-nons**) fenómeno *m*

**philanthropy** *n* filantropía *f*

**philosophy** *n* (**-phies**) filosofía *f* — **philosopher** *n* filósofo *m*, -fa *f*

**phobia** *n* fobia *f*

**phosphorus** *n* fósforo *m*

**photocopy** *n* (**-copies**) fotocopia *f* — **photograph** *n* fotografía *f*, foto *f* — **photograph** *v* fotografiar — **photographer** *n* fotógrafo *m*, -fa *f* — **photography** *n* fotografía *f*

**phrase** *n* frase *f*

**physical** *adj* físico

**physics** *ns & pl* física *f* — **physicist** *n* físico *m*, -ca *f*

**physiology** *n* fisiología *f*

**physique** *n* físico *m*

**piano** *n* (**-anos**) piano *m* — **pianist** *n* pianista *mf*

**pick** *v* recoger — **pick** *n* *or* **pickax** pico *m*

**pickle** *n* pepinillo *m* (encurtido)

**pick up** *v* levantar

**picnic** *n* picnic *m*

**picture** *n* cuadro *m*; imagen *f*

**pie** *n* pastel *m* (con fruta o carne), empanada *f* (con carne)

**piece** *n* pieza *f*

**piety** *n* piedad *f*

**pig** *n* cerdo *m*, -da *f*; puerco *m*, -ca *f*

**pigeon** *n* paloma *f*

**pigtail** *n* coleta *f*, trenza *f*

**pile** *n* montón *m*, pila *f* — **pile** *v* amontonar, apilar

**pill** *n* pastilla *f*, píldora *f*

**pillow** *n* almohada *f*

**pilot** *n* piloto *mf*

**pin** *n* alfiler *m* — **pin** *v* prender, sujetar (con alfileres)

**pinch** *v* pellizcar — **pinch** *n* pellizco *m*

**pineapple** *n* piña *f*, ananás *m*

**pink** *n* rosa *m*, rosado *m* — **pink** *adj* rosa, rosado

**pioneer** *n* pionero *m*, -ra *f*

**pipe** *n* tubo *m*, caño *m*; pipa *f* (para fumar) — **pipeline** *n* conducto *m*, oleoducto *m* (para petróleo)

**pistol** *n* pistola *f*

**piston** *n* pistón *m*

**pit** *n* hoyo *m*, fosa *f*

**pizza** *n* pizza *f*

**place** *n* sitio *m*, lugar *m*; asiento *m*; puesto *m*; papel *m*; **take ~** tener lugar; **take the ~ of** sustituir a — **place** *v* poner, colocar; identificar, recordar; **place an order** hacer un pedido — **placement** *n* colocación *f*

**plagiarism** *n* plagio *m*

**plaid** *adj* escocés

**plain** *adj* *n* llanura *f*, planicie *f*

**plan** *n* plan *m*, proyecto *m*; plano *m* — **plan** *v* planear, proyectar; tener planeado; hacer planes

**plane** *n* plano *m*, nivel *m*

**planet** *n* planeta *f*

**plank** *n* tabla *f*

**planning** *n* planificación *f*

**plant** *n* planta *f*

**plantain** *n* plátano *m* (grande)

**plaque** *n* placa *f*

**plaster** *n* yeso *m* — **plaster** *v* enyesar — **plaster cast** *n* escayola *f*

**plastic** *adj* de plástico; plástico, flexible — **plastic** *n* plástico *m*

**plate** *n* plato *m*

**platform** *n* andén *m* (de una estación de ferrocarril)

**platter** *n* fuente *f*

**play** *n* juego *m* — **play** *v* jugar; jugar (deportes, etc.), jugar a (juegos); tocar (música o un instrumento) — **player** *n* jugador *m*, -dora *f* — **playing card** *n* naipe *m*, carta *f* — **playwright** *n* dramaturgo *m*, -ga *f*

**pleasant** *adj* agradable, grato — **please** *v* complacer; satisfacer agradar — **please** *adv* por favor — **pleasure** *n* placer *m*, gusto *m*

**pledge** *n* prenda *f*

**plot** *n* argumento *m* (de una novela, etc.)

**plug** *n* enchufe *m* (eléctrico) — **plug** *v* **plug in** enchufar

**plum** *n* ciruela *f*

**plumber** *n* fontanero *m*, -ra *f*; plomero *m*, -ra *f*

**plunge** *v* sumergir; hundir

**plural** *adj* plural — **plural** *n* plural *m*

**plus** *prep* más

**pocket** *n* bolsillo *m* — **pocketbook** *n* cartera *f*, bolsa *f* — **pocketknife** *n* (**-knives**) navaja *f*

**poem** *n* poema *m* — **poet** *n* poeta *mf*

**point** *n* punto *m*; punta *f*; **be beside the** ~ no venir al caso; **there's no** ~ no sirve de nada — **point** *v* apuntar; *or* **point out** señalar, indicar; **point at** señalar (con el dedo)

**poison** *n* veneno *m* — **poison** *v* envenenar

**poker** *n* póquer *m* (juego de naipes)

**polarize** *v* polarizar

**pole**[1] *n* palo *m*, poste *m*

**pole**[2] *n* polo *m* (en geografía)

**police** *v* mantener el orden en — **police** *ns or pl* **the police** la policía — **policeman** *n* (**-men**) policía *m*

**policy** *n* (**-cies**) política *f*

**polish** *v* pulir; limpiar (zapatos) — **polish** *n* brillo *m*, lustre *m*; betún *m* (para zapatos), cera *f* (para suelos y muebles), esmalte *m* (para las uñas)

**Polish** *adj* polaco — **Polish** *n* polaco *m* (idioma)

**polite** *adj* cortés — **politeness** *n* cortesía *f*

**political** *adj* político — **politician** *n* político *m*, -ca *f* — **politics** *ns & pl* política *f*

**poll** *n* encuesta *f*, sondeo *m*; encuestar, sondear

**pollute** *v* contaminar — **pollution** *n* contaminación *f*

**pool** *n* billar *m*; *or* **swimming** ~ piscina *f*

**poor** *adj* pobre; malo — **poorly** *adv* mal

**popcorn** *n* palomitas *fpl*

**pope** *n* papa *m*

**popular** *adj* popular — **popularity** *n* popularidad *f*

**population** *n* población *f*

**porcelain** *n* porcelana *f*

**port** *n* puerto *m*

**portable** *adj* portátil

**porter** *n* maletero *m*, mozo *m* (de estación)

**portion** *n* porción *f*

**portrait** *n* retrato *m*

**portray** *v* representar, retratar; interpretar (un personaje)

**Portuguese** *adj* portugués — **Portuguese** *n* portugués *m* (idioma)

**pose** *v* plantear (una pregunta, etc.), representar (una amenaza); posar; ~ **as** hacerse pasar por

**position** *n* posición *f*; puesto *m*

**positive** *adj* positivo

**possess** *v* poseer — **possessive** *adj* posesivo

**possible** *adj* posible — **possibility** *n*
(**-ties**) posibilidad *f*

**postal** *adj* postal — **postcard** *n* tarjeta *f*
postal

**poster** *n* cartel *m*

**posterity** *n* posteridad *f*

**posthumous** *adj* póstumo

**postpone** *v* aplazar

**postwar** *adj* de (la) posguerra

**pot** *n* olla *f* (de cocina)

**potato** *n* (**-toes**) patata *f*, papa *f*

**pottery** *n* cerámica *f*

**pound**[1] *n* libra *f* (unidad de dinero o de
peso)

**pound**[2] *v* golpear

**poverty** *n* pobreza *f*

**powder** *v* empolvar — **powder** *n* polvo
*m*

**power** *n* poder *m*; fuerza *f*; potencia *f*
(política); energía *f* — **powerful** *adj*
poderoso — **powerless** *adj* impotente

**practical** *adj* práctico

**practice** *or* **practise** *v* practicar; practicar — **practice** *n* práctica *f*

**prank** *n* travesura *f*

**pray** *v* rezar; ∼ **for** rogar — **prayer** *n*
oración *f*

**preach** *v* predicar

**precaution** *n* precaución *f*

**precedent** *n* precedente *m*

**precious** *adj* precioso

**precipitation** *n* precipitación *f*; preci-
pitaciones *fpl* (en meteorología)

**precise** *adj* preciso — **precision** *n* precisión *f*

**precocious** *adj* precoz

**predict** *v* pronosticar, predecir — **prediction** *n* pronóstico *m*, predicción *f*

**predominant** *adj* predominante

**preface** *n* prefacio *m*, prólogo *m*

**prefer** *v* preferir

**prefix** *n* prefijo *m*

**pregnancy** *n* (**-cies**) embarazo *m* —
**pregnant** *adj* embarazada

**prehistoric** *adj* prehistórico

**prejudice** *n* prejuicio *m*; perjuicio *m*

**preliminary** *adj* preliminar

**premarital** *adj* prematrimonial

**premature** *adj* prematuro

**premise** *n* premisa *f* (de un argumento);
∼**s** *npl* recinto *m*, local *m*

**premium** *n or* **insurance** ∼ prima *f* (de
seguro)

**prepare** *v* preparar; prepararse —
**preparation** *n* preparación *f*

**preposition** *n* preposición *f*

**prescription** *n* receta *f*

**presence** *n* presencia *f*

**present**[1] *adj* actual; **be** ∼ **at** estar presente en — **present** *n* presente *m*; **at
present** actualmente

**present**[2] *n* regalo *m* — **presentation** *n*
presentación *f*

**preserve** *v* conservar; mantener

**president** *n* presidente *m*, -ta *f* — **presidency** *n* (**-cies**) presidencia *f*

**press** *v* apretar; presionar — **pressure** *n*
presión *f* — **pressure** *v* presionar,
apremiar

**prestige** *n* prestigio *m*

**pretend** *v* fingir

**pretext** *n* pretexto *m*

**pretty** *adj* lindo, bonito

**prevent** *v* impedir — **prevention** *n* prevención *f*

**previously** *adv* anteriormente

**price** *n* precio *m*

**prickly** *adj* espinoso

**pride** *n* orgullo *m*

**priest** *n* sacerdote *m*

**primary** *adj* primario; principal

**primitive** *adj* primitivo

**principal** *adj* principal

**principle** *n* principio *m*

**print** *v* imprimir (libros, etc.); escribir
con letra de molde — **printer** *n* impresora *f* (máquina) — **printing** *n* impresión *f*; imprenta *f* (profesión); letras
*fpl* de molde

**priority** *n* (**-ties**) prioridad *f*

**prison** *n* prisión *f*, cárcel *f* — **prisoner** *n*
preso *m*, -sa *f*

**privacy** *n* intimidad *f* — **private** *adj* privado

**privilege** *n* privilegio *m*

**prize** *n* premio *m*

**pro** *n* **the** ∼**s and cons** los pros y los contras

**probability** *n* (**-ties**) probabilidad *f*

**problem** *n* problema *m*

**procedure** *n* procedimiento *m*

**proceed** *v* proceder — **proceedings** *npl* proceso *m* (en derecho)

**process** *n* proceso *m*; **in the** ∼ **of** en vías de — **process** *v* procesar

**proclaim** *v* proclamar

**produce** *v* producir; causar; presentar, mostrar; poner en escena (una obra de teatro) — **produce** *n* productos *mpl* agrícolas — **product** *n* producto *m*

**profession** *n* profesión *f* — **professional** *adj* profesional — **professional** *n* profesional *mf* — **professor** *n* profesor *m*, -sora *f*

**profile** *n* perfil *m*

**profit** *n* beneficio *m*, ganancia *f* — **profit** *v* sacar provecho (de), beneficiarse (de) — **profitable** *adj* provechoso

**profound** *adj* profundo

**prognosis** *n* (**-noses**) pronóstico *m*

**program** *n* programa *m* — **program** *v* programar

**progress** *n* progreso *m*; avance *m* — **progress** *v* progresar, avanzar

**prohibit** *v* prohibir — **prohibition** *n* prohibición *f*

**project** *n* proyecto *m* — **projection** *n* proyección *f* — **projector** *n* proyector *m*

**prologue** *n* prólogo *m*

**prolong** *v* prolongar

**promise** *n* promesa *f* — **promise** *v* prometer

**promote** *v* ascender (a un alumno o un empleado); promover, fomentar; promocionar — **promoter** *n* promotor *m*, -tora *f*; empresario *m*, -ria *f* (en deportes) — **promotion** *n* ascenso *m* (de un alumno o un empleado); publicidad *f*, propaganda *f*

**prompt** *v* apuntar (a un actor, etc.); puntual

**prong** *n* punta *f*, diente *m*

**pronoun** *n* pronombre *m*

**pronounce** *v* pronunciar — **pronouncement** *n* declaración *f* — **pronunciation** *n* pronunciación *f*

**proof** *n* prueba *f* — **proof** *adj* **proof against** a prueba de

**propaganda** *n* propaganda *f*

**propeller** *n* hélice *f*

**property** *n* (**-ties**) propiedad *f*; inmueble *m*

**proportion** *n* proporción *f*; parte *f* — **proportional** *adj* proporcional

**proposal** *n* propuesta *f*

**propose** *v* proponer; ∼ **to do** pensar hacer; proponer matrimonio — **proposition** *n* proposición *f*

**proprietor** *n* propietario *m*, -ria *f*

**prose** *n* prosa *f*

**prosecute** *v* procesar

**prospect** *n* perspectiva *f*

**prosper** *v* prosperar — **prosperity** *n* prosperidad *f* — **prosperous** *adj* próspero

**prostitute** *n* prostituta *f*

**protagonist** *n* protagonista *mf*

**protect** *v* proteger — **protection** *n* protección *f* — **protective** *adj* protector — **protector** *n* protector *m*, -tora *f*

**protest** *n* protesta *f* — **protest** *v* protestar — **protester** *or* **protestor** *n* manifestante *mf*

**protrude** *v* sobresalir

**proud** *adj* orgulloso

**prove** *v* probar

**proverb** *n* proverbio *m*, refrán *m*

**provide** *v* proveer

**provision** *n* provisión *f*, suministro *m*; ∼**s** *npl* víveres *mpl* — **provisional** *adj* provisional

**provoke** *v* provocar — **provocation** *n* provocación *f*

**proximity** *n* proximidad *f*

**prudent** *adj* prudente

**prune** *n* ciruela *f* pasa

**pseudonym** *n* seudónimo *m*

**psychiatrist** *n* psiquiatra *mf*

**psychology** *n* psicología *f* — **psychological** *adj* psicológico — **psychologist** *n* psicólogo *m*, -ga *f*

**puberty** *n* pubertad *f*

**public** *adj* público — **public** *n* público *m* — **publication** *n* publicación *f* — **publicity** *n* publicidad *f*

**publish** *v* publicar — **publisher** *n* editor *m*, -tora *f* (persona)

**pudding** *n* budín *m*, pudín *m*

**puddle** *n* charco *m*

**Puerto Rican** *adj* puertorriqueño

**pull** *n* tirón *m* — **pull** *v* tirar (de)

**pulse** *n* pulso *m*

**pumpkin** *n* calabaza *f*, zapallo *m*

**punch** *v or* **paper** ~ perforadora *f*

**punctual** *adj* puntual — **punctuality** *n* puntualidad *f*

**punctuation** *n* puntuación *f*

**punish** *v* castigar — **punishment** *n* castigo *m* — **punitive** *adj* punitivo

**pupil**[1] *n* alumno *m*, -na *f* (de colegio)

**pupil**[2] *n* pupila *f* (del ojo)

**puppet** *n* títere *m*

**puppy** *n* (**-pies**) cachorro *m*, -rra *f*

**purchase** *v* comprar — **purchase** *n* compra *f*

**pure** *adj* puro

**puree** *n* puré *m*

**purify** *v* (**-fied**) purificar — **purification** *n* purificación *f*

**purity** *n* pureza *f*

**purple** *n* morado *m*

**purpose** *n* propósito *m*; determinación *f*; **on** ~ a propósito

**purse** *n or* **change** ~ monedero *m*

**pursue** *v* perseguir — **pursuit** *n* persecución *f*

**push** *v* empujar; apretar; presionar; empujar — **push** *n* empujón *m*

**put** *v* (**put**) poner; meter; decir; ~ **one's mind to** proponerse hacer

**puzzle** *v n* rompecabezas *m*

# Q

**q** *n* (**q's** *or* **qs**) q *f*, decimoséptima letra del alfabeto inglés

**quack** *n* charlatán *m*, -tana *f*

**qualification** *n* requisito *m*; ~**s** *npl* capacidad *f*; **without** ~ sin reservas — **qualify** *v* (**-fied**) clasificarse (en deportes) — **qualified** *adj* capacitado

**quality** *n* (**-ties**) calidad *f*; cualidad *f*

**quantity** *n* (**-ties**) cantidad *f*

**quarrel** *n* pelea *f*, riña *f* — **quarrel** *v* pelearse, reñir

**quarter** *n* cuarto *m* (en matemáticas); moneda *f* de 25 centavos; barrio *m*; ~ **after three** las tres y cuarto; ~**s** *npl* alojamiento *m* — **quarter** *v* dividir en cuatro partes — **quarterly** *adv* cada tres meses — **quarterly** *adj* trimestral

— **quarterly** *n* (**-lies**) publicación *f* trimestral

**quartet** *n* cuarteto *m*

**queen** *n* reina *f*

**query** *n* (**-ries**) pregunta *f* — **query** *v* (**-ried**) preguntar; cuestionar

**quest** *n* búsqueda *f*

**question** *n* pregunta *f*; cuestión *f*; **be out of the** ~ ser indiscutible; **call into** ~ poner en duda; **without** ~ sin duda — **question** *v* preguntar; cuestionar; interrogar — **question mark** *n* signo *m* de interrogación — **questionnaire** *n* cuestionario *m*

**quick** *adj* rápido; agudo — **quick** *n* **to the quick** en lo vivo — **quickly** *adv* rápidamente

**quiet** *n* silencio *m*; tranquilidad *f* —
  **quiet** *adj* silencioso; tranquilo; callado;
  discreto (dícese de colores, etc.) —
  **quiet** *v* hacer callar; calmar; *or* **quiet**
  **down** calmarse

**quit** *v* (**quit**) parar; dimitir, renunciar; dejar,
  abandonar; ~ **doing** dejar de hacer
**quota** *n* cuota *f*, cupo *m*
**quotation** *n* cita *f*; presupuesto *m* —
  **quote** *v* citar; cotizar (en finanzas)

# R

**r** *n* (**r's** *or* **rs**) r *f*, decimoctava letra del alfabeto inglés
**rabbit** *n* conejo *m*, -ja *f*
**race¹** *n* raza *f*; **human** ~ género *m* humano
**race²** *n* carrera *f* (competitiva) — **race** *v*
  correr (en una carrera); ir corriendo —
  **racehorse** *n* caballo *m* de carreras
**racial** *adj* racial — **racism** *n* racismo *m*
  — **racist** *n* racista *mf*
**rack** *n* **luggage** ~ portaequipajes *m*
  ~**ed with** atormentado por
**racket** *n* raqueta *f* (en deportes)
**radar** *n* radar *m*
**radiance** *n* resplandor *m* — **radiate** *v*
  irradiar
**radio** *n* (**-dios**) radio *mf* (aparato), radio *f*
  (medio) — **radio** *v* transmitir por radio
**raft** *n* balsa *f*
**rag** *n* trapo *m* — **ragged** *adj* irregular;
  andrajoso, harapiento
**rage** *n* cólera *f*, rabia *f* — **rage** *v* estar furioso
**raid** *n* invasión *f* (militar); asalto *m* (por
  delincuentes), redada *f* (por la policía)
  — **raid** *v* invadir; asaltar
**rail** *n* barra *f*; pasamanos *m*; riel *m*; **by** ~
  por ferrocarril — **railing** *n* baranda *f*
  (de un balcón), pasamanos *m* (de una
  escalera) — **railroad** *n* ferrocarril *m*
**rain** *n* lluvia *f* — **rain** *v* llover — **rain-**
  **bow** *n* arco *m* iris — **raincoat** *n* impermeable *m* — **rainfall** *n* precipitación *f*
  — **rainy** *adj* lluvioso

**raise** *v* levantar; criar; cultivar; aumentar
  — **raise** *n* aumento *m*
**raisin** *n* pasa *f*
**rally** *v* (**-lied**) unirse, reunirse — **rally** *n*
  (**-lies**) reunión *f*, mitin *m*
**RAM** *n* RAM *f*
**ramble** *v* pasear; *or* ~ **on** divagar —
  **ramble** *n* paseo *m*, excursión *f*
**ramp** *n* rampa *f*
**ranch** *n* hacienda *f* — **rancher** *n* hacen-
  dado *m*, -da *f*
**random** *adj* aleatorio; **at** ~ al azar
**range** *n* pradera *f*; cocina *f*; amplitud *f*; *or*
  **mountain** ~ cordillera *f* — **range** *v* extenderse — **ranger** *n* *or* **forest ranger**
  guardabosque *mf*
**rank** *n* fila *f*; rango *m* (militar); ~**s** *npl*
  soldados *mpl* rasos — **rank** *v* clasi-
  ficar(se)
**rap** *n* *or* ~ **music** rap *m*
**rapid** *adj* rápido
**rapport** *n* **have a good** ~ entenderse
  bien
**rare** *adj* excepcional; raro; poco cocido
  (de la carne) — **rarely** *adv* raramente
  — **rarity** *n* (**-ties**) rareza *f*
**rash¹** *adj* imprudente, precipitado
**rash²** *n* sarpullido *m*, erupción *f*
**raspberry** *n* (**-ries**) frambuesa *f*
**rat** *n* rata *f*
**rate** *n* velocidad *f*, ritmo *m*; tipo *m*, tasa
  *m* (de interés, etc.); tarifa *f*; **at any** ~
  de todos modos — **rate** *v* considerar;
  merecer

**rather** *adv* bastante **I'd ~ ...** prefiero **...; or ~** o mejor dicho

**rating** *n* clasificación *f*; **~s** *npl* índice *m* de audiencia

**rational** *adj* racional — **rationalize** *v* racionalizar

**raw** *adj* crudo; inexperto; **~ materials** materias *fpl* primas

**ray** *n* rayo *m*

**razor** *n* maquinilla *f* de afeitar — **razor blade** *n* hoja *f* de afeitar

**reach** *v* alcanzar; extenderse; *or* **~ out** extender; llegar a (un acuerdo, un límite, etc.); contactar — **reach** *n* alcance *m*; **within reach** al alcance

**reaction** *n* reacción *f* — **reaction** *n* (**-aries**) reaccionario *m*, -ria *f* — **reactor** *n* reactor *m*

**read** *v* (**read**) leer — **readable** *adj* legible — **reader** *n* lector *m*, -tora *f* — **reading** *n* lectura *f*

**readily** *adv* de buena gana; fácilmente

**ready** *adj* listo, preparado; dispuesto; **get ~** prepararse — **ready** *v* (**readied**) preparar

**real** *adj* verdadero, real; auténtico — **real** *adv* muy — **realism** *n* realismo *m* — **realist** *n* realista *mf* — **reality** *n* (**-ties**) realidad *f*

**realize** *v* darse cuenta de; realizar

**really** *adv* verdaderamente

**rear** *n* parte *f* de atrás; trasero *m*

**rearrange** *v* reorganizar, cambiar

**reason** *n* razón *f*; razonar — **reasonable** *adj* razonable — **reasoning** *n* razonamiento *m*

**rebel** *n* rebelde *mf* — **rebellion** *n* rebelión *f*

**rebuild** *v* (**-built**) reconstruir

**recall** *v* llamar (al servicio, etc.); recordar

**receipt** *n* recibo *m*; **~s** *npl* ingresos *mpl*

**receive** *v* recibir — **receiver** *n* receptor *m* (de radio, etc.); *or* **telephone receiver** auricular *m*

**recent** *adj* reciente — **recently** *adv* recientemente

**receptacle** *n* receptáculo *m*, recipiente *m*

**reception** *n* recepción *f* — **receptionist** *n* recepcionista *mf*

**recharge** *v* recargar — **rechargeable** *adj* recargable

**recipe** *n* receta *f*

**recipient** *n* recipiente *mf*

**recite** *v* recitar (un poema, etc.) — **recital** *n* recital *m*

**reckon** *v* calcular; considerar

**reclaim** *v* reclamar; recuperar

**recline** *v* reclinarse

**recognition** *n* reconocimiento *m* — **recognizable** *adj* reconocible — **recognize** *v* reconocer

**recommend** *v* recomendar — **recommendation** *n* recomendación *f*

**reconsider** *v* reconsiderar

**record** *v* anotar, apuntar; registrar; grabar (música, etc.) — **record** *n* documento *m*; registro *m*; disco *m* (de música, etc.); **world record** récord *m* mundial; *or* **tape record** grabadora *f* — **recording** *n* disco *m* — **record player** *n* tocadiscos *m*

**recover** *v* recobrar; recuperarse — **recovery** *n* recuperación *f*

**rectangle** *n* rectángulo *m* — **rectangular** *adj* rectangular

**rector** *n* párroco *m* (clérigo); rector *m*, -tora *f* (de una universidad) — **rectory** *n* (**-ries**) rectoría *f*

**recuperate** *v* recuperar(se) — **recuperation** *n* recuperación *f*

**recur** *v* repetirse — **recurrence** *n* repetición *f* — **recurrent** *adj* que se repite

**recycle** *v* reciclar

**red** *adj* rojo — **red** *n* rojo *m* — **redhead** *n* pelirrojo *m*, -ja *f*

**redo** *v* (**-did; -done**) hacer de nuevo

**reduce** *v* reducir; adelgazar — **reduction** *n* reducción *f*

**refer** *v* **~ to** referirse a — **reference** *n* referencia *f*; consulta *f*

**referee** *n* árbitro *m*, -tra *f* — **referee** *v* arbitrar

**refill** *v* rellenar — **refill** *n* recambio *m*

**reflect** *v* reflejar(se) — **reflection** *n* reflexión *f*; reflejo *m* — **reflector** *n* reflector *m*

**reflex** *n* reflejo *m* — **reflexive** *adj* reflexivo

**reform** *v* reformar — **reform** *n* reforma *f*

**refrain** *v* ~ **from** abstenerse de

**refresh** *v* refrescar — **refreshments** *npl* refrigerio *m*

**refrigerate** *v* refrigerar — **refrigeration** *n* refrigeración *f* — **refrigerator** *n* nevera *f*, refrigerador *m*, frigorífico *m*

**refuel** *v* llenar de carburante; repostar

**refund** *v* reembolsar — **refund** *n* reembolso *m*

**refuse** *v* rehusar, rechazar; negarse; ~ **to do** negarse a hacer — **refusal** *n* negativa *f*

**regain** *v* recuperar, recobrar

**regard** *n* consideración *f*; estima *f*; **in this** ~ en este sentido; ~**s** *npl* saludos *mpl*; **regarding** *prep* respecto a — **regardless** *adv* a pesar de todo — **regardless of** *prep* sin tener en cuenta; a pesar de

**region** *n* región *f* — **regional** *adj* regional

**register** *n* registro *m* — **register** *v* registrar (a personas), matricular (vehículos); certificar (correo); inscribirse, matricularse — **registration** *n* inscripción *f*, matriculación *f* — **registry** *n* (**-tries**) registro *m*

**regret** *v* lamentar — **regret** *n* arrepentimiento *m*; pesar *m* — **regrettable** *adj* lamentable

**regular** *adj* regular; habitual — **regular** *n* cliente *mf* habitual — **regularity** *n* regularidad *f*

**rehabilitate** *v* rehabilitar — **rehabilitation** *n* rehabilitación *f*

**rehearse** *v* ensayar — **rehearsal** *n* ensayo *m*

**reign** *n* reinado *m* — **reign** *v* reinar

**reinforce** *v* reforzar — **reinforcement** *n* refuerzo *m*

**reject** *v* rechazar — **rejection** *n* rechazo *m*

**relate** *v* relatar; relacionar; ~ **to** estar relacionado con — **relation** *n* relación *f*; pariente *mf*; **in relation to** en relación con — **relationship** *n* relación *f*; parentesco *m* — **relative** *n* pariente *mf* — **relative** *adj* relativo — **relatively** *adv* relativamente

**relax** *v* relajar(se) — **relaxation** *n* relajación *f*

**release** *v* liberar, poner en libertad; soltar (un freno, etc.); despedir

**relevant** *adj* pertinente — **relevance** *n* pertinencia *f*

**reliable** *adj* fiable (de personas), fidedigno (de información, etc.) — **reliability** *n* (**-ties**) fiabilidad *f* (de una cosa), responsabilidad *f* (de una persona) — **rely** *v* (**-lied**) **rely on** depender de; confiar (en)

**relief** *n* alivio *m*; ayuda *f*; relevo *m* — **relieve** *v* aliviar

**religion** *n* religión *f* — **religious** *adj* religioso

**remain** *v* quedar(se); seguir, continuar — **remainder** *n* resto *m*

**remark** *n* comentario *m*, observación *f* — **remark** *v* *or* **remark on** observar — **remarkable** *adj* extraordinario, notable

**remedy** *n* (**-dies**) remedio *m* — **remedy** *v* (**-died**) remediar

**remember** *v* recordar; acordarse (de) — **remembrance** *n* recuerdo *m*

**remind** *v* recordar — **reminder** *n* recordatorio *m*

**remote** *adj* remoto — **remote control** *n* control *m* remoto

**remove** *v* quitar(se); sacar — **removable** *adj* separable, de quita y pon

**rendition** *n* interpretación *f*

**renew** *v* renovar

**renovate** v renovar — **renovation** n renovación f

**renown** n renombre m — **renowned** adj célebre, renombrado

**rent** n alquiler m, arrendamiento m, renta f; **for ~** se alquila — **rent** v alquilar — **rental** n alquiler m — **rental** adj de alquiler — **renter** n arrendatario m, -ria f

**repair** v reparar, arreglar — **repair** n reparación f, arreglo m

**repeat** v repetir — **repeat** n repetición f

**repetition** n repetición f

**replace** v reponer; reemplazar, sustituir; cambiar — **replacement** n sustitución f; sustituto m, -ta f (persona); or **replacement part** repuesto m

**reply** v (**-plied**) contestar, responder — **reply** n (**-plies**) respuesta f

**report** n informe m; rumor m; or **news ~** reportaje m; **weather ~** boletín m meteorológico — **report** v anunciar; informar; **report for duty** presentarse — **reporter** n periodista mf; reportero m, -ra f

**represent** v representar; presentar — **representation** n representación f

**repress** v reprimir — **repression** n represión f

**reproduce** v reproducir(se) — **reproduction** n reproducción f

**republic** n república f

**reputation** n reputación f

**request** n petición f — **request** v pedir

**require** v requerir; necesitar — **requirement** n necesidad f; requisito m

**rescue** v rescatar, salvar — **rescue** n rescate m

**research** n investigación f — **research** v investigar — **researcher** n investigador m, -dora f

**resemble** v parecerse a — **resemblance** n parecido m

**reserve** v reservar — **reserve** n reserva f — **reserved** adj reservado

**reset** v (**-set**) volver a poner (un reloj etc.)

**residence** n residencia f — **reside** v residir

**resign** v dimitir; renunciar; **~ oneself to** resignarse a

**resistant** adj resistente

**resolve** v resolver

**resort** n recurso m; or **tourist ~** centro m turístico

**resource** n recurso m

**respect** n respeto m; **in some ~s** en algún sentido — **respect** v respetar

**respiration** n respiración f — **respiratory** adj respiratorio

**response** n respuesta f — **respond** v responder — **responsibility** n (**-ties**) responsabilidad f — **responsible** adj responsable

**rest** n descanso m — **rest** v descansar; **rest on** depender de

**restaurant** n restaurante m

**restful** adj tranquilo, apacible

**restless** adj inquieto, agitado

**restore** v devolver; restablecer

**restrain** v contener; **~ oneself** contenerse

**restriction** n restricción f — **restrict** v restringir — **restricted** adj restringido

**result** v resultar — **result** n resultado m; **as a result of** como consecuencia de

**resume** v reanudar; continuar

**résumé** or **resume** or **resumé** n currículum m (vitae)

**retire** v jubilarse, retirarse (de un trabajo) — **retirement** n jubilación f

**retrieve** v cobrar, recuperar

**return** v volver, regresar; devolver — **return** n regreso m, vuelta f; **in return for** a cambio de

**reveal** v revelar

**reverse** adj inverso, contrario — **reverse** n dorso m, revés m; or **reverse gear** marcha f atrás

**review** n revisión f; resumen m; repaso m

(para un examen) — **review** *v* examinar; repasar (una lección); reseñar

**revise** *v* revisar, corregir (una publicación) — **revision** *n* corrección *f*, modificación *f*

**revival** *n* reanimación *f*, reactivación *f*

**revolution** *n* revolución *f* — **revolutionary** *adj* revolucionario

**reward** *v* recompensar — **reward** *n* recompensa *f*

**rewrite** *v* (-wrote; -written) volver a escribir

**rhyme** *n* rima *f* — **rhyme** *v* rimar

**rhythm** *n* ritmo *m*

**rib** *n* costilla *f*

**ribbon** *n* cinta *f*

**rice** *n* arroz *m*

**rich** *adj* rico — **richness** *n* riqueza *f*

**rid** *v* (**rid**) librar; **get** ∼ **of** deshacerse de

**riddle** *n* adivinanza *f*

**ride** *v* (**rode; ridden**) montar (a caballo, en bicicleta), ir (en auto, etc.); recorrer — **ride** *n* paseo *m*, vuelta *f*; aparato *m* (en un parque de diversiones) — **rider** *n* jinete *mf* (a caballo); ciclista *mf*, motociclista *mf*

**ridiculous** *adj* ridículo — **ridicule** *n* burlas *fpl* — **ridicule** *v* ridiculizar

**rifle** *n* rifle *m*, fusil *m*

**right** *adj* bueno, justo; correcto; apropiado, adecuado; recto; **be** ∼ tener razón; bien *m*; **on the** ∼ a la derecha — **right** *adv* bien; inmediatamente — **right–hand** *adj* derecho — **right–handed** *adj* diestro — **rightly** *adv* justamente; correctamente

**rigid** *adj* rígido

**ring**[1] *v* (**rang; rung**) sonar (de un timbre, etc.); tocar (un timbre, etc.) — **ring** *n* llamada *f* (por teléfono)

**ring**[2] *n* anillo *m*, sortija *f*; aro *m*; círculo *m* — **ringlet** *n* rizo *m*, bucle *m*

**rink** *n* pista *f* (de patinaje)

**rinse** *n* enjuague *m*

**ripe** *adj* maduro; ∼ **for** listo por — **ripen** *v* madurar

**rise** *v* (**rose; risen**) levantarse; salir (del sol, etc.); subir — **rise** *n* subida *f*; aumento *m*

**risk** *n* riesgo *m* — **risk** *v* arriesgar — **risky** *adj* arriesgado, riesgoso

**rival** *n* rival *mf* — **rival** *adj* rival

**river** *n* río *m*

**road** *n* carretera *f*; calle *f*; camino *m* — **roadway** *n* carretera *f*

**roast** *v* asar(se) (carne, etc.), tostar (café, etc.) — **roast** *n* asado *m* — **roast beef** *n* rosbif *m*

**robot** *n* robot *m*

**robust** *adj* robusto

**rock**[1] *n or* ∼ **music** música *f* rock

**rock**[2] *n* roca *f* (sustancia); piedra *f* — **rocky** *adj* rocoso

**rocking chair** *n* mecedora *f*

**role** *n* papel *m*

**roll** *n* rollo *m* (de película, etc.); rodar; ∼ **around** revolcarse; ∼ **over** darse la vuelta; ∼ **up** enrollar (papel, etc.), arremangar (una manga) — **roller** *n* rodillo *m*; rulo *m* — **roller coaster** *n* montaña *f* rusa — **roller–skate** *v* patinar (sobre ruedas) — **roller skate** *n* patín *m* (de ruedas)

**Roman Catholic** *adj* católico

**romance** *n* romanticismo; novela *f* romántica

**Romanian** *adj* rumano — **Romanian** *n* rumano *m* (idioma)

**romantic** *adj* romántico

**roof** *n* tejado *m*, techo *m*; ∼ **of the mouth** paladar *m* — **rooftop** *n* tejado *m*, techo *m*

**room** *n* cuarto *m*, habitación *f*; dormitorio *m* — **roommate** *n* compañero *m*, -ra *f* de cuarto

**rooster** *n* gallo *m*

**root** *n* raíz *f*

**rope** *n* cuerda *f* — **rope** *v* atar (con cuerda)

**rose** *n* rosa *f* (flor), rosa *m* (color) — **rose** *adj* rosa — **rosebush** *n* rosal *m*

**rotate** *v* girar — **rotation** *n* rotación *f*

**rough** *adj* áspero; accidentado; agitado; duro; brusco; aproximado; ∼ **draft** borrador *m* — **roughly** *adv* bruscamente; aproximadamente — **roughness** *n* aspereza *f*

**round** *adj* redondo — **round** *n* asalto *m* (en boxeo), vuelta *f* (en juegos) — **round** *v* doblar; *or* **round off** redondear — **round–trip** *n* viaje *m* de ida y vuelta

**route** *n* ruta *f*; *or* **delivery** ∼ recorrido *m*

**routine** *n* rutina *f* — **routine** *adj* rutinario

**row**[1] *v* ∼ **a boat** remar — **rowboat** *n* bote *m* de remos

**row**[2] *n* fila *f* (de gente o asientos), hilera *f* (de casas, etc.)

**rowdy** *adj* escandaloso, alborotador

**rub** *v* frotar; ∼ **in** aplicar frotando

**rubber** *n* goma *f*, caucho *m*; ∼**s** *npl* chanclos *mpl* — **rubber band** *n* goma *f* (elástica) — **rubber stamp** *n* sello *m* (de goma)

**rubbish** *n* basura *f*; tonterías *fpl*

**rude** *adj* grosero, mal educado; brusco — **rudely** *adv* groseramente — **rudeness** *n* grosería *f*, mala educación *f*

**rug** *n* alfombra *f*, tapete *m*

**rugged** *adj* fuerte

**ruin** *n* ruina *f* — **ruin** *v* arruinar

**rule** *n* regla *f*; dominio *m*; **as a** ∼ por lo general — **rule** *v* gobernar — **ruler** *n* regla *f* (para medir)

**rumor** *n* rumor *m*

**run** *v* (**ran**; **run**) correr; funcionar; extenderse; ∼ **away** huir; ∼ **into** tropezar con; ∼ **into** chocar contra ∼ **out of** quedarse sin ∼ **over** atropellar — **run** *n*; carrera *f*

**runner** *n* corredor *m*, -dora *f*

**runway** *n* pista *f* de aterrizaje

**rupture** *n* ruptura *f* — **rupture** *v* romper; reventar

**rural** *adj* rural

**rush** *v* apresurar, apurar; asaltar — **rush** *n* prisa *f*, apuro *m* — **rush** *adj* urgente

**Russian** *adj* ruso — **Russian** *n* ruso *m* (idioma)

# S

**s** *n* (**s's** *or* **ss**) s *f*, decimonovena letra del alfabeto inglés

**sacred** *adj* sagrado

**sacrifice** *n* sacrificio *m* — **sacrifice** *v* sacrificar

**sad** *adj* triste — **sadden** *v* entristecer

**sadness** *n* tristeza *f*

**safe** *adj* seguro; ileso — **safe** *n* caja *f* fuerte — **safeguard** *n* salvaguarda *f* — **safely** *adv* sin peligro — **safety** *n* seguridad *f*

**sail** *n* vela *f* (de un barco); **go for a** ∼ salir a navegar; **set** ∼ zarpar — **sail** *v* navegar — **sailboat** *n* velero *m* — **sailor** *n* marinero *m*

**saint** *n* santo *m*, -ta *f*

**sake** *n* **for goodness'** ∼**!** ¡por Dios!

**salad** *n* ensalada *f*

**salary** *n* (**-ries**) sueldo *m*

**sale** *n* venta *f*; **for** ∼ se vende; **on** ∼ de rebaja — **salesman** *n* (**-men**) vendedor *m*, dependiente *m* — **saleswoman** *n* (**-women**) vendedora *f*, dependienta *f*

**saliva** *n* saliva *f*

**salt** *n* sal *f* — **salt** *v* salar — **salty** *adj* salado

**salvage** *n* salvamento *m* — **salvage** *v* salvar

**salvation** *n* salvación *f*

**same** *adj* mismo; **be the** ∼ **(as)** ser igual (que); **the** ∼ **thing (as)** la misma cosa (que) — **same** *pron* **the same** lo mismo

**sample** *n* muestra *f*

**sand** *n* arena *f* — **sand** *v* lijar (madera) — **sandy** *adj* arenoso

**sandal** *n* sandalia *f*

**sandwich** *n* sandwich *m,* bocadillo *m*

**sane** *adj* cuerdo

**sanitary** *adj* sanitario; higiénico — **sanitary napkin** *n* compresa *f* (higiénica) — **sanitation** *n* sanidad *f*

**Santa Claus** *n* Papá *m* Noel

**satellite** *n* satélite *m*

**satire** *n* sátira *f* — **satiric** *or* **satirical** *adj* satírico

**satisfaction** *n* satisfacción *f* — **satisfactory** *adj* satisfactorio — **satisfy** *v* (**-fied**) satisfacer — **satisfying** *adj* satisfactorio

**Saturday** *n* sábado *m*

**Saturn** *n* Saturno *m*

**sauce** *n* salsa *f* — **saucepan** *n* cacerola *f* — **saucer** *n* platillo *m*

**sauna** *n* sauna *mf*

**sausage** *n* salchicha *f*

**savage** *adj* salvaje, feroz — **savage** *n* salvaje *mf*

**save** *v* salvar; guardar; ahorrar (dinero, tiempo, etc.) — **save** *prep* salvo

**saw** *n* sierra *f*

**say** *v* (**said**) decir; marcar (de relojes, etc.); **that is to ~** es decir — **saying** *n* refrán *m*

**scale** *v* escalar

**scan** *v* escanear (en informática)

**scandal** *n* escándalo *m;* habladurías *fpl*

**Scandinavian** *adj* escandinavo

**scar** *n* cicatriz *f*

**scarce** *adj* escaso — **scarcely** *adv* apenas — **scarcity** *n* escasez *f*

**scare** *v* asustar; **be ~d of** tener miedo a — **scare** *n* susto *m;* pánico *m* — **scary** *adj* que da miedo

**scarf** *n* (**scarves**) *or* **scarfs** bufanda *f;* pañuelo *m*

**scene** *n* escena *f* — **scenery** *n* decorado *m;* paisaje *m* — **scenic** *adj* pintoresco

**schedule** *n* programa *m;* horario *m* — **schedule** *v* planear, programar

**scheme** *n* plan *m;* esquema *f*

**scholar** *n* erudito *m,* -ta *f* — **scholarship** *n* beca *f*

**school** *n* escuela *f*

**science** *n* ciencia *f* — **scientific** *adj* científico — **scientist** *n* científico *m,* -ca *f*

**scissors** *npl* tijeras *fpl*

**scoop** *n* pala *f*

**scoot** *v* ir rápidamente — **scooter** *n* patinete *m; or* **motor scooter** escúter *m*

**scope** *n* alcance *m;* posibilidades *fpl*

**score** *n* (**scores**) puntuación *f;* resultado *m* — **score** *v* marcar, anotarse (un tanto); sacar (una nota); marcar (en deportes)

**Scot** *n* escocés *m,* -cesa *f* — **Scottish** *adj* escocés

**scout** *n* explorador *m,* -dora *f*

**scramble** *v* trepar; **~ for** pelearse por; mezclar — **scrambled eggs** *npl* huevos *mpl* revueltos

**scrap** *n* pedazo *m*

**scrape** *v* rascar; rasparse (la rodilla, etc.); *or* **~ off** raspar; **~ together** reunir — **scrape** *n* rasguño *m*

**scratch** *v* arañar; rayar; rascarse (la cabeza, etc.); **~ out** tachar — **scratch** *n* arañazo *m*

**scream** *v* gritar, chillar — **scream** *n* grito *m,* chillido *m*

**screen** *n* pantalla *f*

**screw** *n* tornillo *m* — **screw** *v* atornillar

**script** *n* escritura *f;* guión *m* (de cine, etc.)

**scuff** *v* raspar, rayar

**sculpture** *n* escultura *f*

**sea** *n* mar *mf* — **seafood** *n* mariscos *mpl* — **seagull** *n* gaviota *f* — **seashell** *n* concha *f* (marina) — **seashore** *n* orilla *f* del mar — **seasick** *adj* mareado; **be**

**seasick** marearse — **seasickness** *n* mareo *m*

**seal**[1] *n* foca *f* (animal)

**seal**[2] *n* sello *m*

**search** *v* registrar; ∼ **for** buscar — **search** *n* búsqueda *f*

**season** *n* estación *f* (del año) — **seasoning** *n* condimento *m*

**seat** *n* asiento *m* — **seat** *v* **be seated** sentarse — **seat belt** *n* cinturón *m* de seguridad

**second** *adj* segundo — **second** *or* **secondly** *adv* en segundo lugar — **second** *n* segundo *m*, -da *f*; segundo *m* — **secondary** *adj* secundario — **secondhand** *adj* de segunda mano

**secret** *adj* secreto — **secret** *n* secreto *m*

**secretary** *n* (**-taries**) secretario *m*, -ria *f*; ministro *m*, -tra *f* (del gobierno)

**secretly** *adv* en secreto

**sect** *n* secta *f*

**section** *n* sección *f*, parte *f*

**sector** *n* sector *m*

**security** *n* (**-ties**) seguridad *f*; garantía *f* — **secure** *adj* seguro — **secure** *v* asegurar

**see** *v* (**saw; seen**) ver; entender; ∼ **you later!** ¡hasta luego!

**seed** *n* semilla *f*; germen *m*

**seek** *v* (**sought**) *or* ∼ **out** buscar; pedir

**seem** *v* parecer

**segregate** *v* segregar — **segregation** *n* segregación *f*

**seldom** *adv* pocas veces, raramente

**select** *adj* selecto — **select** *v* seleccionar — **selection** *n* selección *f* — **selective** *adj* selectivo

**self** *n* (**selves**) ser *m* — **selfish** *adj* egoísta — **selfishness** *n* egoísmo *m* — **selfless** *adj* desinteresado — **self–service** *adj* de autoservicio

**sell** *v* (**sold**) vender(se) — **seller** *n* vendedor *m*, -dora *f*

**semester** *n* semestre *m*

**semicolon** *n* punto y coma *m*

**semifinal** *n* semifinal *f*

**seminar** *n* seminario *m*

**senate** *n* senado *m* — **senator** *n* senador *m*, -dora *f*

**send** *v* (**sent**) mandar, enviar; ∼ **away for** pedir; ∼ **back** devolver (mercancías, etc.); ∼ **for** mandar a buscar — **sender** *n* remitente *mf*

**senior** *n* superior *m*; estudiante *mf* de último año (en educación); *or* ∼ **citizen** persona *f* mayor

**sensation** *n* sensación *f* — **sensational** *adj* sensacional

**sense** *n* sentido *m*; sensación *f* — **sense** *v* sentir — **senseless** *adj* sin sentido; inconsciente — **sensible** *adj* sensato, práctico — **sensibility** *n* sensibilidad *f* — **sensitive** *adj* sensible; susceptible — **sensitivity** *n* sensibilidad *f* — **sensual** *adj* sensual

**sentence** *n* frase *f*; sentencia *f* — **sentence** *v* sentenciar

**sentiment** *n* sentimiento *m*; opinión *f* — **sentimental** *adj* sentimental — **sentimentality** *n* sentimentalismo *m*

**separation** *n* separación *f* — **separate** *v* separar(se); distinguir — **separate** *adj* separado; aparte

**September** *n* septiembre *m*

**sequence** *n* orden *m*; secuencia *f* (de números o escenas)

**Serb** *or* **Serbian** *adj* serbio

**serene** *adj* sereno — **serenity** *n* serenidad *f*

**sergeant** *n* sargento *mf*

**series** *n* (**series**) serie *f*

**serious** *adj* serio — **seriously** *adv* seriamente

**sermon** *n* sermón *m*

**serve** *v* servir — **server** *n* camarero *m*, -ra *f*; servidor *m* (en informática) — **serving** *n* porción *f*, ración *f*

**service** *n* servicio *m*; **armed** ∼**s** fuerzas *fpl* armadas — **service** *v* revisar (un vehículo, etc.) — **service station** *n* estación *f* de servicio

**session** *n* sesión *f*

**set** *v* (**set**) **setting** *v or* ∼ **down** poner; ∼ **up** montar, armar; ∼ **up** establecer; ponerse (del sol, etc.); ∼ **in** empezar — **set** *n* juego *m* (de platos, etc.); set *m* (en tenis, etc.) — **setting** *n* escenario *m*

**settle** *v* asentarse (de polvo, colonos, etc.); fijar, decidir; resolver; calmar; ∼ **down** calmarse; ∼ **in** instalarse — **settlement** *n* pago *m*; colonia *f*, poblado *m*; acuerdo *m*

**seven** *adj* siete — **seven** *n* siete *m* — **seven hundred** *adj* setecientos — **seventeen** *adj* diecisiete — **seventeenth** *adj* decimoséptimo — **seventh** *adj* séptimo — **seventieth** *adj* septuagésimo — **seventy** *adj* setenta — **seventy** *n* (**-ties**) setenta *m*

**several** *adj* varios — **several** *pron* varios, varias

**sew** *v* (**sewed; sewn** *or* **sewed**) coser

**sewing** *n* costura *f*

**sex** *n* sexo *m* — **sexism** *n* sexismo *m*

**shade** *n* sombra *f; or* **window** ∼ persiana *f* — **shade** *v* proteger de la luz — **shadow** *n* sombra *f*

**shake** *v* (**shook; shaken**) sacudir; agitar; ∼ **hands with** dar la mano a; temblar — **shake** *n* sacudida *f* — **shaker** *n*; **salt shaker** salero *m*; **pepper shaker** pimentero *m* — **shaky** *adj* tembloroso

**shame** *n* vergüenza *f*; **what a** ∼! ¡qué lástima! — **shame** *v* avergonzar — **shameful** *adj* vergonzoso — **shameless** *adj* desvergonzado

**shampoo** *v* lavar (el pelo) — **shampoo** *n* (**-poos**) champú *m*

**shape** *v* formar; **be** ∼**d like** tener forma de; *or* ∼ **up** tomar forma — **shape** *n* forma *f*

**share** *n* porción *f* — **share** *v* compartir; dividir

**shark** *n* tiburón *m*

**sharp** *adj* afilado; puntiagudo; agudo — **sharp** *adv* **at two o'clock sharp** a las dos en punto — **sharpen** *v* afilar (un cuchillo, etc.), sacar punta a (un lápiz) — **sharpener** *n or* **pencil sharpener** sacapuntas *m*

**shave** *v* (**shaved; shaved** *or* **shaven**) afeitar(se); cortar — **shave** *n* afeitada *f* — **shaver** *n* máquina *f* de afeitar

**she** *pron* ella

**sheet** *n* sábana *f* (de la cama); hoja *f* (de papel)

**shelf** *n* (**shelves**) estante *m*

**shell** *n* concha *f*; caparazón *m* (de un crustáceo, etc.); cáscara *f* (de un huevo, etc.) — **shell** *v* pelar (nueces, etc.)

**shepherd** *n* pastor *m* — **shepherd** *v* conducir, guiar

**shield** *n* escudo *m* — **shield** *v* proteger

**shift** *v* cambiar; mover(se) — **shift** *n* cambio *m*; turno *m* (de trabajo) — **shifty** *adj* sospechoso

**shimmer** *v* brillar, relucir

**shin** *n* espinilla *f*

**shine** *v* (**shone** *or* **shined**) brillar; alumbrar (una luz) — **shine** *n* brillo *m* — **shiny** *adj* brillante

**ship** *n* barco *m*, buque *m*; ∼ *v* transportar, enviar (por barco) — **shipbuilding** *n* construcción *f* naval — **shipment** *n* envío *m* — **shipping** *n* transporte *m*; barcos *mpl*

**shirt** *n* camisa *f*

**shiver** *v* temblar (del frío, etc.) — **shiver** *n* escalofrío *m*

**shock** *n* choque *m*; golpe *m* emocional; shock *m* (en medicina)

**shoe** *n* zapato *m* — **shoelace** *n* cordón *m* (de zapato) — **shoemaker** *n* zapatero *m*, -ra *f*

**shoot** *v* (**shot**) disparar (en deportes, caza, etc.)

**shop** *n* tienda *f*; taller *m* — **shop** *v* hacer compras; **go shopping** ir de compras — **shopkeeper** *n* tendero *m*, -ra *f* — **shopper** *n* comprador *m*, -dora *f*

**shore** *n* orilla *f*

**short** *adj* corto; bajo (de estatura); brusco; **a** ∼ **time ago** hace poco —

**shortcake** n tarta f de fruta — **short-coming** n defecto m — **shorten** v acortar — **shortly** adv dentro de poco — **shortness** n lo corto (de una cosa), baja estatura f (de una persona) — **shorts** npl shorts mpl, pantalones mpl cortos

**shot** n disparo m, tiro m — **shotgun** n escopeta f

**shoulder** n hombro m — **shoulder blade** n omóplato m

**shout** v gritar — **shout** n grito m

**shove** v empujar — **shove** n empujón m

**shovel** n pala f

**show** v (**showed; shown** or **showed**) mostrar; enseñar; demostrar; proyectar (una película), dar (un programa de televisión); ~ **off** hacer alarde de; notarse, verse; lucirse; ~ **up** aparecer — **show** n demostración f; exposición f; espectáculo m (teatral), programa m (de televisión, etc.)

**shower** n ducha f; fiesta f — **shower** v regar; ducharse

**shrink** v (**shrank; shrunk** or **shrunken**) encoger(se) (de ropa), reducirse (de números, etc.); or ~ **back** retroceder

**shrivel** v or ~ **up** arrugarse, marchitarse

**shuffle** v barajar (naipes), revolver (papeles, etc.); caminar arrastrando los pies

**shun** v evitar, esquivar

**shut** v (**shut**) cerrar; ~ **up** encerrar; or ~ **down** cerrarse; ~ **up!** ¡cállate!

**shy** adj tímido — **shyness** n timidez f

**sick** adj enfermo

**side** n lado m; ~ **by** ~ uno al lado de otro — **sidewalk** n acera f — **sideways** adj & adv de lado

**sigh** v suspirar — **sigh** n suspiro m

**sight** n vista f; espectáculo m; lugar m de interés (turístico)

**sign** n signo m; letrero m; seña f, señal f — **sign** v firmar (un cheque, etc.)

**signal** n señal f — **signal** v hacer señas a; señalar; señalizar (en un vehículo)

**signature** n firma f

**significance** n significado m; importancia f — **significant** adj importante — **signify** v (**-fied**) significar

**silence** n silencio m — **silence** v silenciar — **silent** adj silencioso; callado

**silk** n seda f — **silky** adj sedoso

**silly** adj tonto, estúpido

**silver** n plata f — **silverware** n plata f — **silvery** adj plateado

**similar** adj similar, parecido — **similarity** n (**-ties**) semejanza f, parecido m

**simple** adj simple; sencillo — **simplicity** n simplicidad f, sencillez f — **simplify** v (**-fied**) simplificar — **simply** adv sencillamente; realmente

**simultaneous** adj simultáneo

**sin** n pecado m — **sin** v pecar

**since** adv or ~ **then** desde entonces — **since** conj; desde que; ya que, como — **since** prep desde

**sincere** adj sincero — **sincerely** adv sinceramente — **sincerity** n sinceridad f

**sing** v (**sang** or **sung; sung**) cantar

**singer** n cantante mf

**single** adj solo, único; soltero — **single** n soltero m, -ra f; or **single room** habitación f individual — **single** v **single out** escoger; señalar

**singular** adj singular — **singular** n singular m

**sink** v (**sank** or **sunk; sunk**) hundir(se) (en un líquido); bajar, caer — **sink** n or **kitchen sink** fregadero m; or **bathroom sink** lavabo m, lavamanos m

**sinner** n pecador m, -dora f

**sir** n sir m (en un título); señor m (tratamiento)

**sister** n hermana f — **sister–in–law** n (**sisters– . . .** ) cuñada f

**sit** v (**sat**) or ~ **down** sentar(se); estar (ubicado)

**site** n sitio m, lugar m

**situation** *n* situación *f*

**six** *adj* seis — **six** *n* seis *m* — **six hundred** *adj* seiscientos — **sixteen** *adj* dieciséis — **sixteenth** *adj* decimosexto — **sixth** *adj* sexto — **sixtieth** *adj* sexagésimo — **sixtieth** *n* sexagésimo *m*, -ma *f* (en una serie) — **sixty** *adj* sesenta — **sixty** *n* (**-ties**) sesenta *m*

**size** *n* tamaño *m*, talla *f* (de ropa), número *m* (de zapatos); magnitud *f* — **size** *v* **size up** evaluar

**skate** *n* patín *m* — **skate** *v* patinar — **skateboard** *n* monopatín *m* — **skater** *n* patinador *m*, -dora *f*

**skeleton** *n* esqueleto *m*

**sketch** *n* esbozo *m*, bosquejo *m* — **sketch** *v* bosquejar

**ski** *n* (**skis**) esquí *m* — **ski** *v* esquiar — **skier** *n* esquiador *m*, -dora *f*

**skill** *n* habilidad *f*, destreza *f*; técnica *f* — **skilled** *adj* hábil

**skillful** *adj* hábil, diestro

**skin** *n* piel *f* — **skin** *v* despellejar — **skinny** *adj* flaco

**skip** *v* ir brincando; saltarse — **skip** *n* brinco *m*, salto *m*

**skirt** *n* falda *f*

**skull** *n* cráneo *m* (de una persona viva), calavera *f* (de un esqueleto)

**sky** *n* (**skies**) cielo *m* — **skylight** *n* claraboya *f*, tragaluz *m* — **skyline** *n* horizonte *m*

**slacks** *npl* pantalones *mpl*

**slap** *v* dar una bofetada a — **slap** *n* bofetada *f*, cachetada *f*

**Slavic** *adj* eslavo

**sled** *n* trineo *m*

**sleep** *n* sueño *m*; **go to** ~ dormirse — **sleep** *v* (**slept**) dormir — **sleepy** *adj* somnoliento, soñoliento

**sleeve** *n* manga *f* — **sleeveless** *adj* sin mangas

**slender** *adj* delgado

**slice** *v* cortar — **slice** *n* trozo *m*, rebanada *f* (de pan, etc.), tajada *f* (de carne)

**slide** *v* (**slid**) deslizarse — **slide** *n* deslizamiento *m*; tobogán *m* (para niños); diapositiva *f* (fotográfica)

**slight** *adj* ligero, leve; delgado — **slightly** *adv* ligeramente, un poco

**slim** *adj* delgado — **slim** *v* adelgazar

**slip** *v* resbalarse; deslizar — **slip** *n* error *m*, desliz *m*

**slipper** *n* zapatilla *f*, pantufla *f*

**slit** *n* rendija *f*; corte *m*, raja *f* — **slit** *v* (**slit**) cortar

**slot** *n* ranura *f*

**slow** *adj* lento; **be** ~ estar atrasado (de un reloj) — **slow** *v* retrasar, retardar; *or* **slow down** ir más despacio — **slowly** *adv* lentamente, despacio — **slowness** *n* lentitud *f*

**small** *adj* pequeño, chico

**smart** *adj* listo, inteligente; elegante — **smartly** *adv* elegantemente

**smash** *n* golpe *m*; choque *m* — **smash** *v* romper; aplastar; hacerse pedazos; **smash into** estrellarse contra

**smell** *v* (**smelled** *or* **smelt**) oler — **smell** *n* (sentido *m* del) olfato *m*; olor *m* — **smelly** *adj* maloliente

**smile** *v* sonreír — **smile** *n* sonrisa *f*

**smoke** *n* humo *m* — **smoke** *v* fumar — **smoker** *n* fumador *m*, -dora *f*

**smooth** *adj* liso (de superficies), suave (de movimientos), tranquilo (del mar) — **smooth** *v* alisar — **smoothly** *adv* suavemente — **smoothness** *n* suavidad *f*

**snack** *n* refrigerio *m*, tentempié *m*

**snake** *n* culebra *f*, serpiente *f*

**snappy** *adj* rápido; elegante

**snarl** *v* gruñir — **snarl** *n* gruñido *m*

**sneakers** *npl* tenis *mpl*, zapatillas *fpl*

**sneaky** *adj* solapado

**sneeze** *v* estornudar — **sneeze** *n* estornudo *m*

**sniff** *v* oler

**snoop** *v* husmear — **snoop** *n* fisgón *m*, -gona *f*

**snooze** *v* dormitar — **snooze** *n* siestecita *f*, siestita *f*

**snore** *v* roncar — **snore** *n* ronquido *m*

**snow** *n* nieve *f* — **snow** *v* nevar — **snowfall** *n* nevada *f* — **snowman** *n* muñeco *m* de nieve — **snowplow** *n* quitanieves *m* — **snowstorm** *n* tormenta *f* de nieve — **snowy** *adj* **a snowy day** un día nevoso

**so** *adv* también; así; por lo tanto; *or* ~ **much** tanto; *or* ~ **very** tan; **and** ~ **on** etcétera; **I think** ~ creo que sí — **so** *conj*; así que; *or* **so that** para que; **so what?** ¿y qué? — **so** *adj* cierto — **so** *pron* **or so** más o menos

**soap** *n* jabón *m*

**soccer** *n* fútbol *m*

**social** *adj* social — **social** *n* reunión *f* social — **sociable** *adj* sociable — **society** *n* (**-eties**) sociedad *f* — **sociology** *n* sociología *f*

**sock** *n* (**socks**) calcetín *m*

**socket** *n or* **electric** ~ enchufe *m*, toma *f* de corriente

**soda** *n or* ~ **pop** refresco *m*, gaseosa *f*; *or* ~ **water** soda *f*

**sofa** *n* sofá *m*

**soft** *adj* blando; suave — **softball** *n* softbol *m* — **soft drink** *n* refresco *m* — **soften** *v* ablandar(se); suavizar(se) — **softly** *adv* suavemente — **software** *n* software *m*

**soggy** *adj* empapado

**soil** *v* ensuciar — **soil** *n* tierra *f*

**solar** *adj* solar

**soldier** *n* soldado *mf*

**sole**[1] *n* planta *f* (del pie), suela *f* (de un zapato)

**sole**[2] *adj* único — **solely** *adv* únicamente, sólo

**solid** *adj* — **solid** *n* sólido *m*

**solitary** *adj* solitario — **solitude** *n* soledad *f*

**solo** *n* (**solos**) solo *m*

**solution** *n* solución *f* — **soluble** *adj* soluble — **solve** *v* resolver

**some** *adj* un; algo de, un poco de; unos; algunos — **some** *pron* algunos, unos; un poco, algo — **somebody** *pron* alguien — **someday** *adv* algún día — **somehow** *adv* de algún modo; **somehow or other** de alguna manera u otra — **someone** *pron* alguien

**something** *pron* algo; ~ **else** otra cosa — **sometime** *adv* algún día, en algún momento — **sometimes** *adv* a veces — **somewhat** *adv* algo — **somewhere** *adv* en alguna parte, en algún lado; **somewhere around** alrededor de

**son** *n* hijo *m*

**song** *n* canción *f*

**son–in–law** *n* (**sons–** . . . ) yerno *m*

**soon** *adv* pronto; dentro de poco; **as** ~ **as** en cuanto; **as** ~ **as possible** lo más pronto posible

**soothe** *v* calmar

**sophomore** *n* estudiante *mf* de segundo año

**sore** *adj* ~ **throat** dolor *m* de garganta — **sore** *n* llaga *f* — **sorely** *adv* muchísimo

**sorry** *adj* lamentable; **feel** ~ **for** compadecer; **I'm** ~ lo siento — **sorrow** *n* pesar *m*, pena *f*

**sort** *n* tipo *m*, clase *f*; **a** ~ **of** una especie de — **of a** ~ de alguna clase — **sort** *v* clasificar — **sort of** *adv* algo; más o menos

**SOS** *n* SOS *m*

**so–so** *adj or adv* así así

**soul** *n* alma *f*

**sound** *n* sonido *m* — **sound** *v* hacer sonar, tocar (una trompeta, etc.); sonar; parecer

**soundly** *adv* sólidamente; profundamente

**soup** *n* sopa *f*

**sour** *adj* agrio

**source** *n* fuente *f*, origen *m*

**south** *adv* al sur — **south** *adj* (del) sur — **south** *n* sur *m* — **South African**

*adj* sudafricano — **South American**
*adj* sudamericano — **southerly** *adv or
adj* del sur — **southern** *adj* del sur,
meridional

**souvenir** *n* recuerdo *m*

**space** *n* espacio *m*; sitio *m*, lugar *m* —
**space** *v* espaciar — **spaceship** *n* nave
*f* espacial

**spaghetti** *n* espaguetis *mpl*

**Spaniard** *n* español *m*, -ñola *f*

**Spanish** *adj* español — **Spanish** *n*
español *m* (idioma)

**spark** *n* chispa *f* — **spark** *v* chispear,
echar chispas; despertar (interés), provocar (crítica) — **sparkle** *v* destellar,
centellear — **sparkle** *n* destello *m*, centelleo *m*

**speak** *v* (**spoke; spoken**) hablar; hablar
(un idioma); decir; ~ **out against** denunciar; ~ **up** hablar más alto; ~ **up
for** defender — **speaker** *n* orador *m*,
-dora *f*; hablante *mf* (de un idioma); altavoz *m*

**special** *adj* especial — **specialist** *n*
especialista *mf* — **specialization** *n* es-
pecialización *f* — **specialize** *v* espe-
cializarse — **specially** *adv* especialmente — **specialty** *n* (**-ties**) especialidad *f*

**species** *ns & pl* especie *f*

**specify** *v* (**-fied**) especificar — **specific**
*adj* específico — **specifically** *adv* es-
pecíficamente; expresamente — **specification** *n* especificación *f*

**spectacle** *n* espectáculo *m* — **spectacular** *adj* espectacular

**speech** *n* habla *f*; discurso *m*

**speed** *n* rapidez *f*; velocidad *f* — **speed**
*v* (**sped** *or* **speeded**) conducir a exceso de velocidad; *or* **speed up** acelerar — **speed limit** *n* velocidad *f*
máxima — **speedy** *adj* **speedier, -est**
rápido

**spell** *v* escribir (las letras de); *or* ~ **out**
deletrear; significar

**spelling** *n* ortografía *f*

**spend** *v* (**spent**) gastar (dinero); pasar
(las vacaciones, etc.); ~ **time on**
dedicar tiempo a

**spice** *n* especia *f* — **spice** *v* condimen-
tar, sazonar — **spicy** *adj* picante

**spider** *n* araña *f*

**spill** *v* derramar(se)

**spin** *v* (**spun**) girar; hilar (lana, etc.) —
**spin** *n* vuelta *f*, giro *m*

**spinach** *n* espinacas *fpl*

**spine** *n* columna *f* vertebral; espina *f*

**spiral** *adj* de espiral, en espiral

**spirit** *n* espíritu *m* — **spiritual** *adj* espiritual — **spirituality** *n* (**-ties**) espiritualidad *f*

**spite** *n* **in** ~ **of** a pesar de — **spite** *v* fastidiar

**splash** *v* salpicar — *n* salpicadura *f*;
mancha *f* (de color, etc.)

**splendor** *n* esplendor *m* — **splendid** *adj*
espléndido

**split** *v* (**split**) partir; *or* ~ **up** dividir(se);
partirse, rajarse

**spoil** *v* estropear; consentir, mimar

**sponge** *n* esponja *f*

**sponsor** *n* patrocinador *m*, -dora *f* —
**sponsor** *v* patrocinar — **sponsorship**
*n* patrocinio *m*

**spontaneous** *adj* espontáneo

**spoon** *n* cuchara *f* — **spoonful** *n*
cucharada *f*

**sport** *n* deporte *m* — **sportsman** *n*
(**-men**) deportista *m* — **sportswoman**
*n* (**-women**) deportista *f* — **sporty** *adj*
deportivo

**spot** *n* mancha *f*; punto *m*; lugar *m*, sitio
*m*; **in a tight** ~ en apuros — **spot** *v*
manchar; ver, descubrir — **spotless**
*adj* impecable — **spotlight** *n* foco *m*,
reflector *m*; **be in the spotlight** ser el
centro de atención

**spouse** *n* cónyuge *mf*

**spray**[1] *n* ramillete *m*

**spray**[2] *n* rocío *m*; *or* **aerosol** ~ spray
*m*; *or* ~ **bottle** atomizador *m* — **spray**

*v* rociar (una superficie), pulverizar (un líquido)

**spread** *v* (**spread**) propagar(se) (enfermedades), difundir(se) (noticias, etc.); *or* ~ **out** extender(se); untar (con mantequilla, etc.) — **spread** *n* propagación *f*, difusión *f*; extensión

**spring** *v* (**sprang** *or* **sprung; sprung**) saltar; ~ **from** surgir de — **spring** *n* manantial *m* (de aguas); primavera *f* (estación); salto *m*; elasticidad *f* — **springtime** *n* primavera *f* — **springy** *adj* mullido

**sprinkle** *v* salpicar, rociar; espolvorear — **sprinkle** *n* llovizna *f*

**sprint** *v* correr

**sprout** *v* brotar

**spy** *v* (**spied**) ver, divisar; ~ **on** espiar a — **spy** *n* espía *mf*

**squadron** *n* escuadrón *m* (de soldados), escuadra *f* (de aviones o naves)

**square** *n* cuadrado *m*; plaza *f* (de una ciudad) — **square** *adj* cuadrado — **square root** *n* raíz *f* cuadrada

**squeak** *v* chillar — **squeak** *n* chillido *m*

**squeeze** *v* apretar; exprimir (frutas, etc.); extraer (jugo, etc.) — **squeeze** *n* apretón *m*

**squirrel** *n* ardilla *f*

**stab** *n* puñalada *f*

**stable** *n* establo *m* (para ganado) — **stable** *adj* estable — **stability** *n* estabilidad *f* — **stabilize** *v* estabilizar

**stadium** *n* (**-dia** *or* **-diums**) estadio *m*

**staff** *n* (**staffs** *or* **staves**) bastón *m*; (**staffs**) personal *m* — **staff** *v* proveer de personal

**stage** *n* escenario *m* (de un teatro); etapa *f* — **stage** *v* poner en escena

**stagger** *v* tambalearse — **stagger** *n* tambaleo *m*

**stair** *n* escalón *m*, peldaño *m*; ~**s** *npl* escalera(s) *f(pl)* — **staircase** *n* escalera(s) *f(pl)* — **stairway** *n* escalera(s) *f(pl)*

**stalk** *n* tallo *m* (de una planta)

**stamp** *n* timbre *m*; *or* **postage** ~ sello *m*, estampilla *f* — **stamp** *v* franquear (una carta); sellar

**stand** *v* (**stood**) estar de pie, estar parado; estar; seguir vigente; reposar; ~ **aside** *or* ~ **back** apartarse; ~ **out** sobresalir; *or* ~ **up** ponerse de pie, pararse; poner, colocar; soportar — **stand** *n* puesto *m*; posición *f*; **stands** *npl* tribuna *f* — **stand by** *v* mantener (una promesa, etc.) — **stand up** *v* **stand up for** defender

**standard** *n* norma *f*; criterio *m*; ~ **of living** nivel *m* de vida — **standard** *adj* estándar — **standardize** *v* estandarizar

**standing** *n* posición *f*

**standpoint** *n* punto *m* de vista

**star** *n* estrella *f* — **star** *v* estar protagonizado por; **star in** protagonizar

**stare** *v* mirar fijamente — **stare** *n* mirada *f* fija

**starlight** *n* luz *f* de las estrellas

**starry** *adj* estrellado

**start** *v* empezar, comenzar; salir; *or* ~ **up** arrancar; empezar, comenzar; provocar; *or* ~ **up** montar; *or* ~ **up** arrancar (un motor, etc.) — **start** *n* principio *m*

**starve** *v* morirse de hambre; privar de comida — **starvation** *n* inanición *f*, hambre *f*

**state** *n* estado *m*; **the States** los Estados Unidos — **state** *v* decir; exponer — **statement** *n* declaración *f*; *or* **bank statement** estado *m* de cuenta — **statesman** *n* (**-men**) estadista *mf*

**station** *n* estación *f* (de trenes, etc.); condición *f* (social); canal *m* (de televisión), emisora *f* (de radio)

**statistic** *n* estadística *f*

**statue** *n* estatua *f*

**stature** *n* estatura *f*, talla *f*

**status** *n* situación *f*; *or* **social** ~ estatus *m*; **marital** ~ estado *m* civil

**stay** *v* quedarse, permanecer; alojarse; ~ **awake** mantenerse despierto; ~ **in**

quedarse en casa — **stay** *n* estancia *f*, estadía *f*; suspensión *f*

**steady** *adj* firme, seguro; fijo; responsable; constante — **steady** *v* (**steadied**) mantener firme; calmar (los nervios) — **steadily** *adv* progresivamente; sin parar; fijamente

**steak** *n* bistec *m*, filete *m*

**steal** *v* (**stole; stolen**) robar

**steam** *n* vapor *m* — **steam** *v* echar vapor; cocer al vapor; **steam up** empañar

**steel** *n* acero *m*

**steering wheel** *n* volante

**stem**[1] *n* tallo *m* (de una planta), pie *m* (de una copa)

**stem**[2] *v* contener, detener

**step** *n* paso *m*; escalón *m*; ∼ **by** ∼ paso por paso; **take** ∼**s** tomar medidas — **step** *v* dar un paso; **step back** retroceder; **step down** retirarse — **step up** *v* aumentar

**stepbrother** *n* hermanastro *m* — **stepdaughter** *n* hijastra *f* — **stepfather** *n* padrastro *m* — **stepmother** *n* madrastra *f* — **stepsister** *n* hermanastra *f* — **stepson** *n* hijastro *m*

**stereo** *n* (**stereos**) estéreo *m* — **stereo** *adj* estéreo

**sterile** *adj* estéril — **sterility** *n* esterilidad *f* — **sterilization** *n* esterilización *f* — **sterilize** *v* esterilizar

**stern** *adj* severo, adusto

**stew** *n* estofado *m*, guiso *m* — **stew** *v* estofar, guisar; cocer; preocuparse

**stick**[1] *n* palo *m*; bastón *m*

**stick**[2] *v* (**stuck**) pegar; clavar; poner; ∼ **out** sacar (la lengua, etc.) — **sticky** *adj* pegajoso

**stiff** *adj* rígido, tieso; forzado

**stigmatize** *v* estigmatizar

**still** *adj* inmóvil; callado — **still** *adv* todavía, aún; de todos modos, aún así

**stimulate** *v* estimular — **stimulant** *n* estimulante *m* — **stimulation** *n* estimulación *f* — **stimulus** *n* (**-li**) estímulo *m*

**sting** *v* (**stung**) picar — **sting** *n* picadura *f*

**stingy** *adj* tacaño — **stinginess** *n* tacañería *f*

**stink** *v* (**stank** *or* **stunk; stunk**) apestar, oler mal — **stink** *n* hedor *m*, peste *f*

**stir** *v* remover, revolver; mover; incitar

**stitch** *n* puntada *f* — **stitch** *v* coser

**stock** *n* existencias *fpl*; acciones *fpl*; **out of** ∼ agotado; **take** ∼ **of** evaluar — **stock** *v* surtir, abastecer; **stock up on** abastecerse de

**stocking** *n* media *f*

**stocky** *adj* robusto, fornido

**stomach** *n* estómago *m* — **stomachache** *n* dolor *m* de estómago

**stone** *n* piedra *f*; hueso *m* (de una fruta), pepa — **stony** *adj* pedregoso

**stop** *v* tapar; impedir; parar, detener(se); dejar de — **stop** *n* parada *f*, alto *m*; **put a stop to** poner fin a — **stoplight** *n* semáforo *m* — **stoppage** *n* *or* **work stoppage** paro *m*

**store** *v* guardar (comida, etc.), almacenar (datos, mercancías, etc.) — **store** *n* reserva *f*; tienda *f* — **storage** *n* almacenamiento *m* — **storehouse** *n* almacén *m* — **storekeeper** *n* tendero *m*, -ra *f*

**storm** *n* tormenta *f*, tempestad *f* — **storm** *v* asaltar — **stormy** *adj* tormentoso

**story** *n* (**stories**) cuento *m*; historia *f*

**stove** *n* estufa *f* (para calentar); cocina *f*

**straight** *adj* recto, derecho; lacio (del pelo) — **straight** *adv* derecho — **straightaway** *adv* inmediatamente — **straightforward** *adj* franco; claro, sencillo

**strain** *v* forzar (la vista o la voz); ∼ **a muscle** sufrir un esguince — **strain** *n* tensión *f*; esguince *m*

**strand** *n* hebra *f*

**strange** *adj* extraño, raro; desconocido — **strangely** *adv* de manera extraña — **stranger** *n* desconocido *m*, -da *f*

**strap** *n* correa *f*; *or* **shoulder** ∼ tirante

*m* — **strap** *v* sujetar con una correa — **strapless** *n* sin tirantes

**strategy** *n* (**-gies**) estrategia *f* — **strategic** *adj* estratégico

**strawberry** *n* (**-ries**) fresa *f*

**stream** *n* arroyo *m*, riachuelo *m*; chorro *m*, corriente *f* — **stream** *v* correr

**street** *n* calle *f* — **streetlight** *n* farol *m*

**strength** *n* fuerza *f*; fortaleza *f*; resistencia *f*, solidez *f*; intensidad *f* — **strengthen** *v* fortalecer; reforzar

**stress** *n* tensión *f*; acento *m* (en lingüística) — **stress** *v* enfatizar; *or* **stress out** estresar — **stressful** *adj* estresante

**stretch** *v* estirar(se) (músculos, elástico, etc.); extender(se)

**strict** *adj* estricto — **strictly** *adv* **strictly speaking** en rigor

**strike** *v* (**struck**) **struck; striking** *v* golpear; *or* ~ **against** chocar contra; *or* ~ **out** tachar; dar (la hora); golpear; atacar; declararse en huelga — **strike** *n* golpe *m*; huelga *f*, paro *m* (de trabajadores); ataque *m* — **striker** *n* huelgista *mf*

**string** *n* cordel *m*; sarta *f* (de perlas, insultos, etc.), serie *f* (de eventos, etc.); ~**s** *npl* cuerdas *fpl* (en música)

**strip**[1] *v* quitar; desnudar

**strip**[2] *n* tira *f*

**stripe** *n* raya *f*, lista *f* — **striped** *adj* a rayas, rayado

**stroke** *v* acariciar

**stroll** *v* pasearse — **stroll** *n* paseo *m* — **stroller** *n* cochecito *m* (para niños)

**strong** *adj* fuerte — **strongly** *adv* profundamente; totalmente; enérgicamente

**structure** *n* estructura *f*

**struggle** *v* forcejear; luchar — **struggle** *n* lucha *f*

**stubborn** *adj* terco, obstinado

**student** *n* estudiante *mf*; alumno *m*, -na *f* (de un colegio) — **study** *n* (**studies**) estudio *m* — **study** *v* (**studied**) estudiar

**stuff** *n* cosas *fpl*; cosa *f* — **stuff** *v* rellenar; meter — **stuffing** *n* relleno *m* — **stuffy** *adj* pesado, aburrido

**stumble** *v* tropezar

**stupid** *adj* estúpido — **stupidity** *n* tontería *f*, estupidez *f*

**style** *n* estilo *m*; moda *f*; **be in** ~ estar de moda — **style** *v* peinar (pelo), diseñar (vestidos, etc.) — **stylist** *n* estilista *mf*

**subconscious** *adj* subconsciente — **subconscious** *n* subconsciente *m*

**subject** *n* sujeto *m*; tema *m* — **subjective** *adj* subjetivo

**subordinate** *adj* subordinado — **subordinate** *n* subordinado *m*, -da *f* — **subordinate** *v* subordinar

**subscribe** *v* ~ **to** suscribirse a (una revista, etc.), suscribir (una opinión, etc.) — **subscriber** *n* suscriptor *m*, -tora *f* (de una revista, etc.); abonado *m*, -da *f* (de un servicio) — **subscription** *n* suscripción *f*

**substance** *n* sustancia *f*

**substitute** *n* sustituto *m*, -ta *f* (de una persona); sucedáneo *m* (de una cosa) — **substitute** *v* sustituir — **substitution** *n* sustitución *f*

**subterranean** *adj* subterráneo

**subtitle** *n* subtítulo *m*

**subtle** *adj* sutil — **subtlety** *n* (**-ties**) sutileza *f*

**subtraction** *n* resta *f* — **subtract** *v* restar

**suburb** *n* barrio *m* residencial, suburbio *m*; **the** ~**s** las afueras

**subway** *n* metro *m*

**succeed** *v* tener éxito (de personas), dar resultado (de planes, etc.) — **success** *n* éxito *m* — **successfully** *adv* con éxito

**such** *adj* tal; ~ **as** como — **such** *pron* tal; **and such** y cosas por el estilo; **as such** como tal — **such** *adv* muy

**suck** *v* *or* ~ **on** chupar — **sucker** *n* chupón *m* — **suction** *n* succión *f*

**sudden** *adj* repentino — **suddenly** *adv* de repente

**suffer** *v* sufrir; tolerar — **suffering** *n* sufrimiento *m*

**sufficient** *adj* suficiente — **sufficiently** *adv* (lo) suficientemente

**sugar** *n* azúcar *mf* — **sugary** *adj* azucarado

**suggestion** *n* sugerencia *f*; indicio *m* — **suggest** *v* sugerir; indicar

**suicide** *n* suicidio *m* (acto); suicida *mf* (persona)

**suit** *n* traje *m* (ropa) — **suit** *v* adaptar; ser apropiado para; convenir a (de fechas, etc.), quedar bien a (de ropa) — **suitable** *adj* apropiado — **suitcase** *n* maleta *f*, valija *f*

**suite** *n* suite *f* (de habitaciones); juego *m* (de muebles)

**sulky** *adj* malhumorado

**sum** *n* suma *f* — **sum** *v* **sum up** resumir — **summarize** *v* resumir — **summary** *n* (**-ries**) resumen *m*

**summer** *n* verano *m*

**summon** *v* llamar (a algún), convocar (una reunión); citar (en derecho)

**sun** *n* sol *m* — **sunbeam** *n* rayo *m* de sol — **sunburn** *n* quemadura *f* de sol — **sunlight** *n* sol *m* (luz *f* del) — **sunny** *adj* soleado — **sunrise** *n* salida *f* del sol — **sunset** *n* puesta *f* del sol — **sunshine** *n* sol *m*, luz *f* del sol

**Sunday** *n* domingo *m*

**superior** *adj* superior — **superior** *n* superior *m* — **superiority** *n* superioridad *f*

**superlative** *adj* superlativo (en gramática); excepcional — **superlative** *n* superlativo *m*

**supermarket** *n* supermercado *m*

**supervisor** *n* supervisor *m*, -sora *f*

**supper** *n* cena *f*, comida *f*

**supplement** *n* suplemento *m* — **supplement** *v* complementar — **supplementary** *adj* suplementario

**supply** *v* (**-plied**) suministrar; ~ **with** proveer de — **supply** *n* (**-plies**) suministro *m*; **supply and demand** oferta y demanda; **supplies** *npl* provisiones *fpl*, víveres *mpl* — **supplier** *n* proveedor *m*, -dora *f*

**support** *v* apoyar; mantener (una familia, etc.); sostener — **support** *n* apoyo *m* (moral), ayuda *f* (económica); soporte *m*

**suppose** *v* suponer; **be** ~**d to** tener que — **supposedly** *adv* supuestamente

**suppress** *v* reprimir; suprimir (noticias, etc.) — **suppression** *n* supresión *f* (de información)

**supreme** *adj* supremo — **supremacy** *n* (**-cies**) supremacía *f*

**sure** *adj* seguro — **sure** *adv* por supuesto, claro — **surely** *adv* seguramente

**surface** *n* superficie *f*

**surgeon** *n* cirujano *m*, -na *f* — **surgery** *n* (**-geries**) cirugía *f*

**surname** *n* apellido *m*

**surpass** *v* superar

**surprise** *n* sorpresa *f*; **take by** ~ sorprender — **surprise** *v* sorprender — **surprising** *adj* sorprendente

**surrender** *v* entregar, rendir(se) — **surrender** *n* rendición *m* (de una ciudad, etc.), entrega *f* (de posesiones)

**surround** *v* rodear — **surroundings** *npl* ambiente *m*

**survey** *v* medir (un solar); inspeccionar

**survive** *v* sobrevivir (a) — **survival** *n* supervivencia *f* — **survivor** *n* superviviente *mf*

**susceptible** *adj* ~ **to** propenso a — **susceptibility** *n* (**-ties**) propensión *f* (a enfermedades, etc.)

**suspect** *adj* sospechoso — **suspect** *n* sospechoso *m*, -sa *f* — **suspect** *v* sospechar (algo), sospechar de (algún) — **suspicion** *n* sospecha *f* — **suspicious** *adj* sospechoso; suspicaz

**suspend** *v* suspender — **suspense** *n* incertidumbre *m*; suspenso *m*, suspense *m* (en el cine, etc.) — **suspension** *n* suspensión *f*

**sustain** *v* sostener; sufrir

**swallow** *v* tragar — **swallow** *n* trago *m*

**swamp** *n* pantano *m*, ciénaga *f* — **swamp** *v* inundar — **swampy** *adj* pantanoso, cenagoso

**swan** *n* cisne *f*

**swap** *v* intercambiar — **swap** *n* cambio *m*

**swarm** *n* enjambre *m*

**sway** *n* balanceo *m* — **sway** *v* balancearse; influir en

**swear** *v* (**swore; sworn**) jurar; decir palabrotas — **swearword** *n* palabrota *f*

**sweat** *v* (**sweat** *or* **sweated**) sudar — **sweat** *n* sudor *m* — **sweater** *n* suéter *m* — **sweatshirt** *n* sudadera *f* — **sweaty** *adj* sudado

**Swedish** *adj* sueco — **Swedish** *n* sueco *m* (idioma)

**sweep** *v* (**swept**) barrer; ∼ **aside** apartar; ∼ **through** extenderse por — **sweeping** *adj* amplio; extenso

**sweet** *adj* dulce; agradable — **sweet** *n* dulce *m* — **sweeten** *v* endulzar — **sweetener** *n* endulzante *m* — **sweetheart** *n* novio *m*, -via *f*; cariño *m* — **sweetness** *n* dulzura *f*

**swell** *v* (**swelled; swelled** *or* **swollen**) *or* ∼ **up** hincharse; aumentar, crecer — **swell** *n* oleaje *m* (del mar) — **swelling** *n* hinchazón *f*

**swift** *adj* rápido — **swiftly** *adv* rápidamente

**swim** *v* (**swam; swum**) **swimming** nadar; dar vueltas — **swim** *n* baño *m*; **go for a swim** ir a nadar — **swimmer** *n* nadador *m*, -dora *f*

**swindle** *v* estafar, timar

**swing** *v* (**swung**) balancear(se), oscilar; girar; hacer oscilar; arreglar — **swing** *n* vaivén *m*, balanceo *m*; cambio *m*; columpio *m* (para niños)

**swirl** *v* arremolinarse — **swirl** *n* remolino *m*; espiral *f*

**Swiss** *adj* suizo

**switch** *n* cambio *m*; interruptor *m*, llave *f* (de la luz, etc.) — **switch** *v* cambiar de; intercambiar; **switch on** encender, prender; **switch off** apagar; sacudir (la cola, etc.); cambiar; intercambiarse — **switchboard** *n* centralita *f*, conmutador *m*

**swivel** *v* girar (sobre un pivote)

**swoon** *v* desvanecerse

**sword** *n* espada *f*

**syllable** *n* sílaba *f*

**symbol** *n* símbolo *m* — **symbolic** *adj* simbólico — **symbolism** *n* simbolismo *m* — **symbolize** *v* simbolizar

**symmetry** *n* simetría *f*

**sympathy** *n* comprensión *f*; **sympathies** *npl* simpatías *fpl* — **sympathize** *v* **sympathize with** compadecerse de; comprender

**symptom** *n* síntoma *m*

**synonym** *n* sinónimo *m* — **synonymous** *adj* sinónimo

**synthesis** *n* (**-theses**) síntesis *f* — **synthesize** *v* sintetizar — **synthetic** *adj* sintético

**Syrian** *adj* sirio

**syrup** *n* jarabe *m*

**system** *n* sistema *m*; organismo *m*; **digestive** ∼ aparato *m* digestivo — **systematic** *adj* sistemático

# T

**t** *n* (**t's** *or* **ts**) t *f*, vigésima letra del alfabeto inglés

**table** *n* mesa *f*; tabla *f*; ∼ **of contents** índice *m* de materias — **tablecloth** *n* mantel *m* — **tablespoon** *n* cuchara *f* grande; cucharada *f* (cantidad)

**tablet** *n* pastilla *f*

**taboo** *adj* tabú — **taboo** *n* tabú *m*

**tacit** *adj* tácito

**tact** *n* tacto *m* — **tactful** *adj* diplomático, discreto

**tactical** *adj* táctico — **tactic** *n* táctica *f*

**tag** *n* etiqueta *f* — **tag** *v* etiquetar

**tail** *n* cola *f*

**tailor** *n* sastre *m*, -tra *f*

**take** *v* (**took; taken**) tomar; llevar; sacar; ∼ **a bath** bañarse; ∼ **a walk** dar un paseo; ∼ **off** quitar, quitarse (ropa); ∼ **on** asumir (una responsabilidad, etc.); ∼ **out** sacar; ∼ **place** tener lugar; ∼ **off** despegar (de aviones, etc.)

**talcum powder** *n* polvos *mpl* de talco

**tale** *n* cuento *m*

**talent** *n* talento *m* — **talented** *adj* talentoso

**talk** *v* hablar; ∼ **about** hablar de; discutir — **talk** *n* conversación *f*; charla *f* — **talkative** *adj* hablador

**tall** *adj* alto; **how** ∼ **are you?** ¿cuánto mides?

**tally** *n* (**-lies**) cuenta *f*; concordar, cuadrar

**tampon** *n* tampón *m*

**tan** *v* broncearse — **tan** *n* bronceado *m*

**tangle** *v* enredar — **tangle** *n* enredo *m*

**tank** *n* tanque *m*, depósito *m*; tanque *m* (militar) — **tanker** *n* buque *m* tanque; *or* **tanker truck** camión *m* cisterna

**tape** *n* cinta *f* — **tape** *v* pegar con cinta; grabar

**target** *n* blanco *m*; objetivo *m*

**tariff** *n* tarifa *f*, arancel *m*

**tart** *n* pastel *m*

**tartan** *n* tartán *m*

**task** *n* tarea *f*

**taste** *v* probar; saber — **taste** *n* gusto *m*, sabor *m*; **in good/bad taste** de buen/mal gusto — **tasteful** *adj* de buen gusto — **tasteless** *adj* sin sabor

**tax** *v* gravar; poner a prueba — **tax** *n* impuesto *m* — **taxation** *n* impuestos *mpl* — **tax–exempt** *adj* libre de impuestos

**taxi** *n* (**taxis**) taxi *m*

**tea** *n* té *m* — **teacup** *n* taza *f* de té — **teapot** *n* tetera *f*

**teach** *v* (**taught**) enseñar, dar clases (de una asignatura) — **teacher** *n* profesor *m*, -sora *f*; maestro *m*, -tra *f* (de niños pequeños) — **teaching** *n* enseñanza *f*

**team** *n* equipo *m* — **team** *vi or* **team up** asociarse — **teammate** *n* compañero *m*, -ra *f* de equipo — **teamwork** *n* trabajo *m* de equipo

**tear¹** *v* (**tore; torn**) romper, rasgar; ∼ **down** derribar; ∼ **up** romper (papel, etc.); romperse, rasgarse; ir a toda velocidad

**tear²** *n* lágrima *f* — **tearful** *adj* lloroso

**tease** *v* tomar el pelo a, burlarse de; fastidiar

**teaspoon** *n* cucharita *f*

**technical** *adj* técnico — **technician** *n* técnico *m*, -ca *f*

**technique** *n* técnica *f*

**technological** *adj* tecnológico — **technology** *n* (**-gies**) tecnología *f*

**teddy bear** *n* oso *m* de peluche

**teenage** *or* **teenaged** *adj* adolescente — **teenager** *n* adolescente *mf* — **teens** *npl* adolescencia *f*

**telecommunication** *n* telecomunicación *f*

**telephone** *n* teléfono *m* — **telephone** *v* llamar por teléfono

**televise** *v* televisar — **television** *n* televisión *f*

**tell** *v* (**told**) decir; contar; saber — **teller** *n or* **bank teller** cajero *m*, -ra *f*

**temper** *n* **have a bad** ∼ tener mal genio; **lose one's** ∼ perder los estribos — **temperament** *n* temperamento *m*

**temperature** *n* temperatura *f*; **have a** ∼ tener fiebre

**tempest** *n* tempestad *f*

**temple** *n* templo *m*; sien *f* (en anatomía)

**temporarily** *adv* temporalmente — **temporary** *adj* temporal

**tempt** *v* tentar — **temptation** *n* tentación *f*

**ten** *adj* diez — **ten** *n* diez *m*

**tend**[1] *v* cuidar

**tend**[2] *v* ~ **to** tender a — **tendency** *n* (**-cies**) tendencia *f*

**tender** *adj* tierno; dolorido

**tenderness** *n* ternura *f*

**tennis** *n* tenis *m*

**tense** *n* tiempo *m* — **tense** *adj* tenso — **tension** *n* tensión *f*

**tent** *n* tienda *f* de campaña

**tenth** *adj* décimo — **tenth** *n* décimo *m*, -ma *f* (en una serie)

**term** *n* término *m*; período *m*; **be on good ~s** tener buenas relaciones

**terminate** *v* terminar(se); poner fin a — **termination** *n* terminación *f*

**terrain** *n* terreno *m*

**terrible** *adj* espantoso, terrible — **terribly** *adv* terriblemente

**terrific** *adj* tremendo; estupendo

**terrify** *v* (**-fied**) aterrar, aterrorizar — **terrifying** *adj* aterrador

**territory** *n* (**-ries**) territorio *m*

**terror** *n* terror *m* — **terrorism** *n* terrorismo *m* — **terrorist** *n* terrorista *mf* — **terrorize** *v* aterrorizar

**test** *n* examen *m*, prueba *f*; análisis *m* (en medicina) — **test** *v* probar; examinar; analizar (la sangre, etc.)

**testament** *n* testamento *m*

**testify** *v* (**-fied**) testificar

**testimony** *n* (**-nies**) testimonio *m*

**text** *n* texto *m* — **textbook** *n* libro *m* de texto

**than** *conj & prep* que, de

**thank** *v* agradecer, dar (las) gracias a; ~ **you!** ¡gracias! — **thankful** *adj* agradecido — **thanks** *npl* gracias

**Thanksgiving** *n* día *m* de Acción de Gracias

**that** *pron* (**those**) ése, ésa, eso; aquél, aquélla, aquello; **like that** así; **that is** es decir — **that** *conj* que — **that** *adj* (**those**) ese, esa; aquel, aquella; **that one** ése, ésa — **that** *adv* tan

**the** *art* el, la, los, las; por — ~ *adv*

**theater** *or* **theatre** *n* teatro *m*

**their** *adj* su, sus, de ellos, de ellas — **theirs** *pron* (el) suyo, (la) suya, (los) suyos, (las) suyas

**them** *pron* los, las; les, se; ellos, ellas

**theme** *n* tema *m*; trabajo *m* (escrito)

**themselves** *pron* se; ellos mismos, ellas mismas; sí (mismos), sí (mismas)

**then** *adv* entonces; luego, después; además — **then** *adj* entonces

**thence** *adv* de ahí (en adelante)

**theology** *n* (**-gies**) teología *f* — **theological** *adj* teológico

**theoretical** *adj* teórico — **theory** *n* (**-ries**) teoría *f*

**therapeutic** *adj* terapéutico — **therapist** *n* terapeuta *mf* — **therapy** *n* (**-pies**) terapia *f*

**there** *adv* *or* **over** ~ allí, allá; *or* **right** ~ ahí; **who's** ~? ¿quién es? — **there** *pron* **there is/are** hay — **thereafter** *adv* después — **thereby** *adv* así — **therefore** *adv* por lo tanto

**thermometer** *n* termómetro *m*

**thermos** *n* termo *m*

**thesaurus** *n* (**-sauri** *or* **-sauruses**) diccionario *m* de sinónimos

**thesis** *n* (**theses**) tesis *f*

**they** *pron* ellos, ellas

**thick** *adj* grueso; espeso — **thickness** *n* grosor *m*, espesor *m*

**thief** *n* (**thieves**) ladrón *m*, -drona *f*

**thigh** *n* muslo *m*

**thin** *adj* delgado; claro, aguado; fino

**thing** *n* cosa *f*; **for one** ~ en primer lugar

**think** *v* (**thought**) pensar; creer; ~ **about** *or* ~ **of** pensar en; ~ **of** acordarse de; **what do you** ~ **of it?** ¿qué te parece?

**third** *adj* tercero — **third** *n* tercero *m*, -ra *f* (en una serie) — **Third World** *n* Tercer Mundo *m*

**thirst** *n* sed *f* — **thirsty** *adj* sediento

**thirteen** *adj* trece — **thirteen** *n* trece *m* — **thirteenth** *adj* décimo tercero treceavo *m* (en matemáticas)

**thirty** *adj* treinta — **thirty** *n* (**thirties**) treinta *m* — **thirtieth** *adj* trigésimo treintavo *m* (en matemáticas)

**this** *pron* (**these**) éste, ésta, esto; **like ⁓** así — **this** *adj* (**these**) este, esta

**thorn** *n* espina *f*

**though** *conj* aunque — **though** *adv* sin embargo; **as though** como si

**thought** *n* pensamiento *m*; idea *f* — **thoughtful** *adj* pensativo

**thousand** *adj* mil — **thousand** *n* mil *m* — **thousandth** *adj* milésimo

**thread** *n* hilo *m*; rosca *f* (de un tornillo)

**threat** *n* amenaza *f* — **threaten** *v* amenazar

**three** *adj* tres — **three** *n* tres *m* — **three hundred** *adj* trescientos — **three hundred** *n* trescientos *m*

**thrill** *v* emocionar — **thrill** *n* emoción *f* — **thriller** *n* película *f* de suspenso

**throat** *n* garganta *f*

**through** *prep* por, a través de; entre; a causa de; durante — **through** *adv* de un lado a otro (en el espacio), de principio a fin (en el tiempo); completamente — **throughout** *prep* por todo (un lugar), a lo largo de (un período de tiempo)

**throw** *v* (**threw; thrown**) tirar, lanzar; **⁓ away** *or* **⁓ out** tirar, botar

**thumb** *n* (dedo *m*) pulgar *m* — **thumb** *vt* *or* **thumb through** hojear

**thunder** *n* truenos *mpl* — **thunderbolt** *n* rayo *m*

**Thursday** *n* jueves *m*

**thus** *adv* así; por lo tanto

**tic** *n* tic *m* (nervioso)

**tick** *n* tictac *m* (sonido)

**ticket** *n* pasaje *m* (de avión), billete *m* (de tren, avión, etc.), boleto *m* (de tren o autobús); entrada *f* (al teatro, etc.); multa *f*

**tie** *n* atadura *f*, cordón *m*; lazo *m*; empate *m* (en deportes); corbata *f* — **tie** *v* atar, amarrar

**tiger** *n* tigre *m*

**tight** *adj* apretado; ajustado, ceñido — **tighten** *v* apretar; tensar — **tightly** *adv* bien, fuerte

**time** *n* tiempo *m*; época *f*; **at ⁓s** a veces; **at this ⁓** en este momento; **for the ⁓ being** por el momento; **have a good ⁓** pasarlo bien; **many ⁓s** muchas veces **on ⁓** a tiempo — **time** *v* tomar el tiempo a (algún), cronometrar (una carrera, etc.) — **timeless** *adj* eterno — **timely** *adj* oportuno — **timer** *n* temporizador *m*, avisador *m* (de cocina) — **times** *prep*; **3 times 4 is 12** 3 por 4 son 12 — **timetable** *n* horario *m*

**tiny** *adj* diminuto, minúsculo

**tip**¹ *v* inclinar

**tip**² *n* punta *f*

**tip**³ *n* consejo *m* — **tip** *v* **tip off** avisar

**tip**⁴ *v* dar una propina a — **tip** *n* propina *f*

**tire**¹ *n* neumático *m*, llanta *f*

**tire**² *v* cansar(se) — **tired** *adj* **tired of** cansado de, harto de; **tired out** agotado — **tireless** *adj* incansable

**tissue** *n* pañuelo *m* de papel; tejido *m* (en biología)

**title** *n* título *m* — **title** *v* titular

**to** *prep* a; hacia; para; hasta; **a quarter ⁓ seven** las siete menos cuarto

**toast** *v* tostar (pan, etc.); brindar por (una persona) — **toast** *n* pan *m* tostado, tostadas *fpl*; brindis *m* — **toaster** *n* tostador *m*

**today** *adv* hoy — **today** *n* hoy *m*

**toe** *n* dedo *m* (del pie)

**together** *adv* juntos; **⁓ with** junto con

**toilet** *n* baño *m*, servicio *m*; inodoro *m* (instalación) — **toilet paper** *n* papel *m* higiénico

**token** *n* ficha *f* (para un tren, etc.)

**tolerance** *n* tolerancia *f* — **tolerant** *adj* tolerante — **tolerate** *v* tolerar

**toll** *n* peaje *m*

**tomato** *n* (**-toes**) tomate *m*

**tomb** *n* tumba *f*, sepulcro *m* — **tombstone** *n* lápida *f*

**tomorrow** *adv* mañana — **tomorrow** *n* mañana *m*

**ton** *n* tonelada *f*

**tongue** *n* lengua *f*

**tonight** *adv* esta noche — **tonight** *n* esta noche *f*

**too** *adv* también; demasiado

**tool** *n* herramienta *f* — **toolbox** *n* caja *f* de herramientas

**tooth** *n* (**teeth**) diente *m* — **toothache** *n* dolor *m* de muelas — **toothbrush** *n* cepillo *m* de dientes — **toothpaste** *n* pasta *f* de dientes, pasta *f* dentífrica

**top**[1] *n* parte *f* superior; cima *f*, cumbre *f*; tapa *f*, cubierta *f*; **on ~ of** encima de — **top** *adj* de arriba, superior; mejor

**top**[2] *n* trompo *m* (juguete)

**topic** *n* tema *m*

**torment** *n* tormento *m*

**tornado** *n* (**-does** *or* **-dos**) tornado *m*

**tortilla** *n* tortilla *f*

**tortoise** *n* tortuga *f* (terrestre)

**torture** *n* tortura *f* — **torture** *v* torturar

**total** *adj* total — **total** *n* total *m*

**touch** *v* tocar — **touch** *n*; tacto *m* (sentido); toque *m*; pizca *f*; **keep in touch** mantenerse en contacto

**tough** *adj* duro; fuerte; severo; difícil — **toughen** *vt or* **toughen up** endurecer — **toughness** *n* dureza *f*

**tour** *n* viaje *m* (por un país, etc.), visita *f* (a un museo, etc.); gira *f* (de un equipo, etc.) — **tour** *v* viajar; hacer una gira (de equipos, etc.); viajar por, recorrer — **tourist** *n* turista *mf*

**toward** *or* **towards** *prep* hacia

**towel** *n* toalla *f*

**tower** *n* torre *f*

**town** *n* pueblo *m*; ciudad *f*

**toxic** *adj* tóxico

**toy** *n* juguete *m* — **toy** *v* **toy with** juguetear con

**trace** *n* rastro *m*, señal *f*

**track** *n* pista *f*; sendero *m*; *or* **railroad ~** vía *f* (férrea)

**trade** *n* oficio *m*; comercio *m*; industria *f*; cambio *m* — **trade** *v* comerciar; **trade something with** cambiar algo a — **trademark** *n* marca *f* registrada

**tradition** *n* tradición *f* — **traditional** *adj* tradicional

**traffic** *n* tráfico *m* — **traffic** *v* **traffic in** traficar con — **traffic light** *n* semáforo *m*

**tragedy** *n* (**-dies**) tragedia *f* — **tragic** *adj* trágico

**trailer** *n* remolque *m*; caravana *f* (vivienda)

**train** *n* tren *m* — **train** *v* adiestrar, entrenar (atletas, etc.); apuntar; prepararse, entrenarse (en deportes, etc.) — **trainer** *n* entrenador *m*, -dora *f*

**traitor** *n* traidor *m*, -dora *f*

**trampoline** *n* trampolín *m*

**tranquillity** *or* **tranquility** *n* tranquilidad *f* — **tranquil** *adj* tranquilo — **tranquilize** *v* tranquilizar — **tranquilizer** *n* tranquilizante *m*

**transaction** *n* transacción *f*

**transatlantic** *adj* transatlántico

**transfer** *v* transferir (fondos, etc.) — **transfer** *n* transferencia *f* (de fondos, etc.), traslado *m* (de una persona); boleto *m* (para hacer transbordo); calcomanía *f*

**transform** *v* transformar — **transformation** *n* transformación *f*

**transit** *n* tránsito *m*; transporte *m* — **transition** *n* transición *f* — **transitive** *adj* transitivo — **transitory** *adj* transitorio

**translate** *v* traducir — **translation** *n* traducción *f* — **translator** *n* traductor *m*, -tora *f*

**transmit** *v* transmitir — **transmission** *n* transmisión *f*

**transparent** *adj* transparente — **transparency** *n* (**-cies**) transparencia *f*

**transport** *v* transportar — **transport** *n* transporte *m*

**trap** *n* trampa *f* — **trap** *v* atrapar

**trash** *n* basura *f*

**trauma** *n* trauma *m* — **traumatic** *adj* traumático

**travel** *v* viajar — **travel** *n* viajes *mpl* — **traveler** *or* **traveller** *n* viajero *m*, -ra *f*

**tray** *n* bandeja *f*

**treachery** *n* traición *f* — **treacherous** *adj* traidor

**treason** *n* traición *f* (a la patria)

**treasure** *n* tesoro *m* — **treasure** *v* apreciar — **treasurer** *n* tesorero *m*, -ra *f*

**treat** *v* tratar; considerar

**treatment** *n* tratamiento *m*

**treaty** *n* (**-ties**) tratado *m*

**tree** *n* árbol *m*

**tremble** *v* temblar

**tremendous** *adj* tremendo

**trend** *n* tendencia *f*; moda *f*

**trial** *n* juicio *m*, proceso *m*; prueba *f*

**triangle** *n* triángulo *m*

**tribe** *n* tribu *f*

**trick** *n* trampa *f*; broma *f*; truco *m* — **trick** *v* engañar — **trickery** *n* engaño *m*

**tricky** *adj* **trickier; -est** astuto, taimado

**tricycle** *n* triciclo *m*

**trillion** *n* billón *m*

**trim** *v* recortar; adornar — **trim** *adj* esbelto; arreglado — **trim** *n* adornos *mpl*

**trio** *n* (**trios**) trío *m*

**trip** *n* viaje *m*

**triumph** *n* triunfo *m* — **triumph** *v* triunfar — **triumphal** *adj* triunfal

**trivial** *adj* trivial

**troop** *n* escuadrón *m* (de caballería), compañía *f* (de soldados) — **trooper** *n* soldado *m*; *or* **state trooper** policía *mf* estatal

**tropic** *n* trópico *m*

**trot** *n* trote *m* — **trot** *v* trotar

**trouble** *v* preocupar; molestar — **trouble** *n* problemas *mpl*; molestia *f*; **be in trouble** estar en apuros

**trousers** *npl* pantalón *m*, pantalones *mpl*

**truck** *n* camión *m*; carro *m* — **trucker** *n* camionero *m*, -ra *f*

**true** *adj* verdadero; fiel; auténtico

**truly** *adv* verdaderamente

**trumpet** *n* trompeta *f*

**trunk** *n* tronco *m*; baúl *m* (equipaje); maletero *m* (de un auto)

**trust** *n* confianza *f*; esperanza *f*; crédito *m* — **trust** *v* confiar (en); esperar; fiarse de (en frases negativas)

**truth** *n* verdad *f*

**try** *v* (**tried**) tratar (de), intentar

**T–shirt** *n* camiseta *f*

**tub** *n* cuba *f*, tina *f*; envase *m*; bañera *f*

**tube** *n* tubo *m*

**tuberculosis** *n* tuberculosis *f*

**tubing** *n* tubería *f*

**Tuesday** *n* martes *m*

**tuition** *n* enseñanza *f*; *or* ∼ **fees** matrícula *f*

**tulip** *n* tulipán *m*

**tumble** *v* caerse — **tumble** *n* caída *f*

**tumor** *n* tumor *m*

**tumult** *n* tumulto *m*

**tuna** *n* (**-na** *or* **-nas**) atún *m*

**tune** *n* melodía *f* — **tune** *v* afinar; **tune in** sintonizar

**tunnel** *n* túnel *m*

**turkey** *n* (**-keys**) pavo *m*

**turn** *v* hacer girar (una rueda, etc.), volver (la cabeza, una página, etc.); dar la vuelta a (una esquina); torcer; ∼ **down** rechazar; bajar; ∼ **in** entregar; ∼ **off** cerrar (una llave), apagar (la luz, etc.); ∼ **on** abrir (una llave), encender, prender (la luz, etc.); ∼ **out** echar; producir; *or* ∼ **over** dar la vuelta a, voltear; ∼ **over** entregar; girar, dar vueltas; *or* ∼ **around** darse la vuelta, volverse; ∼ **into** convertirse en; ∼ **out** resultar; ∼ **up** aparecer — **turn** *n* vuelta *f*; cambio *m*; curva *f*

**turtle** *n* tortuga *f* (marina) — **turtleneck** *n* cuello *m* de tortuga

**twelve** *adj* doce — **twelve** *n* doce *m* — **twelfth** *adj* duodécimo — **twelfth** *n* duodécimo *m*, -ma *f* (en una serie); doceavo *m* (en matemáticas)

**twenty** *adj* veinte — **twenty** *n* (**-ties**) veinte *m* — **twentieth** *adj* vigésimo — **twentieth** *n* vigésimo *m*, -ma *f* (en una serie); veinteavo *m* (en matemáticas)

**twice** *adv* dos veces

**twilight** *n* crepúsculo *m*

**twin** *n* gemelo *m*, -la *f*; mellizo *m*, -za *f* — **twin** *adj* gemelo, mellizo

**twinkle** *v* brillar (de los ojos) — **twinkle** *n* centelleo *m*, brillo *m* (de los ojos)

**twist** *v* retorcer; girar; torcerse — **twist** *n* vuelta *f*; giro *m*

**two** *adj* dos — **two** *n* (**twos**) dos *m* — **twofold** *adj* doble — **twofold** *adv* al doble — **two hundred** *adj* doscientos — **two hundred** *n* doscientos *m*

**type** *n* tipo *m* — **type** *v* escribir a máquina — **typewriter** *n* máquina *f* de escribir

**typical** *adj* típico, característico

# U

**u** *n* (**u's** *or* **us**) u *f*, vigésima primera letra del alfabeto inglés

**UFO** *n* (**UFO's** *or* **UFOs**) ovni *m*, OVNI *m*

**ugly** *adj* feo

**ultimate** *adj* final, último; máximo; fundamental

**umbrella** *n* paraguas *m*

**umpire** *n* árbitro *m*, -tra *f* — **umpire** *v* arbitrar

**unacceptable** *adj* inaceptable

**unafraid** *adj* sin miedo

**unattached** *adj* suelto; soltero

**unattractive** *adj* poco atractivo

**unauthorized** *adj* no autorizado

**unavailable** *adj* no disponible

**unavoidable** *adj* inevitable

**unaware** *adj* inconsciente; **be ~ of** ignorar — **unawares** *adv* **catch . . . unawares** agarrar a . . . desprevenido

**unbalanced** *adj* desequilibrado

**unbearable** *adj* inaguantable, insoportable

**unbelievable** *adj* increíble

**unbending** *adj* inflexible

**unborn** *adj* aún no nacido

**unbreakable** *adj* irrompible

**unbroken** *adj* intacto; continuo

**unbutton** *v* desabrochar, desabotonar

**uncalled–for** *adj* inapropiado, innecesario

**uncertain** *adj* incierto; **in no ~ terms** de forma vehemente — **uncertainty** *n* (**-ties**) incertidumbre *f*

**unchanged** *adj* igual, sin alterar — **unchanging** *adj* inmutable

**uncivilized** *adj* incivilizado

**uncle** *n* tío *m*

**unclear** *adj* poco claro

**uncomfortable** *adj* incómodo; inquietante, desagradable

**uncommon** *adj* raro

**unconcerned** *adj* indiferente

**unconditional** *adj* incondicional

**unconscious** *adj* inconsciente

**unconventional** *adj* poco convencional

**uncover** *v* destapar; descubrir

**undecided** *adj* indeciso

**undeniable** *adj* innegable

**under** *adv* debajo; menos; *or* **~ anesthetic** bajo los efectos de la anestesia **~ 20 minutes** menos de 20 minutos; **~ the circumstances** dadas las circunstancias

**underdeveloped** *adj* subdesarrollado

**underground** *adv* bajo tierra; **go ~** pasar a la clandestinidad — **underground** *adj* subterráneo; secreto, clandestino — **underground** *n* movimiento *m* clandestino

**underneath** *adv* debajo, abajo — **underneath** *prep* debajo de, abajo de

**underpants** *npl* calzoncillos *mpl*, calzones *mpl*

**undershirt** *n* camiseta *f*

**understand** *v* (**-stood**) comprender, entender

**understatement** *n* **that's an** ~ decir sólo eso es quedarse corto

**underwater** *adj* submarino — **underwater** *adv* debajo (del agua)

**underwear** *n* ropa *f* interior

**undo** *v* (**-did; -done**) deshacer, desatar; reparar (daños, etc.)

**undress** *v* desnudar(se)

**uneasy** *adj* incómodo; inquieto; agitado

**uneducated** *adj* inculto

**unemployed** *adj* desempleado — **unemployment** *n* desempleo *m*

**unexpected** *adj* inesperado

**unfair** *adj* injusto — **unfairness** *n* injusticia *f*

**unfaithful** *adj* infiel

**unfasten** *v* desabrochar (ropa, etc.); desatar (una cuerda, etc.)

**unfavorable** *adj* desfavorable

**unfeeling** *adj* insensible

**unfit** *adj* impropio; no apto, incapaz

**unfold** *v* extenderse; desarrollarse; desplegar(se), desdoblar; revelar (un plan, etc.)

**unforgettable** *adj* inolvidable

**unforgivable** *adj* imperdonable

**unfortunate** *adj* desgraciado, desafortunado; inoportuno

**ungrateful** *adj* desagradecido

**unharmed** *adj* salvo, ileso

**uniform** *adj* uniforme — **uniform** *n* uniforme *m*

**unilateral** *adj* unilateral

**uninhabited** *adj* deshabitado, despoblado

**union** *n* unión *f*; *or* **labor** ~ sindicato *m*, gremio *m*

**unique** *adj* único

**unit** *n* unidad *f*; módulo *m* (de un mobiliario)

**unite** *v* unir(se) — **unity** *n* unidad *f*; acuerdo *m*

**universe** *n* universo *m* — **universal** *adj* universal

**university** *n* (**-ties**) universidad *f*

**unjust** *adj* injusto

**unkempt** *adj* despeinado (del pelo)

**unknown** *adj* desconocido

**unless** *conj* a menos que, a no ser que

**unlike** *adj* diferente — **unlike** *prep* a diferencia de

**unlimited** *adj* ilimitado

**unlock** *v* abrir (con llave)

**unlucky** *adj* de mala suerte (de un número, etc.)

**unmarried** *adj* soltero

**unmistakable** *adj* inconfundible

**unnatural** *adj* anormal; afectado, forzado

**unnecessary** *adj* innecesario

**unpleasant** *adj* desagradable

**unreal** *adj* irreal

**unsanitary** *adj* antihigiénico

**unsettled** *adj* inestable; agitado, inquieto; variable (del tiempo)

**unstable** *adj* inestable

**untidy** *adj* desordenado (de una sala, etc.), desaliñado (de una persona)

**untie** *v* desatar

**until** *prep* hasta — **until** *conj* hasta que

**untimely** *adj* prematuro; inoportuno

**untroubled** *adj* tranquilo; **be** ~ **by** no estar afectado por

**untrue** *adj* falso

**unused** *adj* nuevo; **be** ~ **to** no estar acustumbrado a

**unusual** *adj* poco común, insólito

**unwanted** *adj* superfluo (de un objeto), no deseado (de un niño, etc.)

**unwieldy** *adj* difícil de manejar

**unwilling** *adj* poco dispuesto — **unwillingly** *adv* de mala gana

**unworthy** *adj* be ~ of no ser digno de

**up** *adv* arriba; hacia arriba; ~ **here/there** aquí/allí arriba; ~ **until** hasta — **up** *adj* levantado; terminado; **be up against** enfrentarse con; **be up on** estar al corriente de; **it's up to you** depende de tí; **the sun is up** ha salido el sol — **up** *prep* **go up the river** ir río arriba

**update** *v* poner al día, actualizar — **update** *n* puesta *f* al día

**upgrade** *v* elevar la categoría de (un puesto, etc.), mejorar (una facilidad, etc.)

**uphill** *adv* cuesta arriba — **uphill** *adj* en subida; **be an uphill battle** ser muy difícil

**upon** *prep* en, sobre; ~ **leaving** al salir

**upper** *adj* superior — **upper** *n* parte *f* superior (del calzado, etc.)

**uppercase** *adj* mayúsculo

**upper class** *n* clase *f* alta

**upright** *adj* vertical; derecho; recto, honesto — **upright** *n* montante *m*, poste *m*

**upset** *v* (**-set**) volcar; alterar, inquietar; trastornar — **upset** *adj* alterado; **have an upset stomach** estar mal del estómago — **upset** *n* trastorno *m*

**upside down** *adv* al revés; **turn** ~ volver — **upside–down** *adj* al revés

**upstairs** *adv* arriba — **upstairs** *adj* de arriba — **upstairs** *ns & pl* piso *m* de arriba

**upward** *adj* ascendente, hacia arriba

**urban** *adj* urbano

**urgency** *n* urgencia *f* — **urgent** *adj* urgente; **be urgent** urgir

**Uruguayan** *adj* uruguayo

**us** *pron* nos; nosotros, nosotras; **both of** ~ nosotros dos; **it's** ~! ¡somos nosotros!

**usage** *n* uso *m*

**use** *v* usar; ~ **up** agotar, consumir — **use** *n* uso *m* — **used** *adj* usado; **be used to** estar acostumbrado a — **useful** *adj* útil, práctico — **usefulness** *n* utilidad *f* — **useless** *adj* inútil — **user** *n* usuario *m*, -ria *f*

**usher** *v* acompañar, conducir; ~ **in** hacer entrar — **usher** *n* acomodador *m*, -dora *f*

**usual** *adj* habitual, usual; **as** ~ como de costumbre

**utility** *n* (**-ties**) utilidad *f*; *or* **public** ~ empresa *f* de servicio público

**utilize** *v* utilizar

# V

**v** *n* (**v's** *or* **vs**) v *f*, vigésima segunda letra del alfabeto inglés

**vacant** *adj* libre; desocupado; vacante (dícese de un puesto); ausente (dícese de una mirada) — **vacancy** *n* (**-cies**) (puesto *m*) vacante *f*; habitación *f* libre (en un hotel, etc.)

**vacate** *v* desalojar, desocupar

**vacation** *n* vacaciones *fpl*

**vaccine** *n* vacuna *f*

**vacuum** *n* vacío *m* — **vacuum cleaner** *n* aspiradora *f*

**vain** *adj* vanidoso; **in** ~ en vano

**valid** *adj* válido

**valley** *n* (**-leys**) valle *m*

**value** *n* valor *m* — **value** *v* valorar — **valuable** *adj* valioso

**van** *n* furgoneta *f*, camioneta *f*

**vanguard** *n* vanguardia *f*

**vanilla** *n* vainilla *f*

**vanity** *n* (**-ties**) vanidad *f*; *or* ~ **table** tocador *m*

**vapor** *n* vapor *m*

**variable** *adj* variable — **variable** *n* variable *f* — **variant** *n* variante *f* — **variety** *n* (**-ties**) variedad *f*; surtido *m*; clase *f*

**vary** *v* (**varied**) variar

**vase** *n or* **flower** ∼ florero *m*

**VCR** *or* **videocassette recorder** *n* vídeo *m*, videograbadora *f*

**vegetable** *adj* vegetal — **vegetable** *n* vegetal *m* (planta); **vegetables** *npl* verduras *fpl* — **vegetarian** *n* vegetariano *mf* — **vegetation** *n* vegetación *f*

**vehicle** *n* vehículo *m*

**veil** *n* velo *m* — **veil** *v* cubrir con un velo; velar

**vein** *n* vena *f*; veta *f* (de un mineral, etc.)

**velocity** *n* velocidad *f*

**venetian blind** *n* persiana *f* veneciana

**Venezuelan** *adj* venezolano

**vengeance** *n* venganza *f*; **take** ∼ **on** vengarse de

**ventilate** *v* ventilar — **ventilation** *n* ventilación *f* — **ventilator** *n* ventilador *m*

**venture** *v* arriesgar; aventurar (una opinión, etc.); atreverse — **venture** *n or* **business venture** empresa *f*

**Venus** *n* Venus *m*

**verb** *n* verbo *m* — **verbal** *adj* verbal

**verify** *v* (**-fied**) verificar

**versatile** *adj* versátil

**verse** *n* verso *m*; poesía *f*; versículo *m* (en la Biblia)

**version** *n* versión *f*

**vertical** *adj* vertical — **vertical** *n* vertical *f*

**vertigo** *n* vértigo *m*

**very** *adv* muy; **the** ∼ **same thing** la misma cosa ∼ **much** mucho; ∼ **well** muy bien — **very** *adj* mismo; solo, mero

**veteran** *n* veterano *m*, -na *f*

**veterinarian** *n* veterinario *m*, -ria *f* — **veterinary** *adj* veterinario

**veto** *n* (**-toes**) veto *m* — **veto** *v* vetar

**vibrate** *v* vibrar — **vibration** *n* vibración *f*

**vice** *n* vicio *m*

**vice president** *n* vicepresidente *m*, -ta *f*

**victim** *n* víctima *f*

**victory** *n* (**-ries**) victoria *f*

**video** *n* video *m*, vídeo *m* — **video** *adj* de video — **videocassette** *n* videocasete *m*

**Vietnamese** *adj* vietnamita

**view** *n* vista *f*; opinión *f*; **come into** ∼ aparecer; **in** ∼ **of** en vista de (que) — **view** *v* ver; considerar — **viewer** *n or* **television viewer** televidente *mf* — **viewpoint** *n* punto *m* de vista

**vigil** *n* vela *f* — **vigilance** *n* vigilancia *f* — **vigilant** *adj* vigilante

**vigor** *n* vigor *m* — **vigorous** *adj* vigoroso; enérgico

**vinegar** *n* vinagre *m*

**violate** *v* violar — **violation** *n* violación *f*

**violence** *n* violencia *f* — **violent** *adj* violento

**violet** *n* violeta *f* (flor), violeta *m* (color)

**violin** *n* violín *m* — **violinist** *n* violinista *mf*

**VIP** *n* (**VIPs**) VIP *mf*

**virtual** *adj* virtual

**virtue** *n* virtud *f*; **by** ∼ **of** en virtud de

**virus** *n* virus *m*

**visible** *adj* visible; evidente

**vision** *n* visión *f*; **have** ∼**s of** imaginarse — **visionary** *adj* visionario

**visit** *v* visitar; hacer una visita — **visit** *n* visita *f*

**visor** *n* visera *f*

**vista** *n* vista *f*

**visual** *adj* visual

**vital** *adj* vital; esencial — **vitality** *n* vitalidad *f*, energía *f*

**vitamin** *n* vitamina *f*

**vocabulary** *n* (**-laries**) vocabulario *m*

**vocal** *adj* vocal; vociferante — **vocal cords** *npl* cuerdas *fpl* vocales — **vocalist** *n* cantante *mf*, vocalista *mf*

**vocation** *n* vocación *f*

**vogue** *n* moda *f*, boga *f*; **in** ∼ de moda, en boga

**voice** *n* voz *f* — **voice** *v* expresar

**volley** *n* (**-leys**) descarga *f* (de tiros); torrente *m* (de insultos, etc.); volea *f* (en deportes) — **volleyball** *n* voleibol *m*

**volume** *n* volumen *m*

**voluntary** *adj* voluntario — **volunteer** *n* voluntario *m*, -ria *f* — **volunteer** *v* ofrecer(se) (a)

**vomit** *n* vómito *m* — **vomit** *v* vomitar

**vote** *n* voto *m*; derecho *m* al voto — **vote** *v* votar

**vow** *n* voto *m*, promesa *f* — **vow** *v* jurar

**vulnerable** *adj* vulnerable

# W

**w** *n* (**w's** *or* **ws**) w *f*, vigésima tercera letra del alfabeto inglés

**wade** *v* caminar por el agua; *or* ~ **across** vadear

**waft** *v* llevar por el aire; flotar

**wage** *n or* **wages** *npl* salario *m*

**wager** *n* apuesta *f* — **wager** *v* apostar

**waist** *n* cintura *f*

**wait** *v* esperar — **wait** *n* espera *f* — **waiter** *n* camarero *m*, mozo *m* — **waiting room** *n* sala *f* de espera

**wake** *v* (**woke; woken** *or* **waked**) despertar; *or* ~ **up** despertarse

**waken** *v* despertar(se)

**walk** *v* caminar, andar; pasear; caminar por; sacar a pasear (a un perro) — **walk** *n* paseo *m*; camino *m*; andar *m* — **walker** *n* paseante *mf*; excursionista *mf*

**wall** *n* muro *m* (exterior), pared *f* (interior), muralla *f* (de una ciudad)

**wallet** *n* billetera *f*, cartera *f*

**want** *v* querer; necesitar; carecer de — **want** *n* necesidad *f*; falta *f*; deseo *m*

**war** *n* guerra *f*

**wardrobe** *n* armario *m*; vestuario *m*

**warehouse** *n* almacén *m*, bodega *f*

**warm** *adj* caliente; tibio; cariñoso; **I feel** ~ tengo calor — **warm** *vt or* **warm up** calentar(se); **warm to** tomar simpatía a (algún), entusiasmarse con (algo)

**warn** *v* advertir, avisar — **warning** *n* advertencia *f*, aviso *m*

**warranty** *n* (**-ties**) garantía *f*

**wash** *v* lavar(se); arrastrar; ~ **away** llevarse; ~ **over** bañar — **wash** *n* lavado *m*; ropa *f* sucia — **washing machine** *n* máquina *f* de lavar, lavadora *f* — **washroom** *n* servicios *mpl* (públicos), baño *m*

**wasp** *n* avispa *f*

**waste** *v* desperdiciar, derrochar, malgastar; ~ **time** perder tiempo — **waste** *adj* de desecho — **waste** *n* derroche *m*, desperdicio *m*; desechos *mpl* — **wastebasket** *n* papelera *f*

**watch** *v* mirar; ~ **out!** ¡ten cuidado!, ¡ojo!; *or* ~ **over** vigilar, cuidar; reloj; velar — **watch** *n* vigilancia *f*; guardia *mf* — **watchful** *adj* vigilante — **watchman** *n* (**-men**) vigilante *m*, guarda *m*

**water** *n* agua *f* — **water** *v* regar (el jardín, etc.); **water down** diluir, aguar; lagrimar (de los ojos) — **waterfall** *n* cascada *f*, salto *m* de agua — **watermelon** *n* sandía *f* — **waterpower** *n* energía *f* hidráulica — **waterproof** *adj* impermeable — **watery** *adj* aguado, diluido; desvaído (de colores)

**wave** *v* agitar; ondular — **wave** *n* ola *f* (de agua); onda *f*

**wax** *n* cera *f* (para pisos, etc.) — **wax** *v* encerar

**way** *n* camino *m*; manera *f*, modo *m*; **by the** ~ a propósito, por cierto; **by** ~ **of** vía, pasando por; **come a long** ~ hacer grandes progresos **get in the** ~ meterse en el camino

**we** *pron* nosotros, nosotras

**weak** *adj* débil; aguado — **weakness** *n* debilidad *f*; flaqueza *f*, punto *m* débil

**wealth** *n* riqueza *f* — **wealthy** *adj* rico

**weapon** *n* arma *f*

**wear** *v* (**wore; worn**) llevar (ropa, etc.),

calzar (zapatos); ～ out gastar — **wear** n uso m

**weariness** n cansancio m

**weave** v (**wove** or **weaved; woven** or **weaved**) tejer (tela); entretejer — **weave** n tejido m

**web** n red f

**wedding** n boda f, casamiento m

**wedge** n cuña f; porción f, trozo m — **wedge** v apretar (con una cuña); meter

**Wednesday** n miércoles m

**week** n semana f — **weekend** n fin m de semana — **weekly** adv semanalmente — **weekly** adj semanal — **weekly** n (-**lies**) semanario m

**weep** v (**wept**) llorar

**weigh** v pesar; sopesar; ～ **down** sobrecargar (con una carga), abrumar (con preocupaciones, etc.)

**weight** n peso m; **gain** ～ engordar; **lose** ～ adelgazar

**welcome** v dar la bienvenida a, recibir — **welcome** adj bienvenido; **you're welcome** de nada — **welcome** n bienvenida f, acojida f

**welfare** n bienestar m; asistencia f social

**well**[1] adv (**better; best**) bien; bastante; **as** ～ también; **as** ～ **as** además de — **well** adj bien — **well** interj bueno; ¡vaya!

**well**[2] n pozo m — **well** vi or **well up** brotar, manar

**well–being** n bienestar m — **well–done** adj bien hecho; bien cocido (de la carne, etc.) — **well–off** adj acomodado

**Welsh** adj galés — **Welsh** n galés m (idioma); **the Welsh** los galeses

**west** adv al oeste — **west** adj oeste, del oeste — **west** n oeste m

**wet** adj mojado; lluvioso; ～ **paint** pintura f fresca — **wet** v (**wet** or **wetted**) mojar, humedecer

**whale** n ballena f

**what** adj qué; cualquier — **what** pron qué; lo que; **what for?** ¿por qué?; **what if** y si — **whatever** adj cualquier; **there's no chance whatever** no hay ninguna posibilidad; **nothing whatever** nada en absoluto — **whatever** pron lo que; qué; **whatever it may be** sea lo que sea

**wheat** n trigo m

**wheel** n rueda f; or **steering** ～ volante m (de automóviles, etc.), timón m (de barcos) — **wheel** v empujar (algo sobre ruedas); or **wheel around** darse la vuelta f — **wheelchair** n silla f de ruedas

**when** adv cuándo — **when** conj cuando — **when** pron cuándo — **whenever** adv cuando sea — **whenever** conj cada vez que; **whenever you like** cuando quieras

**where** adv dónde; ～ **are you going?** ¿adónde vas? — **where** conj or pron donde — **wherever** adv en cualquier parte; dónde, adónde — **wherever** conj dondequiera que

**whether** conj si; ～ **you like it or not** tanto si quieras como si no

**which** adj qué, cuál; **in** ～ **case** en cuyo caso — **which** pron cuál; que, el (la) cual — **whichever** adj cualquier — **whichever** pron el (la) que, cualquiera que

**while** n rato m; **be worth one's** ～ valer la pena; **in a** ～ dentro de poco — **while** conj mientras; mientras que; aunque — **while** v **while away the time** matar el tiempo

**whim** n capricho m, antojo m — **whimsical** adj caprichoso, fantasioso

**whine** v gimotear; quejarse — **whine** n quejido m, gemido m

**whip** v azotar; batir (huevos, crema, etc.); agitarse; ～ **up** avivar, despertar — **whip** n látigo m

**whirlwind** n torbellino m

**whisper** v cuchichear, susurrar — **whisper** n susurro m

**whistle** v silbar, chiflar; pitar (de un tren, etc.) — **whistle** n silbido m, chiflido m (sonido); silbato m, pito m (instrumento)

**white** adj blanco — **white** n blanco m

(color); clara *f* (de huevos) — **whiteness** *n* blancura *f*

**who** *pron* quién; que, quien — **whoever** *pron* quienquiera que, quien; quién

**whole** *adj* entero; intacto; **a ~ lot** muchísimo — **whole** *n* todo *m*; **as a whole** en conjunto; **on the whole** en general — **wholesaler** *n* mayorista *mf*

**whom** *pron* a quién; de quién, con quién, en quién; que, a quien

**whose** *adj* de quién; cuyo — **whose** *pron* de quién

**why** *adv* por qué — **why** *n* (**whys**) porqué *m* — **why** *conj* por qué — **why** *interj* ¡vaya!, ¡mira!

**wide** *adj* ancho; amplio, extenso; *or* ~ **of the mark** desviado — **wide** *adv* **wide apart** muy separados; **far and wide** por todas partes; **wide open** abierto de par en par — **widespread** *adj* extendido

**widow** *n* viuda *f* — **widow** *v* dejar viuda — **widower** *n* viudo *m*

**width** *n* ancho *m*, anchura *f*

**wife** *n* (**wives**) esposa *f*, mujer *f*

**wig** *n* peluca *f*

**wild** *adj* salvaje; agreste; desenfrenado; al azar; frenético; extravagante — **wild** *adv* **run wild** volver al estado silvestre (de las plantas), desmandarse (de los niños) — **wildlife** *n* fauna *f*

**will**[1] *v* (**would**) querer — **will** *v aux* **tomorrow we will ...** mañana iremos de . . . ; **you will do as I say** harás lo que digo

**will**[2] *n* voluntad *f*; testamento *m*; **free ~** libre albedrío *m*

**win** *v* (**won**) ganar; conseguir; **~ over** ganarse a — **win** *n* triunfo *m*, victoria *f*

**wind**[1] *n* viento *m*; aliento *m*; flatulencia *f*; **get ~ of** enterarse de

**wind**[2] *v* (**wound**) serpentear; enrollar; **~ a clock** dar cuerda a un reloj

**window** *n* ventana *f* (de un edificio o una computadora), ventanilla *f* (de un vehículo), vitrina *f* (de una tienda)

**windpipe** *n* tráquea *f*

**windshield** *n* parabrisas *m*; **~ wiper** limpiaparabrisas *m*

**wing** *n* ala *f*; **under one's ~** bajo el cargo de algún — **winged** *adj* alado

**wink** *v* guiñar — **wink** *n* guiño *m*

**winner** *n* ganador *m,* -dora *f* — **winning** *adj* ganador; encantador

**winter** *n* invierno *m* — **winter** *adj* invernal, de invierno

**wipe** *v* limpiar; **~ away** enjugar (lágrimas), borrar (una memoria); **~ out** aniquilar, destruir — **wipe** *n* pasada *f* (con un trapo, etc.)

**wire** *n* alambre *m*; cable *m* (eléctrico o telefónico); telegrama *m* — **wire** *v* instalar el cableado en (una casa, etc.); atar con alambre; enviar un telegrama a — **wireless** *adj* inalámbrico

**wisdom** *n* sabiduría *f*

**wise** *adj* sabio; prudente

**wit** *n* ingenio *m*; agudeza *f*

**with** *prep* con; **~ you** contigo

**withdraw** *v* (**-drew; -drawn**) retirar; apartarse

**within** *adv* dentro — **within** *prep* dentro de; a menos de; dentro de, en menos de; **within reach** al alcance de la mano

**without** *adv* **do ~** pasar sin algo — **without** *prep* sin

**withstand** *v* (**-stood**) aguantar; resistir

**witness** *n* testigo *mf*; testimonio *m* — **witness** *v* ser testigo de; atestiguar (una firma, etc.)

**witticism** *n* agudeza *f,* ocurrencia *f*

**witty** *adj* ingenioso, ocurrente

**wolf** *n* (**wolves**) lobo *m,* -ba *f*

**woman** *n* (**women**) mujer *f*

**wonder** *n* maravilla *f,* asombro *m* — **wonder** *v* preguntarse — **wonderful** *adj* maravilloso, estupendo

**wood** *n* madera *f* (materia); leña *f*; *or* **~s** *npl* bosque *m* — **wood** *adj* de madera

**wool** *n* lana *f* — **woolen** *or* **woollen** *adj* de lana — **woolen** *n* lana *f* (tela) — **woolly** *adj* lanudo

**word** *n* palabra *f*; noticias *fpl*; **~s** *npl* letra *f* (de una canción, etc.) — **word**

**processing** *n* procesamiento *m* de textos — **word processor** *n* procesador *m* de textos

**work** *n* trabajo *m*; empleo *m*; obra *f* (de arte, etc.) — **work** *v* trabajar — **worker** *n* trabajador *m*, -dora *f*; obrero *m*, -ra *f* — **working** *adj* que trabaja (de personas), de trabajo (de la ropa, etc.); **be in working order** funcionar bien — **working class** *n* clase *f* obrera — **workingman** *n* (**-men**) obrero *m* — **workman** *n* (**-men**) obrero *m*; artesano *m* — **workshop** *n* taller *m*

**world** *n* mundo *m*; **think the ⁓ of someone** tener a algún en alta estima — **world** *adj* mundial, del mundo — **worldwide** *adv* en todo el mundo — **worldwide** *adj* global, mundial

**worm** *n* gusano *m*, lombriz *f*; **⁓s** *npl* lombrices *fpl* (parásitos)

**worry** *v* (**-ried**) preocupar(se), inquietar(se) — **worry** *n* (**-ries**) preocupación *f* — **worried** *adj* preocupado — **worrisome** *adj* inquietante

**worse** *adv* peor — **worse** *adj* peor; **from bad to worse** de mal en peor; **get worse** empeorar — **worse** *n* **the worse** el (la) peor, lo peor; **take a turn for the worse** ponerse peor — **worsen** *v* empeorar

**worship** *v* adorar; practicar una religión — **worship** *n* adoración *f*, culto *m*

**worst** *adv* peor — **worst** *adj* peor — **worst** *n* **the worst** lo peor, el (la) peor

**worth** *n* valor *m* (monetario); mérito *m*, valía *f*; **ten dollars' ⁓ (of)** diez dólares de — **worth** *prep* **it's worth $10** vale $10; **it's worth doing** vale la pena hacerlo — **worthless** *adj* sin valor; inútil — **worthy** *adj* **-thier; -est** digno

**would** *past of* **will he ⁓ often take his children to the park** solía llevar a sus hijos al parque; **⁓ you kindly help me with this?** ¿tendría la bondad de ayudarme con esto?

**wound** *n* herida *f* — **wound** *v* herir

**wrap** *v* envolver; **⁓ up** dar fin a — **wrap** *n* prenda *f* que envuelve (como un chal); envoltura *f* — **wrapper** *n* envoltura *f*, envoltorio *m* — **wrapping** *n* envoltura *f*, envoltorio *m*

**wreck** *n* **be a nervous ⁓** tener los nervios destrozados — **wreck** *v* destrozar (un automóvil), naufragar (un barco)

**wrench** *v* arrancar (de un tirón); torcerse — **wrench** *n* tirón *m*, jalón *m*; torcedura *f*; *or* **monkey wrench** llave *f* inglesa

**wrestle** *v* luchar — **wrestler** *n* luchador *m*, -dora *f* — **wrestling** *n* lucha *f*

**wretch** *n* desgraciado *m*, -da *f* — **wretched** *adj* despreciable; desdichado **wretched weather** tiempo *m* espantoso

**wrinkle** *n* arruga *f* — **wrinkle** *v* arrugar(se)

**wrist** *n* muñeca *f*

**write** *v* (**wrote; written**) escribir — **writer** *n* escritor *m*, -tora *f* — **writing** *n* escritura *f*

**wrong** *n* injusticia *f*, mal *m*; agravio *m* (en derecho); **be in the ⁓** haber hecho mal — **wrong** *adj* malo; inadecuado, inapropiado; incorrecto, equivocado; **be wrong** no tener razón — **wrong** *adv* mal, incorrectamente — **wrong** *v* ofender, ser injusto con — **wrongful** *adj* injusto; ilegal

# X

**x** *n* (**x's** *or* **xs**) — x *f*, vigésima cuarta letra del alfabeto inglés

**X ray** *n* rayo *m* X; *or* **⁓ photograph** radiografía *f* — **x-ray** *v* radiografiar

# Y

**y** *n* (**y's** *or* **ys**) y *f*, vigésima quinta letra del alfabeto inglés

**yard** *n* yarda *f* (medida)

**yawn** *v* bostezar — **yawn** *n* bostezo *m*

**year** *n* año *m*; **she's ten ⁓s old** tiene diez años; **I haven't seen them in ⁓s** hace siglos que no los veo — **yearbook** *n* anuario *m* — **yearling** *n* animal *m* menor de dos años — **yearly** *adv* anualmente; **three times yearly** tres veces al año — **yearly** *adj* anual

**yearn** *v* anhelar — **yearning** *n* anhelo *m*, ansia *f*

**yellow** *adj* amarillo — **yellow** *n* amarillo *m*

**yes** *adv* sí; **say ⁓** decir que sí — **yes** *n* sí *m*

**yesterday** *n* ayer *m*; **the day before ⁓** anteayer — **yesterday** *adv* ayer

**yet** *adv* aún, todavía; sin embargo; **has he come ⁓?** ¿ya ha venido?; **not ⁓** todavía no; **⁓ more problems** más problemas aún — **yet** *conj* pero

**yield** *v* producir; **⁓ the right of way** ceder el paso; ceder — **yield** *n* rendimiento *m*, rédito *m* (en finanzas)

**yoga** *n* yoga *m*

**yogurt** *n* yogur *m*, yogurt *m*

**yolk** *n* yema *f* (de un huevo)

**you** *pron* tú; vos; ustedes *pl;* vosotros, vosotras *pl*; usted, ustedes *pl*; te, les *pl* (*se* before *lo, la, los, las*), os *pl*; lo, la; los, las *pl*; ti; vos; ustedes *pl;* vosotros, vosotras *pl*; usted, ustedes *pl*; **with ⁓** contigo; con ustedes *pl;* con vosotros, con vosotras *pl*; **with ⁓** con usted, con ustedes *pl*; **⁓ never know** nunca se sabe

**young** *adj* joven; **my ⁓er brother** mi hermano menor; **she is the ⁓est** es la más pequeña; **the ⁓** los jóvenes — **young** *npl* jóvenes *mfpl* (de los humanos), crías *fpl* (de los animales) — **youngster** *n* chico *m*, -ca *f*; joven *mf*

**your** *adj* tu; su, vuestro; su; **on ⁓ left** a la izquierda

**yours** *pron* (el) tuyo, (la) tuya, (los) tuyos, (las) tuyas; (el) suyo, (la) suya, (los) suyos, (las) suyas; (el) vuestro, (la) vuestra, (los) vuestros, (las) vuestras; (el) suyo, (la) suya, (los) suyos, (las) suyas

**yourself** *pron* (**yourselves**) te, se *pl*, os *pl*; se; tú mismo, tú misma; usted mismo, usted misma; ustedes mismos, ustedes mismas *pl;* vosotros mismos, vosotras mismas *pl*

**youth** *n* juventud *f*; joven *m* — **youthful** *adj* juvenil, de juventud; joven

**yucca** *n* yuca *f*

**Yugoslavian** *adj* yugoslavo

# Z

**z** *n* (**z's** *or* **zs**) z *f*, vigésima sexta letra del alfabeto inglés

**zeal** *n* fervor *m*, celo *m*

**zero** *n* (**-ros**) cero *m*

**zigzag** *n* zigzag *m* — **zigzag** *v* zigzaguear

**zip code** *n* código *m* postal

**zipper** *n* cremallera *f*, cierre *m*

**zone** *n* zona *f*

**zoology** *n* zoología *f*

# Common Spanish Abbreviations

| Spanish Abbreviation | Expansion | English Abbr. | English Equivalent |
|---|---|---|---|
| **abr.** | abril | **Apr.** | April |
| **A.C., a.C.** | antes de Cristo | **BC** | before Christ |
| **a. de J.C.** | antes de Jesucristo | **BC** | before Christ |
| **ago.** | agosto | **Aug.** | August |
| **Apdo., Aptdo.** | apartado (de correos) | — | P.O. box |
| **aprox.** | aproximadamente | **approx.** | approximately |
| **A.T.** | Antiguo Testamento | **O.T.** | Old Testament |
| **atte.** | atentamente | — | sincerely |
| **atto., atta.** | atento, atenta | — | kind, courteous |
| **av., avda.** | avenida | **ave.** | avenue |
| **a/v.** | a vista | — | on receipt |
| **Bo** | banco | — | bank |
| **c/, C/** | calle | **st.** | street |
| **C** | centígrado, Celsius | **C** | centigrade, Celsius |
| **C.** | compañía | **Co.** | company |
| **CA** | corriente alterna | **AC** | alternating current |
| **cap.** | capítulo | **ch., chap.** | chapter |
| **c.c.** | centímetros cúbicos | **cu. cm** | cubic centimeters |
| **CC** | corriente continua | **DC** | direct current |
| **Cd.** | ciudad | — | city |
| **CE** | Comunidad Europea | **EC** | European Community |
| **cf.** | confróntese | **cf.** | compare |
| **cg.** | centígramo | **cg** | centigram |
| **CI** | coeficiente intelectual *or* de inteligencia | **IQ** | intelligence quotient |
| **Cía.** | compañía | **Co.** | company |
| **cm.** | centímetro | **cm** | centimeter |
| **Cnel.** | coronel | **Col.** | colonel |
| **col.** | columna | **col.** | column |
| **Com.** | comandante | **Cmdr.** | commander |
| **comp.** | compárese | **comp.** | compare |
| **Cor.** | coronel | **Col.** | colonel |
| **C.P.** | código postal | — | zip code |
| **cta.** | cuenta | **ac., acct.** | account |
| **cte.** | corriente | **cur.** | current |
| **c/u** | cada uno, cada una | **ea.** | each |
| **CV** | caballo de vapor | **hp** | horsepower |
| **d.C.** | después de Cristo | **AD** | anno Domini (in the year of our Lord) |
| **dcha.** | derecha | — | right |
| **d. de J.C.** | después de Jesucristo | **AD** | anno Domini (in the year of our lord) |
| **dep.** | departamento | **dept.** | department |
| **dic.** | diciembre | **Dec.** | December |
| **dir.** | director, directora | **dir.** | director |
| **dir.** | dirección | — | address |

| SPANISH ABBREVIATION AND EXPANSION | | ENGLISH EQUIVALENT | |
|---|---|---|---|
| **do.** | domingo | **Sun.** | Sunday |
| **dpto.** | departamento | **dept.** | department |
| **Dr., Dra.** | doctor, doctora | **Dr.** | doctor |
| **dto.** | descuento | — | discount |
| | | | |
| **E, E.** | Este, este | **E** | East, east |
| **Ed.** | editorial | — | publishing house |
| **Ed., ed.** | edición | **ed.** | edition |
| **edif.** | edificio | **bldg.** | building |
| **edo.** | estado | **st.** | state |
| **EEUU, EE.UU** | Estados Unidos | **US, U.S.** | United States |
| **ej.** | por ejemplo | **e.g.** | for example |
| **E.M.** | esclerosis multiple | **MS** | multiple sclerosis |
| **ene.** | enero | **Jan.** | January |
| **etc.** | etcétera | **etc.** | et cetera |
| **ext.** | extensión | **ext.** | extension |
| | | | |
| **F** | Fahrenheit | **F** | Fahrenheit |
| **FC** | ferrocarril | **RR** | railroad |
| **feb.** | febrero | **Feb.** | February |
| **FF AA, FF.AA.** | Fuerzas Armadas | — | armed forces |
| | | | |
| **g., gr.** | gramo | **g., gm, gr.** | gram |
| **G.P.** | giro postal | **M.O.** | money order |
| **Gral.** | general | **gen.** | general |
| | | | |
| **h.** | hora | **hr.** | hour |
| **Hnos.** | hermanos | **Bros.** | brothers |
| | | | |
| **i.e.** | esto es, es decir | **i.e.** | that is |
| **incl.** | inclusive | **incl.** | inclusive, inclusively |
| **Ing.** | ingeniero, ingeniera | **eng.** | engineer |
| **izq.** | izquierda | **l** | left |
| | | | |
| **juev.** | jueves | **Thurs.** | Thursday |
| **jul.** | julio | **Jul.** | July |
| **jun.** | junio | **Jun.** | June |
| | | | |
| **kg.** | kilogramo | **kg** | kilogram |
| **km.** | kilómetro | **km** | kilometer |
| **km/h** | kilómetros por hora | **kph** | kilometers per hour |
| **kv, kV** | kilovatio | **kw, kW** | kilowatt |
| | | | |
| **l.** | litro | **l, lit.** | liter |
| **Lic.** | licenciado, licenciada | — | *usually indicates a college graduate* |
| **Ltda.** | limitada | **Ltd.** | limited |
| **lun.** | lunes | **Mon.** | Monday |
| | | | |
| **m** | masculino | **m** | masculine |
| **m** | metro | **m** | meter |
| **m** | minuto | **m** | minute |
| **mar.** | marzo | **Mar.** | March |

| SPANISH ABBREVIATION AND EXPANSION | | ENGLISH EQUIVALENT | |
|---|---|---|---|
| **mart.** | martes | **Tues.** | Tuesday |
| **mg.** | miligramo | **mg** | milligram |
| **miérc.** | miércoles | **Wed.** | Wednesday |
| **min** | minuto | **min.** | minute |
| **mm.** | milímetro | **mm** | millimeter |
| **Mons.** | monseñor | **Msgr.** | monsignor |
| | | | |
| **N, N.** | Norte, norte | **N, no.** | North, north |
| **n/** | nuestro | — | our |
| **n.º** | número | **no.** | number |
| **N. de (la) R.** | nota de la redacción | — | editor's note |
| **NE** | nordeste | **NE** | northeast |
| **NN.UU.** | Naciones Unidas | **UN** | United Nations |
| **NO** | noroeste | **NW** | northwest |
| **nov.** | noviembre | **Nov.** | November |
| **N.T.** | Nuevo Testamento | **N.T.** | New Testament |
| **ntra., ntro.** | nuestra, nuestro | — | our |
| **NU** | Naciones Unidas | **UN** | United Nations |
| **núm.** | número | **num.** | number |
| | | | |
| **O, O.** | Oeste, oeste | **W** | West, west |
| **oct.** | octubre | **Oct.** | October |
| **OEA, O.E.A.** | Organización de Estados Americanos | **OAS** | Organization of American States |
| **OMS** | Organización Mundial de la Salud | **WHO** | World Health Organization |
| **ONG** | organización no gubernamental | **NGO** | non-governmental organization |
| **ONU** | Organización de las Naciones Unidas | **UN** | United Nations |
| **OTAN** | Organización del Tratado del Atlántico Norte | **NATO** | North Atlantic Treaty Organization |
| | | | |
| **p.** | página | **p.** | page |
| **P, P.** | padre (*in religion*) | **Fr.** | father |
| **pág.** | página | **pg.** | page |
| **pat.** | patente | **pat.** | patent |
| **PCL** | pantalla de cristal líquido | **LCD** | liquid crystal display |
| **P.D.** | post data | **P.S.** | postscript |
| **p. ej.** | por ejemplo | **e.g.** | for example |
| **PNB** | Producto Nacional Bruto | **GNP** | gross national product |
| **p°** | paseo | **Ave.** | avenue |
| **p.p.** | porte pagado | **ppd.** | postpaid |
| **PP, p.p.** | por poder, por poderes | **p.p.** | by proxy |
| **prom.** | promedio | **av., avg.** | average |
| **ptas., pts.** | pesetas | — | |
| | | | |
| **q.e.p.d.** | que en paz descanse | **R.I.P.** | may he/she rest in peace |
| | | | |
| **R, R/** | remite | — | sender |
| **ref., ref.ª** | referencia | **ref.** | reference |
| **rep.** | república | **rep.** | republic |

| SPANISH ABBREVIATION AND EXPANSION | | ENGLISH EQUIVALENT | |
|---|---|---|---|
| r.p.m. | revoluciones por minuto | rpm. | revolutions per minute |
| rte. | remite, remitente | — | sender |
| | | | |
| s. | siglo | c., cent. | century |
| s/ | su, sus | — | his, her, your, their |
| S, S. | Sur, sur | S, so. | South, south |
| S. | santa, santo | St. | saint |
| S.A. | sociedad anónima | Inc. | incorporated (company) |
| sáb. | sábado | Sat. | Saturday |
| SE | sudeste, sureste | SE | southeast |
| seg. | segundo, segundos | sec. | second, seconds |
| sep., sept. | septiembre | Sept. | September |
| s.e.u.o. | salvo error u omisión | — | errors and omissions excepted |
| Sgto. | sargento | Sgt. | sergeant |
| S.L. | sociedad limitada | Ltd. | limited (corporation) |
| S.M. | Su Majestad | HM | His Majesty, Her Majesty |
| s/n | sin número | — | no (street) number |
| s.n.m. | sobre el nivel de mar | a.s.l. | above sea level |
| SO | sudoeste/suroeste | SW | southwest |
| Sr. | Señor | — | Mr. |
| Sra. | Señora | — | Mrs., Ms. |
| Srta. | señorita | — | Miss |
| S.R.C. | se ruega contestación | R.S.V.P. | please reply |
| ss. | siguientes | — | the following ones |
| SS, S.S. | Su Santidad | H.H. | His Holiness |
| Sta., Sto. | santa, santo | St. | saint |
| | | | |
| t, t. | tonelada | t., tn. | ton |
| TAE | tasa anual efectiva | APR | annual percentage rate |
| tb. | también | — | also |
| tel., Tel. | teléfono | tel. | telephone |
| Tm. | tonelada métrica | MT | metric ton |
| Tn. | tonelada | t., tn | ton |
| trad. | traducido | tr., trans., transl. | translated |
| | | | |
| UE | Unión Europea | EU | European Union |
| Univ. | universidad | Univ., U. | university |
| UPC | unidad procesadora central | CPU | central processing unit |
| Urb. | urbanización | — | residential area |
| | | | |
| v | versus | v., vs. | versus |
| v | verso | v., ver., vs. | verse |
| v. | véase | vid. | see |
| Vda. | viuda | — | widow |
| v.g., v.gr. | verbigracia | e.g. | for example |
| vier., viern. | viernes | Fri. | Friday |
| V.M. | Vuestra Majestad | — | Your Majesty |
| V°B°, V.°B.° | visto bueno | — | OK, approved |
| vol, vol. | volumen | vol. | volume |
| vra., vro. | vuestra, vuestro | — | your |